WITHDRAWN
UTSA LIBRARIES

Emerging Strategies
in
Social Psychological Research

Emerging Strategies
in
Social Psychological Research

Edited by
G. P. Ginsburg

University of Nevada, Reno

JOHN WILEY & SONS
Chichester · New York · Brisbane · Toronto

LIBRARY
The University of Texas
At San Antonio

Copyright © 1979 by John Wiley & Sons Ltd.

All rights reserved.

No part of this book may be reproduced by any means, nor transmitted, nor translated into a machine language without the written permission of the publisher.

Library of Congress Cataloging in Publication Data:
Main entry under title:

   Emerging strategies in social psychological research.

   Includes indexes.
   1. Social psychology—Research—Addresses, essays, lectures. I. Ginsburg, Gerald Phillip, 1932–
HM251.E66   301.1'07'2   78-18506

ISBN 0 471 99690 4

Photosetting by Thomson Press (India) Limited, New Delhi and printed in Great Britain by The Pitman Press, Bath.

CONTRIBUTORS

MICHAEL ARGYLE   *Department of Experimental Psychology, University of Oxford, Oxford, England*

CARL W. BACKMAN   *Department of Sociology, University of Nevada, Reno, Nevada, USA*

DAVID D. CLARKE   *Department of Experimental Psychology, University of Oxford, Oxford, England*

PETER COLLETT   *Department of Experimental Psychology, University of Oxford, Oxford, England*

JOSEPH P. FORGAS   *School of Psychology, The University of New South Wales, Kensington, New South Wales, Australia*

R. HARRÉ   *Subfaculty of Philosophy, University of Oxford, Oxford, England*

G. P. GINSBURG   *Department of Psychology, University of Nevada, Reno, Nevada, USA*

ADAM KENDON   *Department of Anthropology, Australian National University, Canberra, Australia*

DON MIXON   *Department of Psychology, University of Massachusetts-Boston, Boston, Massachusetts, USA*

MICHAEL SCAIFE   *Department of Social Psychology, School of Social Sciences, University of Sussex, Falmer, Brighton*

J.-P. DE WAELE   *Vrije Universitet, Brussels, Belgium*

CONTENTS

1 Introduction and overview 1
   G. P. Ginsburg
2 Sequences in social behaviour as a function of the situation . . 11
   Michael Argyle
3 The linguistic analogy or when is a speech act like a morpheme? . 39
   David D. Clarke
4 Some theoretical and methodological aspects of the use of film in the study of social interaction 67
   Adam Kendon
5 Observing infant social development: theoretical perspectives, natural observation, and video recording 93
   Michael Scaife
6 The effective use of role-playing in social psychological research . 117
   G. P. Ginsburg
7 Understanding shocking and puzzling conduct 155
   Don Mixon
8 Autobiography as a psychological method 177
   J.-P. De Waele and R. Harré
9 The repertory grid in psychological research 225
   Peter Collett
10 Multidimensional scaling: a discovery method in social psychology . 253
   Joseph P. Forgas
11 Epilogue: a new paradigm? 289
   Carl W. Backman

Author Index 305

Subject Index 313

1

INTRODUCTION AND OVERVIEW

G. P. Ginsburg

This book deals with a number of social psychological research procedures that are coming to the fore today and are likely to become important and standard procedures in the near future. These are *emerging* procedures, at least as far as social psychological investigation is concerned. Guidelines for their application appear to be needed and this volume is designed to meet that need. Furthermore, the procedures appear to be emerging within the context of an increasing awareness of the importance of the settings within which actions occur and of the meanings of the actions to the participants. The guidelines offered in this book reflect that growing awareness.

An overview of the material covered in the book will be presented later in this introduction. First, however, it might be of value to trace the origin of the book and to identify its major themes and objectives in more detail.

ORIGIN, THEMES, AND OBJECTIVES

This book is based in part on a workshop of the British Psychological Society held at Oxford University in November 1975. The workshop was organized by Peter Collett of Oxford's Department of Experimental Psychology, with the help of Michael Argyle and other colleagues, and was entitled 'New Developments in Social Psychological Methods'. The workshop was quite successful, judging from the attendance of over two hundred people and the interest reflected in participation and comments.

In subsequent discussions, Argyle, Collett, and I agreed that it would be of value to put together a book based on the workshop, containing the same themes and meeting the same investigative needs. The book, we felt, should offer a set of guidelines, both conceptual and methodological, which would reflect emerging strategies in our field and would prove useful in the conduct and teaching of social psychological research. This constitutes the primary orientation of the book.

The underlying theme of the 1975 BPS workshop was the recognition that procedures and conceptions of social psychological research were changing and that the emerging strategies had attendant problems as well as potentials. Discussion of these strategies and articulation of guidelines for their use and interpretation were goals of the workshop and are objectives of this book as well. At a more detailed level, discussions during and after the workshop indicated that considerable attention was being given to certain properties of social behaviour, and that a number of research strategies were being developed (or imported) in full recognition of those properties. For example, a number of the participants discussed strategies in which it was presumed that people are active agents, capable of making plans and pursuing objectives, of acting as well as reacting, of doing things for reasons as well as having been forced to do them by causes. The theme of active agency is common across most of the contributed chapters in this volume, too.

Another theme in most of the workshop papers, and in this book as well, was that the meanings of actions, events and settings were important. Most of the procedures incorporated that theme. A third theme which ran through the workshop was the conceptual presumption that actions generally occur in interactional *sequences*, which are embedded in *episodes*. Episodes, in turn, unfold and are completed within *settings* or situations. The meanings of actions help to complete and form the settings within which the episodes unfold. Again, this theme is common to many of the chapters in the book.

The investigative strategies and concrete procedures discussed at the workshop have considerable potential to facilitate our study and understanding of action as meaningful, of sequences of interaction, of episodes of action, and of settings. The procedures treated in the book include film and video recording, sequence analysis, role-playing, a special approach to the construction of biographies, and scaling and statistical procedures for the descriptive analysis of persons, interactions and situations. The cinematic procedures allow us to capture and replay an episode or skill as it emerges over time, whether briefly, as in an encounter, or during many months, as in an infant learning to play 'peek-a-boo'. Role-playing, if used properly, affords the opportunity for precise experimental analysis and for the synthesis of the social phenomenon of interest. The biographical technique requires careful orchestration between the living person and the biographical team of clinical and social scientists; but it can yield a construction of the meanings of critical social acts in the person's life, and thereby generate a powerful understanding of that person. The statistical technique, multidimensional scaling, allows for an objective analysis of the settings of social acts. The scaling procedure presumes that the person is an agent who actively construes his world, and it makes possible a systematic description of his construals. Finally, the analysis of sequences makes use of a linguistic analogy and potentially can reveal underlying structures of interaction.

In addition to the procedural chapters, there are two more conceptually oriented contributions. One offers an overarching conception of action as a situated, embedded phenomenon, and suggests guidelines for attending to rules, roles, physical and social features of the setting, and skills of the person, all of which are important in understanding any particular instance of behaviour. The other conceptual chapter critically examines the knowledge generated by our conventional experimental procedures, and suggest alternatives which would allow us to study shocking and puzzling behaviours.

Thus, the book is designed to provide guidelines for the effective application of certain cinematic, biographical, role-playing and statistical techniques to the study of meaningful, situated action. Moreover, the book recommends somewhat non-conventional frameworks for the interpretation and assessment of the knowledge we generate. These frameworks are much more in accord with current thinking in the philosophy of science than is the rather creaky rhetoric of positivism which still prevails in our field. However, the frameworks recommended by some of the contributors to this book are not yet widely accepted and may still be in the process of formation. Of course, that is consistent with the 'emergent' orientation of the book.

OVERVIEW OF CONTENTS

The first substantive chapter following this Introduction is by Michael Argyle. In it, Argyle argues that sequences of social behaviour are a function of the situations in which they occur, and he urges that more serious conceptual and investigative attention be directed to the analysis of situations. Seven separate but interdependent components of situations will yield a full account of any particular situation: the behavioural elements used within it, the goals or motivations of the participants, the rules which guide the content and styles of performance, the framework of roles, the physical setting and equipment involved in the situation, the cognitive concepts or knowledge necessary or pertinent to action within the situation, and the skills necessary or relevant to effective performance. An understanding of a behavioural sequence not only requires an analysis of the situation in which the sequence occurs, but also requires a 'chunking' of the sequence into *episodes*. The identification of episodes is difficult, conceptually and methodologically, and strategies for accomplishing that task are still emerging, as Argyle discusses in detail; but there is no longer any doubt that episodes constitute a critical unit of analysis and can be found even in the social behaviour of young infants. Touching on a theme common to many chapters in this book, Argyle suggests that the episode is a basic unit of social behaviour and that smaller behavioural elements take their meaning and order from the episode which they are creating and should not be considered in isolation from it.

Argyle also stresses the importance of *rules* as underlying or background guides for action, and recommends how one might go about studying them. Rules are especially important in the production of behaviour. However, in addition to rules, individual differences in pertinent skills must be recognized, especially in less formally structured situations, and so must the nature and extent of interdependency of the actors.

Michael Argyle is probably best known in experimental social psychology for his extensive work on non-verbal communication and his equilibrium model of social interaction. His chapter in this book represents a major conceptual advance, blending as it does his careful empirical orientation with a comprehensive theoretical analysis of situations and a recognition of the importance of rules, meanings and the presumption of the person as an active agent, in a coherent effort to understand any sequence of social behaviour.

David Clarke's chapter focuses more explicitly on the search for structure in face-to-face interaction. Conversations, for example, appear to have a pattern and to adhere to some principle of order. Clarke uses a linguistic analogy to investigate the nature of the pattern to which conversations adhere and the nature of the generative and interpretive processes by which conversations are created and understood. Within the framework of that analogy, he elaborates upon the potentials and difficulties of a structural analysis of a body of social interaction—for example, as might be available in a videotape and transcript of a conversation. Clarke first demonstrates how a pattern might be revealed by having competent members of a culture reconstruct a conversation from a randomly shuffled set of its component utterances. A similar procedure would entail giving a person either the verbal or non-verbal content of an interaction and ask him to specify the structure of the other content. Other uses of reconstruction also are described, but the essence of the procedure is to reveal those relationships between elements of the behavioural stream which are tacitly known by the person by having him reconstitute the stream from an array of its component parts.

Clarke also discusses the importance of being able to synthesize, create a conversation, based on one's presumed understanding of the structural principles through which the conversation was generated. The accomplishment of such a synthesis—that is, the ability to produce a text which adheres to some presumptive principle of structure, and to demonstrate its comprehensibility and realism—is a strong test of one's understanding. Clarke describes several techniques by which synthesis may be attempted, and procedures for testing the adequacy of the outcomes. He then turns to the segmentation of a recorded sequence and differentiates between segmentations which use the knowledge of the native actor and those which are based on the external and more formal scrutiny of the analyst. Clarke gives priority to the former and provides a number of illustrative empirical examples.

The greatest difficulty in applying the linguistic analogy to social behaviour probably arises from the unavoidable necessity of classifying behavioural elements, of placing elements into classes within any one of which the elements are equivalent. Clustering procedures are recommended as means of establishing equivalence relations. From this step, one can proceed to the detection of orderliness in such 'strings' of events as conversations, using any one or more of several techniques which Clarke describes. The chapter ends with a discussion of mechanisms by which social action might be produced and interpreted and a model which contains those mechanisms and is compatible with the constraints of the linguistic analogy. The model is especially noteworthy in its blend of cognitive and motor skills with an *active* rather than reactive nature and with a capacity for growth and maturation.

The third substantive chapter is written by Adam Kendon. It systematically discusses the use of film in the study of social interaction. As Kendon makes clear, the filmed record may prove as important for social psychology as the microscope proved for the biological sciences—but only to the extent that it is used within an appropriate conceptual framework. Kendon reviews many recent projects which reveal how interacting people relate their actions to each other so as to accomplish orderly interaction of the sort that is familiar and common to us all. However, the capacity of film and video techniques to reveal such processes was made manifest only after a particular theoretical viewpoint emerged, a viewpoint which focused on the behavioural relationship between interactors.

A very wide variety of behaviours, persons, sequences and settings have been subjected to cinematic analysis, and Kendon reviews these in some detail; but his major emphasis in the chapter is on 'context analysis'. Context analysis is embedded in a conceptual framework taken from symbolic interactionism in social psychology, cybernetics, and structural linguistics. People are seen as participants in complex systems of behavioural relationship, and *not* as isolated senders and receivers of discrete messages. When two people are in each other's presence, *all* of their behaviours are sources of information to each other, even their silences. Furthermore, the actions of each can be understood only in relation to the actions of the other, as in formal systems of feedback, information exchange and control. Moreover, each action is multiply informative, and the meaning of each may be influenced radically not only by what preceded it in the sequence but by its relationship with concurrent items and even by future items. Context analysis also presumes that behaviour is hierarchically organized, and that at any level the organization has a characteristic or customary structure. What occurs in interaction is usually comprehensible and commonplace. All of this is taken into account in context analysis and is combined with systematic procedures of transcribing the actions in the filmed record and delineating structural units.

The theoretical and procedural complexities of context analysis are described lucidly by Kendon, but always from the perspective that context analysis is *necessary* in making informed use of the filmed record. Furthermore, context analysis influences how film or video records should be made, as well as how they should be analysed. The guidelines which Kendon offers from that framework are at variance with practices followed by some other users of film techniques.

For example, Kendon cautions especially against prejudging the research questions by moving one's camera as a function of one's insights and understandings in the field. Such movement reveals a good bit about the cameraman's experience of the event, but seriously biases later analysis by selectively structuring the spectator's view of the interaction. Kendon also offers concrete references to techniques and apparatus for filming which should be of value to anyone seriously interested in producing and analysing filmed records.

The value of filmed records and context analysis is made clear in the extensive discussion by Kendon of recent discoveries using filmed specimens. It now is clear that interactors are highly sensitive to each other's behaviours and are integrated into temporally extended systems of relationships at several different levels of organization simultaneously. Kendon is sufficiently struck by this to wonder whether we should ask how individuals emerge from the continual and pervasive communicative systems of our species, rather than the more common reverse question of how individuals manage to communicate with each other.

Michael Scaife's chapter continues the emphasis on the visual recording, but focuses on video instead of film and on studies of social development of the infant and child. The latter emphasis requires a consideration of much longer time-spans than were considered by Kendon. Of course the videotaping cannot be continuous over such periods, for example, twenty months of an infant's life. Scaife points out that microanalysis of the videotapes of infant behaviour is likely to be sterile unless it is based on some theoretical perspective concerning infant biosocial development. He chooses two perspectives to illustrate the issues which arise in trying to understand in systematic fashion the social development of the infant. In one perspective, investigators are interested in identifying potential important events and processes and in tracing forward their developmental effects. Special attention is given to the reciprocal nature of early social interaction. The second perspective is more recent in origin, and investigators operating within it attempt to identify particular social accomplishments and then to trace the origins of those accomplishments by going backwards in time. Clearly, a long-term videotape file on a given infant, extending from ages 10 to 24 months, would be extremely useful within this perspective. There are many pitfalls in such retrospective analyses; but as Scaife shows, some of the pitfalls can be circumvented, and the potential biases of the strategy can be minimized by combining it with other, more deliberately experimental designs to check one's emerging understanding.

The two perspectives, and the problems associated with the mere fact of being observed, are illustrated in Scaife's discussion of object exchange. The infant develops skill at a complex, social game only over time, and the process of development of that social skill can be examined by repeated, selective reference to the videotape record, starting with clear demonstrations of the skill and working backwards in time to watch its early, primitive, awkward origins. Such strategies, of course, are applicable to a wide variety of developmental social processes, such as the emergence of group norms, as well as to the social development of the infant. However, as both Scaife and Kendon argue, the use of the technologies will be of little value unless done within a theoretical framework.

The next two chapters, by myself and Mixon respectively, raise basic questions about the sorts of knowledge we generate through conventional laboratory experimentation in social psychology. In my chapter, I argue that conventional social psychological experiments, and especially experiments using deception, contain inherent and unavoidable ambiguities. Furthermore, they are based upon and are interpreted within a framework which construes people as unrealistically simplistic objects and denies their capacity to act as active, planning agents. The experiment does not give the 'subject' the opportunity to exercise his full capacities of planning and coping with regard to the topic of actual interest in the experiment; yet, the experimenter uses the experiment as a basis for making statements about human nature with regard to that very topic. We should acknowledge the fact that social psychological experiments cannot be used as ultimate criteria for assessing the knowledge gained through other research strategies.

One set of alternative research strategies is role-playing, and I suggest that the variety of techniques available within the broad set can yield considerable knowledge about human action. There are important limitations to role-playing, and the knowledge generated is inherently ambiguous; but so is the knowledge generated by any of our investigative strategies. If used properly, role-playing allows very precise control of the setting, of the actions open to the participants in the scenario, and of the time-frame covered by the scenario. Using recent conceptual analyses of role-playing, a variety of procedures and applications are proposed, along with several examples of role-play studies by which our understandings have been extended.

Mixon develops the argument that scientists are engaged, constantly, in the creation and application of analogies which derive from a process which we do understand and are applied as models to facilitate our understanding of events or processes which are enigmatic to us. Moreover, those human actions which are enigmatic—puzzling to us, or perhaps even shocking—often are so because of morally toned expectations on our parts about how people should behave in specified settings. For example, the notion of conformity is morally toned: in our culture, it is felt that people generally should not 'conform', should not do something they do not agree with just because others do it. Such 'should not' claims imply the existence of some model of how a person should act in the setting of interest. Mixon argues that experimentation often contains such implicit models within the design, instructions, and interpretations by the experimenter. The results may reflect the operation of a set of prescriptive moral rules which guide actions in such settings and to which all competent members of the culture are sensitive; and the results may not reflect the operation of the particular causal mechanism specified by the investigator. Mixon argues further that much of the conduct of interest in social psychology is governed by roles and rules, and that it is of interest to social psychologists to discover the rules which govern the actions of particular role holders in specifiable settings and to investigate the conditions under which the rules are transgressed. He, too, recommends role-playing as one potentially powerful strategy and compares the understandings obtained from a series of deception experiments of harmful obedience with the understandings generated by his own role-playing investigations.

Mixon and I give emphasis to increasing our knowledge about social events, sequences or settings which have occurred but are not well understood. Somewhat less emphasis is given to the discovery of new social patterns or phenomena. Both chapters emphasize the importance of taking into account the meanings and contexts of actions when attempting to understand a social event. This emphasis is common to most of the chapters and constitues a major theme of the book itself.

In their chapter, Jean-Pierre De Waele and Rom Harré introduce the idea of the assisted autobiography. The rationale of the procedures and the interpretation of the resulting understandings derive in part from Harré's ethogenic approach. However, the detailed development of the procedures has taken place, under De Waele's supervision, in a European prison system, with cooperative murderers as the autobiographers. The autobiographer offers a brief written account of his life from which the project chief extracts nine different themes (such as socioeconomic living conditions; goals, aspirations, and conflicts). Each theme is given to a different person on the project team who reconstructs a biography from it. The project personnel negotiate compatible biographies among themselves in small groups of two or three, and these then are discussed with the autobiographer and new biographies are negotiated. The discussions are conducted within the framework of 'focused account eliciting interviews', which involves the elicitation of accounts from the autobiographer and a negotiation of those accounts with team members. The autobiographer is a collaborative participant in the creation of an account of his past, not a 'subject' being studied by an investigator.

De Waele and Harré point out that the past of an individual is not a relic which he carries with him in the present. Instead, it is part of the living present; at any moment of the present, the past is a reconstruction which transcends prior reconstructions of it by virtue of new data and new viewpoints. The process of assisted autobiographical reconstruction changes the team and the focal participant, and the reconstructable past itself, by virtue of the continual negotiation of accounts of the past. The strategy also is an expensive one: a team of twelve professionals (physicians, sociologists, psychologists) may work for a year with a single prisoner. But the final product appears to have immense potential for the understanding of the life, the resources, the susceptibilities, and perhaps the likely future of a particular person. The strategy manifests the importance of the personal meanings of actions, of the cultural setting as a source of those meanings, and of the person as an active agent in the creation and modification of those meanings as he continues to live his life.

The conception of the person as an agent who makes sense of the world by actively construing it underlies the use of the Role Repertory Grid, which Peter Collett discusses in his chapter. In order to understand the choices and actions of a person, it is necessary to understand the meanings which events, actions and alternatives have for him. Those meanings inhere in the systematic way in which he construes people and events in his world, and the repertory grid can be used to reveal that construct system. The repertory grid is a matrix technique which discloses the repertoire and systemic properties of a person's constructs. It is not a new technique, having been in occasional use for over twenty years; but most of its applications have been in clinical psychology, especially in the study of schizophrenia. Relatively little use of it has been made in social psychology. The technique is based on the premise of the person as an active construer with the capacities to plan and anticipate, and it thereby is compatible with the 'active agency' theme which we see emerging in the field. The technique deserves more serious attention by social psychologists, and it has been included in this book to facilitate its incorporation into their investigative armamentarium.

Collett discusses in detail the procedures and pitfalls in designing, using and analysing a grid. The content of one person's grid can be compared with that of another person; the patterns of association between constructs within a single grid can be extracted; and the total structure of the matrix can be used to estimate the simplicity or complexity of the person's construct system—the degree of complexity inherent in the meanings which people and events have for him. The potential strengths and the encountered difficulties of the grid technique are covered by Collett in his discussion of selected research applications. Greatest attention is given to its use in the study of schizophrenic thought disorder, a field in which it has been very widely applied and has given rise to sharp and extensive debate. Collett's review of that debate highlights the benefits which can derive from the repertory grid, but his discussion also urges reasonable caution in interpretations and awareness of ambiguities.

In the final substantive chapter of the book, Joseph Forgas argues that the emerging recognition of the person as an active agent and of the importance of personal meanings to an understanding of action frequently carries with it journalistic and anecdotal methods. However, more rigorous descriptive techniques are readily available. Forgas suggest that multidimensional scaling (MDS) is eminently suited to the complex tasks of naturalistic descriptions called for by the emerging conceptions, and that MDS is especially useful for the quantitative study of social episodes and the factors which influence their perception. Perceived social structures and implicit theories of personality also are susceptible to discovery and analysis by MDS.

Forgas briefly traces the development of MDS methods over the last twenty-five years and distinguishes among the different approaches. He then identifies a number of potential uses of MDS in social psychological research. These include the discovery of previously unknown structures, such as the structure of a social episode; the quantitative representation of phenomenological reality; the development of taxonomies of situations; and the use of the coordinates of the multidimensional space generated by MDS as input data for further analyses, including the testing of hypotheses. The procedural steps of MDS are described, and the ease of interpretation, as well as the limitations, of the outputs of MDS are considered in detail.

To date, MDS techniques have been used in the study of person perception, implicit personality theory, stereotypes, political behaviour and perception, the structure of emotions, and social structure. However, as the MDS techniques become more familiar and routinized, their applicability will be extended even further; and as Forgas suggests, the most promising extension is to the study of social episodes—another of the basic themes of this volume.

The final, review chapter by Carl Backman is more of an analysis, interpretation and prognostication for the field than a straightforward summary of the book. Backman spent a year at Oxford, prior to the BPS workshop which stimulated this volume, and worked closely with Argyle and his group, and with Harré as well. He saw the early emergence of a number of the themes and strategies presented in this book, and his review and predictions for the future capitalize upon that perspective and upon his extensive involvement in the contemporary history of empirical social psychology.

2

SEQUENCES IN SOCIAL BEHAVIOUR AS A FUNCTION OF THE SITUATION

Michael Argyle

INTRODUCTION

The situation has long been overlooked and underestimated by social psychologists, despite lip-service to the contrary. Social psychologists have paid little attention to the ways in which social behaviour is affected by the situations in which it takes place. Fortunately, this is changing, as a result of increased interest in behaviour in natural settings, the rise of environmental psychology and concern with personality–situation interaction. My main concern in this chapter is with sequences of social behaviour, and to show that they are a function of situations. In order to do so, I shall develop the further concepts of *episodes, rules*, and *skilled play within the rules*, and I shall discuss some of the theoretical problems and the research methods which have been developed in this area.

SITUATIONS

Recent research on personality–situation interaction has tried to apportion variance between personality and situation; this requires a categorizing of situations, or the use of dimensions of situations like formal–informal. Other research in this tradition has shown how behaviour is a function both of personality and situational variables—which requires dimensions of situations. These two approaches show the extent to which behaviour is a function of personality traits, situational dimensions, and interaction between them; it also shows the nature of the functional relationships involved (Endler and Magnusson, 1976). However, it is now realized that this 'interactionist' approach is open to a number of objections (Argyle, 1976). In particular the actual forms of behaviour which occur in different situations may be quite different, so that the approach is limited to universal aspects of behaviour like anxiety, amount of speech, and so on. Further, the dimensions which characterize situations provide very poor predictors of behaviour in concrete situations.

Dominant approaches to the measurement of situations

While there is no agreed way of conceptualizing and measuring situations, there are several dominant approaches.

Assessment of the physical aspects of situations

Environmental psychologists are concerned with objectively measurable aspects of situations (Proshansky et al., 1970). Direct measures of the physical features of situations are often objected to on the ground that the situation has to be perceived and interpreted by participants before their behaviour can be affected. Nevertheless, a number of regularities have been discovered by environmental psychologists about the ways in which people respond to the physical aspects of situations, such as distance, density of people, and temperature.

In addition, the physical features of situations have symbolic qualities, and these also have a regular effect, at least within a given culture, because of their common social meaning. Thus physical proximity produces intimacy via the first process; but sitting in certain kinds of chair or position at a table signifies dominance via the second (Argyle, 1975).

Subjective dimensions and affective reactions

The main approach which has emerged out of the personality-situation work has been that of multidimensional scaling (MDS), where dimensions are extracted from the perceived similarity of situations. This is discussed by Forgas in Chapter 10. A good example is the work of Wish (1975) who finds that people construe social situations in terms of variables like cooperative–competitive, or friendly–hostile, equal–unequal, intense–superficial, formal–informal and social–task. These subjective dimensions have been found in several studies and they correspond to familiar dimensions in social psychology. However, if we want to predict behaviour, understand situations, or teach people how to cope with particular situations, these dimensions are not sufficient, and they may not be the most important features of situations. Take a particular combination—task, unequal, formal, cooperative and intense. This includes such situations as teaching, psychotherapy, doctor–patient encounters, religious confession, selection interviews and supervision of work. Each of these situations is totally different in terms of the goals of the encounters, the behaviour which is appropriate, and the rules which must be followed. Perhaps situations cannot be reduced to dimensions (as in physics), and perhaps they are more like the discrete, discontinuous elements of chemistry, each with its internal structure and properties, but describable in terms of general laws nevertheless.

However, subjective and phenomenological approaches need not be limited to global or affective reactions, and we turn to more detailed perceptions of situations.

More detailed analysis of subjective perceptions of situations

Obviously everyone who goes to see the doctor or to teach someone knows a great deal more about such situations than is encompassed by the dimensional scheme described above. They would know, for example, that you might be expected to take your clothes off in one situation, and write on the blackboard in the other. This knowledge may be widely shared, and could be elicited by standard techniques of interview, or more sophisticated procedures like the Semantic Differential and Repertory Grid (see Collett, Chapter 9 in this volume).

Many investigators have argued for a phenomenological approach to situations on the grounds that behaviour depends on how things are perceived and interpreted. On the other hand there is now extensive evidence that people do not have access to the causes of much of their behaviour, or to the cognitive processes involved—they only have access to the cognitive products (Nisbett and Wilson, unpublished, 1976). An example of this is the syntax of language, to which people conform without being able to state the rules. Here there is an objective system, which can be discovered by methods other than phenomenology. However, the distinction between objective and subjective becomes very blurred, if the rules can be elicited from subjects by asking them to judge instances of rule-breaking.

Using behaviour as means of classifying situations

Another way which has been used to classify situations has been in terms of some aspects of the response to them. Frederickson (1972) suggested the use of three-way factor analysis, which produces factors for person, situations, and types of response. Frederickson and his colleagues placed subjects in simulated and realistic job settings, in which they were asked to behave as if they were actually working on the job, and used this kind of analysis for the ways in which items were handled; factors included problems permitting routine solutions, requiring solution of personnel problems, among other items. Endler and Hunt (1966, 1968) in a series of studies have used the same method to analyse types of anxiety response as a function of persons and situations. This method has the advantage that it does not assume that the same behaviour will appear in all situations, and provides a way of discovering the types of behaviour which are used. However, as a measure of situations this general method leaves much to be desired. If our aim is to discover the ways in which behaviour is produced by situations ($B = f(S)$), and to explain how situations produce the behaviour they do, then we need an analysis of situations which is independent of behaviour.

A new approach to the analysis of situations

We have now opened the way to an analysis of situations not in terms of affective dimensions or of behaviour, but in terms of various procedures used by the investigator, which include finding shared perceptions as well as assessment of objective features.

We argued that the dimensions of situations produced by subjective ratings led to groupings of situations where the behaviour taking place is very different. We argued that situations may be discrete, just as ice-hockey and cricket are. The question we may ask is what knowledge and skills does one need to know in order to play a particular game? We have also kept in mind the needs of mental patients who have difficulties with social behaviour—often with particular situations or types of situation (Trower, Bryant, and Argyle, 1977). What knowledge and skills do they need to be taught? My view is that neither affective dimensions, nor measures based on the behaviour taking place are of much help, but that a number of other features of situations are essential.

We should emphasize here that situations, like selection interviews, teaching, and so on, are not static. They have developed as part of the culture in the course of history, and members of the culture learn about them as part of their socialization. However, they are constantly changing, for example, as new relations between teachers and pupils emerge. In addition quite new situations are invented, like the meetings of encounter groups. At any particular social event there has to be some agreement of the 'definition of the situation', and the precise form which it will take. When we speak of assessing a situation we include the assessment of a particular occasion, as well as of typical selection interviews etc. in a particular subculture.

Elements of behaviour used

By an element is meant a type of utterance (questions, jokes, requests, etc.), a type of non-verbal social act (head nods, smiles, shifts of proximity, etc.), and combinations of the two. There are elements of different sizes—singing a hymn, singing one verse, singing one line, for example. However, for many purposes the more useful size to work with is that of a single utterance, with its non-verbal accompaniments, or a non-verbal equivalent (such as a head nod for 'yes'). Utterances also can be divided into smaller elements of different kinds, for example a statement followed by a question. In that case, the utterance would consist of two elements linked 'proactively'. Each situation defines certain social acts as relevant and meaningful. This is partly because the same elements are expressed in different ways—giving directions on the parade ground and to a group of research workers for example. It also is partly because a different range of elements is used—there is no dancing in church, and there are no prayers, sermons or hymn-singing at a dance.

So we have a new interactionist equation:

$$\text{behavioural categories} = f(S).$$

This has been confirmed in a series of our studies in which the main categories have been established for interviews, tutorials, conversation over coffee, buying and selling, etc.

The categorization of behaviour is of crucial importance for sequence analysis, as David Clarke shows (Chapter 3 in this volume). My view is somewhat different from his, since I think that the categories are different in different situations. The only way in which universal categories can be used is by keeping to categories of a high degree of generality, like Bales' (1950) category 5, 'gives opinion', which could include a sermon, an interpretation by a psychoanalyst, and so on.

In addition to having a characteristic repertoire of elements, situations also have a repertoire of *episodes*, which as we shall see can be regarded as higher-order elements. The repertoire for a particular situation can be discovered by one of the techniques described later (pp. 18–21).

Goals or motivations of participants

Lewin (1935) tried to explain behaviour in terms of the structure of the individual's life-space, which consisted mainly of goals and obstacles. His method of assessing the life-space was, unfortunately, to infer it from the subsequent behaviour. Murray (1938) offered an early analysis of person–situation interactions, in terms of the needs of persons and environmental 'press', that is, the capacity of the situation to meet or frustrate those needs. He did not, however, suggest how press should be measured. If we want to describe a game, it is essential to be able to state what the players are trying to do, what their 'goals' are. In a sales situation, an essential component is the fact that one person is trying to buy (to get the right thing for a low price), and the other to sell (to make as much profit as possible). A more sophisticated analysis would reveal that the salesperson is also trying to satisfy the customer, so that she will come again, and tell her friends. Indeed in every social encounter each participant is motivated in some way, is concerned with the anticipated rewards and costs. As yet there are no sophisticated methods of assessing this aspect of situations, though common experience provides likely hypotheses, and skilled interviewing could verify these in many cases. On the other hand some aspects of motivation are largely unconscious, and other approaches may be necessary, such as comparing the appeal of a situation for individuals high and low in various drives, though there are problems about measuring these too. What motivations are aroused and satisfied by a dinner party, for example, and what is the range of individual differences?

Rules

With exactly the same goals being sought, situations may differ greatly according to the rules which are followed. For example, buying and selling may be done by auction, bargaining, self-selection as in a supermarket, and individual selling with fixed prices. The sequence of events that take place is totally different in each case. Rules, and methods of discovering them, will be discussed at more length below. The rules of a game are interconnected; if one is changed, others often have to be changed too—they form a system. The rules of social situations probably form systems in a similar way.

Tasks

Several writers have suggested classifications of situations in terms of the main activity taking place. Krause (1970) for example suggested the following categories: joint working, trading (negotiating), fighting, teaching, serving, self-disclosure, and play. To this would need to be added purely social activity, family life, and rituals. However, tasks are probably covered by the components of situations we have presented already—elements, goals and rules, so we propose to omit them.

Roles

Most situations recognize or generate social roles, whereby different people present have to keep different rules, or pursue different goals. The buyer and salesman follow different rules and goals. In a committee the chairperson, secretary, treasurer and other members may have similar goals, but the rules for them are different. At a dinner party the roles of guest and host are created by the situation, while the more general social roles of different ages and sex are also important.

Physical setting and equipment

Games like hockey, ice-hockey and football are rather similar in their goals and rules, but differ greatly in their physical setting and the equipment used. The equipment makes certain social acts possible—as in the case of the blackboard, slide-projector, etc., used for lectures. The physical setting can create certain kinds of social relationship, intimacy, for example. And it can symbolize certain kinds of social activity by the way rooms are furnished and decorated; a room can thereby suggest love, interrogation, important decision-taking, etc. Such physical settings are usually the residues from past activities; they convey a kind of non-verbal message about what has been going on, but they can also be deliberately contrived.

Barker and Wright (1954) in their analysis of situations emphasized the physical aspects of 'behaviour settings', but combined this with the observed behaviour patterns—which we argued should not be used as a part of the analysis of situations.

Cognitive concepts

To take part in Scottish dancing, for instance, one must know the significance of 'second corner',' 'the ladies side' etc.; to play cricket one must know what an 'innings' and an 'over' are. We suggest later that more expert and experienced performers use more elaborate concepts; for example, in Scottish dancing using terms such as 'poussette' and 'rondel', in chess 'fork', 'discovered check', 'open game', and 'Sicilian defence', or the terms used in different schools of psychotherapy to describe the state of the patient or the therapy—'resistance' and 'negative transference'.

We also conceptualize the other people in a way varying with the situation. In recent and unpublished experiments by Argyle, Forgas and Ginsburg we have found that the trait-dimensions which people use to classify others are quite different for different situations; thus the members of the same group were thought of at the pub in terms of *evaluation* as an enjoyable companion, and *extraversion*, while at a seminar they were thought of in terms of *dominance, creativity*, and *supportiveness*. Similarly members of different groups are thought of in terms of different traits, in the same situations.

Skills

In order to take part in any situation it is necessary to possess certain skills, in addition to knowing the rules and so on. In order to play ice-hockey it is necessary to be able to skate, and in order to take part in a party, a committee meeting, or any other social situation it is necessary to possess a minimal amount of the relevant social skills. However, participants vary greatly in their skills, and in their style of performance, and are often competing within the framework of shared rules. Indeed, this may be an essential feature of the situation, as in games.

Our seven components of situations (omitting tasks) between them give a complete account of situations. They are not independent, however, but form a system in which each component depends on, and could be deduced from, the others. This suggests a new line of research on situations—change one component and see how the others are affected. When we understand the properties of situations we shall be able to predict such consequences.

EPISODES

In order to understand the sequence of events in a situation, it is necessary to divide it up into episodes. The reason is that there are often several periods of interaction of quite different kinds within a situation, which cannot be treated as a continuous or homogeneous series. Watson and Potter (1962) may have been the first to use this concept, and they did so in order to describe the different things that happened in a single situation—parties. They listed eight types of episodes, such as 'hosting', and 'cumulative presenting' (a series of jokes, stories, etc.). Bjerg (1968) offered another scheme for classifying the episodes or 'agons' in the conversation of married couples in a waiting-room situation—such as teasing, consoling, and giving advice.

Harré and Secord (1972) gave the concept of episode a central part in their conceptual analysis of social behaviour, defining it as *'any* sequence of happenings . . . which has some principle of unity' (p. 154). They suggest several such principles—where some person has carried out some plan, where there is a beginning and end, and where there are formal rules, governing the conduct of the episode. We shall now discuss the different ways of defining episodes. We shall see that a very similar concept emerges from quite different empirical procedures, and that there has been a considerable degree of convergence here.

Empirical identification of episodes

Episodes as perceived by observers

Dickman (1963) showed an eight-minute film, and made a hundred and forty-four cards which described the events in it. Subjects were asked to group the cards to make single events. Newtson (1973) showed five-minute videotapes to subjects and asked them to press a button at the ends of units of action. These and other studies on 'chunking' show that (a) there is a fairly high degree of agreement on where the unit-boundaries fall, but (b) there are individual differences in the size of unit used, so that some subjects do not recognize minor boundaries; (c) subjects can be instructed to use units of different sizes; (d) some sequences are more readily and reliably chunkable than others (Collett and MacPhail, unpublished).

However, in these studies the units chosen were rather small—seventeen seconds on average for Newtson, and twenty-five seconds for Dickman. There is no reason why the same methods could not be used for the kind of party episodes described by Watson and Potter, or other extended social acts.

When units are primarily marked by a pattern of movements they can be more easily seen in speeded-up film: Hass (1970) found that the larger (repeated) units of a newspaper seller's activities only became visible in this way.

Episodes as reported by the participants

Harré and Secord (1972) suggest that episodes may be based on the plans of individuals, for example the performance of Berne-type 'games'. This can only happen if one person is in charge (a teacher, for example), or if he succeeds in keeping the initiative as in Berne's games. A skilled performer can control a complete episode even when the others present behave in a variable way. There is extensive evidence in psychology to the effect that individual skilled and verbal behaviour is planned and has a hierarchical structure (Miller, Galanter, and Pribram, 1966). Familiar episodes have 'scripts'; that is, actors have clear expectations about the sequence of events, based on numerous experiences of the episode in the past (Schank, 1975). Various sizes of plans used by teachers have been described, such as Taba's (1966) 'teaching module' and Smith *et al.*'s 'venture' (1967)—both referring to a planned section of the lesson aimed at certain goals. Such episodes are not only planned but announced. There are no agreed research methods for defining episodes via plans. One technique is to play back the videotape of an encounter, to stop it periodically, and interview a participant about his plans at that point. However, there is a danger here; he may make up plans which he did not have at the time. Clarke has devised a piece of equipment on which subjects can indicate aspects of their plans at the time, such as the estimated length of time before something will happen.

Episodes as derived from sequence analysis

Most forms of sequence analysis consist of finding the main categories of behaviour in use in a situation, and finding a Markov chain of the transition probabilities that act A by X will lead to acts, A, B, C, etc. by Y or further acts by X himself. In this method it is possible to use different categories of acts for X and Y, as in teacher–pupil interaction (Flanders, 1970). This method has been much used in the study of animal behaviour, both for single animals (for example, grooming), and more than one animal (such as courtship) (Bateson, 1973). It is fairly clear, however, that a simple first-order Markov chain cannot do justice to sequences of animal behaviour (Dawkins, 1976) so that it seems unlikely that they will do justice to sequences of human social behaviour either.

Several animal studies have found that the pattern of transition probabilities shifts from time to time, as the action enters a new phase. One repeated cycle of behaviour gives way to a different one. It is possible to find transition probabilities for these larger units. Dawkins (1976) describes this as a hierarchy of decisions—first to enter a particular phase, and then to select a particular move. There is greatest uncertainty at the beginning of a phase, since the high transition frequencies only occur within phases. This is non-Markovian since there is a series of decisions, and an earlier decision affects a larger chunk of following moves.

In his 'chunking' experiments Newtson and Engquist (1976) also found that the breakpoints provide more information than points within units; a series of slides of the breakpoints was regarded as more intelligible, led to a more accurate description of behaviour, was remembered better, and their omission was detected more often. It has been found that there is increased gaze, and usually mutual gaze, at the ends of utterances, at greetings and farewells, and at other transition points. This may be because of the greater amount of information available at these points (Argyle and Cook, 1976).

A similar pattern of shifting from cycle to cycle has been found in the classroom. Flanders (1970) reports cycles of events like these shown in Figure 2.1.
Again there may be several different cycles, for example

(a) Question (Teacher)—Answer (Pupil)
(b) Lecture (T)—Question (T)—Answer (P)
(c) Lecture (T)—Question (T)—Answer (P)—Question or other initiation (P)—Response to P's ideas (T).

A teacher might start a lesson with a quick question-answer episode (a), and later shift to more complex sequences like (b) and (c).

How do these episodes consisting of repeated cycles come to a stop? This

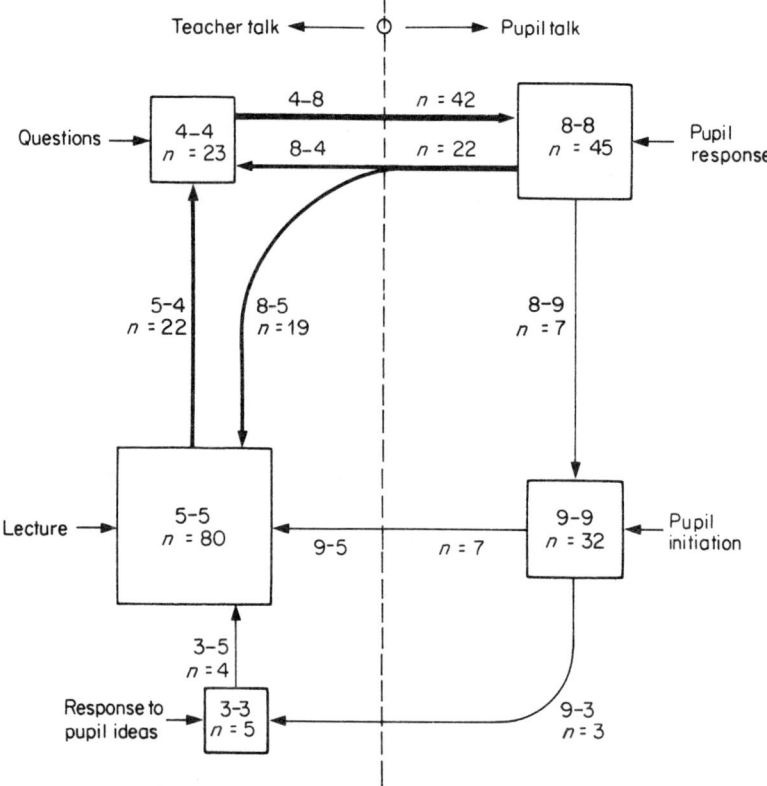

Figure 2.1 Cycle of interaction in the classroom (Flanders, *Analyzing Teacher Behaviour*, 1970 Addison-Wesley, Reading, Mass.)

requires the postulation of a series of goals and subgoals; when an episode has reached its particular goal, there is a shift to another episode. An example is a teacher coming to the end of a planned section of a lesson, having got as far as she had intended. This corresponds to the hierarchy of goals in individual skill performance, which we shall discuss later.

So far we have discussed episodes which consist of repeated cycles. However, some important social episodes are once-through affairs, as with greetings, farewells, and Goffman's 'remedial sequence' (1971). These do not fit a Markovian model either. Greetings, as described by Kendon and Ferber (1973), consist of four main, and complex, moves: mutual gaze–wave–smile–vocalization/physical approach–aversion of gaze–grooming/mutual gaze–bodily contact–smile–vocalization/orientation shift–conversation. Both gaze and smile occur twice, at different points in the sequence, as parts of more complex social acts.

Some situations seem to involve a combination of recycling and once-through episodes. For example a selection interview goes through four main episodes: Opening—interviewer asks questions—candidate asks questions—close. The second and third episodes, however, consist of repeated cycles of the form: question/reply/comment–follow up question/new reply, etc.

There are a number of other approaches to sequence analysis, which are discussed both by Dawkins and by Clarke, but all involve the discovery of episodic units of some kind.

Episodes as derived from rules of sequence

The shortest episode of this kind is the 'adjacency pair', such as question–answer, where the first leads to expectation of the second, and the second is pointless and incomplete without the first (Harvey Sacks, Lecture Notes, Oxford University, 1972). The criterion of what should follow what is now acceptability as discourse, or more generally as social behaviour, rather than of transitional probabilities. Questions can lead to several acceptable sequiturs, including further questions: $Q_1-Q_2-A_2-A_1$, which is a case of 'embedding'. It also can lead to a combined answer and second question: Q_1-A_1/Q_2-A_2 (Merrit, 1976). Such double moves, or 'proactive' sequences, play an important part in social behaviour. Producing a straight piece of information, except in response to a question, can bring conversation to a halt. Such information should be followed proactively by a second move, such as a question, to which others can respond. A somewhat longer episode occurs when one person indicates some plan, which requires a further move on his part. For example, the doctor asks the patient to take his clothes off; the patient does so: what must the doctor do now? In this and other ways, short sections of episodes are constructed out of social acts that must follow each other for the sequence to make sense as social behaviour.

The signalling of episodes

How are episodes started? Sometimes there is someone in charge, who has the power to direct operations. He may do this by verbal 'structuring' or 'framing', as when a teacher explains what the lesson will be about (Bellack *et al.*, 1966). Or he can simply signal the episode by getting on with it, as when an interviewer starts asking questions. He can signal it non-verbally, as when an interviewer starts the second phase by sitting upright and looking more businesslike. If there is no-one in charge the episodes have to be negotiated. One person suggests or begins a particular episode (for example, tells funny story at a party, starts serious discussion of politics at dinner); the others may accept, reject, or try to modify the suggested episode. Sometimes, as Harré and Secord (1972) point out, there are formal rules governing the conduct of the episode, as in ceremonies and games. The beginning and end of episodes may be indicated by the change of topic or activity, but they are also signalled by such non-verbal cues as change of position in space, change of posture, and so on. Scheflen (1965) and Kendon (1970) suggest that there is a hierarchy of verbal and non-verbal units, where the larger verbal units (giving a lecture, for example) correspond to the larger non-verbal units. There is some controversy over exactly how closely the smaller verbal and non-verbal elements coincide (Argyle, 1975); but Erickson (1975), for example, reports some evidence on the linkage between topic shifts and posture shifts.

Episodes in infant social behaviour

Confirmation of the value of the episode as a unit of analysis has come, rather unexpectedly, from the study of infant social behaviour. Richards (1971) reports that the social behaviour of infants of two to three months, with their mothers, consists of certain repeated cycles of smiling, looking and vocalizing, in which the behaviour of the two is closely coordinated. Bruner (1975) reports that at six to seven months infant behaviour with the mother takes the form of repeated cycles like 'peek-a-boo', and handing objects backwards and forwards. Garvey (1974) found that at three-and-a-half to five-and-a-half years children spend much of their time in fantasy play, in which standard episodes from adult life are re-enacted—shopping, going to the doctor, and so on. The two or more children present play the different roles, use special voices, convert toys into props, and go through appropriate cycles of episodes. These authors have suggested that one of the functions of play is practice with rules, including discovering the limits to variation within the rules. Adult episodes are perhaps different from most of these infant and child sequences in that real decisions are taken, and in that there is not *just* repetition, but variations on a theme, within the rules.

Evidence from a variety of sources has been assembled to show the importance of the episode as a unit of social behaviour. The research on infancy suggests that the episode may be the basic unit of social behaviour. That is to say, social behaviour has a *gestalt* quality, in which the smallest units only occur as part of larger sequences, and take their point and meaning from those sequences. The components of episodes take their meaning and order from the episode, and should not be considered in isolation.

THE RULES OF SITUATIONS AND EPISODES*

Sociologist, linguists, philosophers, and now psychologists have argued that man is a rule-following creature, and that his behaviour should be explained in terms of underlying rules. This view is partly based on the analogy between social behaviour and language, the analogy with games, and the analogy with formal social events. Language, games and formal events are themselves forms of social behaviour, each has known rules, and in the first two cases at least these rules are *generative*, in other words, a finite set of rules generates a possibly infinite set of possible sentences or games. The actors can move in different ways within the rules, according to their goals, styles and skill.

The arguments for applying this model to other forms of social behaviour are that people can sometimes state the rules, the rules are sometimes used in planning their behaviour, sanctions may be applied to those who break rules, people try to find out what the rules are, tell others about them, and sometimes conceal them. It is further maintained that to establish rules is basic to human society, and to follow them basic to human nature. Bach (1975) argues that rules are a special kind of norm, which 'entail special social obligations', either to coordinate behaviour (for example, driving on the left), to produce cooperation (for example, anti-litter), to apportion duties (division of labour), or as regulations imposed by authority.

The rules of language are rather different: they are generative rules, whereby ideas are translated into sentences in a 'top-to-bottom' rather than 'left-to-right' manner. The rules are not primarily about the order of words, since the same set of words can express more than one idea, and the same idea can be expressed by different words. Speakers of a language can tell when the rules have been broken, but cannot usually state the rules. Linguists find sets of rules which would account for the set of sentences regarded as acceptable, but it is not known whether these are the rules used by speakers in generating their speech.

Clarke (Chapter 3 in this volume) suggests that the key to explaining sequences of social behaviour lies in discovering such generative rules for social behaviour. These would explain the implicit knowledge which we all have about whether sequences are appropriate or inappropriate. However, this grammar of social behaviour has yet to be discovered.

It would be absurd to try to carry out an empirical study of the behaviour of cricket players, or people at an auction sale, without first finding the rules. On the

---

*I am indebted to the collection of papers edited by Peter Collett (1977).

other hand the importance of rules is greater in some situations than others. Price and Bouffard (1974) asked subjects to rate the appropriateness of fifteen kinds of behaviour in fifteen situations. It was found that the situations varied greatly in 'constraint' (that is, the number of things not permitted). At one extreme were church services and job interviews, at the other were being in one's own room, or in a park. Probably the importance of rules, the applicability of the model, is greatest in formal situations. In any case rules do not tell the whole story—there is also play within them.

Rules and empirical laws

Rules are usually contrasted with empirical laws of nature. An example of a rule is 'Secretaries should arrive at work by 9 am'; an example of a law is 'If a response is reinforced, its probability of occurrence is increased'. We have to add, in the case of such psychological laws, 'over a certain range of conditions, and in the absence of interfering processes'. Furthermore, 'empirical laws' are abstractions by scientists working within a given tradition. Rules are the conventional practices of a particular social group; they could be different and usually are in other groups, they are not true or false, they can be broken; if they are broken, someone can be held responsible. Laws describe regularities and functional relationships; if they are broken, it means the law is wrong.

Harré and Secord (1972) argue that behaviour is either produced by causal mechanisms or by the following of rules to seek a goal. They contrast the biological causal process whereby two people become parents, with the rule-following sequences whereby they got married. However, even the biological process of procreation involves rule-governed behaviour, the performance of meaningful social acts, and the following of 'scripts' (Gagnon, 1974). I would argue that *all* sequences of events require explanation, and that marriage involves causal processes (for example, about the effects of rituals). In the case of such complex, higher-order, non-physiological sequences of events we have to operate at the level of meanings, such as 'being married', but that is what cognitive psychology is about. And we have to take account of the operation of rules which are themselves arbitrary, have complex historical origins, and are not simply part of psychology.

If a regularity is observed in human behaviour, for example, secretaries coming to work at 9 am, how do we decide whether this is due to a rule or a law? We would say there is a rule if people can state it, report using it to plan their behaviour, tell when it is broken, or apply sanctions when it is broken. Could there be universal rules? There may be, but they then would surely be laws as well. Could a natural law become labelled as a rule (Fox, 1976), so that the rule is 'behaviour-fitting', but not 'behaviour-guiding' (Lindsay, 1976)? Some decision might be made here by trying to find out how far the rule had actually guided behaviour. Mann (1970) reports the rules governing behaviour in Australian football queues. These are clearly rules, since sanctions are used against those who break them. Fox (1976) argues that the apparently disorderly behaviour at certain Irish 'fights' is rule-governed, although this is not realized by those involved or by casual observers. This is not such a clear case since no evidence is presented of sanctions, recognition when the rules are broken, or knowledge of the rules. In both these cases the rules are claimed to form a coherent system, in much the same way as are the rules of grammar or games. They are also claimed to be functional, for example, in controlling aggression. The rule system is now being offered as a theory about the situation, and hence is like empirical laws and their explanatory hypotheses. Thus, in these cases the rules appear to be based on empirical laws.

There may be some instances which have claims to be both rules and laws. However, I see no reason why a law could not also be a rule. In any case rules are themselves natural phenomena, in that social psychologists have studied the conditions under which rules (or 'norms') develop, though they have not found out much about their contents. This enables us to dodge the problems which Harré and Secord discuss—that most episodes of human life seem to be 'enigmatic', because it is not clear whether they are governed by rules or laws. However, that is only a problem for social scientists, not for the actors. For them, the performance of most episodes is habitual or routine, and they need not worry whether rules or laws are involved.

A person may follow, or be influenced by, a rule without knowing what the rule is. A good example of this is grammar, where the rules can be stated by very few people. However, most people can recognize when these rules are broken, so that they have knowledge of a sort. A person may fail to keep to a rule, either because he does not know about it, or because he is influenced by another rule, or conflicting motivation, or because he lacks the ability to do what is required. In the latter cases the rule still serves as a 'subjective yardstick in the evaluation of behaviour' (Collett, 1977, p. 14), in other words, he may feel guilty or inadequate, or judge the behaviour of others as unsatisfactory.

Clearly there are a number of ways in which the existence of rules affects behaviour, and a number of questions which can be raised in relation to them, such as how children change with age in their relation to rules, and which kinds of personality appeal to rules most (Robinson, 1976). One of the most important roles of rules is in the production of behaviour, as will be elaborated below.

Research methods for studying rules

We need first to make some conceptual distinctions.

(1) In studies in which we asked subjects to rate instances of rule-breaking on a number of scales, the main factor found was degree of disruptiveness. At one pole were rules *intrinsic* to situations, where breaking them brought things to a

complete stop—for example, candidate at interview insists on asking all the questions; at the other pole were conventions—for example, candidate wears no shoes. This brings us to a fundamental point about social behaviour—unless those present agree to keep to the intrinsic rules, no game or social behaviour can take place. In games there is a clear distinction between, for example, using a tennis racquet or wearing trousers of the wrong colour at cricket. However, in the case of social situations we found that this is a continuous, not a dichotomous variable. That is, breakage of some of the rules at interviews or at dinner parties created intermediate degrees of disruption.

(2) Some rules regulate what should happen, while others define terms. The regulatory rules of cricket require constitutive rules defining 'over', 'no-ball', etc. It can be seen how the rules may comprise a complex cognitive structure, which is mastered by the players, and used in the production of behaviour.

(3) Some behaviour is *prescribed*, some is *proscribed* (prohibited); we may add that some is permitted. In each case we may be referring to an episode, situation or a group of situations.

(4) Rules may refer to different content areas—the elements of behaviour, sequences, mood, etc.

(5) There may be different sanctions, which in turn might lead people to regard different rules differently, such as legal, moral, etiquette, or rules of games (against cheating).

The research worker may want to find out several things about rules: the content of the main intrinsic rules which apply to a situation or group of situations, the amount of latitude allowed in behaviour, the sanctions which follow rule-breaking, the authority or other source of the rule, the extent to which people are aware of it.

The research methods which are appropriate for studying empirical laws are not suited to the study of rules. Empirical laws depend upon the observation of empirical regularities, but uniformity of behaviour does not always correspond to the presence of rules, and vice versa, and the relation between rules and behaviour may be complex, as in cricket. So the simple observation of empirical regularities is not the way to study rules. Instead, several other approaches may be suggested.

Rule-breaking

One of the main criteria for the existence of rules is the observed use of sanctions for breaking them, so observational methods can be used as by Mann (1970). The experimental breaking of rules was first used by Garfinkel (1963), in an experiment on noughts and crosses, where the experimenter placed his mark on one of the lines. We have used this method in a more controlled experimental way to study the rules of interruption—an example of a sequence rule. Subjects were asked to judge experimentally varied instances of interruption. It was found that interruption is most acceptable at the end of a sentence rather than at the end of a phrase, though this was better than the middle of a phrase, and that it was irrelevant how long the person interrupted had been speaking (Argyle, 1975).

Study of mobile individuals

This method makes use of the fact that rules are different in different groups. Garfinkel and Stoller (Garfinkel, 1967) interviewed Agnes who had a sex change, and we have done less dramatic studies of newcomers to Oxford. This could be extended to the study of individuals who enter the same host group from different source groups, since each direction of mobility will presumably produce sensitivity to different rules.

Standardized questionnaire procedures

Argyle, Campbell, and White are now studying the rules of a number of situations by a two-stage process. First a sample of people from the appropriate subculture are asked to provide prescriptive and proscriptive rules 'which are of some importance' (that is, are intrinsic) for each situation. They are also asked for rules which apply to groups of situations, using a hierarchical classification based on perceived similarity of situations. A second set of judges then rates the applicability of each rule to every situation. This generates a further hierarchical classification of situations—a dendrogram—based on the operation of common rules. It also generates a set of rules at all levels of generality. This method shows which rules apply, and are more or less distinctive, in each situation, as well as the generality of the rules found.

Similar methods are being used for finding the rules governing sequences. The situation is described, part of a sequence is shown, and subjects are asked to say what must, may or may not happen next.

The study of sanctions

Forgas, Ginsburg, and Argyle are using similar methods for the study of sanctions. A large collection of types of sanctions for rule-breaking is being assembled and will be treated by multidimensional scaling (MDS). The main types of sanction for different situations and types of rule-breaking are being found.

I hope that the discussion above makes clear that rules play an important part in individual behaviour, though the behaviour in question, like all behaviour, is still governed by empirical laws, and is capable of explanation in the usual ways. Rules are an essential component of situations and episodes, and need to be established before we can understand or predict behaviour in them. Some situations are more rulebound than others, and in all situations we need to study behaviour *within* the rules as well—the result of individual goals, style and skill.

THE SKILLS OF INDIVIDUAL PERFORMANCE WITHIN THE RULES

We have pointed out that rules provide an account of only some aspects of behaviour in different situations, and that there is varied play within the rules. We suggested that rules are more important in 'formal' situations, where the scope for individual variation is less. These would also be types of situations where there is more situational (S) variance, and less person (P) and $P \times S$ variance. There are different elements of behaviour in different situations, and there are so many aspects of person which affect behaviour in particular situations that it is hard to imagine the necessary list of P variables—including ability at croquet, attitude toward Mexicans, etc., which are of overriding importance in *some* situations.

The social skills model

This model was elaborated by Argyle and Kendon (1967) and Argyle (1969) and will not be described at length here.

Interactors have goals, which they attempt to attain by skilled acts, which are continually modified as a result of feedback. The skilled acts have a hierarchical structure, the largest units including cognitive plans with a corresponding hierarchy of goals and subgoals. However, skilled behaviour operates within the rules and other properties of situations, in several ways.

Choice of goals

As we have seen, situations have characteristic goals for the occupants of each position. The actual goals chosen are typically a subdivision of these, for

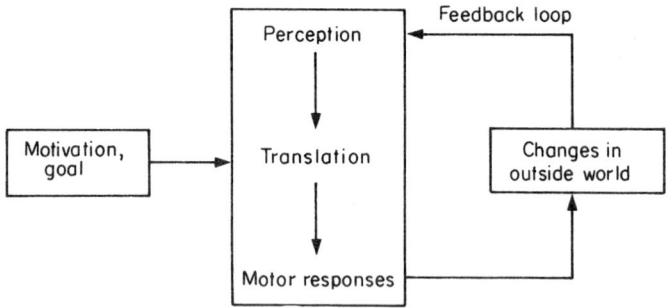

Figure 2.2 Motor skill model (from Argyle, 1969, 1972; reproduced by permission of Penguin Books Ltd)

example, a teacher wants to teach a particular area of knowledge. When goals deviate from those appropriate to the situation, there is likely to be trouble.

Cognitive planning of skilled behaviours

In order to make a move at chess, for example, a player must know the rules and appreciate the state of play. He must have a cognitive map of the situation, and how it has developed so far. In social behaviour generally, in order to produce an acceptable and effective social act, it is necessary to understand the rules and other aspects of the situation, as well as what has gone before. A person who has failed to appreciate correctly the nature of the situation will not know what to do in it. One common source of social inadequacy we have found is inability to deal with particular situations like parties or interviews, through not having understood the nature of the situation.

Use of elements (choice of moves)

Interactors may use only those elements of behaviour which are permitted in a particular situation (or episode). Part of the skill consists in the effective production of these elements.

Use of means–end sequences

Some moves like asking questions, or giving reinforcement, have much the same consequences in all situations. Others vary with the situation, and the skilled performer knows which ones to use. Extensive research has been done for example on the techniques on the part of teachers which are most effective in the classroom (Rosenshine, 1971), and on the skills of industrial supervisors (Argyle, 1972).

Use of episodes

Part of social skill consists of being able to use appropriate episodes, such as those with repeating cycles. We described above some of the cycles observed in the classroom. Flanders (1970) describes the technique for shifting from one cycle to another.

Reactive and other sequences

The four types of interaction distinguished by Jones and Gerard (1967) show how skilled processes operate in different kinds of interaction.

In asymmetrical contingency (teaching, for example), one interactor has a plan to which others merely respond; in mutual contingency (such as bargaining) both do; and so on. The social skill model fits best those cases where goals and planning, rather than simply reacting, are involved. A common source of incompetence is acting only in a reactive way, and not exercising sufficient control over others, as is reflected for example by high scores on external control (Phares, 1976).

Social effectiveness and inadequacy

Social effectiveness is most easily defined and measured for professional roles like teacher or interviewer. We may also speak of effectiveness in a variety of everyday encounters, though here *lack* of it is more easily recognized, resulting in isolation, failure to communicate effectively or persuade, and so on. Let us confine the discussion to effectiveness in the performance of a specific role in a particular situation. The criterion of effectiveness is then success in attaining the normally accepted goals of that situation. Our experience in training mental patients and others by social skills training suggests that inadequacy may take a wide variety of forms, about twenty-five in all. These are related to situations in several ways.

(1) Lack of understanding of the situation and its rules, for example, thinking a selection interview is for vocational guidance.

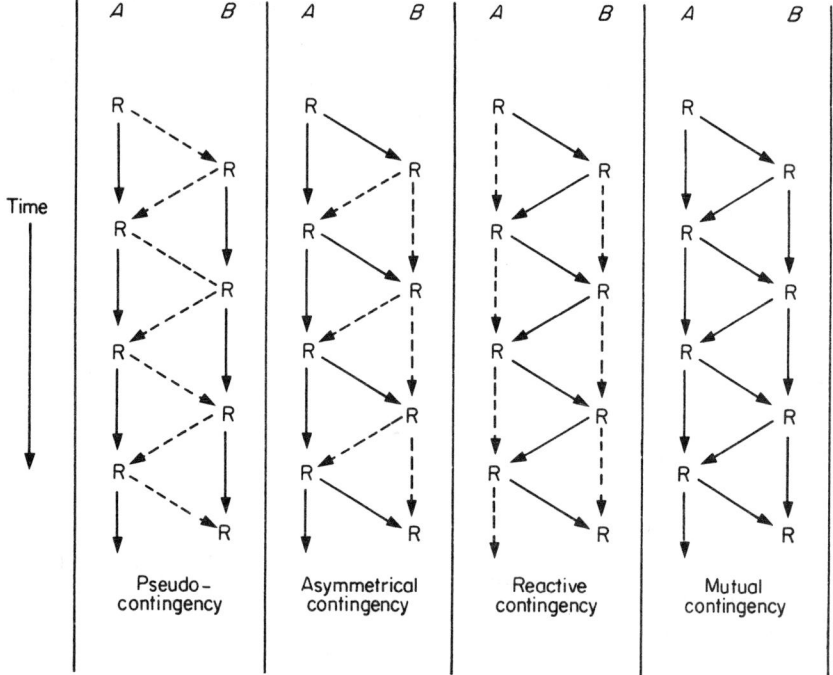

Figure 2.3 Classes of social interaction in terms of contingency (Jones and Gerard, 1967)

(2) Lacking the skills required in a situation, for example, not being able to speak in the manner required for public speaking. Alternatively there may be ignorance of what the effective skills are, of chairmanship perhaps.

(3) Lacking other personal properties needed for success in a situation—attractiveness, the right social class, age, beliefs, etc.

(4) Lacking more universal social skills like rewardingness and effective use of non-verbal signals (Trower, Bryant, and Argyle, 1977).

SEQUENCES OF BEHAVIOUR IN SITUATIONS

The analysis of sequences of social behaviour cannot be done without taking the properties of the situation into account. In order to show how this is done, we will consider separately the four kinds of social interaction contingencies mentioned above.

Pseudo-contingency

Here neither interactor is reacting to the other, except as regards timing. Examples are people acting in a play, or enacting a ritual, like greeting and saying farewell. Greetings and farewells are a little different, in that there is some variation and interaction. Such formal sequences are taken by Harré and Secord (1972) and Goffman (1971) as a model for other situations; our view is that they lack some of the key properties of other kinds of sequence. In pseudo-contingencies, the sequence is totally predictable from the rules; there is no variation within the rules, except in style.

Reactive contingency

Here each person reacts to the last move by the other. Examples are rambling conversations. The sequence is limited by the universal rules of all social behaviour, and the particular rules of the situation, which will allow only certain kinds of utterances, for example, and certain sequences. Thus a conversation in a pub is somewhat different from a conversation at a polite dinner party. In either case the sequence could be described, and to a limited extent predicted by the rules governing which sequences are allowable as sensible sequences of social behaviour and the probabilities (in each situation) that the allowable moves will be made. Both rules and probabilities can vary with the cultural setting, as shown by Keenan's (1976) study of conversation in Malagasy: there is no obligation to produce informative replies to questions. This is a deviation from what appears to be a rule in most Western cultural settings.

Asymmetrical contingency

Here only one person has a plan, while the others are mainly reacting to what he

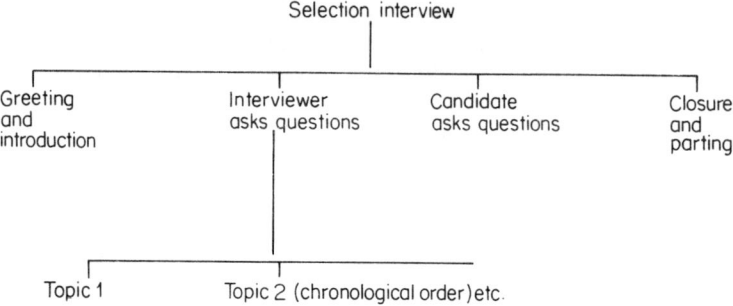

Figure 2.4 Plans in the selection interview

does. Examples are teaching and interviewing. The kind of plan an interviewer might have is shown in Figure 2.4.

The interviewer's performance fits the social skill model, which of course allows for *some* reaction on the part of the interviewee to the other's responses. The social skill model is not sufficient to tell us about the sequence of events: the person in charge reacts to the other (a) by rules of sequence—questions lead to answers, including some rules which may be unique to the situation; and (b) by feedback, which modifies his own planned sequence of behaviour. It will be noticed that the interviewer creates four main episodes, two of which have definite subepisodes; and he must move within the rules and in accordance with other properties of the situation, as described above.

Mutual contingency

Here each interactor has plans, each is an autonomous initiator of social-skill sequences. Examples are negotiation and discussion. This is a much more difficult kind of sequence to analyse. There is both cooperation and competition, the former over keeping to the rules of social behaviour in general and also those of the situation, and the latter in that the interactors usually have somewhat incompatible goals. Again the moves by each interactor, and the sequences of moves, are restricted by the rules of the situation. An example is an auction sale, where the rules of sequence are as shown in Figure 2.5. (There is a further rule: bid *more* than the last person.) In so far as there are clear episodes, the same principle can be taken further—there is predictability from the rules of the episode. If it is found that sequences in a particular situation have a clear hierarchical structure, this is one source of prediction.

A first-order Markov-chain approach will not help much, since both interactors are pursuing persistent plans. Higher-order Markov chains do better, and Altmann (1965) found that taking account of four previous acts led to good prediction. Clarke (1975) found that fourth-order artificial dialogues (in which three previous utterances were supplied) were indistinguishable from real ones.

			Following act				
			1	2	3	4	5
Preceding act	Auctioneer	1. Offers object for sale			✓	✓	✓
		2. States latest bid			✓	✓	✓
		3. Closes bidding	✓				
	Customer A	4. Bids		✓	✓		✓
	Customer B	5. Bids		✓	✓	✓	

Figure 2.5 Rules of sequence in auction sales

We can also make some use of universal principles of sequence which apply in all situations. It is not our present concern to consider whether these exist, or what they are, but likely candidates are (a) response-matching, (b) the effects of reinforcement, (c) certain utterance sequences, like question–answer, (d) certain principles of non-verbal communication, and its linkage with speech, and (e) the alternation of utterances. In addition there are further rules, not all of which have been identified. A second move should be 'coherent with', that is, be a sensible response to the move before. This is a difficult concept to define, but would include not shifting to a different topic or activity and the completion of adjacency pairs and similar units and the persistence of plans, where a previous move by a person entailed further acts on his part.

So far we have been thinking of sequences in terms of the repeated, probabilistic use of certain categories of behaviour. However, there is another aspect of sequences: the progressive buildup of cognitive contents, or other aspects of the situation, just as a game of chess develops. Each utterance has an inner structure, in that it builds on ideas which are shared by speaker and listener, and successive utterances add to this shared material (Rommetveit, 1974). In order to understand an utterance it is necessary to construct a cognitive map of the contents, based on the 'frame' within which it is set, such as the background idea of the conversation (Minsky, 1975). Each move, whether verbal or not, requires an understanding of the situation, and of the state of play. The relation between two people may change as interaction proceeds, and the pay-off matrix of possible rewards shifts towards the expectation of greater rewards as friendship develops (Huesmann and Levinger, 1976). An episode of a school lesson may follow from a plan in the mind of the teacher, to develop a certain level of understanding of some topic, and the episode continues, in a cyclic manner, until this is achieved.

We see then that in order to explain or predict a sequence of social behaviour we have to take account of the situation, in several ways. We need to know:

(1) Which of the four contingency types the sequence approximates. This may shift from episode to episode.

(2) The rules of the situation, the elements of behaviour, and the sequences permitted (this is sufficient for pure cases of Type I).

(3) Information about the Markovian probabilities, perhaps up to fourth-order, for the probable sequences (first-order is sufficient for Type II).

(4) The goals of the interactors (combined with first-order probabilities, for Type III).

(5) For Type IV, higher-order Markov tables can be used. Another approach is via the hierarchical episodic structure, with stronger rules within episodes.

(6) Where there is a continuous buildup of cognitions or relationships, this may be taken account of as one of the goals of interaction (as in teaching), or there may be rules about it; but in any case a new kind of category must be introduced.

CONCLUSION

We have argued that to understand sequences of social behaviour, a detailed analysis must first be made of situations, and we presented a new approach to doing so. Situations, however, contain a number of different episodes, which need to be taken separately, though *their* sequence also can be studied. Situations resemble games, and in certain respects language: in each case the sequence is partly a function of rules, and methods were described for finding them; however, we also need to explain why there is a particular set of rules. We must also take account of varied play within the rules, and various aspects of individual plans, style, and effectiveness were introduced. To explain or predict an actual sequence of events we need to know about situations, episodes, rules and the individuals concerned. Use can be made of Markovian rules and probabilities, but these have to be applied differently for different kinds of encounter.

References

Altmann, S. A., 1965, Sociobiology of rhesus monkeys II. Stochastics of social communication, *Journal of Theoretical Biology*, **8**, 490–522.
Argyle, M., 1969, *Social Interaction*, London: Methuen; New York: Aldine.
Argyle, M., 1972, *The Social Psychology of Work*, Harmondsworth: Penguin Books.
Argyle, M., 1975, *Bodily Communication*, London: Methuen.
Argyle, M., 1976, Personality and social behaviour, in R. Harré (ed.), *Personality*, Oxford: Blackwells.
Argyle, M. and Cook, M., 1976, *Gaze and Mutual Gaze*, Cambridge University Press.
Argyle, M. and Kendon, A., 1967, The experimental analysis of social performance, *Advances in Experimental Social Psychology*, **3**, 55–98.

Bach, K., 1975, Analytical social philosophy—basic concepts, *Journal for the Theory of Social Behaviour*, **5**, 189–214.
Bales, R. F., 1950, *Interaction Process Analysis*, Reading, Mass.: Addison-Wesley.
Barker, R. G. and Wright, H. F., 1959, *Midwest and its Children: the Psychological Ecology of an American Town*, Evanston, Ill.: Row, Peterson.
Bakson, P. P. G., 1973, Internal influences on early learning in birds, in R. A. Hinde and J. Stevenson-Hinde (eds.), *Constraints on Learning: Limitations and Predispositions*, New York: Academic Press, 101–116.
Bellack, A. A. et al., 1966, *The Language of the Classroom*, New York: Teachers College Press.
Bjerg, K., 1968, Interplay-analysis. A preliminary report on an approach to the problems of interpersonal understanding, *Acta Psychologica*, **28**, 201–245.
Bruner, J., 1975, The ontogenesis of speech acts, *Journal of Child Language*, **2**, 1–19.
Clarke, D. D., 1975, The use and recognition of sequential structure in dialogue, *British Journal of Social and Clinical Psychology*, **14**, 333–339.
Collett, P., 1977, (ed.) *Social Rules and Social Behaviour*, Oxford: Blackwells.
Dawkins, R., 1976, Hierarchical organisation: a candidate principle for ethology, in P. P. G. Bateson and R. Hinde (eds.), *Growing Points in Ethology*, Cambridge University Press.
Dickman, H. R., 1963, The perception of behavioral units, in R. G. Barker (ed.), *The Stream of Behaviour*, New York: Appleton-Century-Crofts.
Endler, N. S. and Hunt, J. McV., 1966, Sources of behavioural variance as measured by the S–R Inventory of anxiousness, *Psychological Bulletin*, **65**, 336–346.
Endler, N. S. and Hunt, J. McV., 1968, S–R variations of hostility and comparison of the properties of variance from persons, response, and situation for hostility and anxiousness, *Journal of Personality and Social Psychology*, **9**, 309–315.
Endler, N. S. and Magnusson, D., 1976, *Interactional Psychology and Personality*, Washington: Hemisphere.
Erickson, F., 1975, One function of proxemic shifts in face-to-face interaction, in A. Kendon et al. (eds.), *Organisation of Behavior in Face-to-Face Interaction*, The Hague and Paris: Mouton.
Flanders, N. A., 1970, *Analyzing Teaching Behavior*, Reading, Mass.: Addison-Wesley.
Fox, R., 1977, The inherent rules of violence, in P. Collett (ed.), *Social Rules and Social Behaviour*, Oxford: Blackwells, pp. 132–149.
Frederickson, N., 1972, Toward a taxonomy of situations, *American Psychologist*, **27**, 114–123.
Gagnon, J. H., 1974, Scripts and the coordination of sexual conduct, in J. K. Cole and R. Dienstbier (eds.), *Nebraska Symposium on Motivation, 1973*, Lincoln: University of Nebraska Press.
Garfinkel, H., 1963, Trust and stable action, in O. J. Harvey (ed.), *Motivation and Social Interaction*, New York: Ronald.
Garfinkel, H., 1967, *Studies in Ethnomethodology*, Englewood Cliffs, NJ.: Prentice-Hall.
Garvey, C., 1974, Some properties of social play, *Merrill-Palmer Quarterly*, **20**, 163–180.
Goffman, E., 1971, *Relations in Public*, London: Allen Lane, Penguin Press.
Hass, H., 1970, *The Human Animal*, New York and London, Putnam's.
Harré, R. and Secord, P. F., 1972, *The Explanation of Social Behaviour*, Oxford: Blackwells.
Huesmann, L. R. and Levinger, G., 1976, Incremental exchange theory: a formal model for progression in dyadic social interaction, *Advances in Experimental Social Psychology*, **9**, 192–229.
Jones, E. E. and Gerard, H. B., 1967, *Foundations of Social Psychology*. New York: Wiley.

Keenan, F. O., 1976, On the universality of conversational implications. *Language and Society*, **5**, 67–80.

Kendon, A., 1970, Movement coordination in social interaction, *Acta Psychologica*, **32**, 100–125.

Kendon, A., 1972, Some relationships between body motion and speech, in A. Siegman and B. Pope. (eds.), *Studies in Dyadic Interaction*, Elmsford, NY: Pergamon.

Kendon, A. and Ferber, A., 1973, A description of some human greetings, in R. P. Michael and J. H. Crook (eds.), *Comparative Ecology and Behaviour of Primates*, London: Academic Press.

Krause, M. S., 1970, Use of social situations for research purposes, *American Psychologist*, **25**, 748–753.

Lewin, K., 1935, *A Dynamic Theory of Personality*, New York: McGraw-Hill.

Lindsay, R., 1977, Rules as a bridge between speech and action, in P. Collett (ed.), *Social Rules and Social Behaviour*, Oxford: Basil Blackwell, pp. 150–173.

Mann, L., 1970, The social psychology of waiting lines, *American Scientist*, **58**, 390–398.

Merritt, M., 1976, On questions following answers in sensible encounters, *Language and Society*, **5**, 315–357.

Miller, G. A., Galanter, E. and Pribram, K. H., 1966, *Plans and the Structure of Behavior*, New York: Holt.

Minksy, M., 1975, A framework for representing knowledge, in P. H. Winston (ed.), *The Psychology of Computer Vision*, New York: McGraw-Hill.

Murray, H. A., 1938, *Explorations in Personality*, New York: Cambridge University Press.

Newtson, D., 1973, Attribution and the unit of perception of ongoing behavior, *Journal of Personality and Social Psychology*, **28**, 28–38.

Newtson, D., and Engquist, G., 1976, The perceptual organization of ongoing behavior. *Journal of Experimental Social Psychology*, **12**, 436–450.

Nisbett, R. E. and Wilson, T. D., 1976, Telling more than we can know: self perception and the representativeness heuristic, unpublished, University of Michigan.

Phares, E. J., 1976, *Locus of Control in Personality*, Morristown, NJ: General Learning Press.

Price, R. H. and Bouffard, D. L., 1974, Behavioral appropriateness and situational constraints as dimensions of social behavior. *Journal of Personality and Social Psychology*, **30**, 579–586.

Proshansky, H. M. et al. (eds.), 1970, *Environmental Psychology: Man and his Physical Setting*, New York: Holt, Rinehart and Winston.

Richards, M. P. M., 1971, Social interaction in the first weeks of human life, *Psychiat. Neurol. Neurochir.*, **74**, 35–42.

Robinson, P., 1977, The rise of the rule: Mode or node?, in P. Collett (ed.), *Social Rules and Social Behaviour*, Oxford: Basil Blackwell, pp. 70–87.

Rommetveit, R., 1974, *On Message Structure*, London: Wiley.

Rosenshine, B., 1971, *Teaching Behaviour and Student Achievement*, Slough: NFER.

Schank, R. C., 1975, The role of memory in language processing, in C. Cofer and R. Atkinson (eds.), *The Status of Human Memory*, New York: W. H. Freeman.

Scheflen, A. E., 1965, *Stream and Structure of Communicational Behavior*, Commonwealth of Pennsylvania: Eastern Pennsylvania Psychiatric Institute.

Slater, P. J. B., 1973, Describing sequences of behavior, in P. P. G. Bateson and P. H. Klopfer (eds.), *Perspectives in Ethology*, New York and London: Plenum Press.

Smith, B. O. et al., 1967, *A Study of Strategies of Teaching*, Urbana, Ill.: Bureau of Educational Research, University of Illinois.

Taba, H., 1966, *Teaching Strategies and Cognitive Functioning in Elementary School*

Children, USOE Cooperative Research Project, No. 2404, San Francisco State College.

Trower, P., Bryant, B. and Argyle, M., 1977, *Social Skills and Mental Health*, London: Methuen.

Watson, J. and Potter, R. J., 1962, Analytic unit for the study of interaction, *Human Relations*, **15**, 245–263.

Wish, M., 1975, Role and personal expectations about interpersonal communication, US–Japan Seminar (roneoed), University of California, San Diego.

3

THE LINGUISTIC ANALOGY OR WHEN IS A SPEECH ACT LIKE A MORPHEME?

David D. Clarke

The central phenomenon in human social life is face-to-face interaction. Two or more people gather together in the same place at the same time, they communicate, and particularly they converse. The properties of such conversations are to some extent familiar to every layman. We all recognize, for example, that they are governed by some principle of order. They are certainly not just a random collection of remarks. However, the nature of the non-randomness does not seem to be a part of the layman's knowledge, or at least not a part on which he can comment spontaneously. There are two essential mysteries in conversation, and it will require special techniques to unravel them: the nature of the pattern to which conversations conform, and the nature of the generative and interpretative processes by which they are created and understood. This is the familiar distinction between a behavioural *product* (the structure of conversation) and generative or interpretative *process*.

What then is the relation between product and process, and how should we find out more about both? According to Harré and Secord (1972) and Harré (1976) it is necessary to appreciate the essentially metaphorical nature of scientific investigation, if we are to progress in social psychology and to emulate the successes of the advanced sciences. An understanding of human social behaviour will derive, at least in the early stages, from the construction of suitable metaphors, or icons. Harré says our discovery procedure should go like this: first there should be a critical description of the product of the system we are studying (the product in this case being conversation and the system being the cerebral mechanisms which produce it). Then, rather than making deductions directly about the generative process, which would be a naive simplification of the means by which processes are elucidated by products, we should next turn to a source of analogy, choosing something which is better understood than our subject matter, and which could be plausibly said to share many of its important features. Using our understanding of that source we can then construct an icon, which is a hypothetical generative process or device, whose properties we can exactly define. In some cases the source of the iconic model will be the same as the subject matter. Then the icon is called a homeomorph. In other cases the source and the subject matter are different, and the icon is called a paramorph.

A famous paramorphic model will serve to illustrate the stages in this discovery procedure. When the Austrian monk, Gregor Mendel, studied the genetics of pea plants in his monastery garden, he started, one assumes, with a description of the phenomenon or 'the product' he wished to explain. He observed that the properties of filial plants related to those of their parents in ways which might seem curious at first sight. They were not, for example, a mixture of parental attributes. Red flowers crossed with white flowers did not give pink, but a mixture of red and white flowers, and furthermore the mixture occurred in a fixed proportion. Clearly at that time, any inference about the actual genetic process in the plants was out of the question. Processes of molecular biology as we now understand them, were conceptually and technologically beyond Mendel's reach. In offering us the picture of the gene he was not describing a structure within the plant cell of which he had any direct knowledge, but rather he was coining a metaphor whose source was card-playing and whose properties, like those of a card game, included discrete messages having certain values that could not combine—a relation of dominance and recession as between trump cards and lower suits, and so on. From the elaborated form of this icon, which was an imaginary model of a process that could give rise to plants like those he observed, Mendel was able to derive further testable predictions about successive generations of plants. In this way he and his followers could modify the icon, refine it and produce a better fit to the empirical data, in spite of its essentially metaphorical character. It was only with the advent of modern biochemistry that metaphor became fact, and the gene, the master card in Mendel's analogy, was found to have physical embodiment in the structure of the DNA molecule.

The point of the linguistic analogy with human social interaction is to suggest that we can use our elaborate linguistic knowledge as a homeomorphic icon for conversation, and possibly as a paramorphic icon for other forms of communication and social activity. Perhaps we could write a grammar of face-to-face interaction whose output would resemble the observed forms of behaviour which are so familiar, just as Mendel's card-playing picture of plant genetics was able to model and predict the observable features of character inheritance. It would then be an empirical question as to whether our grammar were adequate in the sense that it would produce all and only those conversations which were recognized by the native speaker as acceptable simulations of human talk.

The analogy could be taken further still. We might find that linguistics served as a useful model not only for the linguistic facts of conversation in the homeomorphic sense, but as a paramorph for human transaction of many kinds and on many scales, ranging from the minutia of dyadic exchange to the frightening complexity of large scale intergroup and international conflicts.

ANALOGY AND DISANALOGY

If we were to adopt the linguistic analogy, or the structuralist perspective on interaction, what would be likened to what? Clearly the striking similarities between sentences and interactions include their diachronic structures. This means that each consists of an ordered set of events forming structures *in time* whose meanings depend on the temporal arrangement of their parts. Sentences and conversations share a communicative function and hence a semantic structure, defining the relations between the form of events which occur and are transmitted from one individual to another, and the meaning which can (or would, or should) be attached to those events. The basic unit of description, which would be a morpheme for the grammarian, could well be the *speech act* or *social act* for the social psychologist.

The idea of an act comes from philosophical work on speech and behaviour. Austin (1962) criticized the traditional conception of sentence meaning as inadequate. He claimed that sentences as propositions to be evaluated by their truth or falsity only captured one aspect of the meaning of utterance use. Beyond this propositional or constative aspect of sentences lay the ground of performative use, in which utterances were not used just to declare the truth of certain states of the world, but also to perform social actions such as promising, undertaking, bequeathing, threatening, inviting, and so on. Furthermore Austin proposed a two-fold division of these performatives into *illocutions*, which were those aspects of the utterance performed *in* its saying, and *perlocutions*, those aspects which might possibly be achieved *by* its saying. So, for example, to urge somebody would be an illocution, because one only has to use the appropriate form of words in order to carry out the act of urging completely and successfully. To persuade somebody, however, there must be comprehension and acceptance of the part of the listener, so this is a perlocution. The absolute distinctions between constative and performative utterances was withdrawn by Austin in the latter part of his book, since all utterances appear to have a constative content and a performative force. Units of speech defined by their performative force have come to be known as speech acts (Searle, 1965, 1969 and 1975). The more general notion of a social act is found in the work of Harré and Secord (1972) as part of an act/action structure. This is a hierarchical conceptual scheme for the understanding of behaviour having as its lowest level movement or behaviour such as holding out the hand, gripping the hand of another and oscillating both up and down—a physical description making no reference to the meaning or conventional use of that action. The next level of description is that of the *action* which is a small meaningful unit, in this case that of hand-shaking, which, in its turn, is seen as part of the *act* which is the overall ritual of greeting. While act and action are seen as two separate kinds of event by Harré and Secord it seems preferable to think of them as relations that can exist between adjacent levels of description anywhere in the pyramid of behavioural description. So while *handshake* may be to *greeting* as *action* is to *act*, so *greeting* may be to *entertaining a friend* as *action* is to *act*.

In a way this hierarchical structure of action is like the hierarchical structure of language, in which small, physically defined, meaningless units (*phonemes*) combine to form minimal units of meaning (*morphemes*). Their combination to form the larger constructions of the language is the essence of syntactic structure. So it is reasonable to suppose that the starting point for the construction of a grammar of social action will be minimal units of meaningful social activity such as greeting, threatening, inviting, insulting, questioning, undertaking, and so on.

As we know the redeployment of units in different orders changes the meaning of sentences or other sequences of events (known generally as strings). The same morphemes in a different order constitute a different sentence. The same speech acts in a different order constitute a different conversation. But that is not all. There are some orders of morpheme which do not constitute a sentence at all. There are probably some orders of speech act which do not constitute a sensible conversation at all. That is to say that the process which regulates the production of orderly strings of morphemes or speech acts does not only recognize the semantic differences between one well-formed string and another, but also the syntactic differences between those orderings which are legitimate uses of the code and those which are not. Now while it is difficult and perhaps unwise to suggest a strict distinction between semantics and syntax, it is still the case that interaction and language share certain principles of order which differentiate on the one hand between those strings of units which are permissible and those which are not, and on the other hand between those which convey a particular meaning and those whose meaning is different.

A detailed description of the permissible forms, or of the meanings which derive from a given form can be given more easily if we idealize the problem, and assume that there is an unequivocal answer to these issues, corresponding to the opinions of a perfect speaker or actor in a homogeneous community. Such an idealization is rather like the physicists' model of a notional inelastic string, running over a frictionless pulley. We all realize of course that no string is inelastic, no pulley frictionless; and similarly no one person's judgment is the perfect arbiter of linguistic or behavioural propriety. But a useful approximation to the real world can be made by ignoring such complications at some stages of theoretical model building.

There are two other distinctions dating back to Saussure (1916, reissued 1974) which have proved invaluable in the description of linguistic phenomena, and have formed standard resources of structural analysis in other branches of semiology (the science of signs). Saussure distinguished between studies of a language as it exists at a particular point in time, which he called *synchronic*, and those which trace its evolution over time, which he called *diachronic*. The use of those terms can now be extended to distinguish any instantaneous structure such as the components of a body posture or the expressive elements of the facial mask, from structures which exist in time like a spoken sentence or a conversation. Saussure also distinguished between two classes of relations which could exist between words. On the one hand were the *syntagmatic* relations existing between the different words of the same syntagm or sentence. So in a sentence like '*The cat sat on the mat*', '*the*' and '*cat*' and '*sat*' have to be related in a certain way for that string to be a sentence and for it to be a sentence bearing a particular meaning. '*Cat*', however, brings to mind a number of alternative words with which it might be associated. These latter *paradigmatic* relations were originally called 'associative' by Saussure. '*Cat*', '*dog*', '*pet*', '*animal*', and so on come to mind as similar words and more importantly as interchangeable words within the structure of that particular syntagm. This raises the idea that the syntagm is defined by relations not between particular words but between paradigmatic equivalence classes, made up of sets of words whose properties of combination are identical. Consequently the study of event class sequences becomes the central topic in the structural analysis of social interaction and it merits some further discussion.

Sequence analysis cannot be performed directly on the behavioural events themselves because they do not recur. Instead each event must be conceived of as a member of a class where the class recurs but the individual members do not. Clearly if that classification is to the basis of a sequence analysis, it must be built upon those features of the behavioural events which determine their deployment in sequences. Some will turn out to be irrelevant. A piece of human behaviour is a thing of many parts and many facets. Some have a bearing on when that piece of behaviour will occur or when it could properly occur, and others do not.

Consider a tangible case. Let us suppose that the structure being analysed were not the sequence of human behaviour, or of morphemes in a sentence, but the structure of coaches and trucks making a railway train. If there, as here, the objective were to write some kind of formalization which would describe all and only those strings (trains) which could be formed, we should have to attend to the nature of the coupling between coaches when classifying them. Other factors such as their colour, length, number of wheels, shape of windows, type of furnishings, and so on, would be quite irrelevant. The only important things would be the determinants of which coaches could couple with which others. Now it may be the case that one coach, having different couplings at either end, would mimic the coupling properties of a whole string of trucks whose exposed end couplings were the same as those of the single coach. The point being that the equivalence in coupling does not only exist between one unit, coach, speech act, morpheme, or whatever, and another, but sometimes between one and several. A string of events can have the same combinational characteristics as a single event.

If the railwaymen were not able to inspect the couplings directly, as we are not in the case of speech acts, he could determine which coaches, or strings of coaches were equivalent by the following means. If he were to take a train which had been successfully coupled and remove one coach from the middle, he could then determine by trial and error which other coaches or strings of coaches would be put in its place while the firm coupling of the train as a whole (which is equivalent in this analogy to the well-formedness of a sentence or behaviour sequence) was preserved. This notion of classification by substitutability, otherwise known as the test of commutation, is one way in which the structural analyst can ensure that the equivalence classes he uses contain events which are equivalent in the one vital respect of being similar in their properties of combination.

Let us revert from the study of trains to the study of conversations. The same test can be applied. If a well-formed conversation is taken and each item compared with those which could have taken its place, then sets of functionally equivalent items may be drawn up. However it is not enough simply to list those items and take the list as the definition of the category, because a further problem arises. Each functional category is associated not so much with items which it contains, as with the use to which those items would be put in the particular context from which they came. In a different context the same items could have a different function and would therefore have to be regarded as members of a different class. A piece of behaviour out of its context does not bear the hallmark of its functional category. For instance, the sentence 'It's three o'clock' might well serve as a reproach when said to someone arriving late; a reminder when said to someone with a bus to catch at five past three; an answer when given in response to the question 'Do you have the time, please?' and so on.

The sets of items of behaviour found to be structurally equivalent according to the criteria of mutual replaceability should then be identified by a description of the functional properties which define the set. So the resulting event categories might be labelled (for instance) threat, promise, initiation, insult, and so on.

Once the individual events of the behaviour stream have been cast into categories in this way the remaining stage of description is to give a summary statement of the pattern of temporal or sequential relations that can exist between items of different classes. There are three main ways of doing this. The first method, which we might call analytical, takes as its strategic point a corpus of recorded material which can then be broken into units, classified, and subjected to sequence analysis. Individual techniques of doing this will be discussed later on. Alternatively one can adopt an experimental approach, in which a particular relation is postulated, such as that a will always follow b, and never follow anything else. The experimental test of this is clearly to set up a number of occasions on which b occurs, in all of which cases a should be its sequitur, and a number of occasions on which things other than b occur, in all of which cases the sequitur should be something other than a. Finally one can write a simulation. This would require specifying a set of rules (hypothetical, generative procedures, computer programs or algorithms) supposed to produce all and only those sequences of behaviour which are examples of realistic human action. Such rules would perform several functions. They would provide a description of the pattern of the behaviour stream or 'product' in so far as the outputs of the simulation and the human actor are identical. Secondly, they would form a generative icon, a metaphor for the process of production in the human actor. And lastly, in so far as their iconic imagery could be refined and perfected, they would ultimately come to be the isomorph of the generative process by which human behaviour is actually created. The rules which constitute the icon should include rules of production and rules of interpretation, so as to account for the genesis of actions and interpretations of action.

Descriptions of linguistic units (and by analogy of behavioural units as well) may be *emic* or *etic* (Pike, 1967). That is to say, the descriptions may be based on behavioural groups or categories which are apparent to the native actor, or categories inferred by the analyst from objectively observed discontinuities in the physical nature of actions. Emic classifications, when available, tend to provide a better access to the structure of the signalling system, at least as it appears to the native user. For example, the phonemic identity between the vowel sounds in *hat, sat, had* and *lad* would often provide a better basis for the classification of speech sounds, than the fact that they are made phonetically (physically) different by the accoustic contexts in which they occur. Similarly, in the case of social action it would often be important to know that drinking from a glass held in the left hand is equivalent to drinking from a glass held in the right, as far as the actors' judgments of meaning and propriety are concerned, while the physical or etic distinctiveness of the two acts is relatively unimportant. In short, the classifications of events needed for a grammar of action must distinguish between the *acts* which can be performed in a culture but not between the (semantically) equivalent means by which each can be performed.

As a further resolution for a grammar of action, we might attempt a description of *competence* rather than *performance* (Chomsky, 1965). This would provide a model of the underlying knowledge required by an actor to be competent in the terms of a given community, rather than a detailed account of the uses to which his knowledge was actually put. Stated in generative terms, such a competence model would also produce idealized behaviour strings, whose acceptability to the native actor would determine the adequacy of the model. It would not attempt to simulate the properties of incoherence and ineptitude which may well be features of a real behavioural corpus. It is worth noting that the discovery procedure for such a model need not involve the critical description of real corpora, and the induction of general principles from them. On the contrary it can be a matter of working directly with the generative rules which will produce outputs acceptable to the native actor. For instance a system of generative rules which included the constraint that every question must be followed immediately by its answer, would not produce all the acceptable arrangements of question and answer (and would probably produce a number of configurations which were unacceptable). A different set of questions and answer rules would fare better, such as

$$q = \xi \rightarrow q + X + \xi$$
$$X + \xi \rightarrow a + \xi$$
$$\rightarrow Y + a + \xi$$
$$Y \rightarrow q + a$$
$$\rightarrow q + Y + a$$

where q and a represent questions and answers.

In all these respects there seems to be an interesting analogy to be drawn between the temporal structure of social behaviour and that of English sentences. However, there are disanalogies as well, which is only reasonable. If it were not so the analogy would cease to be an analogy and become an identity. A sentence, for example, is the product of one person while an interaction is produced by several. In other words the rule system has to take account of changes of actor as well as changes of action. The way in which particular events are associated with their category, which we might call paradigmatic relations or constitutive rules (Searle, 1965) are more dependent on context in the case of interaction than in the case of sentences. In addition to those features of linguistic analysis which are suitable for sentences but not for social behaviour, there are other features which may be suitable for neither, such as the tendency to study complete written forms which have different properties and problems from those posed by the incomplete and ongoing sequences of behaviour in which speaker and listener continually deal.

So far we have seen that language and social behaviour share certain important properties which suggest that a linguistic analysis of social behaviour will prove fruitful. Social behaviour, like language, consists of acts, arrayed in time so as to convey meanings. Some arrangements are permissible uses, others are not. Some allowable constructions convey one meaning, others convey other meanings. In short there is a kind of syntax and a semantics of action.

Having set the conceptual stage then for a structural analysis of social interaction, let us consider one concrete problem and some of the techniques which are available for its solution. Suppose that a corpus of interaction is available in the form of a videotape and transcript, and we are to perform a structural analysis. A number of problems would arise which can now be posed and answered in general terms.

RECONSTRUCTION

It is often difficult to establish that a particular aspect of the behavioural record is patterned. One might be in doubt for example as to whether the events that made up the behavioural stream really did follow one another in a non-random succession. Let us suppose that they do, but that the nature of the non-randomness is unknown. The obvious solution, of describing the nature of the pattern, or postulating the nature of the pattern and checking to see whether the behavioural record is so constructed, is inappropriate at this early stage, since no clear descriptions of the pattern is available. However, it is probably also the case that the pattern is familiar to the native actor although he cannot give a summary statement of its properties. His knowledge of behaviour sequences can be used as a resource as well as a topic of our study. Just as the native speaker's ability to tell a sentence from a non-sentence becomes one of the instruments of linguistic analysis, so the native actor's ability to recognize sensible interaction should be one of our principle resources. Furthermore, we can tell whether any two facets of the behavioural system are reliably associated in a way which is familiar to the actor, by ascertaining whether he can reproduce one when provided only with the other. For instance, it may be the case that speech acts follow one another in an orderly pattern; or to put it another way, the sequence of words that is used to form an utterance is dependent on the context in which it is used. In so far as that is true, it should be possible when given the individual utterances (or turns at talking) which make up a passage of dialogue in random order, to reconstruct the context of each, in other words to reconstruct the original sequences in which they were spoken. This turns out to be possible with English dialogue (Clarke, 1975a). In one part of that study, for example, ten subjects were given twenty cards in random order, knowing that they bore twenty successive utterances from a real conversation. Two cards from the set of twenty read:

'What are you doing on Saturday night?'

and

'Going to dinner which is at seven o'clock and then doing a ... singing in a concert'.

After all ten subjects had placed the twenty utterances in the order they presumed to represent the original conversation, it turned out that eight of the ten subjects had put these two utterances together in that order (a result with a probability of less than 10^{-8} of occurring by chance alone).

The technique of reconstruction could be used in a number of other ways as well. Let us suppose we wanted to know whether the non-verbal accompaniments of speech were reliably associated with the occurrence of sentence and clause boundaries. Again we could present the subject with one and see if he were able to replicate the other reliably. We might for example take a complete record of the behaviour stream, in which both the location of phrase and clause boundaries and the nature of non-verbal display were known, present the non-verbal information to a group of subjects on videotape for example and ask them to indicate whereabouts they thought phrase and clause boundaries were occurring. Their accuracy could then be checked against the original record. (This use of the reconstruction procedure was suggested to me by Peter McPhail).

An advantage of this technique is that the criterion is always the reconstruction of a real sequence of behaviour which has actually occurred, so we are left in little doubt about the degree to which the subjects' judgements conform to the structure of at least one specific episode of real behaviour.

The technique of reconstruction might also be viewed as a kind of filtration process in which a particular structured object, namely the behavioural record, is passed through a filter. The filter in this case is the experimental procedure whereby a limited amount of information about the behaviour is passed to the subject. It is then an empirical question as to whether other classes of information have been blocked by the filter or carried through in the form of the material given to the subjects.

The essence of the reconstruction procedure is to find those relations between elements of the behaviour stream which are known (albeit tacitly) to subjects, by getting the subjects to reconstitute the actual relations of a given behavioural episode from an array of its component parts.

ANALYSIS BY SYNTHESIS

Let us suppose that the existence of some pattern has been detected in the behaviour stream. For instance, it might be the case that subjects were able to reconstitute the structure of the behaviour stream from its parts. This would not indicate which structural principles of behaviour the subjects were employing. Perhaps they know that X always leads to Y in a conversation, or X is followed by Y unless there has been a Z in the last five events. We would need to know which regularities of the behaviour stream make such reconstructions possible. We would need to know which facets of behaviour are related and in what ways. A straightforward analysis poses problems in deciding the class to which each event belongs, and whether or not a systematic relation exists between events. How, for example, could one decide rigorously how many preceding lines of conversation each new line was derived from. This is particularly difficult as it is not enough just to show that two lines are related. One has to show that the relation cannot be explained away by the information carried in the intervening lines. In the extract:

$1A$: 'Would you like some tea?'
$2B$: 'Yes, thank you, I would love a cup of tea.'
$3A$: 'I am afraid we only have tinned milk.'

it could be argued that line 3 is related to lines 2 and 1. Yet in so far as all the information from line 1 that is relevant to our understanding of line 3 is contained in or implied by line 2, we could say that line 3 is related only to line 2.

The problem becomes more manageable if one relinquishes the attempt at analysis and turns to synthesis instead. It may not be possible to tell whether a corpus of dialogue contains relations between lines which are not adjacent, for example, but it is possible to produce texts which comply with this constraint and then assess their realism. So to determine the number of preceding speech acts which should be considered in explaining the presence of each act in an orderly string or conversation, one can ask a number of subjects to provide what seems a plausible next speech act for a conversation about which they know nothing at all. Alternatively they may know the one immediately preceding speech act, or two, or three, etc. (This is similar to the technique used by Miller and Selfridge, 1950, for the word-by-word construction of various orders of statistical approximation to English sentences.) The newly elongated string is then shown to the next subject, but with the omission of the first act. So he too produces a new act in the knowledge of n antecedents. In this way a text or narrative, or whatever, may be built up in such a way that each item relates to only the n preceding ones. In Miller and Selfridge's terminology this would make it an $(n+1)$th order of approximation.

The various examples of different orders can then be judged blindly (in ignorance of the order of approximation which they represent) by a group of judges whose ability to distinguish between realistic and unrealistic examples of interaction is now a resource rather than a topic of investigation. Using this procedure it has been demonstrated that realism increases with orders of approximation up to about the fourth order (Pease and Arnold, 1973; Clarke, 1975b).

Other patterns may be imposed upon the behaviour stream to see whether its realism is enhanced or impaired. One can discover whether or not linear relations between items are a necessity or whether relations can span an intervening string of unrelated acts, as suggested by Jefferson (1972). Examples may be shown to subjects in which two question/answer pairs are arranged in a linear fashion as in example (1) below, nested as in (2) or cross-nested as in (3):

(1) $1A$: 'What is the time?'
    $2B$: 'It's three o'clock.'
    $3B$: 'Why do you want to know?'
    $4A$: 'I have a bus to catch.'
(2) $1A$: 'What is the time?'
    $2B$: 'Why do you want to know?'
    $3A$: 'I have a bus to catch.'
    $4B$: 'It's three o'clock.'
(3) $1A$: 'What is the time?'
    $2B$: 'Why do you want to know?'
    $3B$: 'It's three o'clock.'
    $4A$: I have a bus to catch.'

It seems that for examples such as these the linear structure is seen as most realistic by subjects. The nested structure is less realistic but not significantly so, and the cross-nested structure is significantly less realistic than both the others (Clarke, 1975b). This suggests that a rule limiting use of cross-nesting would be a necessary feature of an action grammar.

In its most elaborate form this synthetic approach is the method of simulation (either on computer or by a rule system) and has the status of an iconic model in Harré's scheme (1976). With an elaborate simulation there may be some doubt as to how well it matches the properties of the real thing. One criterion for deciding is taken from Turing's (1950) discussion of the means of establishing whether a computer is behaving as an intelligent being. The Turing test is performed by confronting subjects with a text or a live channel of communication which is governed on some occasions by a person and on others by a 'person-simulation'. When the judge fails to discriminate with greater than chance accuracy, the simulation could be said to succeed.

A simple simulation of discourse might be constructed by taking a finite set of speech act categories (Clarke, 1976) and other events such as speaker changes and specifying a 'transitional probability' that each will be a sequitur to every other. A simple computer model of this sort produced sequences such as:

```
        #
    A   COMPLAIN
        CONTINUE
    B   DENY
        TERMINATE
        #
    A   COMPLAIN
    B   QUESTION
    A   REFUSE
        APOLOGIZE
```

where A and B are the names of speakers and # is a topic delimiter. The approach of analysis by synthesis allows us to examine the consequences of making certain assumptions about the genesis of behaviour. Generative models or simulations working on certain principles can be shown to produce a set of output behaviour sequences which are unlike those of people. Such models are then said to be inadequate. Other models may reproduce certain crucial properties of human behaviour (such as the use of nested structures) and hence prove adequate in this respect. It is most important to note, however, that a generative model whose output resembles human behaviour does not necessarily use the same generative operations. In this regard a generative model of human action may be seen as a summary description of the behaviour stream, but not of the psychological processes which produce it.

Analysis by synthesis, as I have called this approach (after Neisser, 1967) provides a direct application of hypotheticodeductive methodology to the study of complex diachronic structures in the stream of human behaviour.

SEGMENTATION OF STRINGS

So far the methods discussed have been addressed to general issues, such as whether the 'code' of English discourse relates each speech act to one or more antecedents. We should now consider the quasi-linguistic analysis of *particular* texts and behavioural records. In doing this we must first take account of the fact that linguistics, and structural analyses generally, deal in discontinuities. They recognize discrete events and classes of event rather than continuous changes between types or over time. We must therefore take the behaviour stream, whose name rightly suggests a continuous flow, and recode it as a series of units: pools and waterfalls if you like, rather than a 'stream' as such.

In practice this is not too difficult for the verbal record which tends to be somewhat discontinuous and lumpy anyway, but it is much harder for non-verbal behaviour. There are two ways of approaching the problem, which in linguistic terminology might be called *emic* and *etic* respectively (Pike, 1967). The first uses the knowledge of the native actor as a resource and places interunit boundaries as appropriate in his system of interpretation. The etic method uses the objective scrutiny of the analyst as its resource and places boundaries where the greatest physical discontinuities are apparent. Emic methodology, therefore, provides semantically differentiated units, while etic methodology gives formally differentiated elements. The two do not necessarily correspond. It cannot be overemphasized that the structural analysis of behaviour is as much a description of behavioural semantics as used by a particular community, as it is of the physical reality of the behavioural objects created interactively in public space. Emic methodology should therefore be given prior but not sole consideration.

Emic procedures for behaviour segmentation may be found in the work of Dickman (1963) and Newtson (1973). In Dickman's technique subjects saw a sequence of behaviours on film and then again as a set of cards, each of which represented a small segment of the action. The whole set of cards was presented in the order of the original behaviour so subjects had only to cut the pack into a series of smaller piles to indicate how they had perceived the segmental structure of the original film. Newtson used a method in which subjects pressed buttons to indicate junctures (perhaps the behavioural equivalent of phrase boundaries) whilst viewing a videotape of the behaviour sequences in question. Compared with Dickman's procedure, Newtson's method has the disadvantage of introducing a delay in the placing of each unit boundary which is due in part to the reaction latency of the subject, and in part to the difficulty of knowing that a unit of activity has really ended, until after it has become quite clear that a new unit has begun. The advantage of Newtson's method is that it can be used on the first viewing of the materials. This compels the subject to react to his *knowledge* of past and present, and his *anticipation* of the future, as would normally be the case. Techniques such as Dickman's that require a previous acquaintance with a film record, allow the subject to interpret each moment in a *knowledge* of the 'future' which is clearly unnatural. This is really another instance of the difference between judgements of a frozen sentence or behavioural record, when all moments from the real-time progression are represented simultaneously, and judgements of 'live' action where the present is perceptible, the past can only be recalled with imperfect accuracy, and the future only anticipated. (I am grateful to G. P. Ginsburg for stressing this distinction in personal communications.)

Let us keep the difficulties of a valid segmentation in mind, and pass on to the next stage of structural analysis—the assignment of each behavioural event in the record to an equivalence class. This turns out to be the crucial step where the quality of the final picture is largely determined.

CATEGORIZATION OF ELEMENTS

As we saw earlier in the discussion of *syntagmatic* and *paradigmatic* structure, there is a crucial relation between the way in which items of behaviour combine to form structurally integrated diachronic wholes, and the way in which items of behaviour form equivalence classes (units which enable us to form general structural descriptions from individual series of unique events). The essential point is that items of behaviour must be placed in the same equivalence class if and only if they are treated similarly in all respects by the sequencing rules. In practice this means that those elements which are true members of the same category will always have the same conditions of occurrence, being all permissible or all impermissible on any occasion. Those which are jointly permissible on some occasions but not others, are clearly distinguished by the rules of sequence and must therefore be assigned to different classes. Otherwise the rules cannot be accurately described in terms of this set of event categories.

In principle, it is a straightforward matter to take a behavioural event, consider all other forms which are equivalent in so far as they are always sensible and permissible substitutes, and call the set an equivalence class. Often there is a clear distinction between pairs of behaviours which are equivalent (such as drinking with a glass in the right hand and drinking with a glass in the left hand) and others which are not equivalent (such as eating with a fork and eating with the fingers). Notice, however, that the 'different' behaviours are no more physically distinct than the equivalent behaviours. This reflects the way in which emic taxonomy rests on different criteria from those used in a physicalistic or etic taxonomy.

In practice things are not so easy, since the particular form of words or movements being classified may well have a different significance when used in different contexts. Since it is equivalence of significance which determines the limits of the equivalence class, it is necessary that events be classified under circumstances which permit the recognition of event significances. In other words the classification must be performed on events as seen in their contexts, and not as isolated extracts of the text or the behavioural record viewed out of context.

For example it is one thing to ask about utterances which would be equivalent to

> 'It's three o'clock.'

when viewed out of context. Its equivalents could be

> 'Where on earth have you been?'
> 'Hurry up, or we shall be late.'

or

> 'Just think, Tom will just be landing at Kennedy Airport at this moment,'

depending on whether it was used as a reproach, a reminder, or a cue to shared imaginations of a friend's adventures. It is quite a different matter to ask for equivalents for the same utterance when taken in the context

> 'Do you have the time, please?'
> 'It's three o'clock.'

This sensitivity to context affects the identification of equivalence classes, as we have seen, and it also affects their notation. In symbolic systems where syntactic class membership is not context sensitive, each class can be represented by a list of members. This is largely true of languages like English, where words such as *engine, leg* or *door* are all nouns whatever their context, so a list of similar words provides a useful definition of the concept of noun. However there are exceptions like *hand, light* and *clip* which can be nouns or verbs depending on their context.

When class membership *is* context sensitive, the classes must be represented by lists of members in contexts, or by general descriptions of the distinctive features which distinguish members of the class from non-members. There could be general illustrationary labels such as 'greetings' or 'invitation'. The contexts which determine the force and the equivalence relations of an item include the future as well as the past. In the case of a sequence like

> 'What are you doing on Saturday evening?'
> 'Singing in a concert, why?'
> 'Because there's this party you're invited to.'

it is clear that the first question is a 'pre-invitation question'. It is a 'set-up' for a later invitation of the kind a young man might use when he wants (a) to avoid a direct rebuff to an invitation on the grounds that the young lady is irrevocably committed to the idea of washing her hair that night, and (b) to deny her the opportunity of evaluating the details of the invitation before deciding whether she is free. In deciding on an equivalence class for the question 'What are you doing on Saturday evening?' it is essential to recognize its proactive nature and to class it with utterances like 'Got any plans for the weekend?' rather than with such things as 'What did you do last Saturday night?'

The judgments concerning the substitutability of a given set of speech acts, on which the equivalence classifications are based, can be made by the analyst or by a group of subjects acting as judges. In the former case the presentation of results is simple. There would be one set of equivalence classes, partitioning the universe of discourse, and these could be used in sequence analyses as described below. A group of subjects on the other hand, are liable to produce different judgments of equivalence which will require integrating into some summary statement. A cluster analysis provides a convenient way of doing this (Miller, 1969; Jardine and Sibson, 1971). In its simplest form (otherwise known as a single-linkage cluster analysis) the technique can be used as follows. The data would consist of a number of different partitions of the universe of speech acts into equivalence classes, one partition for each subject. This could be achieved by giving subjects a number of cards, each representing a speech act or speech act type, and having each subject sort the cards into piles of equivalent instances. It would be easy to record which items a subject had placed in the same category. That representation of the data would then be converted to a form in which the number of subjects putting any pair of elements in the same category could be identified. This is usually done by drawing up a lower triangular matrix, whose rows and columns are labelled with the names of all the items, and whose cells contain the number of subjects who placed each pair of items in the same class. This technique is described in more detail in Miller (1969). The highest cell value can then be taken to indicate that the items naming its row and column form a cluster whose 'strength' is represented by the cell value. That cluster of two items is then viewed as a single item, later joined by others in so far as they are frequently classed with *either* of its members. (The distinctive characteristic of single-linkage clustering is that new items may accrue to a cluster when they are sufficiently similar to *any* of its previous members.) In this way a hierarchical picture of similarities, or dendrogram, may be built up. A single set of categories for further use is then formed by setting a certain level of similarity which defines a particular section through the dendrogram, and hence a particular set of clusters.

For example, suppose there were five behavioural items in question, *a, b, c, d*, and *e*, and ten subjects had been asked to place them in groups of equivalent items. A table could then be drawn showing the number of subjects who regarded any pair of items as equivalent.

The greatest similarity exists between items *a* and *d*, since they were seen as equivalent by eight out of ten subjects. Consequently *a* and *d* are shown on the dendogram (Figure 3.1) as being joined at level 8. The next greatest similarity is between *c* and *e* which join at level 6. Now we see at level 5 that *c* and *d* should be united, but because this is single-linkage analysis, this is taken to mean that the cluster of *a* and *d* (to which *d* now belongs) and the cluster of *c* and *e* (to which *c*

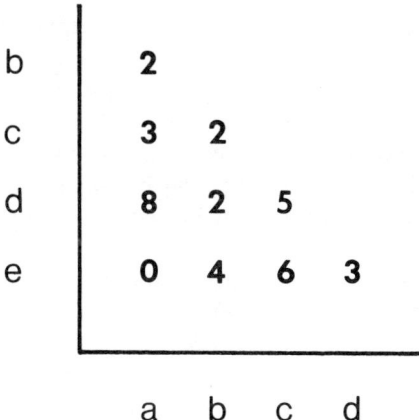

Table 3.1 Lower triangular matrix of hypothetical similarity measures between elements a, b, c, d, and e

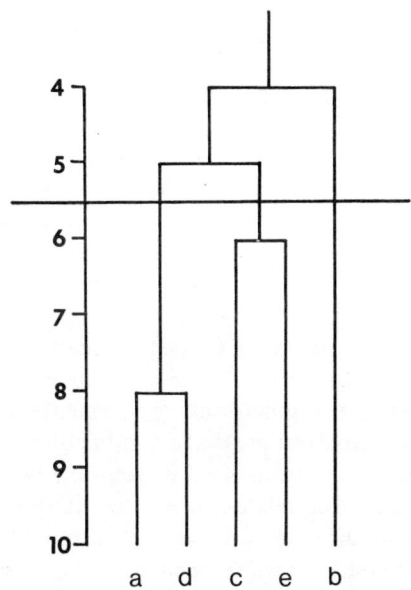

Figure 3.1 Dendrogram showing single linkage cluster analysis of elements a, b, c, d, and e, from the similarity measures in Table 3.1

now belongs) should be united at level 5. Finally b is joined to this large cluster at level 4. Values below 4 in the matrix never enter into the construction of the dendrogram in this case. Now a line drawn horizontally through the dendrogram at level 5.5, say, will form a partition of the set of events a, b, c, d and e into three clusters or families: a and d; c and e; and b.

The process of cluster analysis is like that of arranging elements in a space in such a way that the distance between the two members of every pair is proportional to their dissimilarity, or the inverse of the number of subjects putting them in the same category. The closely knit groups of points in space then represent the equivalence classes of items as represented by the pooled judgments of all subjects. The items which are found by this procedure to exceed some criterion of similarity are then regarded as equivalent in subsequent stages of analysis.

Once the paradigmatic or equivalence relations of the behaviour stream have been established, and each item or event has been identified as a member of its class, the behaviour stream may be recoded as a succession of class members, plus some indication of the relations existing between them. It should then be possible to start screening the strings of events so described for principles of 'syntactic' orderliness.

THE DETECTION OF SEQUENTIAL PATTERNS

There are three principal strategies for the detection of orderliness in strings; analysis, experimentation, and synthesis. The analytical methods are largely those of the ethologists (such as Altman, 1965; Hutt and Hutt, 1970; Slater, 1973; Van Hooff, 1973; Van der Kloot and Morse, 1975; and Dawkins, 1976). They fall into three subcategories: correlation methods, transitional frequency analysis and time-interval analyses. In a typical correlational analysis one might take two classes of behaviour, and correlate their frequencies of occurrence in a number of time-intervals. Presumably those behavioural classes having the greatest correlation of frequencies of occurrence are those with the greatest functional similarity. A transitional frequency analysis consists of a record (usually a matrix) of the number of times each item of behaviour has been observed to follow every other item (or every combination of n previous items). The shortcomings of such analyses are that a number of previous items have to be considered in specifying the occasion of use of each behaviour and a data dilution occurs: n^2 cells are required to relate n behaviour classes to the one preceding event. $n^{(m+1)}$ cells are required to relate each item to m predecessors. Another problem is that the method assumes *stationarity* or an invariance of transitional probabilities over time. This assumption is seldom met by behavioural data. For example, in the structure of a sentence the probability of any two given words occurring one after the other does not remain constant as the sentence proceeds.

The method is also limited to the description of those event series where the most closely contiguous items are the most intimately related. Stochastic models of language fell into disuse after Chomsky (1957) pointed out that English sentences often fail to display this property. The sentence, 'The book, which I bought in town the day it rained so hard and soaked my new mackintosh and caused me to miss the last bus home at some considerable inconvenience, is on the table', has a structure in which 'The book is on the table' is the basic unit with a long digression in the middle. This sort of construction cannot be captured easily by stochastic models of determinate order, operating only on the spoken words or terminal elements. Since digression and resumption of ongoing themes is also common in the behaviour stream, this may be as unsuitable as the sentence for stochastic analysis.

Time-interval analyses are essentially frequency distributions of the occurrence of time intervals of different lengths between specified pairs of events, such as successive occurrences of a particular event. In one such technique, the log survivor analysis, a geometrical convenience is used to make the data more readily interpretable. A plot of the log of the proportion of time-intervals exceeding a duration t against the values of t gives rise to a straight line in the case of randomly spaced behaviours. This makes the recognition of randomness, clumping and overspacing much easier in the resulting graphical displays. The technique is summarized in Figure 3.2.

These analytical techniques can summarize the temporal properties of long strings of events. However, they seldom give an exact specification of those behaviour combinations and structures which represent all and only the members of a set, such as the sentences of a language, or the sensible conversations of a given speech community. To get a little closer to such an exact specification it is often necessary to use experimental techniques. The general methodology of the social psychology experiment is sufficiently familiar to require little further comment here. Its application to this problem concerns a postulated regularity such as 'B occurs always and only after A' in which a variety of occurrences and non-occurrences of A would be introduced into experimental interactions, and the occurrence of B monitored. This kind of experiment would be of greatest interest when the postulated regularity was of a somewhat higher order of complexity. It may be possible to combine analytical procedures with some 'experimental' checks. Computer programs can be written, for example, which will scan the first part of a data string, extract apparent regularities and then test for their validity in the latter part of the string. Alternatively the program can be constructed to work along a string constructing the simplest generalization which is true of all the cases it has met. This is called eliminative induction. Suppose

$$c\ a\ b\ x\ c\ b\ a\ b\ x\ y\ c\ b\ x$$

represents the succession of event classes making up a sequence of social

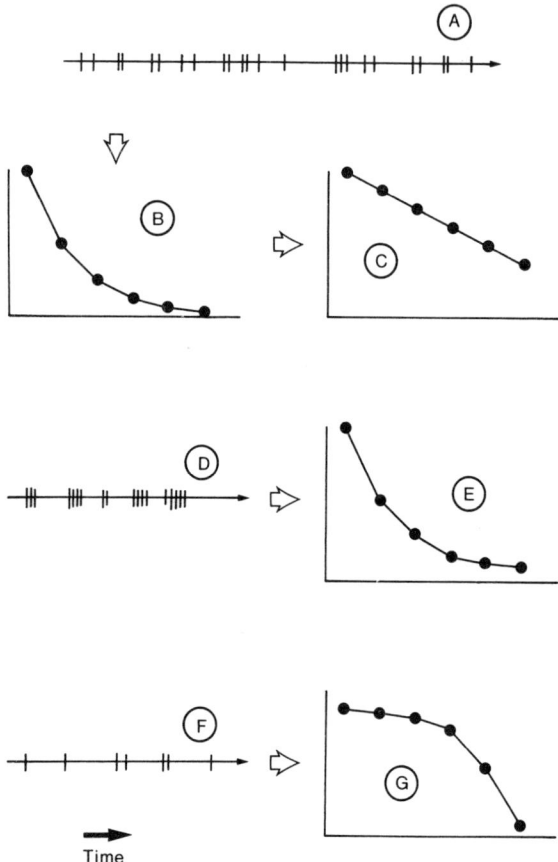

Figure 3.2 (A) A series of events randomly distributed in time. The event has a probability of occurrence in any time interval which does not vary with the length of time since the event last occurred. (B) Percentage of inter-event time intervals larger than t as a function of t. This is a survivor function. (C) Log percentage of inter-event time intervals larger that t as a function of t. This is a log survivor function. Note that the log survivor function for randomly distributed events is a straight line with negative gradient. (D) A series of events occurring in bouts. (E) Log survivor function for bouts of events. (F) A series of events which are over-spaced. (G) Log survivor function for over-spaced events

behaviour. The programme when generating rules for the occurrence of x would scan for the first x and conclude that b is followed by x, or in a more general notation of rewrites

$$b \rightarrow b + x \tag{1}$$

The next occurrence of b, however, does not satisfy this rule, but a comparison of first and second occurrences of b shows that

$$a + b \rightarrow a + b + x \tag{2}$$
$$c + b \rightarrow c + b + \bar{x} \tag{3}$$

satisfies both.

However the third occurrence of x disconfirms (3) but is compatible with

$$x + c + b \rightarrow x + c + b + \bar{x} \tag{4}$$
$$y + c + b \rightarrow y + c + b + x \tag{5}$$

and so by scanning the string, rules numbers (2), (4) and (5) could be constructed which satisfy all occurrences of x.

Once sufficient regularity has been discerned from analysis and experimentation it should be possible to write a rule system which will generate all and only the strings of interest. This might be called a 'grammar' when represented in abstract terms, or a 'simulation' when realized in the form of a computer program. It is essential to note at this stage that such a grammar or simulation is only an *icon*. It generates behavioural replicas by means which are *adequate* in so far as they produce similar outputs to the real social actor. That is not to say that they model the process *in vivo* by which the actor arrives at his performance. Ultimately the icon should be refined until it is demonstrably isomorphic with the actual mechanisms of behaviour production, but that claim should not be read into the statement that a certain rule system can mimic or simulate behaviour to some degree.

In general the techniques of sequence analysis all suffer from a need to compromise between simplifying assumptions which misrepresent the data but allow some summary to be made, and elaborate formulations which need to feed on prohibitive quantities of data. Ideally one would like a procedure which used data economically and produced results which were as complex as the data demand but no more so. Such a technique is the 'melody analysis' described by Dawkins (1976). This takes a series of events, usually coded as integers, and constructs a transitional frequency matrix. If, for example, the most common transition was from event 3 to event 17, the pair (3, 17) would be pointed out together with the number of times it occurred, and then all occurrences of (3, 17) erased from the data record and replaced by a single new code, perhaps 91. Now the process is repeated. The second pass through the data may reveal that the highest frequency transition is now from event 91 to event 91. Translating this back into the original event coding the printout now shows the chain ((3, 17) (3, 17)) and its frequency of occurrence. In this way the procedure can detect any long chains which do occur repeatedly without having to construct a high-order transition matrix, most of which is likely to be wasted.

All the sequence analytical techniques attempt to answer the question, 'In what contexts does each event occur?' The correlational methods are crude and only indicate what other events are likely to be in the vicinity of the event in question, while transitional frequency methods place too much emphasis on the immediately preceding events. Time-interval methods can show whether two events are mutually influencing in the sense that one tends to hasten or delay the occurrence of the other, but still a detailed picture of the structure of events is missing. An experimental approach will only work if suitable hypotheses are available from some inductive procedure and if the antecedent events are manipulable, which they are usually not in the cases of interesting behaviour sequences. A full simulation is even more demanding in that it requires a nearly complete picture of the working of the system as the basis for its program. Given such a picture the simulation can test its adequacy and lead to refinements but it can do little in the early stages to help produce a workable global model.

To date the greatest development has gone into analytical procedures used by ethologists on the stream of animal behaviour (see Slater, 1973).

PRODUCT AND PROCESS

The techniques described so far have been aimed solely at the description of behavioural products. They should result in a set of descriptive or generative specifications capable of distinguishing all instances of the variety of social behaviour in question from all non-instances. What then of the process? Some consideration should be given to the mechanisms by which social action is produced and interpreted. Some light may be cast on this matter by the description of behaviour patterns (the product) since certain kinds of output are only possible given certain classes of device. Further specifications of the properties of a behaviour-generating device would be empirically testable in so far as they implied that detectable constructions would be produced in the behaviour system.

A more direct attack on the cognitive processes of behaviour generation and interpretation may be guided by a general conceptual analysis. The product of such an analysis is set out below.

It is prompted in part by the motor skill model of Argyle (1967) and the control-room model of Tolman (1948). It shows a hypothetical person simulator having as its central feature a (semantic) representation, the embodiment of all the individual's knowledge of himself and the outside world. It is called a

LINGUISTIC ANALOGY OR WHEN IS A SPEECH ACT LIKE A MORPHEME?

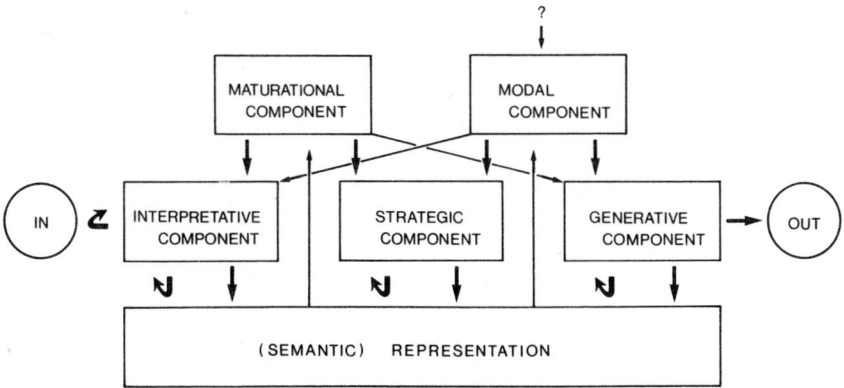

Figure 3.3 Information processing model of the social actor

'(semantic) representation' because the information it contains is largely but not entirely semantic. One could say for example that the information which has been taken in from this chapter by you (the reader) is now part of your world view or (semantic) representation. It is semantic in so far as your recollections will be of points made, and evidence quoted rather than of words used, the placing of items on the pages, the style of typeface, etc. In other words you will store and remember (I hope) what this chapter means, and not what it looks like. For this to be the case there must be a functional unit called the interpretive component which makes sense of input. That is to say it interrogates the input, and then outputs semantic markers to the semantic representation. Two features should be noted. First that the input to this and other components is active, as indicated by the loop-arrow symbol. If one viewed this component in computational terms, that would be equivalent to saying that the algorithm read the input in ways determined by the algorithm itself (as is usually the case in a computer). Secondly, the inputs to the interpretive component include a reading of information previously stored in the semantic representation. This allows the interpretation to be context sensitive, a feature which was mentioned as a difficulty when classifying behaviours in the way the actors interpretive system would do. As it has inputs from the (semantic) representation, the interpretive component can be envisaged as revising and updating the representation even in the absence of external stimuli. This raises another important feature of the schema, namely that the representation is a dynamic, not a static thing. If its contents were ever to be published they would have to be captured by an animated diagram rather than a static one. The moment labelled 'present' would be constantly changing. Events which first entered the map as anticipations of the future would in time be modified and form cognitions of the present and then recollections of the past. The significance of past events would often change so that an old interpretation became replaced by a new one, together with a recollection that it had been a reinterpretation of an older version, and so on.

Our world view, however, is not just a dynamic reinterpretation of present and past. It is also a set of anticipations and plans for the future. These are produced in the diagram by a *strategic component* and realised as particular forms of action by a *generative component* having a symmetrical relation with the interpretive component. Furthermore the device having sensed a change in situation or role should be able to change into a new mode of interpretation, strategy or generation. By the addition of a 'modal component' one can endow the device with the capacity to change between discrete styles of functioning as motives, moods and circumstances changed. The one unspecified input to the modal component raises the very difficult problem of whether this system is open and should be viewed as a cognitive tool which may be used by a person, or whether it would be viewed as a closed system modelling those processes which actually *constitute* a person.

Finally, there is a maturational component, a part of the device sensitive to changes in the semantic representation and capable of producing progressive or irreversible modifications in the interpretive, strategic, generative and modal components.

The advantages of this schema include a number of features of social interaction which it can encompass. The first is the so-called phenomenon of multiple realities. Each device (or actor) constructed according to this schema would have a peculiar set of interpretive procedures, and a peculiar input to those interpretive procedures from the previous state of the semantic representation. Consequently the output from the interpretive component to the semantic representation induced by any event would be peculiar to that individual, and another idiosyncratic piece would accrue to his idiosyncratic picture of reality.

The schema also incorporates active processing. Information coming into the system does not drive the process, but is itself the subject of scanning operations controlled by the system. This is a familiar mode of data access in computer systems.

The schema can incorporate the idea of a behavioural semantic, whereby physical events, movements and behaviours in public space are transformed by the interpretive component to their counterparts in the upper levels of an act/action structure (Harré and Secord, 1972) before being incorporated into the semantic representation.

The modal component makes it possible to explain how certain kinds of experiment are possible. An experimenter's instructions, for example, might be interpreted and entered in the semantic representation as an utterance having a certain force. This could influence the modal component, giving rise to a mode switch in the other components, leading to role-playing or accounting. The latter process may be envisaged as one in which the generative component, which would normally read the semantic representation and base certain actions upon it, now reads the semantic representation and (to some degree) describes it. The schema is even reflexive to the extent that it can explain its own existence. An investigator so constituted could observe a number of behavioural phenomena in his fellows which would be assimilated into the semantic representation. There the interpretive component 'housekeeping' the image would process these events and their apparent explanation to form a more economical model, which the strategic component could select as part of a career strategy, to be implemented by the generative component as a particular published description of the image.

Lastly the scheme incorporates the property of context sensitivity. Each item of information arriving at the interpretive component is processed together with a reading of the existing component of the semantic representation. The interpretation given to an event can therefore depend on the context (including anticipations of the future) in which it occurs. Furthermore the context/input comparison can also result in a reappraisal of the context, so another intriguing property of behavioural semantics can be accounted for, namely the retrospective reinterpretation of past events.

So what is the point of all this speculation about language-like structure in the behaviour stream, and hypothetical generative devices or grammars? There are two points, one academic and the other pragmatic. As academics we need to know what the brain does and how it does it. This, according to Harré's scheme, requires a description of observed behaviour patterns, followed by the choice of a source for a metaphorical system or icon, whose behaviour may be precisely and formally specified. Comparison of iconic and observed patterns would then allow the iconic model to be modified, becoming, one hopes, a closer and closer approximation to the real generative process, by which the actor is empowered to behave as he does. Behaviour sequences are chosen for this study for the general reason that any complex system is best represented to the outsider in the sequential pattern of its output.

> Of all truths relating to phenomena, the most valuable to us are those which relate to the order of their succession. On a knowledge of these is founded every reasonable anticipation of future facts, and whatever power we possess of influencing those facts to our advantage (Mill, 1851).

But an order of succession is not enough, it is too ephemeral. We also need to know the nature of the underlying powers and processes of the individual whereby he tailors his behaviour to his changing circumstances and fortunes.

As pragmatists we must surely take heed to Mill's claim that the succession of events provides us with '... whatever power we possess of influencing those facts to our advantage'. Human behaviour can be very problematic and a source of great suffering. Those who dare intervene to try and improve the situation, for instance in cases of conflict, had better have good grounds for choosing their course of action. They should know what alternatives are open to them in a given situation and what would be the consequences of each *given that situation*. A summary statement of these considerations could turn out to look very much like the 'behavioural grammars' described above.

Naturally this enterprise has its critics. It has been suggested that more account should be taken of the dependence of behaviour on situations (Argyle, Chapter 2 in this volume), and yet if there is a dependable relation between behaviour and situation, there must be a pan-situational process to produce it. Furthermore, in a world where behavioural variations and diversity abound, it seems more fruitful to look for underlying similarities between occasions, than the readily apparent differences. It has also been suggested that by omitting (deliberately) the details of individual differences and the dimensional qualities of events such as duration, a false picture is produced. And yet every model is an approximation. Nothing will ever completely simulate reality except reality itself. It seems quite reasonable to work for a while with an approximation which uses a discrete-stage single-reality system as a model of interaction. Even that is too complicated for comfort, and if further complications prove necessary, they should be added later rather than sooner.

In conclusion then, one can liken social behaviour to language in several crucial respects. Both are the accessible product of an inaccessible process. Both are symbolic systems which may be described by syntactic and semantic constraints, and by certain classes of relation between their component parts such as syntagmatic and paradigmatic structures. Both have a distinct surface (and maybe also deep) structure. Each may be studied by emic or etic procedures. Most importantly, they both present a bewildering array of novel manifestations to the observer, behind which there is almost certainly a principle of order. This *can* be inferred, and it could enable us to shed new light on the working of the brain, and provide a new resource for the management of human affairs.

References

Altman, S. A., 1965, Sociobiology of Rhesus monkeys. II: Stochastics of social communication, *Journal of Theoretical Biology*, **8**, 490–522.
Argyle, M., 1967, *The Psychology of Interpersonal Behaviour*, Harmondsworth: Penguin.
Austin, J. L., 1962, *How to Do Things with Words*, Oxford: Clarendon Press.
Chomsky, N., 1957, *Syntactic Structures*, The Hague: Mouton.
Chomsky, N., 1965, *Aspects of the Theory of Syntax*, The Hague: Mouton.
Clarke, D. D., 1975a, The use and recognition of sequential structure in dialogue, *British Journal of Social and Clinical Psychology*, **14**, 333–339.
Clarke, D. D., 1975b, *The Structural Analysis of Verbal Interaction*, unpublished doctoral dissertation, Oxford University.
Clarke, D. D., 1976, Discourse analysis as third-order psychology. Proceedings of IKP Conference on Gesprächsanalyse, Institut für Kommunicationsforschung und Phonetik der Universität Bonn, October.
Dawkins, R., 1976, Hierarchical organisation: a candidate principle for ethology, in P. P. G. Bateson and R. A. Hinde (eds.) *Growing Points in Ethology*. London: Cambridge University Press.
Dickman, H. R., 1963, The perception of behavioural units, in R. G. Barker (ed.), *The Stream of Behavior*, New York: Appleton-Century-Crofts.

Harré, R. and Secord, P. F., 1972, *The Explanation of Social Behaviour*, Oxford: Blackwells.
Harré, R., 1976, The constructive role of models, in L. Collins (ed.), *The Use of Models in the Social Sciences*, London: Tavistock.
Hutt, S. J. and Hutt, C., 1970, *Direct Observation and Measurement of Behaviour*, Springfield, I11.: Thomas.
Jardine, N. and Sibson, R., 1971, *Mathematical Taxonomy*, London: Wiley.
Jefferson, G., 1972, Side sequences, in D. Sudnow (ed.), *Studies in Social Interaction*, New York: Free Press.
Mill, J. S. 1851, *A System of Logic, Ratiocinative and Inductive*, 3rd edn, London: Parker.
Miller, G. A. and Selfridge, J. A., 1950, Verbal content and the recall of meaningful material, *American Journal of Psychology*, **63**, 176–185.
Miller, G. A., 1969, A psychological method to investigate verbal concepts, *Journal of Mathematical Psychology*, **6**, 169–191.
Neisser, U., 1967, *Cognitive Psychology*, New York: Appleton-Century-Crofts.
Newtson, D., 1973, Attribution and the unit of perception of ongoing behaviour, *Journal of Personality and Social Psychology*, **28**, 28–38.
Pease, K. and Arnold, P., 1973, Approximations to dialogue, *American Journal of Psychology*, **86**, 769–776.
Pike, K. L., 1967, *Language in Relation to a Unified Theory of the Structure of Human Behaviour*, The Hague: Mouton.
Saussure, F. de., 1974, *Cours des linguistique générale*, Lausanne: Bally et Sechehaye, 1916; *Course in General Linguistics*, Glasgow: Fontana.
Searle, J., 1965, What is a speech act? in M. Black (ed.), *Philosophy in America*, London: Allen and Unwin and Cornell University Press.
Searle, J., 1969, *Speech Acts*, London: Cambridge University Press.
Searle, J., 1975, A taxonomy of illocutionary acts, in K. Gunderson (ed.), *Language, Mind and Knowledge*, Minnesota Studies in The Philosophy of Science, vol. 7, University of Minnesota Press.
Slater, P. J. B., 1973, Describing sequences of behaviour, in P. P. G. Bateson and P. H. Klopfer (eds.) *Perspectives in Ethology*, New York: Plenum.
Tolman, E. C., 1948, Cognitive maps in rats and men, *Psychological Review*, **55**, 189–208.
Turing, A. M., 1950, Computing machinery and intelligence, *Mind*, **59**, 433–460.
Van der Kloot, W. and Morse, M. J., 1975, A stochastic analysis of the display behaviour of the red-breasted merganser (*Mergus serrator*), *Behaviour*, **LVI**, 181–216.
Van Hooff, J. A. R. A. M., 1973, A structural analysis of the social behaviour of a semi-captive group of chimpanzees, in M. von Cranach and I. Vine (eds.), *Social Communication and Movement*, London: Academic Press.

4

SOME THEORETICAL AND METHODOLOGICAL ASPECTS OF THE USE OF FILM IN THE STUDY OF SOCIAL INTERACTION

Adam Kendon

INTRODUCTION

There are many different ways in which social interaction may be studied. One question of importance is how people engaging in it relate their actions to one another so as to bring off the orderly occasions of interaction that most of us experience most of the time. A number of studies which have been concerned with this question have undertaken very detailed analyses of the patterning of behaviour in interaction using film or video records so that as many different aspects of behaviour as possible may be taken into account. Such studies have contributed several important discoveries, throwing new light upon the communication systems participants in interaction make use of. In this chapter it will be argued that these discoveries not only required the technical innovation of cinematography, they also required the development of an appropriate theoretical viewpoint. As we shall see, there are many studies of behaviour in which film has been used. It was only after the emergence of a viewpoint in which the *behavioural relationship* between interactants became the primary focus of attention, that film-based studies of social interaction began to appear.

Throughout what follows I shall refer to *film*, but most of what I shall say applies to video recording as well. Both technologies make possible the making of *specimens* of behaviour, and it is with the consequences of this possibility that I am concerned. There are some differences between the two technologies. For example, film is more useful than video for fine-grained behavioural analysis because the resolution of the image is so much greater. Furthermore, there are as yet no slow-motion analysers for video that have anything like the precision and flexibility of film-analysis projectors. On the other hand, video records are immediately retrievable, they are cheaper to make than films, and they can be made under a wider range of circumstances. For a discussion of one situation where video technology is definitely advantageous in comparison to film see Schaeffer (1970, 1975) and McMillan (1974) who describe its use in a study of long-term patterns of space use and other aspects of behaviour of members of a household in their own home.

VARIETIES OF FILM USE IN THE STUDY OF BEHAVIOUR

The use of film for the study of interaction from the point of view of the orientation that is our main concern has developed only within the last two decades. Film technology, however, has been available for more than fifty years and it has been widely used in many different ways in the study of behaviour. Indeed, two of the earliest pioneers of cinematography, Muybridge and Marey, were led to make the inventions they did precisely because they were interested in analysing movement patterns in animals and humans (Muybridge, 1899, 1901; Marey, 1895). Since their work, there has been a continual development in what has come to be known as kinesiology or 'biomechanics' in which film recordings play a very central role (Prost, 1975). Film has been used in the intensive study of human motor development (Ames, 1940, 1944; Gesell and Ames, 1947; Gesell and Halverson, 1942; Gesell and Ilg, 1937). It has also been used extensively in the analysis of motor skills. For a survey of these and other uses of film in research, see Michaelis (1955). The use of film in ethnography and related areas of anthropology is discussed in Hockings (1975).

Of greater relevance to the concerns of this chapter are studies of expressive behaviour using film. Landis (1924), Thompson (1940), Frijda (1953), Haggard and Isaacs (1966), Ekman (1973), and Eibl-Eibesfeldt (1973) have used film in various ways to study facial expression. Hunt (1936), Hunt, Clarke, and Hunt (1936), and Landis and Hunt (1936) used film in their detailed studies of the startle pattern.

Patterns of body movement in their relationship to speech have also been studied with cinematographic and video records. Freedman and Hoffman (1967), Ekman and Friesen (1968), Dittman (1962, 1963, 1972), and Lindenfeld (1971, 1974) have used film records of psychiatric patients in interviews to make detailed counts of the occurrence of various types of hand and other bodily movements which have been related both to speech patterns and to psychiatric condition. Ekman's work on the kinesic symptoms of deceitfulness has also used filmed records as sources of data (Ekman and Friesen, 1974; Ekman, Friesen, and Scherer, 1976).

Condon and Ogston (1966, 1967), and Dendon (1972a, 1975a) have presented detailed descriptive studies of the flow of movement that is concurrent with speech. Kendon, for example, has formulated a phrasal structure for gesticulation and has shown how this structure relates to the phrasal organization of speech. Efron (1941), though he did not use sound film, undertook detailed comparative analyses of gesticulatory styles among East European Jews and Southern Italians in New York City using film records. Lomax and his colleagues (Lomax, 1968) make extensive use of film specimens in their studies of movement styles in different cultures.

Film has also been used as a means of presenting behaviour to observers in investigations concerned with judgemental and perceptual processes. For example, Estes (1938), Frijda (1953), Davitz (1964), and Dittman, Parloff and Boomer (1965), have investigated judgments of emotional expression, disposition and personality in this way. From (1971) used short filmed episodes of behaviour in his pioneering studies of the way a perceiver organizes the flow of behaviour in terms of governing intentions he attributes to the actors he observes. Flapan (1968), using excerpts from cinema films, investigated developmental trends in how children describe the social behaviour of others. Newtson (Newtson, 1976; Newtson and Engquist, 1976) showed short films of people engaged in brief action sequences to subjects and asked them to segment what they saw into successive actions. Similar studies have also been initiated by Collett (Argyle, Clarke, and Collett, 1976). Nielsen (1964) reports a 'self-confrontation' study in which participants in films subsequently watched themselves and gave detailed reports on their own behaviour.

The foregoing, which is not intended as a comprehensive survey, illustrates the variety of ways in which film has been used in studies of human behaviour, where the focus has been on the behaviour of individuals. In the case of the studies of expressive behaviour cited, the main concern has been on how this behaviour expresses an emotion, a current psychological state or disposition. The functioning of behaviour in social interaction is not directly investigated for the most part in the above studies. For this, a different perspective is needed and it is to this that we now turn.

CONTEXT ANALYSIS IN THE STUDY OF SOCIAL INTERACTION: OUTLOOK AND METHODOLOGY

The perspective which gave rise to film-based studies of interaction was provided by a conception of human communication in which people are seen as participants in complex systems of behavioural relationships instead of as isolated senders and receivers of discrete messages. This conception of human communication, which is related to the pragmatic tradition in social philosophy (Mead, 1934) and which is heavily indebted both to concepts derived from information theory and cybernetics (Reusch and Bateson, 1951) and to developments in the method and theory of structural linguistics (Harris, 1951; Trager and Smith, 1951; Pike, 1967), gave rise to a specific methodology for unravelling the organization of communication in interaction. This methodology has been termed 'context analysis'. Its assumptions and procedures were first fully formulated by Scheflen (1966, 1973), though discussions may also be found in Pittinger, Hockett, and Danehy (1960) and Birdwhistell (1970). The general point of view receives extensive discussion in Sebeok, Hayes and Bateson (1964) and a closely similar outlook and methodology is presented by Hall (1974). Goffman's work on face-to-face interaction is closely related to this approach, and his writings continue to be very influential for workers following this orientation (Goffman, 1961, 1963, 1967, 1971, 1974). Discussions of context analysis, and the outlook that informs it, have been published by McQuown (1971), Kendon (1972b), Bär (1974) and McDermott and Wertz (1976).

The central ideas of context analysis arose from a collaboration between two linguists—Charles Hockett and Norman McQuown, two anthropologists—Ray Birdwhistell and Gregory Bateson, and two psychiatrists—Henry Brosin and Frieda Fromm-Reichmann. This collaboration, which took place in 1956 at the Center for Advanced Study in the Behavioural Sciences, revolved around a close examination of a film of a psychiatric interview in which an attempt was made to formulate explicitly all the different ways in which the behaviour of the participants in the interview was significant for each other (McQuown *et al.*, 1971). It was recognized that much more happens in an interview than a series of questions put by the psychiatrist and a series of answers given by the patient. A relationship is entered into and negotiated, and both patient and psychiatrist gain information about one another not only from what is said and how it is said, but from what is not said, and from what is done rather than said. The question was to provide a systematic formulation of what occurred, communicatively, in the interview.

It was recognized by this group that the patient and psychiatrist, besides both using a common language, also made use of voicings, pacings of speech, patterns of pausing, and the like, which could also be analysed, like language itself, into minimally contrasting units which occur in regular, customary patterns (Trager, 1958; McQuown, 1957). Birdwhistell (1952) had likewise developed the view that bodily movement is organized into patterns which function in regular, customary sequences. Thus an attempt was made to apply the methods of contrastive analysis developed in structural linguistics for establishing the significant units of a language, to the full range of behaviour that could be observed in the film.

In addition, the application of ideas from communication theory and cybernetics to the phenomena of human communication (Reusch and Bateson, 1951) led to the recognition that 'communicating' is not an act that one can choose to engage in or not. Rather, so long as one is in the presence of another, all of one's behaviour is a source of information for another, all of the time. To remain silent or immobile in another's presence is as informative as moving or speaking. Obviously, in a co-present situation such information does not flow only one way. If p is continuously informative for q, q is continuously informative for p, so any adjustment p makes to information he receives from q is simultaneously informative for q, and vice versa. Thus people in one another's presence enter into systems of information exchange and reciprocal control. The behaviour of each feeds back to and controls the other. Thus, in analysing what happens in an interview, or any other interaction, we have to consider the behaviour of each in relation to the behaviour of the other.

Furthermore, behaviour always functions communicatively on more than one level at once. When p says something to q, not only do the words uttered convey something, but the very occurrence of the utterance (contrasting with non-occurrence) is informative. Further, p's utterance occurs in some relationship to something that q has done or is doing, and this relationship, contrasting, again, with some other possible kind of relationship, is informative at yet a different level. In addition, any utterance is also said in some tone of voice or other, with some pattern of body motion or other, in the context of some posture and relative spatial position or other—all of which can serve to further inform q about the utterance. Utterances, thus, indeed actions of any sort, are always and unavoidably multiply informative. The significance of any unit of action in the communicative system, thus, cannot be stated except in terms of how it is related to the entire complex of concurrent action and situation.

In the context analysis approach, then, it is assumed that the process of communication is a continuous one and that the behaviour of people in face-to-face interaction is functioning in systems of reciprocal relation. Furthermore, since all behaviour is always a possible source of information, we cannot, at the outset of an investigation, exclude any aspect of behaviour from the possibility that it may be functional in the communicative system. As Scheflen (1966) has put it: 'We do not decide beforehand what is trivial, what is redundant, or what alters the system. This is a *result* of the research' (p. 270).

Second, the recognition that communication must be seen as operating at multiple levels simultaneously means that we must be prepared for the possibility that the meaning of an item of behaviour may be radically altered, not only according to the relationship it has with other items of behaviour that occur in sequence, but also according to the relationship it has with other, concurrent items which, perhaps, can be seen as including it. The analysis of language proposed in structural linguistics had already suggested the concept of the hierarchical organization of behaviour. It is an important feature of the context analysis approach that it sees behaviour in interaction as organized at multiple levels. Units of behaviour are specified at a particular level of organization and are seen as both themselves containing elements or units at lower levels of organization, and at the same time as participating in units at higher organizational levels.

Third, it is assumed that the units into which the behaviour of the participants in interaction is organized, at any level of organization, have a characteristic or customary structure. That is to say, behaviour is not constructed out of units or phrases whose pattern or form is completely different from any that have ever occurred before. Rather, the phrases of behaviour occur in a limited range of forms, which are familiar at least to members of the same communicating group. It is claimed for all of behaviour, as it is claimed for speech, that we may see it in its communicative function, at least, as comprising complex patterns of patterned elements. As Scheflen (1973) has pointed out, the very occurrence of systemic relationships between the behaviour of people, the very phenomenon of interaction, that is, depends upon the ability of people to organize their behaviour into patterns which have a predictable structure and organization. To accomplish a handshake, for instance, the two handshakers must be able to recognize what each is going to do, each step of the way, otherwise neither would be able to coordinate his behaviour with that of the other. But to recognize what the other is doing is possible only to the extent that the other's behaviour is organized into patterns that are familiar. It is one of the principal aims of context analysis to discern and to give an account of the patterns into which behaviour is organized which make communication possible.

It will be seen that, if interaction is to be investigated from this point of view, the availability of film specimens of interaction is essential. If it is assumed that all behaviour is potentially informative, we must have as much of that behaviour as possible available to examine. If it is supposed that behaviour functions communicatively at multiple levels simultaneously, we must be able to compare and contrast extended segments of the flow of behaviour so that we have the opportunity to inspect its organization at various levels. For this kind of analysis it is quite essential to be able to examine and re-examine the same sequence of behaviour. And again, to establish the characteristic or patterned structure of units of behaviour, we must be able to compare behavioural items directly. The film specimen is thus an integral part of the whole procedure. This is acknowledged by Scheflen when, in formulating the operational procedures of context analysis into five steps, as he does (Scheflen, 1973, appendix B) he places 'the acquisition of the audio-visual record of a transaction' as the first of these steps.

The remaining operations of context analysis which Scheflen lists concern the procedures of transcribing or charting the behaviour in the specimen, the delineation of structural units of behaviour and the examination of the communicative or interactional function of these units. Scheflen lists these steps as separate operational procedures which succeed one another in that order. However, as McQuown (1971) has commented, and as Scheflen himself has remarked, one in fact must proceed with several of these operations simultaneously. For example, to make a chart of the behaviour in the specimen presupposes an understanding of the structural units of the behaviour, since any sort of transcription embodies decisions as to what the units are that one is transcribing. Scheflen points out that we have a considerable knowledge of what many of the units of communicational behaviour are, and the first step usually taken in a context analysis is not to make a transcription, but to view many times the specimen we propose to investigate, to become fully familiar with it. As one does this, one begins to notice certain features of the behaviour that appear to repeat themselves, or that occur in a sequence with which one is highly familiar. For example, if we look at films of people greeting one another we will quickly notice certain regularities, such as the repeated occurrence of such highly familiar patterns as smiling, laughing, handwaving, handshaking, embracing, and so on. One may then begin to make a chart of the event in terms of these units. The chart may, at this stage, be quite rough, and in noting down a unit such as 'wave' or 'handshake' one will in fact be noting down units that are quite complex, at a relatively high level of organization. As one proceeds, however, one will find it necessary to work to progressively finer degrees of detail, and subsequent charts may be much more elaborate. Charting or mapping, therefore is a continuous process. The charts or maps one makes of the behaviour are one of the outcomes of the research and they are continuously revised as one's analysis proceeds.

The initial mapping, thus, also constitutes the initial delineation of the structural units. To proceed to the identification of these units requires careful comparisons between recurrent examples to establish that they are in fact the same. Thus, to continue with the greetings example, if one has delineated 'wave' as a tentative unit, one must proceed to compare the various examples of 'waves' that one has available to see whether they are the same. One will find it necessary to analyse 'wave' into a number of components: the lifting of the arm, the successive units of movement the arm engages in when it is lifted, its lowering etc. As one looks at one's examples, one will notice that associated with the arm actions there are vocalizations, movements of the head and patterns of action on the face. One must compare and contrast the various examples of 'waves' to see to what extent these components occur together and in the same way. If they do, then it is this recurrent combination of elements that comprises one's structural unit at a given level of organization. If one finds, on the other hand, that the lifting of the arm is not always accompanied by vocalization or smiling, then these components are not considered an integral part of the unit.

A unit once delineated must then be examined in its context of occurrence. That is, one will notice the place it has in the sequencing of other units that have been delineated. Kendon and Ferber (1973) described the 'wave' as one of a number of behavioural units that occurred at a phase of a greeting transaction in which the participants were still widely separated in space, shortly after they had oriented to one another and looked at one another. From its placement in sequence, and by comparing contrasting instances where, in the same context, different behavioural units occur, and by contrasting the associated patterns of behaviour in the other participant to the transaction, one may establish the difference made by the presence or absence of the unit of behaviour one is studying to the subsequent development of the sequence. It is through this kind of contrastive contextual analysis that one establishes the probable interactive function of the unit being examined. Context analysis, thus, is so called because it insists upon always examining the patterning of units in their contextual relations with other units, and the interactive functioning of behavioural units is derived from the difference their occurrence or non-occurrence makes in otherwise similar contexts. It may be noted that it is but one expression of a rather widespread development, in which human behaviour is viewed in terms of how it functions in systems of relationship between individuals. An early expression of this outlook is found in the work of G. H. Mead (1934), especially in his notion of the 'significant gesture' where, for him, a gesture acquires its meaning only because of the difference it makes to the unfolding 'conversation of gestures' of which it is a part. We find a closely similar view in the work of Malinowski (1923) who developed a 'context theory of meaning' and insisted that acts of speech should be examined in terms of their situation of occurrence. Malinowski's views have had considerable influence in Britain, for example through the development of his views by Firth (1957). Such workers as Halliday (1973), Bernstein (1971), Laver (1975), Brazil (1975), and Sinclair and Coulthard (1975), are pursuing investigations into the interactive functioning of language using procedures and following an outlook that has close affinities with the outlook of context analysis. In the United States Hymes (1974) is well known for his advocacy of the study of 'speech situations' and a good many are working in this direction (see the collection in Gumperz and Hymes, 1972, Bauman and Sherzer, 1974.) It is also notable that there has been a parallel development in linguistic philosophy, stemming from Wittgenstein's (1953) insistence that the 'meaning of a word is its use' and Austin's (1962) work on what are now called 'speech acts' (Searle, 1969).

Finally, developments in 'conversation analysis', though deriving from a very different philosophical tradition (Garfinkel, 1967; Sudnow, 1972; Mehan and Wood, 1975), may also be seen as part of the same general current of thought. For example, when Schegloff and Sacks (1973), and Sacks, Schegloff, and Jefferson (1974) insist as a central point of their methodology that it is the way interactants attend to and treat each other's turns at talk, that is the focus of their analysis, since it is the participants' understandings of each other's behaviour that is wanted for analysis, they are assuming a closely similar orientation—see also the excellent methodological discussion in Schenkein (1972).

MAKING FILMS FOR CONTEXT ANALYSIS

The technical procedures of cinematography, sound recording and videotaping are well described in a variety of handbooks. In recent years, lightweight ciné cameras and highly portable video equipment have become available which make field filming much easier than it used to be (Pincus, 1972; Mercer, 1974; Lipton, 1972; Leviton, 1970).

Here a few general comments will be offered on the approach to be followed if one is making films for context analysis purposes. It will be apparent how the theoretical outlook we have described informs the practicalities of filmmaking.

Ciné photography is usually undertaken for the purpose of making footage which can be edited into what might be called a *made film* which, when viewed by others, either provides an experience for them or in some other way tells a story about what was filmed. It is most important for anyone proposing to make films for context analysis purposes, to remember that the film being made will not have these functions. In shooting the footage, no attempt should be made through the use of camera movements or changes of camera angle, or through the use of multiple short takes, to impose any sort of narrative analysis on the transaction one is filming. In filming a conversation, for example, the camera operator should on no account emphasize a speaker at the expense of his listeners. It may be true that participants in conversation tend to switch their attention from one speaker to the next, and so if one is making a film which is intended to convey to spectators the experience of the conversation, it may be appropriate to concentrate now on one speaker, now on the next, perhaps intercutting appropriate 'reaction shots' of listeners. However, if one is making a film of a conversation for context analysis purposes one should choose the most comprehensive angle possible and then stick to it. As we have seen, what a context analysis aims at is an account of the system of behavioural in-terrelationship, and it adheres to the principle that any of the behaviour *may* play some part in this system. As far as possible, therefore, one must film so that all of the participants in a transaction can be seen all of the time. One must use ciné equipment that allows for very long takes (for example, cameras that have capacities for 364 m (1200 feet) film magazines) and be prepared to simply let the camera run. If possible, filming should begin before the transaction in which one is interested has begun, and it should continue until after the participants have dispersed. As a general rule, one should always film for longer than one thinks is necessary. It is important to avoid switching the camera on and off in accordance with what, to ordinary perception, seems central in interaction. If this is done one will fail to record the behaviour by which the event was set up and by which it was brought to an end. Furthermore, the resulting record will not permit the event to be analysed in terms of the behavioural organization that constituted it.

It is obvious that the camera cannot record a truly comprehensive view of any event. The limitations of a film recording must be fully recognized but attempts to overcome them, for example by moving around with the camera while one is filming, should be avoided at all costs. Ideally, one should make use of several cameras. This would make it possible to film the same event from more than one direction, and one could also at the same time film in close-up, for example, to record the more subtle details of facial behaviour. Usually one cannot afford such luxuries, or the exigencies of the situation are such that the practicalities of working with several cameras are too great to overcome. Therefore, one must try to decide in advance what is the best position and angle for the main questions one will be asking in the analysis, and then film as consistently as possible from this viewpoint.

The points we have been making here may appear obvious, yet one recent paper (Williams and Feld, 1975) has actually recommended that in making 'researchable film' one should aim to generate 'footage that shows the filmer's through-the-camera experience of the event/he is filming/' (p. 31). Now if one were going to investigate the cameraman's experience of the event this is, of course, just the strategy one should adopt. However, for the purposes of making footage suitable for the analysis of the behavioural organization of the interaction it would be quite inappropriate. What the context analysis filmmaker must do is to try to select the angle and position that will include as much of the behaviour as possible. Having decided on the most inclusive angle, however, no further attempt to structure the spectator's view of the material filmed should be made. To try to do this will prejudge the very questions one is after.

A question that is frequently raised is that of whether or not one should try to conceal the activity of filming. It is often suggested that the presence of a camera will so distort the behaviour that it will not be 'natural'. Undoubtedly, the presence of cameras does have an effect on people's behaviour. There are, however, ways of minimizing these effects which fall far short of concealment or deception and for most purposes these are much to be preferred. If concealment or deception is used, one must bear in mind both the poor ethics of this practice and the possibility that if one is found out the consequences could be serious.

The best way to minimize the effects of the presence of camera is probably habituation. If one is going to record routine events, for example, one should place the equipment in the site some considerable time before one begins to film. When the equipment first appears, people may pay it considerable attention, but quite quickly they will find it necessary to get on with whatever they need to do regardless of whether the camera is working or not. Even when people are fully habituated, however, one should avoid making the act of filming conspicuous. Cameras should be placed as far away as possible (distance can be compensated for by the use of tele-lenses). If possible they should be mounted on a tripod and allowed to run with as little attention from the cameraman as possible.

If the event is not routine, it is best to make sure the participants know in advance that filming is going to take place so that they will not be surprised by it. Best results can be obtained if one is able to film an event that the participants intend to engage in anyway, in the locale they had intended to use. Even conversations staged in the laboratory can provide valid material, however. The activity of filming may affect what people say, but the detailed way in which each organizes his speech and concurrent kinesics as he engages in conversation is not likely to be very much affected.

TECHNICAL PROCEDURES AND APPARATUS FOR ANALYSIS

A projection print of the film that is to be used for analysis should be overprinted with frame numbers which appear at the top of the picture when the film is projected. This may be accomplished by preparing a second ('B') roll which then can be used for any research prints to be used. This procedure, originated by Van Vlack at the Eastern Pennsylvania Psychiatric Institute in Philadelphia, (Van Vlack, 1966) is used routinely by several workers in the field. It enables the referencing of sequences which have been analysed, as a quick method of deriving the time any sequence takes, and it is also a great aid in plotting out maps of the filmed behaviour. A frame-numbering device is now available for videotape and this will prove much more satisfactory than using a special effects generator to overprint minutes and seconds.

For actual procedures of film analysis, some kind of equipment is necessary by which the film can be viewed both at normal speed and in slow motion and frame by frame. There are available film analysis projectors which permit the film to be viewed at any speed up to twenty-four frames per second (normal sound film projection speed) and which can at the same time be viewed at different rates (L-W Athena 224A, Selectaframe, and Lafayette Analyser are widely used US models). It is also possible to use editing tables for analysis purposes. Editing tables (for example the Steenbeck or Moviola), while they permit viewing of the film at speeds greater than normal projection speed, and while they are much less likely to damage film, have the disadvantage that they are not adapted for projection and they show only a small and rather poorly focused image. In contrast, projectors, though they are noisey, generate heat and have a greater potential for damaging film, provide a large, bright, sharp image. They are also somewhat cheaper than editing tables, take up much less space and are portable.

Automatic analysis projectors are ideal for true frame-by-frame analysis and for viewing extended segments of film at slow speeds, thus making possible the inspection of complicated events. However, if one wishes to establish the boundaries of movement phrases, it is better to use an apparatus that permits the film to be viewed several frames at a time, but at full speed, so that the movement on the film can be perceived as such, and not as a series of positional displacements. For this purpose it is better to use a manually controlled analysis projector, in which the film is advanced by turning a handle. Such a projector, at one time manufactured as a Time and Motion Study Projector by Bell and Howell, can now be had only by custom adaptation. With the skilled use of such a manual projector, a movement phrase analysis becomes very easy to carry out. It has been used in the several studies published by Condon and his co-workers and also by Kendon in several studies (see below). A detailed comparative discussion of automatic and manual projectors and of the techniques of movement phrase boundary analysis (as distinct from frame-by-frame analysis) can be found in Kendon (1977c).

How one proceeds with an analysis will depend, of course, on what the object of the analysis is. An important part of the procedure in any context analysis, as we have seen, is the mapping of the behaviour structure. It is of inestimable help to lay out on a time-chart the various behavioural events, both vocalic and kinesic, that have been recorded on the film. Exactly what transcription procedures one will make use of will depend very much upon the level of detail at which one is proposing to work. Although for speech there are well-established notation systems both for the segmental phonemes and for suprasegmental or prosodic phenomena (Jones, 1966; Pike, 1946; Kingdon, 1958) and for paralinguistic phenomena (Crystal and Davy, 1969), such is not the case for bodily movement. Although a number of systems have been devised, each of them has its limitations since they have been evolved for different special purposes and there is, as yet, no generally agreed upon system. (For a comparative discussion of some of these systems see Bouissac 1973; systems of notation have been proposed and published by Laban, 1956; Hutchinson, 1970; Benesh, 1956; and Eshkol and Wachmann, 1958. These have not been widely used by researchers in communicative behaviour who appear, for the most part, to make use of *ad hoc* systems.

One quite general point may be made in reference to the question of transcription systems, however. A transcription system embodies a theory as to what constitutes the significant units of which the phenomenon being transcribed is made up. A live issue in research is the question as to what systems of units behaviour is to be seen as being organized into. One should by wary, therefore, of becoming too attached to a particular transcription system and, more particularly, of first trying to transform one's entire specimen into the form of a transcript and then working exclusively from it, rather than in constant reference to the original specimen.

A final point deserving comment is the question of the reliability of one's transcriptions. Data pertaining to this question are rarely presented, presumably because it is felt that, since one is making transcriptions from specimens, one can continually check back with the original material and so correct any errors. Where one is attempting to plot the precise location of the boundary of a movement phrase, however, there is bound to be some irreducible margin of error. This margin of error will vary according to the clarity of the image and the kind of movement boundary from which one is working. Changes in direction of movement of a body part can be very gradual, and the location of the change sometimes cannot be arrived at with the same degree of precision as more rapid changes. The investigator should, however, for each specimen he has analysed, present some indication of the margin of error within which he is working. This issue receives some further discussion in Kendon (1977c).

PROBLEMS AND FINDINGS IN FILM-BASED STUDIES OF SOCIAL INTERACTION

The behavioural phenomena of face-to-face interaction are very complex and to attempt to produce detailed systematic descriptions from film specimens is very time-consuming. For this reason, most of the work done by context analysts or by those who follow similar methods has been done with relatively few specimens. This is justified if it is assumed that the specimens are representative of the kind of interaction being studied. It is a basic assumption in this work that human interaction employs a limited repertoire of behavioural units and that there is a limited set of principles by which its organization is governed. Thus these units and principles will be illustrated in any appropriate sample. Obviously, this assumption is subject to continual testing, as more and more examples of interaction are analysed (see Chapter 8 in this volume by DeWaele and Harré for a similar consideration regarding autobiography—Ed.).

The work conducted by context analysts and similar workers has not been experimental in the sense that as yet there are no studies which have attempted to test hypotheses by the manipulation of variables under controlled conditions. A number of workers have, to be sure, filmed *ad hoc* groups in laboratories, but this has been done simply as a means of generating interactional phenomena which were not themselves manipulated in any way. Investigators in this orientation have seen themselves as natural historians of interaction. It is maintained that a thorough acquaintance with the behaviour of interaction is necessary before genuinely new hypotheses can emerge and before one can undertake meaningful experiments to test them.

Most of the studies of interaction done within the context analysis orientation have been concerned with interactional events in which talk is the featured activity and most of the findings, though they tend to focus upon posture, orientation, patterns of looking, gesturing and other kinds of bodily movement, are concerned with the way in which participants organize their behaviour in relation to one another in cooperative behavioural relationships within which talk can be successfully accomplished (cf. Kendon, 1973). It may also be noted that many of these studies have focused upon phenomena that can be observed within quite short time-spans, and one of the main contributions of film-based studies of social interaction has been to show that participants' behavioural coordination is very finely textured (see Chapter 5 in this volume by Scaife for a discussion of longer time-spans—Ed.).

In the following survey we shall indicate the principal issues that have been tackled in film-based studies of interaction. We shall include here the main investigations which have used film specimens for descriptive analyses of interaction, whether or not they explicitly acknowledge the methodology of context analysis.

Presentation, position and point

Scheflen's findings, based on analyses of films of psychotherapy sessions, but presented as having more general implications, may be found in several publications (Scheflen, 1963, 1964, 1965, 1966, 1968, 1969, 1973, 1974). He shows how interactants may be regarded as employing a repertoire of units of communicational behaviour, organized at various levels of complexity. He proposes three organizational levels, termed, in descending order of inclusiveness, the *presentation*, the *position* and the *point*. Each is marked by some constant feature of behaviour which serves as an indicator that the unit is in operation. While it is in operation we may recognize sequences or cycles of behaviour which constitute the unit's enactment and which are themselves units at the level of organization below.

The *presentation* refers to the sustained location and orientation a participant in an interactional event maintains so long as he *is* a participant. Thus, for the duration of an event such as a conversation or a psychotherapy session, the participants maintain a relatively constant spatial and orientational arrangement which disperses once the event is over. While engaged in a presentation a participant may engage in one or more *positions*. A position is a recurrent configuration of behaviour which may be recognized by a sustained posture, which is distinctive, and concurrent with this the individual engages in a distinctive enactment. For example, Scheflen distinguishes narrating and *defending* as positions enacted by one of the participants in the psychotherapy session analysed in Scheflen (1973); *passive protesting* and *contending* for another; *listening* and *explaining* for the therapists (there are nine positions distinguished altogether, but these will suffice here). Each of these different positions are recognizable not only from the kinds of speech acts engaged in, but also from the distinctive sustained posture maintained during them. Scheflen describes how participants in an interaction tend to have a limited repertoire of positions. In the psychotherapy session analysed he shows how the successive phases of the session may be distinguished in terms of the sequencing and cycling of the positions that occur. He suggests that the postural configuration of the position that is held while the position is performed serves as a frame for a stretch of behaviour, indicating that a particular theme is informing the participant's activities. Transactions can be analysed as progressing through several stages, each stage comprising a configuration of positions. The associated postural configuration, thus, can serve to identify for the participants, the stage of the transaction. By shifting into a new posture, an individual participant can signal that he is moving into a new phase of interactional activity.

Within each position, the participant engages in a number of actions which constitute the performance of the position. For example, within the framework of the position *narrating*, the psychotherapy participant referred to above would produce a succession of utterances, addressing first one psychiatrist, then the next. As she sat huddled by her mother in the posture that characterized the position of *passive protesting*, her daughter would grimace, mutter under her breath, sprawl back on the sofa she was sitting on and sit forward again. In other words, *within* a position, marked by a total bodily configuration, a series of one or more actions are performed. These Scheflen calls *points*. Points themselves may be further analysed into components, of course, though Scheflen himself only indicates this. For example, if a point unit is enacted as an utterance, the speech may be analysed into its component phonemic clauses or tone units, which in turn may be analysed into their syllabic and intonational components. Any accompanying gestures can be analysed into gesture phrases and components thereof (Kendon 1972a, 1975a). Once again we see that a unit at one level of organization can be seen as an organization or patterning of units at a lower level of organization.

Formation

Several of Scheflen's concepts and findings (only some of which we have touched on above) have been supported by other studies. Kendon (1977b) has examined the way in which an entire interactional event may be characterized in terms of a jointly sustained spatial–orientational arrangement he has termed a *formation*. He describes in detail the properties of one kind of formation, the F-formation, in which the participants so arrange themselves to have joint and exclusive access to space between them. Kendon further describes how the specific pattern or arrangement of the F-formation remains constant only for a given phase of the interaction. For example, Kendon and Ferber (1973), in their study of greeting encounters, described how the two greeters would assume one pattern of spatial–orientational arrangement for the duration of their initial salutation (such as a handshake), and they would then change and assume a new spatial arrangement for their subsequent conversation. In a study of conversations, Kendon (1977b) also describes how the shape of the arrangement changes with major changes in the topic of the conversation. This is quite comparable to Scheflen's notion that the configuration of presentations constitutes a frame for the encounter as a whole, within which successive configurations of positions, marked in postural arrangements, constitute frames for subperiods of activity within the encounter. Erickson (1975) has described this phenomenon in counselling interviews. McDermott (1976) in a recent study of reading groups in a primary school shows how a period of time at a table by a group, which constitutes the lesson, is divisible into a series of four major phases within which a succession of four *positionings* can be identified. These positionings are configurations of postural arrangements within each of which a different programme of activity proceeds. For example, he distinguishes a positioning (1) in which the children and teacher each focus on their book, while one child reads; in positioning (2) the children bid for, and the teacher decides upon, who next will get a turn to read; in positioning (3) children focus their attention in different directions—this McDermott refers to as 'anarchy'; in positioning (4) the children are waiting for the teacher to come. Each of these positionings has a distinctive pattern of postural arrangements.

McDermott shows, in a detailed analysis, how, once a given positioning is under way—its inception may be marked by an announcement by the teacher, for example—even if the stable pattern of postural orientations characteristic of the positioning is not currently evident, the way each member of the group orients to and moves in relation to movements of the other members, is related to the programme of activity of that positioning and is different from the way they would relate their behaviour in another one. For example, if the prevailing positioning is positioning (1) where the children focus of their books and one child reads, the children coordinate their behaviour in relation to each other's looking or not looking at their books differently from the way they do if the prevailing positioning is, say, positioning (4) waiting for the teacher to come. McDermott's analysis illustrates the way in which people are oriented to one another's actions and are highly sensitive to the implications those actions have for their own options in a given situation.

McDermott's analysis illustrates one aspect of what Scheflen once called *regulatory* communication (Scheflen, 1963). One aspect of regulation that has been most widely investigated is concerned with how taking turns at speaking in conversation is managed. So that an orderly turn-taking in speaking in conversation is achieved, not only must there be a system of turn-taking rules (Sacks, Schegloff, and Jefferson, 1974), but participants must be able to constantly inform one another of their intentions with respect to turn-taking. Thus turn exchanges have been studied and patterns of behaviour associated with them have been described which, it is suggested, may serve as signals of intention to yield the turn, to offer the turn to a specific other, to continue the turn, to request a turn, or to show that one is not attempting to take a turn—that one is continuing as a listener, in effect. This problem was first treated by Nielsen (1964), Kendon (1967), and Yngve (1971). Both Nielsen and Kendon suggested that the patterning of gaze in association with utterances could play a part in turn-signalling. Duncan (1972, 1973, 1974, 1975; Duncan and Niederehe, 1974; Duncan and Fiske, 1977) has presented a series of comprehensive analyses of turn exchanges in two-person conversations, and he has proposed a set of rules or a grammar by which the various signals in the turn-taking system are employed. Wiemann and Knapp (1975) have provided some detailed descriptions of turn-requesting behaviour. Utterance exchange-associated behaviour has been described in children by De Long (1974). Wiener and Devoe (1974) have also described turn-taking behaviour. Baker (in press) has described turn-taking signals in users of American Sign Language.

Studies have also appeared which suggest that the way in which a speaker constructs his turn is highly sensitive to the concurrent behaviour of the listener. Goodwin (1975) reports analyses of three and four-person conversations in which he shows how a current speaker may restructure his turn as he is producing it, according to who at the moment is looking at him and so serving as a recipient. Erickson (1976) has studied interracial counselling interviews and finds that the way in which the counsellor develops his explanations to his client is intimately dependent upon the patterning and variety of discrete listener responses such as headnods and brief utterances that the recipient provides. He suggests that the 'hyper-explanation' and repetition of white interviewers complained of by black clients may be due to the fact that the white counsellor, not appreciating the system of black listener responses, acts as if he has not received any and thus he repeats himself. Another, earlier study along these lines, has also been reported by Birdwhistell (1970).

Other studies of speaker–listener relationships which have examined the flow of behaviour in great detail, show even more clearly the dynamic nature of this relationship. Condon, in a series of papers (Condon, 1970; Condon and Ogston, 1966, 1967, 1971) in which he has undertaken extremely fine-grained analyses of the organization of the flow of movement in speakers and their listeners, reports that speakers and listeners tend to move together in a synchronous relationship. Using a manually operated film projector, he establishes the boundaries of the minimum movement phrases in each segment of the body, and these he compares to the occurrence of boundaries in the concurrent speech flow and also with boundaries in the flow of movement of the speaker's listener. He proceeds, body segment by body segment to establish, over a given stretch of film, whether movement in that body segment remains constant in its direction or speed. When a body segment *changes* in direction or speed of movement, a boundary is marked. The resulting analysis, thus, is a time-based chart of the successive contrasting segments of movement in each body part. This can be matched to a concurrent time-based chart of the concurrent speech segments, and also to a movement phrase boundary chart of the co-interactant's movements. Condon reports a very high degree of boundary coincidence, so that he speaks of the speaker and listener moving together in synchrony.

Examples of such synchrony have also been described by Kendon (1970). In a detailed study of a question–answer–response interchange he showed how the next speaker began his next utterance precisely as the other ended and how the next speaker had, prior to the end of the current turn, begun to move in a pattern which was rhythmically coordinated with the current speaker's speech. He describes how the speaker and listener were not only in synchrony at transition points but that the form of the listener's movements was in part similar to the form of the gestural and postural movements of the speaker. He suggests that such overt synchrony and shared movement morphology could be important in maintaining joint attention and in thus making possible the high degree of coordination that often obtains in utterance exchanges.

Such synchronization of action in interactants has also been described for interaction where speech was not occurring (Kendon, 1973, 1977b). For such synchronization to be achieved, participants in interaction must be able to anticipate rather precisely the temporal trajectory of each other's phrases of action. Martin (1973) has drawn attention to the importance of the rhythmical organization of speech in this regard. Such rhythmical organization is probably also evident in the organization of phrases of bodily movement. A phrase of action once begun, the rhythmical organization governing it can be apprehended by the other and its course of development in time thus anticipated. A process of this sort must be involved if the synchronization that has been observed is to be achieved (Trevarthen, 1975).

A few studies have appeared in which the interaction analysed is not organized around talk as the featured activity of the event. Kendon and Ferber (1973) presented a detailed analysis of the organization of greeting encounters in which they attempted to show the sequential organization of such events. Kendon (1975b) has described the organization of a 'kissing round' from a film of a courting couple in a park. He described the patterning of facial display and its relationship to other events in the interaction, showing that the face functions as a subtle regulatory instrument. Wolff (1973) and Collett and Marsh (1974) have analysed films of pedestrians on crowded pavements, and have discussed the way in which they cooperate to avoid colliding. Ryave and Schenkein (1974) have discussed the achievement of walking in public space, using videotape specimens as a basis for analysis. Aldiss (1975) has presented a detailed study of play-fighting in children, in which he makes extensive use of film specimens.

There are a growing number of studies in which films of mother–infant interaction has been analysed (see Schaffer, 1977). Contrary to widely held belief, these studies demonstrate that even very small infants enter into systems of behavioural relationship with others. Evidently, from the very first infants are able to recognize intentional, communicative action in another, and to organize their own behaviour, albeit in a rudimentary fashion, accordingly. Condon and Sander (1974a, 1974b) have demonstrated interactional synchrony between an infant's movements and human speech. Trevarthen (1975) finds that infants as young as three weeks old organize their behaviour quite differently when they are presented with their mother as compared to when they are presented with an object. Bullowa (1975), working with films of mothers and babies interacting as the mother undresses, baths, dresses and feeds the baby, finds that infants of eight months can engage in complex cooperative interaction with the mother as they are being dressed and undressed. She also describes conversation-like exchanges in interactions with infants only twelve days old. There is, thus, extensive interaction going on between mother and infant well before even the rudiments of recognizable speech is manifested. Bullowa suggests, as does Trevarthen, that the establishment of rhythmical coordination between mother and infant, which both Bullowa and Trevarthen observe as coming about through the mother adapting her cadence of actions to those of the infant, is an essential precursor to the emergence of language. Language emerges first as speech-acts which are meaningful because they are integrated within the framework of an ongoing interactional event between mother and child (Bruner, 1975). The process of language acquisition is thus revealed to be intimately bound up with the development of participation in interaction.

CONCLUSIONS

In this paper we have tried to show that the use of film as a means of making specimens of interactional events which can then be inspected in great detail and at leisure, makes possible discoveries about the nature of the interaction process that would not otherwise be possible. Such discoveries have been made, however, only because investigators have adopted an outlook which directs their attention to *behavioural relationships*. We see, thus, how a technical innovation does not in itself bring about new discoveries. There must also be a theoretical viewpoint providing a rationale for using the innovation in a particular way.

The discoveries made about interaction using film specimens show how complex and multifaceted interaction is. They suggest that co-present individuals are highly attuned to one another's behaviour, and integrated into systems of relationship at several levels of organization at once. They suggest strongly that rather than thinking of individuals first and then asking how it is they manage to communicate with one another, we should think in reverse and ask how *individuals* emerge from the continual and all-pervasive systems of communication human organisms are found to be in.

References

Aldiss, O., 1975, *Play Fighting*, New York: Academic Press.
Ames, Louise B., 1940, The constancy of psychomotor tempo in individual infants, *Journal of Genetic Psychology*, 57, 445–450.
Ames, Louise B., 1944, Early individual differences in visual and motor behavior patterns: a comparative study of two normal infants by the method of cinemanalysis, *Journal of Genetic Psychology*, 65, 219–226.
Argyle, M., Clarke, D., and Collett, P., 1976, *Project on the Sequential Structure of Social Behaviour*, Oxford: University of Oxford, Department of Experimental Psychology, Report to the Social Science Research Council for the period September 1975 to August 1976.
Austin, J. M., 1962, *How to Do Things with Word*, Oxford: Clarendon Press.
Baker, Charlotte, in press, Regulations and turn-taking in American Sign Language Discourse, in Lynn Friedman (ed.), *On the Other Hand: New Perspectives on American Sign Language*, New York: Academic Press.
Bär, E., 1974, Context analysis in psychotherapy, *Semiotica*, 10, 255–281.
Bauman, R. and Sherzer, J. (eds.), 1974, *Explorations in the Ethnography of Speaking*, London: Cambridge University Press.
Benesh, R., 1956, *Introduction to the Benesh Movement Notation*, London: A. & C. Black.
Bernstein, B., 1971, *Class, Codes and Control*, Vol. I, *Theoretical Studies Toward a Sociology of Language*, London: Routledge & Kegan Paul.
Birdwhistell, R. L., 1952, *Introduction to Kinesics*, Washington, DC: US Department of State Foreign Service Institute. Reprinted (1954) University of Louisville, Ky.
Birdwhistell, R. L., 1970, *Kinesics and Context: Essays on Body Motion Communication*, Philadelphia: University of Pennsylvania Press, pp. 163–166.
Bouissac, P., 1973, *La Mesure des Gestes*, The Hague: Mouton.

Brazil, D., 1975, *Discourse Intonation*, Birmingham: English Language Research, Discourse Analysis Monographs No. 1.

Bruner, J. S., 1975, The ontogenesis of speech acts, *Journal of Child Language*, **2**, 1-19.

Bullowa, Margaret, 1975, When infant and adult communicate how do they synchronize their behaviors?, in A. Kendon, R. M. Harris, and Mary Ritchie Key (eds.), *The Organization of Behavior in Face-to-Face Interaction*, The Hague: Mouton (World Anthropology).

Coleman, J. C., 1949, Facial expression of emotion, *Psychological Monographs*, whole No. 296, **63**, 1-36.

Collett, P. and Marsh, P., 1974, Patterns of public behaviour, *Semiotica*, **12**, 281-300.

Condon, W. D., 1970, Method of micro-analysis of sound films of behavior, *Behavior Research Methods and Instrumentation*, **2**, 51-54.

Condon, W. S., in press, Communication and order: the micro 'rhythm hierarchy' of speaker behavior, *Sign Language Studies*.

Condon, W. S. and Ogston, W. D., 1966, Sound film analysis of normal and pathological behavior patterns, *Journal of Nervous Mental Behavior*, **143**, 338-347.

Condon, W. S. and Ogston, W. D., 1967, A segmentation of behavior, *Journal of Psychiatric Research*, **5**, 221-235.

Condon, W. S. and Ogston, W. D., 1971, Speech and body motion synchrony of the speaker-hearer, in D. L. Horton and J. J. Jenkins (eds.), *Perception of Language*, Columbus, Ohio: Charles E. Merrill.

Condon, W. S. and Sander, L., 1974a, Neonate movement is synchronized with adult speech: interactional participation and language acquisition, *Science*, **183**, 99-101.

Condon, W. S. and Sander, L., 1974b, Synchrony demonstrated between movements of the neonate and adult speech, *Child Development*, **45**, 456-462.

Crystal, D. and Davy, D. L., 1969, *Investigating English Style*, Bloomington: Indiana University Press.

Davitz, J., 1964, *Communication of Emotional Meaning*, New York: McGraw-Hill.

Dell, Cecily, 1970, *A Primer for Movement Description: Using Effort-Shape and Supplementary Concepts*, New York: Dance Notation Bureau.

De Long, A., 1974, Kinesic signals at utterance boundaries in preschool children, *Semiotica*, **11**, 43-74.

Dittmann, A. T., 1962, The relationship between body movements and mood in interviews, *Journal of Consulting Psychology*, **26**, 480.

Dittmann, A. T., 1963, Kinesic research and therapeutic processes: further discussion, in P. H. Knapp (ed.), *Expression of the Emotions in Man*, New York: International Universities Press.

Dittmann, A. T., 1972, Speech and body motion, in A. Seigman and B. Pope (eds.), *Studies in Dyadic Communication*, Elmsford, NY: Pergamon Press.

Dittmann, A. T., Parloff, M. B., and Boomer, D. S., 1965, Facial and bodily expression: a study of receptivity of emotional cues, *Psychiatry*, **28**, 239-244.

Duncan, S. D., Jr., 1972, Some signals and rules for taking speaking turns in conversation, *Journal of Personality and Social Psychology*, **23**, 283-292.

Duncan, S. D., Jr., 1973, Towards a grammar for dyadic conversations, *Semiotica*, **9**, 29-46.

Duncan, S. D., Jr., 1974, On the structure of speaker-auditor interaction during speaking turns, *Language and Society*, **3**, 161-180.

Duncan, S. D., Jr., 1975, Interaction units during speaking turns in dyadic, face-to-face conversations, in A. Kendon, R. M. Harris and Mary Ritchie Key (eds.), *The Organization of Behavior in Face-to-Face Interaction*, The Hague: Mouton (World Anthropology).

Duncan, S. D., Jr. and Fiske, D. W., 1977, *Face-to-Face Interaction: Research, Method and Theory*, Hillsdale, NJ: Lawrence Erlbaum.
Duncan, S. D. Jr. and Niederehe, G., 1974, On signalling that it is your turn to speak, *Journal of Experimental Social Psychology*, **10**, 234–247.
Efron, D., 1941, *Gesture, Race and Culture*, New York: Kings Crown Press. Reprinted 1972 as No. 9, *Approaches to Semiotics*, Thomas A. Sebeok (ed.), The Hague: Mouton.
Eibl-Eibesfeldt, I., 1970, *Ethology: The Biology of Behavior*, New York: Holt, Rinehart and Winston.
Eibl-Eibesfeldt, I., 1973, The expressive behaviour of the deaf-and-blind-born, in M. Von Cranach and I. Vine (eds.), *Social Communication and Movement: Studies of Interaction and Expression in Man and Chimpanzee*, London and New York: Academic Press.
Ekman, P. (ed.), 1973, *Darwin and Facial Expression: A Century of Research in Review*, London and New York: Academic Press.
Ekman, P. and Friesen, W., 1968, Nonverbal behaviour in psychotherapy research, in J. Shlien (ed.), *Research in Psychotherapy, III*, Washington, DC: American Psychological Association.
Ekman, P. and Friesen, W., 1974, Detecting deception from the body or face, *Journal of Personality and Social Psychology*, **29**, 288–289.
Ekman, P., Friesen, W. V. and Scherer, K. R., 1976, Body movement and voice pitch in deceptive interaction, *Semiotica*, **16**, 23–28.
Erickson, F., 1975, One function of proxemic shifts in face-to-face interaction, in A. Kendon, R. M. Harris, and Mary Ritchie Key (eds.), *The Organization of Behavior in Face-to-Face Interaction*, The Hague: Mouton (World Anthropology).
Erickson, F., 1976, Talking down and giving reasons: hyper-explanation and listening behavior in inter-racial interviews, paper delivered at the International Conference on Non-Verbal Behaviour, Ontario Institute for Studies in Education, Toronto, Canada.
Eshkol, N. and Wachmann, A., 1958, *Movement Notation*, London: Weidenfeld and Nicolson.
Estes, S. G., 1938, Judging personality from expressive behavior, *Journal of Abnormal and Social Psychology*, **33**, 212–236.
Firth, J. R., 1957, *Papers in Linguistics 1934–1951*, London: Oxford University Press.
Flapan, Dorothy, 1968, *Children's Understanding of Social Interaction*, New York: Teachers College Press, Teachers College, Columbia University.
Freedman, N. and Hoffman, S. P., 1967, Kinetic behavior in altered clinical states: an approach to objective analysis of motor behavior during clinical interviews, *Perceptual and Motor Skills*, **24**, 527–539.
Frijda, N. H., 1953, The understanding of facial expression of emotion, *Acta Psychologica*, **9**, 294–362.
From, F., 1971, *Perception of Other People*, New York: Columbia University Press.
Garfinkel, H., 1967, *Studies in Ethnomethodology*, Englewood Cliffs, NJ: Prentice-Hall.
Gesell, A. and Ames, Louis B., 1947, The development of handedness, *Journal of Genetic Psychology*, **70**, 155–175.
Gesell, A. and Halverson, H. M., 1942, The daily maturation of infant behavior: a cinema study of postures, movements and laterality, *Journal of Genetic Psychology*, **61**, 3–32.
Gesell, A. and Ilg, F. L., 1937, *Feeding Behavior of Infants: A Pediatric Approach to the Mental Hygiene of Early Life*, Philadelphia: J. B. Lippincott.
Goffman, E., 1961, *Encounters*, Indianapolis: Bobbs-Merrill.
Goffman, E., 1963, *Behavior in Public Places*, New York: Free Press of Glencoe.

Goffman, E., 1967, *Interaction Ritual: Essays on Face-to-Face Behavior*, Chicago: Aldine Publishing Co.
Goffman, E., 1971, *Relations in Public*, New York: Basic Books.
Goffman, E., 1974, *Frame Analysis*, New York: Harper and Row.
Goodwin, C., 1975, The interactive construction of the sentence within the turn at talk in natural conversation, paper presented to the 74th Annual meeting of the American Anthropological Association.
Gumperz, J. J. and Hymes, D. (eds.), 1972, *Directions in Sociolinguistics: The Ethnography of Communication*, New York: Holt, Rinehart and Winston.
Haggard, E. A. and Isaacs, K. S., 1966, Micro-momentary facial expressions as indicators of ego mechanisms in psychotherapy, in L. A. Gottichalk and A. H. Auerbach (eds.), *Methods of Research in Psychotherapy*, New York: Appleton-Century-Crofts.
Halliday, M. A. K., 1973, *Explorations in the Functions of Language*, London: Edward Arnold.
Hall, E. T., 1974, *Handbook for Proxemic Research*, Washington, DC: Society for the Anthropology of Visual Communication.
Harris, Z., 1951, *Structural Linguistics*, Chicago: Chicago University Press.
Hockings, P., (ed.), 1975, *Principles of Visual Anthropology*, The Hague: Mouton (World Anthropology).
Hunt, W. A., 1936, Studies of the startle pattern: II bodily pattern, *Journal of Psychology*, **2**, 207–213.
Hunt, W. A., Clarke, Frances M., and Hunt, Edna B., 1936, Studies of the startle pattern: IV infants, *Journal of Psychology*, **2**, 339–352.
Hutchinson, Ann, 1970, *Labanotation or Kinetography Laban: The System of Analyzing and Recording Movement*, New York: Theatre Arn Books.
Hymes, D., 1974, *Foundations in Sociolinguistics* Philadelphia: University of Pennsylvania Press.
Jones, D., 1966, *The Pronounciation of English*, London: Cambridge University Press.
Kendon, A., 1967, Some functions of gaze-direction in social interaction, *Acta Psychologica*, **26**, 22–63.
Kendon, A., 1970, Movement coordination in social interaction, *Acta Psychologica*, **32**, 100–125.
Kendon, A., 1972a, Some relationships between body motion and speech, in A. Seigman and B. Pope (eds.), *Studies in Dyadic Communication*, Elmsford, NY: Pergamon Press.
Kendon, A., 1972b, Review of Ray L. Birdwhistell *Kinesics and Context*, *American Journal of Psychology*, **85**, 441–455.
Kendon, A., 1973, The role of visible behaviour in the organization of face-to-face interaction, in M. Von Cranach and I. Vine (eds.), *Movement and Communication in Man and Chimpanzee*, London and New York: Academic Press.
Kendon, A., 1975a, Gesticulation, speech and the gesture theory of language origins, *Sign Language Studies*, **9**, 349–373.
Kendon, A., 1975b, Some functions of the face in a kissing round, *Semiotica*, **15**, 299–334.
Kendon, A., 1977a, *Studies in the Behavior of Social Interaction*, Lisse: Peter De Ridder Press (Vol. 6, Studies in Semiotics, ed. Thomas A. Sebeck).
Kendon, A., 1977b, The F-formation system: spatial orientational relations in face-to-face interaction, in A. Kendon (1977a).
Kendon, A., 1977c, A note on techniques of film analysis, Appendix, A. Kendon (1977a).
Kendon, A., and Ferber, A., 1973, A description of some human greetings, in R. P. Michael and J. H. Crook (eds.), *Comparative Ecology and Behaviour of Primates*, London and New York: Academic Press.
Kingdon, R., 1958, *The Groundwork of English Intonation*, London: Longmans Green.

Laban, R., 1956, *Principles of Dance and Movement Notation*, London: Macdonald and Evans.
Laban, R., 1964, *The Mastery of Movement*, London: Macdonald and Evans.
Landis, C., 1924, Studies of emotional reactions: II, general behavior and facial expression, *Journal of Comparative Psychology*, **4**, 447–509.
Landis, C. and Hunt, W. A., 1936, Studies of the startle pattern: III, facial pattern, *Journal of Psychology*, **2**, 215–219.
Laver, J., 1975, Communicative functions of phatic communion, in A. Kendon, R. M. Harris, and Mary Ritchie Key (eds.), *The Organization of Behaviour in Face-to-Face Interaction*, The Hague: Mouton (World Anthropology).
Leviton, E., 1970, *An Alphabetical Guide to Motion Picture, Television and Videotape Production*, New York: McGraw-Hill Book Co.
Lindenfeld, Jaqueline, 1971, Verbal and Nonverbal elements in discourse, *Semiotica*, **3**, 223–233.
Lindenfeld, Jaqueline, 1974, Syntactic structure and kinesic phenomena in communicative events, *Semiotica*, **12**, 61–74.
Lipton, L., 1972, *Independent Filmmaking*, San Francisco: Straight Arrow Books.
Lomax, A., 1968, *Folksong Style and Culture*, Washington, DC: American Association for the Advancement of Science, Publ. No. 88.
Malinowski, B., 1923, The problem of meaning in primitive languages, Supplement I, in C. K. Ogden and I. A. Richards, *The Meaning of Meaning*, London: Routledge & Kegan Paul.
Marey, É. J., 1895, *Movement*, New York: D. Appleton.
Martin, J. G., 1973, Rhythmic (hierarchical) versus social structure in speech and other behavior, *Psychological Review*, **79**, 487–509.
Mead, G. H., 1934, *Mind, Self, and Society*, University of Chicago Press.
Mehan, H. and Wood, H., 1975, *The Reality of Ethnomethodology*, New York: John Wiley.
Mercer, J., 1967, *An Introduction to Cinematography*, Champaign, Ill.: Stipes Publishing Co.
Michaelis, A. R., 1955, *Research film in Biology Anthropology, Psychology and Medicine*, New York: Academic Press.
Muybridge, E., 1899, *Animals in Motion*, Reprinted by Dover Publications, New York, 1957.
Muybridge, E., 1901, *The Human Figure in Motion*, Reprinted by Dover Publications, New York, 1955.
McDermott, R. D., 1976, Criteria for an ethnographically adequate description of activities and their contexts, paper presented to the American Anthropological Association, Washington, DC, November.
McDermott, R. D. and Wertz, Marjorie, 1976, Doing the social order: some ethnographic advances from communicational analysis and ethnomethodology, *Reviews in Anthropology*, **3**, 160–174.
McMillan, R. A., 1974, A method for using naturalistic videotape recordings for the study of behavior-space relations in homes, doctoral dissertation, Columbia University, New York.
McQuown, N. A., 1957, Linguistic transcription and specification of psychiatric interview materials, *Psychiatry*, **20**, 79–86.
McQuown, N. A., 1971, Natural history method—a frontier method, in A. R. Mahrer and L. Pearson (eds.), *Creative Developments in Psychotherapy*, Cleveland: The Press of Case Western Reserve University.
McQuown, N., Bateson, G., Birdwhistell, R., Brosin, H., and Hockett, C., 1971, The

natural history of an interview, University of Chicago Microfilm Collection of Manuscripts in Cultural Anthropology, Series 15 (Nos. 95–98).

Newtson, D., 1976, The process of behavior observation, *Journal of Human Movement Studies*, **2**, 114–122.

Newtson, D. and Engquist, Gretchen, 1976, The perceptual organization of ongoing behavior, *Journal of Experimental Social Psychology*, **12**, 436–450.

Nielsen, G., 1964, *Studies in Self-Confrontation*, Copenhagen: Munksgaard.

Pike, K. L., 1946, *The Intonation of American English*, Ann Arbor, Michigan: University of Michigan Press.

Pike, K. L., 1967, *Language in Relation to a Unified Theory of the Structure of Human Behavior*, 2nd Edition, The Hague: Mouton.

Pincus, E., 1972, *Guide to Filmmaking*, New York: New American Library, Signet Books.

Pittinger, R. E., Hockett, C. F., and Danehy, J. J., 1960, *The First Five Minutes*, Ithaca, NY: Paul Martineau.

Prost, J. H., 1975, Filming body behavior, in Paul Hockings (ed.), *Principles of Visual Anthropology*, The Hague: Mouton (World Anthropology).

Reusch, J. and Bateson, G., 1951, *Communication: the Social Matrix of Psychiatry*, New York: W. W. Norton.

Ryave, A. L. and Schenkein, J. N., 1974, Notes on the art of walking, in Roy Turner (ed.), *Ethnomethodology: Selected Readings*, Harmondsworth, Middlesex: Penguin Education.

Sacks, H., Schegloff, E. A. and Jefferson, Gail, 1974, A simplest systematics for the organization of turn taking in conversation, *Language*, **50**, 696–735.

Schaeffer, J. H., 1970, Video-tape techniques in anthropology: the collection and analysis of data, unpublished doctoral dissertation, Columbia University.

Schaeffer, J. H., 1975, Videotape: new Techniques of observation and analysis in anthropology, in P. Hockings (ed.), *Principles of Visual Anthropology*, The Hague: Mouton (World Anthropology).

Schaffer, H. R. (ed.), 1977, *Studies in Mother–Infant Interaction*, London and New York: Academic Press.

Scheflen, A. E., 1963, Communication and Regulation in Psychotherapy, *Psychiatry*, **26**, 126–136.

Scheflen, A. E., 1964, The significance of posture in communication systems, *Psychiatry*, **27**, 316–331.

Scheflen, A. E., 1965, Quasi-courtship behavior in psychotherapy, *Psychiatry*, **28**, 245–257.

Scheflen, A. E., 1966, Natural history method in psychotherapy: communicational research, in L. A. Goltschalk and A. H. Auerback (eds.), *Methods of Research in Psychotherapy*, New York: Appleton-Century-Crofts, 263–289.

Scheflen, A. E., 1968, Human communication: behavioral programs and their integration in interaction, *Behavioral Science*, **13**, 44–55.

Scheflen, A. E., 1969, Behavioral programs in human communication, in W. Gray, F. J. Duhl, and N. D. Rizzo (eds.), *General Systems Theory and Psychiatry*, Boston: Little, Brown and Co.

Scheflen, A. E., 1973, *Communicational Structure: Analysis of a Psychotherapy Transaction*, Bloomington, Indiana: Indiana University Press.

Scheflen, A. E., 1974, *How Behavior Means*, Garden City, NY: Doubleday and Co.

Schegloff, E. A. and Sacks, H., 1973, Opening up closings, *Semiotica*, **8**, 289–327.

Schenkein, J. N., 1972, Towards an analysis of natural conversation and the sense of Heheh, *Semiotica*, **6**, 344–377.

Searle, J. R., 1969, *Speech Acts*, London: Cambridge University Press.

Sebeok, T., Hayes, A. S., and Bateson, Mary C. (eds.), 1964, *Approach to Semiotics*, The Hague: Mouton.
Sinclair, J. McH. and Coulthard, R. M., 1975, *Towards an Analysis of Discourse*, London: Oxford University Press.
Sudnow, D., 1972, *Studies in Social Interaction*, New York: Free Press.
Thompson, Jane, 1940, Development of facial expression of emotion in blind and seeing children, *Archives of Psychology*, 37, 1–47.
Trager, G. L., 1958, Paralanguage: a first approximation, *Studies in Linguistics*, 13, 1–12. Reprinted in Dell Hymes (ed.), *Language in Culture and Society*, New York: Harper and Row.
Trager, G. L. and Smith, H. L., 1951, *An Outline of English Structure*, Norman, Oklahoma: Battenburg.
Trevarthen, C., 1975, Early attempts at speech, in R. Lewis (ed.), *Child Alive*, London: Maurice Temple Smith.
Van Vlack, J., 1966, Filming psychotherapy from the viewpoint of a research cinematographer, in L. A. Gottschalk and A. H. Auerbach (eds.), *Methods of Research in Psychotherapy*, New York: Appleton-Century-Crofts.
Wiemann, J. M., and Knapp, M. L., 1975, Turn Taking in Conversation, *Journal of Communication*, 25, 75–92.
Wiener, M., and Devoe, S., 1974, Regulators, Channels and Communication Disruption, Research Proposal, Clark University, Worcester, Massachusetts.
Wiener, M., Devoe, S., Rubinow, S., and Geller, J., 1972, Nonverbal behavior and nonverbal communication, *Psychological Review*, 79, 185–214.
Williams, C., and Feld, S., 1975, Toward a researchable film language, *Studies in Visual Anthropology*, 2, 25–32.
Wittgenstein, L., 1953, *Philosophical Investigations*, Oxford: Blackwells.
Wolff, M., 1973, Notes on the behavior of pedestrians, in A. Birenbaum and E. Sagar (eds.), *People in Places: The Sociology of the Familiar*, New York: Praeger.
Yngve, V. H., 1971, On getting a word in edgewise, in *Papers from the Sixth Regional Meeting of the Chicago Linguistic Society April 17, 1970*, Chicago: University of Chicago, Department of Linguistics, pp. 567–578.

5

OBSERVING INFANT SOCIAL DEVELOPMENT: THEORETICAL PERSPECTIVES, NATURAL OBSERVATION, AND VIDEO RECORDING

M. Scaife

INTRODUCTION

This chapter is concerned with some of the problems encountered in studying the changes that occur in social interaction between an infant and his parents over the first eighteen months or so of life. It is not intended as a comprehensive review of the field. Nor is it intended as a statement of how research *should* be done. Any *diktat* of this sort is out of the question given our profound ignorance of the period of infancy. What I have done is to outline what seem to be the most influential of current research trends, limiting discussion to a small number of investigators in an attempt to link theory, method and analysis. This task has not been made any easier by the fact that sophistication of theory and of method often seem to be inversely correlated.

THEORETICAL PERSPECTIVES

What is involved in the study of infant socialization? Richards (1974) suggests: 'Our task in the analysis of socialisation is to describe and explain the process by which the single cell that is formed at conception develops into a recognisable human being who can live among and communicate with the fellow members of his society: so we are concerned with the development of the basic human attributes—the skills necessary to take part in human life' (p. 7). This formulation is a convenient one for our purposes since it brings out the importance of considering the relationship between the biological organism and the social world into which he is born. Further, taking the zygote as the point of departure recognizes the potential importance of the period of foetal growth in the socialization process. The various problems of pregnancy and birth itself may all affect subsequent social interactions. The relationship between the neonate and the immediate family is already one with a considerable history. Our concern here, however, is with what occurs during the early part of postnatal life and with some of the differing frameworks within which this period is currently being investigated and interpreted.

The area of research which we designate as 'infancy' is now quite appropriately seen as having common ground with various other areas of social and life sciences. This leads to much more varied and complex accounts of development than the chronological cataloguing of emergence of social behaviours which is found, for instance, in Valentine (1942). In attempting to present some of these various approaches, I shall concentrate mainly on the work of people within developmental psychology itself and in so doing impose a fairly arbitrary division between two areas of research. Firstly, I shall discuss those investigators who seem primarily concerned with the reciprocal nature of behaviour seen in early social interaction, although their views of 'reciprocality' are somewhat different. Two of them, Ainsworth and Trevarthen, have expressly biological perspectives while the third, Schaffer, is ostensibly located more within 'traditional' psychology. Their approaches have many points of difference but they all seem to share a prospective view of the socialization process in the sense that they are concerned with tracing forward the development of the very young infant. The second group, who represent the most recent shifts in research concern, are characterized as retrospective in that they seek to trace the origins of later social accomplishments by looking back in time from the 'mature' state. Their concern is with such things as the 'skills' acquired in infancy which facilitate language acquisition or integration into particular social roles.

Prospective accounts and reciprocal responsiveness

A central thesis of modern biology is the concept of adaptation. The application of this to the study of early infant social development has been marked in recent years. The basic argument which is employed here is a simple, if widely misunderstood one. The organism—infant—is an historical product. His behaviour is the net result of an indefinite period of natural selection whose effects are transmitted via the genetic material. Natural selection has operated 'in favour of' certain behaviour patterns as opposed to others. These behaviours serve the function of adapting the organism to his environment. Since man is (has been) a social creature there is, therefore, adaptation to a social environment. The neonate is already structured to interact with a social world. However, the human infant at least is relatively helpless in physical terms. He must be sustained by another, more capable person. Such an important process cannot be 'left to chance' and, thus, the notion of individuals adapted for infant care is introduced. Such individuals are sensitive to the particular needs of infants, responsive to the infantile behavioural repertoire.

This is basically the position adopted by Ainsworth and her fellow workers. Thus, Ainsworth *et al.* (1974): 'Evolutionary theory suggests that a species characteristic behaviour is adapted to some significant aspect of the environment in which the species evolved, and that social behaviours are adapted to reciprocal behaviours of conspecifics—or of particular classes of conspecifics' (p. 101). Such a model of social interaction has at its base a view of an idealized environment—that corresponding to the result of the authors' speculations on the history of the species. This may lead to some embarrassment in terms of the physical environment—few of us (least of all those in Ainsworth's study) live in the Savannah, for example. However, the 'necessary' social parameters are more easily specified. The adults must be responsive to infant demands and any 'caretaker' that is not is failing to provide the necessary '. . . social environment that approximates to the environment of evolutionary adaptedness' (p. 102). Consequently, '. . . unresponsive mothers may be viewed as the product of developmental anomalies . . .'. The importance of responding is two-fold. Firstly there is the necessity for the infant to be secure and to feel secure. He should be protected from 'dangers' (unspecified) and he must have 'trust' in his mother's continued accessibility and her consistent responses to him. This leads to the second point: this predictability is the *sine qua non* in his decoding the problems of acquiring and understanding a communicative system in its more mature form. As the authors claim, predictability of another '. . . is the first step towards understanding the motivations and set-goals of that figure—a clear step away from 'egocentricity' and towards empathy and understanding and respecting of another's point of view', (p. 127). This view is an extension of, and is usually placed in the context of, what has come to be called 'attachment theory'. The particular theoretical construct of attachment need not concern us here. It has come under some attack (see Bernal, 1974; Clarke and Clarke, 1976) and the phylogenetic-adaptation aspects are separable from it. What is important is the idea of the 'pre-programmed' infant. In the context from which this idea was borrowed, especially early ethological work, the newborn of the species is often endowed with a specific 'pre-disposition to learn' (Lorenz, 1966). In the case of animals this was a predisposition to learn (imprint on) a parent. Ainsworth has, however, extended the idea to human socialization by assuming a similar predisposition on the part of the human infant which facilitates the acquisition of social behaviours themselves—not just the figure to whom they 'should' be addressed. Thus the claim: '. . . it seems likely to us that he will gradually acquire an acceptable repertoire of more 'mature' social behaviours without heroic efforts on the part of his parents specifically to train him to adopt the rules, proscriptions and values that they wish him to absorb . . .' (p. 99).

This formulation leads to a quite clear prescription for research into infant–adult social interactions. Since both infant and parent are preprogrammed for interaction the search is not for the mechanisms by which 'understanding' is achieved, but for what *conditions* best facilitate the transition from the 'loving protective family' into the harsh realities of the wider social world. What maternal practices encourage, or otherwise, the infant with '... a desirable balance between independent competence and harmonious interaction with others?' (p. 126). Thus we are presented with intercorrelations between maternal 'variables', such as rating on scales of sensitivity, acceptance of the infant and co-operation, and such infant variables as compliance to commands.

Such investigations must rely on studying many infants and this is, inevitably, at the expense of finding out anything about the processes of negotiation and individual understanding in particular cases. This is not to say that there is no concern with individual differences but that these are referenced with respect to things like 'deviations from the norm of obedience' (p. 115). In adopting an evolutionary–biological conception of early socialization, Ainsworth *et al.* have also adopted its methodology. Their concern with 'natural' environments has led them to work largely in the home and their data on human socialization do not differ from animal ethology in that they are based largely on observer reports.

A rather different approach to early social interaction based on biological considerations is that of Trevarthen (1975). He makes the following autobiographical comment which I quote by way of illustration: 'Some years ago I began to study infants with the intention of looking for signs of what innate structures of intelligence lay dormant or weakly expressed in them—a biological gift to the beginning human being ... I soon obtained data that made me suspect that much of the innate pattern of human intention and a predisposition to perceive and use the world, including people, had been glossed over in scientific studies of infants' (p. 62). Trevarthen's concern is with the very young infant seen as being highly structured in terms of his behaviour *vis-à-vis* the social world. He emphasizes the basically rhythmic nature of early infant behaviour, using the notions of endogenous pacemakers which are part of the explanatory apparatus of those biologists concerned with periodicity in the neuroendocrine systems. These pacemakers—whatever their particular nature—structure the infant's behaviour in a way that gives it some of the same morphological properties (patterning in space and time) as adult behaviour. This gives adults a basis for interpreting the infant's activity in such terms as '... looking, listening and reaching to touch'. In addition, since the rhythmical properties of the adult's behaviour, the 'input' to the infant, are comparable to the infant's output devices, there is the basis for a potential 'match' from which, somehow, '... the infant builds a bridge to persons'. Objects do not possess such rhythmical properties. Thus the biological structure of the infant and indeed of the adult provides a basis for an initial person/object discrimination.

The innate rhythmic patterns also provide the basis for structuring the interaction itself. In discussing the mother's role Trevarthen says: 'Of course infant communication needs a partner. It depends on a number of special adaptations in the mother's behaviour. Some of these, we find, are almost automatically fulfilled by the normal rhythm and organisation of her voluntary action, others require unconscious alterations in the way the mother would normally communicate' (p. 69). The analysis of interaction, then, is primarily in terms of its microstructure—the systematic study of the details of behaviour in a search for rhythmic relations and ordering, for the close patterning of interpersonal exchanges. Trevarthen's view of the socialization process is one which places such exchanges as a central route to the acquisition of broader social competences, together with 'private experiment' on the infant's part. However despite his insistence on the innateness of what he terms 'human social intelligence', he leaves largely unanswered questions about the nature of the continuity between such phenomena and later social behaviour.

Thus far we have been considering the social development of the infant as studied by observing social interaction. However, the emphasis on the structured infant has also led to experimental approaches largely carried out within the bounds of 'traditional' psychology. Potentially, of course, almost all of the work on infant development in any 'sphere'—cognitive, motor, etc., is relevant material for a proper specification of all the factors impinging on social interaction. Thus Schaffer (1971) correctly points out that '... it is essential to bear in mind that social behaviour does not constitute a class apart from all other forms of behaviour ... cognition and social behaviour are not separate categories ...' (p. 31). Unlike Trevarthan, Schaffer believes the infant to be born asocial and to have to learn a great deal in adjusting to the parent. In setting out the aims of his book, *The Growth of Sociability;* he identified three basic problems: (a) the basis for the infant's initial attraction to human as opposed to inanimate objects; (b) how the infant learns to distinguish familiar from unfamiliar people and (c) what enables the formation of a lasting, emotionally meaningful bond with certain specific individuals. These questions are answered partly by reference to direct experiments on perceptual processes such as the infant's capacity to selectively attend to stimuli organized in a 'facial' arrangement as opposed to equally complex but supposedly non-socially meaningful ones (Fantz, 1961). There are also data on the ability to perform discrimination learning tasks and some reference to Piaget's work on person and object permanence. Schaffer's approach here, then, is basically to assess the infant's capacity for some sort of representation of others but seen within the context of the infant coming to form specific interpersonal bonds. At a general level he shares Ainsworth's preoccupation with the *harmonious* nature of interaction and how this is achieved. This emphasis on the quality of interaction underlies his later work (1975) which deals more with the microanalysis of social interaction itself. The infant, he argues, must come to structure his behaviour so that it fits in with the patterns of behaviour that exist in his social world. Thus: '... an infant does not exist in a vacuum, and the integration of his responses with those of his caretakers becomes one of the major developmental tasks of early childhood'. The aim is to describe '... the fine temporal synchrony that characterises any smooth social interaction ... the most basic feature of any relationship, namely an alteration in the activity of two partners ...' (p. 36). Schaffer believes that the apparent reciprocity of the interactions seen during the first year is largely achieved by the mother fitting in around the infant. His methodology is worth looking at in some detail. It illustrates the way in which a model that emphasizes overt behavioural synchrony can understate infant competence.

Consider the apparently simple problem of how two partners in an interaction come to look at the same thing (looking at something besides each other). The ability to do this, to synchronize visual attention, is potentially important in terms of widening the range of interaction. However this need not concern us at this point. The question is, rather, in what terms are we to account for the development of this phenomenon in adult–infant interaction during the first year of life? Collis and Schaffer (1975) videotaped mothers and infants in a laboratory situation, having in other investigations been struck by the 'extent to which mothers note the focus of their baby's eyes and respond to it by also looking at the same object'. The room was bare save for four toys fixed to a wall. The baby sat on the mother's knee facing the toys and fixations of the objects by each participant were recorded over a six-minute period. The data were analysed to see whether when the infant looked at the same toy his mother would then do so as well (and vice versa) with a frequency greater than expected by chance. The analysis was thus a probability model of contingent behavioural events. The results presented showed that the vast majority of mothers 'showed a significant tendency to follow her infant's gaze to particular toys' but only exceptionally was the reverse true. This was so even of the nearly year-old infants. What are we to make of this finding?

Let us put the question in terms of the authors' rationale for the study. They had hoped, in looking at synchronization of visual attention, to 'substantiate and quantify this phenomenon and to consider its implications for early interactive development'. They certainly substantiated and quantified the mother's apparent following the infant's gaze. But what are the developmental implications? Schaffer (1975) concludes that: 'The baby's visual responses have signal value to the mother, but for his part the infant (*in this situation at least*) remains a largely egocentric creature. The couple's synchrony does not yet reflect true reciprocity' (p. 38, my stress). The quote reveals the easy way in which, despite his own cautions, he slips from a very restricted analysis into a broad characterization of infant social competence. There are various levels on which this may be criticized. Firstly the very nature of the situation ensures that the infant will not pay much attention to the mother and that she looks at him rather than the toys. After all he would have to turn around to see her and the toys could not be of much interest to her except in so far as they interest him. Further, for the infants to be credited with '... any awareness that they may possibly have had of the directive significance of the mother's gaze', they would have had to respond repeatedly and consistently to this signal. Otherwise they could not achieve a behavioural score that exceeded some statistical significance level. So what Schaffer has done is to take the infant's performance in a particular, restricted situation and to infer from the 'absence' of certain behaviours an unwarranted amount about his underlying competence. For it is the latter that 'egocentrism' is concerned with, a psychological construct not a performance measure. To put it crudely, what the infant 'knows' and what he 'does' are different issues to be investigated in different ways. The specification of performance should involve some sort of natural observation (spontaneous behaviour). Getting at competence can be done by inference from such protocols but they are inevitably more or less constrained by sampling considerations. Rather we would wish to use experimental (controlled) investigation to look at what the infant *can* do, even if he only does it once or twice. Conducting quasi-natural observation in a laboratory focusing on what he does not do is not a very fruitful way to proceed.

The alternative may be illustrated by reference to a study conducted by John Churcher and myself on the same problem of 'synchronizing' looking by adult and infant. As a first phase we independently spent a year following the development of several infants by frequent visits to their homes simply watching what was happening, doing informal tests and talking to the parents. This gave us a profile of what we believed the infants were actually doing at various ages. We also formulated an analysis of the abilities we believed to be essential in following another's gaze. Briefly this analysis proposed that the infant should (a) know something about the communicative significance of the particular gesture (the 'look'), and (b) should be able, in order to correctly locate the object of interest, to construct and extrapolate a straight line in space outwards, from the other, to its intersection with an object boundary. This implies both social and spatial knowledge. We had some data on (a) from the home study. We tested (b) in the laboratory in a situation where an adult attempted to direct the infant's attention to various parts of the room 'simply' by looking there himself. We recorded infant eye movements and were thus able to determine when and where he looked. On the majority of occasions the infant would not respond appropriately but when he did look somewhere we could determine its apparent direction—whether or not he correctly located the 'focus of interest'. In fact the room was deliberately kept bare of salient features; the adult looked towards a blank wall. Thus, to arrive at an accurate location, the infant would have to do so precisely by mentally constructing the proposed straight line of sight; he had no assistance from the rest of the environment. This sort of performance measure is, I think, much more obviously a reflection of competence, and success was demonstrated by infants far earlier than one might suppose from Collis and Schaffer's account. The conjunction of in-home observation and then laboratory testing presents a rather more accurate version of infant development. Microanalysis of behaviour, unless it is based on a theoretical developmental analysis, is, in itself, sterile. We can agree with Richards (1974) that 'social communication itself is much more than a simple mutual responsiveness to signals . . .' (p. 91).

Retrospective search for the origins of communicative competence

Amongst the influences causing the marked change in current views of infant social development, one, that of psycholinguistics, has been of particular importance. Research into the acquisition of language has become a growth industry in the last few years. Within this area there has been a shift of emphasis away from structural accounts of early word production, for example, McNeill (1970), and towards consideration of the abilities that are involved in using language as a communication device. The nature of the change may be illustrated by reference to Hymes (1971). In criticizing narrow accounts of the centrally important notions of competence and performance he said: 'We have to account for the fact that a normal child acquires knowledge of sentences, not only as grammatical but also as appropriate. A child acquires a repertoire of speech acts, is able to take part in speech acts and to evaluate the speech acts of others. This is a competence which is integral with the attitudes and values concerning language and integral with competence for the interrelation of language with other codes of communication . . . There are rules of use without which the rules of grammar would be useless' (p. 10). Hymes proposes a wider, sociocultural view which necessarily involves a close consideration of the social context of communication. He says, 'Communicative means generally are viewed in terms of the patterning of communicative acts and purposes . . . One must see the child as acquiring and achieving narrowly linguistic and broadly sociolinguistic (and communicative) competence together' (pp. 23, 24).

Given a move away from the study of purely linguistic phenomena towards communicative competence there is an inevitable interest in the nature of the preverbal communication system of the infant. The potential importance of the latter in affecting and facilitating the acquisition of language becomes a focus of interest. The study of social interaction becomes the search for precedents of language use, a move away from monologic description and towards a view which involves negotiation between partners as its essence. Bruner (1975b) neatly summed up the dissatisfaction with the structural descriptions of early utterances: '. . . the early language for which a grammar is written is the end result of psychological processes leading to its acquisition, and to write a grammar of that language at any point in its development is in no sense to explicate the nature of its acquisition', (p. 256). But how are we to set about investigating the nature of its acquisition? One way this may be done is by analysing the structure of the communicative process and then attempting to understand how the infant uses his knowledge of this as a basis to acquire language itself.

Once one goes beyond the 'signal-consistent response' conceptualization of communication the analysis of social interaction becomes much more complex. There are, however, several different ways in which one might proceed. MacKay (1972), working within a control-systems context, proposes as a minimal definition that communication should be action which is goal-directed with respect to the recipient (receiver). That is to say that the actor should intend some consequence and adjusts his action until the specified goal is attained. Hinde (1972, pp. 86–9) points out several problems with the application of such a model, in particular that empirical correlates of the model are often hard to validate in practice. There are, for instance, problems to do with specifying the nature of the goal itself. This makes for difficulties in using the model for analysis of quite a wide range of behaviour, such as social rituals. However, MacKay does make a very important point when he suggests that the receiver's perception of the actor's behaviour as goal-directed is crucially important in the communication process. In proposing this MacKay is clearly attempting to evolve a model which will go some way to coping with human social behaviour in a more powerful fashion than cause–effect descriptions.

The importance of recipient's interpretation is also emphasized by certain philosophers of language who have been concerned with a 'speech act' theory of meaning. Central to their analysis is the notion of recognition ('uptake') of the actor's intention by the other. This approach has received wide attention (see Bruner, 1975a; Ryan, 1974; Dore, 1975), and I do not intend to pursue many of the details here. What is important is that, as Ryan argues, the speech-act model may provide 'guidelines' for the study of non-linguistic and hence infant social interaction. Specifically she puts forward an analysis by Grice (1957, 1968) as being applicable to '... agent's meaning something by performance of particular actions'. It suggests ways of '... describing what infants have to learn to do' (p. 208). The work of Grice and of Austin (1962) distinguishes between the conventional meaning of a behaviour (in their cases verbal utterances) and the actor's intentions in so behaving. In the case of infants we *might* expect them to have some notion about the possibility of differentially expressing various intentions but not necessarily to have yet acquired conventional means of expression. In such a situation there would be a heavy reliance on the adult as interpreter, and the developmental question for research becomes one of '... identifying and describing the kinds of intention involved, and how the necessary mutual recognition develops' (Ryan, 1974, p. 210). Clearly such a task is going to be both difficult and controversial. Richards (1974) remarks on the particular problems of applying notions like intention and intersubjective understanding, borrowed from their framework of language-use, to the prelinguistic infant. It is not clear that the application of linguistic concepts can be anything more than metaphorical in this situation. This is further exacerbated by the imprecision we find in dealing with the basic concepts even for adults. Thus Rafky (1973) says of intersubjectivity that '... no satisfactory explanation of this phenomenon has yet been offered' (p. 51).

Difficulties of this sort have led to a somewhat guarded response by researchers to the use of analyses which focus on infant intentions *per se*. Thus Bruner (1975b) says 'If only for methodological reasons, I would propose that we avoid *a priori* arguments about 'conscious intent' and 'when' it is born. For questions whose answers are not in principle recognisable are rarely useful, and it is likely that 'consciousness' and 'intention' are opaque in this way' (p. 266). Rather, he believes, it is better to adopt a more functionally based approach to early interaction. This is characterized as doing away with the specification of what the infant 'really' intended and instead focuses on what actually happens: the results of particular behaviours and what functions they seem to serve. Bruner suggests for consideration a list of language functions proposed by Jakobson (1960) which are traced through recurrent, familiar mother–infant interactive situations called 'formats' (Garvey, 1974). The use of adult-based language functions in the analysis of infant behaviour, however, seems to create its own problems. The specification of these functions involves a notion of actor's intent yet Bruner believes that questions about such things are not to be asked of the infant. Further it is not clear how one can attribute any sort of strong continuity, beyond mere chronological succession, to situations where it is the behaviour itself and not the actor's intentions in so behaving that are to be described. Bruner's general theoretical position is complicated. Whilst we shall examine one aspect in some detail later on (the relationship between joint action and language acquisition), no general summary is attempted here. Rather let me preface the remainder of this chapter, the discussion of research methodology, by quoting one of Bruner's 'working assumptions' in investigating prelinguistic communication which sums up the nature of the research enterprise: '... Communication by "other means" precedes linguistic communication and ... in this earlier form it fulfills some of the same functions that will be fulfilled by language proper later' (1976). This is a radical departure from the view of infancy which prevailed a few years ago (in some quarters it still does) and providing evidence is, as we shall see, not easy.

OBSERVING SOCIAL INTERACTION

In this section I shall briefly examine the notion that the basis for research on parent–infant social behaviour should be the observation of 'natural' behaviour. Linked to this is the question of whether it is practically possible to record interaction, unbiased by the process of observation itself.

The commitment to 'natural' behaviour

The term 'natural' seems to have two usages in the area of developmental psychology, although they are often confused. The first meaning is that there is some pattern of social behaviour which will occur automatically, provided that environmental conditions are appropriate, and which is normally assumed to be largely inherited. This we might term 'biologically natural' behaviour. We have already examined such a position in the case of Ainsworth *et al.* (1974), noting their agreement with the theory and methods of animal ethology. They follow Tinbergen (1963) in advocating that the understanding of behaviour is to be achieved only as a carefully phased study, the first, essential part of which is to observe in the natural environment, recording the subject's natural history. Without these data there is the risk of failing to understand the significance of particular behaviours which may be meaningless out of their evolutionary context. In the case of human infants, the home is the closest approximation to this.

The insistence on biologically natural behaviour being that seen only in a natural setting is not always held to. Where there is no reason to believe that interaction will be disrupted by being observed in a strange setting or, alternatively, that a familiar context is somehow necessary, then recording in the laboratory is at least technically attractive. Trevarthen's (1975) work on interpersonal synchrony in early infancy is an example of this. Given the innate ('... natural and unconscious...') basis for behaviour, both parental and infant, the problem is less one of eliciting natural interaction than of recording its details. Thus, once the pair seem to be getting on smoothly, one should be observing natural behaviour. The record then assumes importance as an object of study in its own right, revealing the sophistication of the structure of interaction, rather than serving as data for testing specific hypotheses.

The second sense of 'natural' behaviour is much more of a methodological than biological description. It covers behaviour observed in a variety of studies whose only common denominator is that the researcher purports to give no instruction to the parent unless it is to 'behave as naturally as possible' or some such statement. There is thus no identification of natural behaviour as being that seen in extra-laboratory observation. The distinction essentially is one of procedure rather than of situation. Home observation can be seen as much as an attempt to minimize external (observer) interference as to gather data in an 'ecologically valid' setting. Natural behaviour here is simply what normally goes on. By and large this seems to be the rationale for Bruner's (1975b) in-home study. His emphasis on recurrent interaction routines which often involve familiar environmental props makes the home the best place to record. The availability of the props both promotes the occurrence of the routines and also makes it easier for observers to understand the relevance of the behaviours themselves. Additionally, of course, the parents are more likely to be relaxed in their own homes and so on. It seems likely that the precise nature of the routines—what objects they involve, etc.—is not crucial. The general nature of the interaction, however—parental encouragement, variation or repetition of themes, etc.—is highly important. In this respect the observed behaviour should match that which occurs when the observer is not present.

What this brief discussion has tried to demonstrate is that, for a variety of reasons, there is a widespread commitment to the idea of a normal pattern of behaviour which our research should aim to record. Such a claim has important theoretical and practical consequences which we can only touch on here.

The effects of being observed

The reader will doubtless be pleased that I do not intend to give an extensive catalogue of all possible experimenter/observer effects on behaviour, such as is to be found in Rosenthal (1976). My remarks will be restricted to the potential effects on social interaction of knowing that a (professional) psychologist is observing *and recording* what goes on. I have stressed the recording aspect because I also wish to examine certain common assumptions about the use of permanent audio-visual devices like video. Briefly these assumptions are either: (a) that the presence of an observer with a video camera is no more disturbing than one without *or* (b) that if this is a more disturbing situation, then the effects on behaviour are nonetheless of the same kind as those produced by an observer who records in other ways. In examining these questions I am not suggesting that the discreet silence usually maintained in the literature about such issues reflects a lack of awareness but rather a possibly unwarranted lack of concern.

One major problem arises because of the insularity which often characterizes the description and analysis of infant social interaction. There is little concern with social contexts wider than the immediate domestic environment, and classifying the parents as social class B or whatever often seems to be no more that lip-service. (Even when social class effects seem to be the primary object of study, what is presented is usually nothing beyond a correlation with apparent behavioural differences. There is no investigation into the processes that actually produce the differences.) In an important paper Ingleby (1974) says: '. . . the aim of studying the child as if he and his family were living on a desert island is a futile one: they aren't—and even if they were they would probably still behave as though they weren't (p. 299). The point is that the behaviour which the parent addresses to the child is not only a response to the immediate situation (the infant's needs, the parent's mood, etc.) but also the product of a whole nexus of attitudes, beliefs and pressures whose origins extend far beyond the dyad. Child-rearing is an institution—something with its own pattern of practices, both prescriptive and proscriptive—and parents will have a more or less clearly articulated conception of what is held to be optimal practice. The sources of this knowledge are likely to be various and there are probably frequent conflicts of opinion which arise between personal inclination, family advice and professional wisdom. The resolution of such conflicts are impossible to predict but what is important for research purposes is that parents may well adjust their behaviour towards the infant in the presence of a child psychologist. That is to say they may attempt to behave in the ways advocated by popular handbooks, television documentaries and all the other public pronouncements on 'better-baby' practice. That adjustments in public behaviour do occur in response to a 'professional presence' is surely not in question. Newson and Newson (1963) found a marked discrepancy in the answers to questions asked by health-visitors (local-government officials) than when asked by research psychologists. Newson and Newson assumed that the answers that they (as friendly psychologists) obtained were more accurate, although there is no evidence that they were not simply getting a different set of answers fitted to a different audience. The research psychologist is as much a part of the professional community as the health-visitor.

Arriving at an understanding of the adjustments made by particular individuals would require detailed investigation of their knowledge and sources of advice—an immense task in its own right. However, at a different level of analysis, we can ask what sort of effects are ascribable to the process of observation and recording *per se*. Central to this problem is the obvious fact that the researcher is, in scrutinizing what goes on, doing something which does not occur in normal life, and he does so for purposes which are often not clear to the parents. (In some cases the reasons given to the parents are probably not even credible.) The unsettling effect of being closely observed can be further amplified by the use of a video recorder. This is true because the record is a permanent one and because it is necessarily unselective—capturing everything before the camera. This is a markedly different proposition to someone recording in note form, especially if the potential for public viewing of the tape is a source of anxiety. One common parental reaction to the use of video, initially at least, is to encourage filming of the infant but to eschew such recording of themselves. These same parents, however, often seem to mind far less if the observer is writing things down as they interact with the infant, suggesting that the sort of record kept is itself potentially important to them. After all one cannot write everything down and one cannot view a verbal record. With increasing familiarity (in a longitudinal study, at least) the parents may apparently come to accept the use of video recording although this acceptance may be less wholehearted than one would hope for.

The commonest problem lies in the possibly inhibitory effects of recording but this is by no means the only sort of response. Sometimes the parents seem only too keen to help the research along. In some cases, particularly if the observer has expressed special interest in the infant (rather than in parent–infant interaction itself), the tempo of parental behaviour may be markedly increased. This can be due to the parent attempting to ensure that the baby's attention does not wander, that he continues to demonstrate newly acquired skills, etc. It is all done with the best of intentions but is not likely to be how the pair normally get on. One example of the way in which parental assistance may be misconstrued is afforded by Brown and Bellugi's (1964) report of 'expansions' in parental speech to children just acquiring language. They observed that the parents in their study very frequently responded to the child's short utterances by incorporating what they took the vocalization to mean into a longer utterance of their own—in other words they expanded it. Brown and Bellugi suggested that this phenomenon was of importance in providing a way in which the parent could model appropriate usage for the child. Subsequent studies, especially one by Wells (1974) where the speech was monitored by radio microphone at intervals unpredictable to the parent, failed to confirm the high frequency of such expansions. One possible explanation for this is that the parents in the Brown and Bellugi study were somehow supposing that this was appropriate behaviour and adjusting in the sense discussed previously. A rather more amusing alternative is given by Newport (1976) who suggests that what was happening was that the parents were providing an interpretative commentary as much for the researcher's benefit as for the child's.

The specific and cumulative effects of these problems are, by their very nature, difficult to assess. How can we ever know what effects observation has since it is our very presence that is at issue? The use of recording devices operated unpredictably and without the researcher present is only a partial solution since, by and large, the parents must be aware of the potential for observation. Nor is it possible to, as it were, settle for half the cake and only use the data on the infant while maintaining some reservation as to parental behaviour. Interaction is a supra-individual process and effects on the parent will in turn lead to effects on the infant. There does not seem to be an easy answer.

DESCRIPTION AND ANALYSIS

In the final section of this chapter I wish to turn to some of the problems involved in producing an account of the development of social interaction. Much of the discussion is concerned with observational data recorded on videotape, although the comments are more widely applicable. The topics include the advantages and disadvantages of being able to return repeatedly to a detailed audio-visual record, the ways in which a description might be formulated and the problem of assessing continuity across the record. In examining these issues I shall provide a concrete illustration of analysis largely based on work done at Oxford.

Repeated access to the record

Anyone who has attempted to provide an *in situ* description of social behaviour, writing down details of ongoing interaction as it occurs, is immediately aware of its enormously complex structure. This is just as true of infant social behaviour as it is of adult interaction. There are, for instance, many channels open for communication. The infant's posture, his vocalizations and where he looks are all potential sources of information for the adult. Indeed in the period before language it is usually the totality of the infant's behaviour which the adult uses to interpret the significance of what goes on rather than single cues. Clearly if we are at all interested in providing an account which relates adult interpretation to infant behaviour we need the capacity to produce a detailed description which can potentially encompass all that the infant does. Such a description is not easily obtained without the help of audio-visual records like videotape. There is usually too much happening at the same time for a 'pencil-and-paper' observer to obtain a sufficiently wide coverage. In the latter case it is just not practicable to record details of where the infant looks, what he is saying, what he is holding, etc. from second to second. This may not matter if the investigation is restricted to some narrow topic, such as frequency of smiling. However if there is any concern with reconstructing the detailed course of interaction, then simple recording systems—checklists, audio-tape commentaries—are plainly limited. Coping with the behaviour of one of the participants is difficult enough; recording details of both is often impossible.

By contrast the video observer is free to examine the details of behaviour without having to sacrifice breadth of coverage. He has the option of repeatedly examining the same stretch of tape and is freed from the pressing need to derive coding categories *before* interaction is observed. In not focusing attention on preordained 'items' more notice may be taken of events which are not immediately striking or apparently relevant but later turn out to be important. This advantage is most strikingly seen in the process of tracing the origin of particular behaviours backwards in time. For example, one child developed a gesture of looking at the parent and banging on the floor with his hand apparently in order to get the parent to participate in an object-exchange game. Looking back at previously recorded sessions this behaviour first appeared when the parent had forcibly removed something from the child, only later being 'converted' into a playful signal. Without reviewing the tapes it is likely that the origins of the behaviour would have been missed.

Another advantage of video is the potential for looking at the organization of behaviour over different time-scales. Thus Trevarthen's (1975) work on the synchronous nature of mother–infant interaction, referred to previously, produced evidence of rhythmical patterns with very short cycle times. Such patterns are not easily discernible without going into the fine temporal sequences available for study on a film record. Interestingly, the use of the 'fast-play' facility on a video recorder also allows one to discern patterns which are not immediately apparent at normal viewing speeds. This has received almost no attention and there is little I can say about it directly here. However there seems no reason why we should not use fast-speed viewing as a guide to looking for regularities which might otherwise be discovered only by a complex statistical analysis. It seems eminently plausible that the hierarchical organization which characterizes behaviour should have 'units' organized over quite long periods just as much as it does over very short periods.

Even from the little that has been said so far it is clear that the video-observer has the opportunity to produce a wide variety of descriptions, to try as many analytical schemes as he is capable of deriving. He can always start again. But is this necessarily an unqualified advantage? In a very real sense, viewing the same piece of film is a different enterprise on every occasion that it is seen. The interaction looks different both from the 'real' situation as it occurred and from each subsequent scrutiny of the record. New things 'emerge' from the scene—we see nuances that were missed before or rectify previous errors of judgment. This would seem to be a definite 'plus' but in fact the shifting descriptions of the interaction do not necessarily have some fixed and recognizable end-point. There is often no obvious limit, beyond that imposed by sheer physical exhaustion, to the endless redescription of the behaviour. Yet the descriptions cannot be infinitely long; at some point the process must be terminated. This decision will obviously depend on the ultimate purpose of the study but should always be based on explicit criteria of what is required.

Object-exchange: an example of the analysis of developmental change

There are two points which, while they are extremely obvious, have to be made at the outset. The first is that any analysis should be guided by a prior theoretical account. Merely viewing the tapes with the hope that 'something' will emerge is a profitless enterprise. The second and related point is that the process of behavioural description is necessarily an interpretative one if we are to retain any sense of the social significance of what we observe. It is necessary to accept these points in order to follow the procedure outlined below.

The initial step in coding the behaviour is to look for recurrent situations with an apparently similar structure. These may then be interpreted in terms of their apparent functional significance as Bruner (1975b) does in identifying his 'format-types'. Examples of formats include 'joint attention': attempts to indicate something; 'social interaction': greeting rituals, etc., and 'object interaction': joint activity on an object with some common aim. This sort of division provides a rough taxonomy within which to locate more detailed analysis. It is not amenable for use as a powerful segmentation procedure since decision rules for reliable identification of interaction as being properly 'object' or 'social' are not conveniently formulated. This does not strictly matter since the reason for following through format types at this level of generality is primarily one of convenience, the framework for the isolation of 'lower-level' categories of interaction. A good example of the latter is that of object-exchange, an interaction which fulfils the requirements of recurring throughout the first year and having, at least eventually, an apparently rule-bound form. It can thus be used to explore the general claim that, 'The action seen in play between a mother and her child serves a pragmatic function and such rule-bound sequences as we find ... provide a solid basis for language to enter the routine and, eventually, for language to become the 'carrier' of the action' (Bruner, 1977, p. 287). However the specific importance of the exchange interaction is that it enables the infant to learn '... what might be properly characterised as the pre-linguistic prototype of case grammar: who is the Agent, what is the Action, the Object, the Recipient of Action ...He is learning not only how to carry out joint action but how to represent its relevant segments and how to signal appropriately about them' (1977, p. 282). Given that it is relatively easy to group together all of the instances on the record where (minimally) a successful object exchange, from one person to another, has occurred how might these be analysed?

The first problem is that of the language in which the description of behaviour is to be formulated. Assumptions have to be made about the social knowledge of the reader in order to use functionally based categories which, it is assumed, the reader can identify from his own experience and which are relevant to the reasons for studying the interaction. The descriptions of behaviour incorporate terms like 'offer', 'show', 'accept', 'hand to' even though they may individually cover a wide range of morphological variation. In Bruner's view they serve the distinctions derived from his case grammar/joint action model. The act of exchange may be regarded as incorporating features which include possession, agency, action and object. This allows Bruner to, for instance, directly equate 'agency' with initial possession and subsequent loss of an object, deriving a second-order description from the basic functional terms. Similarly 'recipient' is defined as the new possessor and 'initiator' as the person who attempts to give, take or show the object (1977, p. 293).

The analysis of each exchange can be produced in several ways. Here I shall merely outline one which concentrates on three features of the interaction:

(1) The nature of the exchange. Does the infant, for instance, (a) only take the object, (b) take and return, (c) take one object and return another, (d) is he the initiator of the sequence?

(2) The temporal structure of the exchange. This concentrates on the synchronization of the actions of the two participants. Does the infant show any evidence of waiting for appropriate movements to take or offer or does he, for instance, attempt to grab the object?

(3) The form of vocalizations and their position within the action sequence. This includes both parental speech and infant utterances with especial emphasis on the junctures at which the vocalizations occur, for example, during object transfer, on its receipt, as attempts to prolong exchange, etc.

The pattern of developmental change which emerges has been documented in some detail in Bruner's publications (1975, a and b, 1977) and we need give no more than a brief summary here. The interaction is seen in its earliest forms in the first three months with the infant as a largely passive recipient, the object being pushed into his hand. The timing of exchange is thus controlled exclusively by the parent although usually it will not occur until the infant shows some interest (looking, smiling). However even at this early stage the parent can be said to be dividing the exchange into component sequences, getting the child's attention by waving the object, accompanying the act of transfer with pronounced vocalizations (such as, 'there!'), etc. This 'highlighting' of the phases of the action becomes increasingly elaborate as the child develops the capacity to reach accurately, and therefore actively take objects. The parent may now enforce recognition of the phases by making the infant pause before transfer of the object to him, or waiting for some demand gesture of his part. Gradually the child's behaviour comes to parallel that of the adult in its apparent division into ordered, synchronized actions of demanding/taking/offering/returning, each increasingly stylized in form. The integration of pointing, shifts in gaze direction and word-like forms into the exchange accompany a shift in emphasis in the nature of the enterprise. The important thing becomes, by the end of the first year, the exchange itself and not possession or transfer of a particular object. This is inferred from the fact that the infant will readily give back, or accept, a different object from that previously in circulation.

These sorts of observations represent the data for exploring the child's mastery of the structure of the interaction. If he can successfully maintain a sequence of object exchange he must, it is argued, have a knowledge of the role structure involved and its reversible nature, an appreciation that agents can be recipients and of the non-permanence of possession. This conceptual acquisition is, for Bruner, very important in forming the prelinguistic base for appropriate language use. The child's language is analysed in terms of case-grammatical categories which, as already mentioned, also form the basis for the interpretation of his knowledge of action. This is the means of linking cognitive and linguistic development, distinctions in the former 'domain' being reflected in the latter. We must now ask what problems such an account faces in explaining the process of change itself.

Developmental continuity

The necessarily intermittent and limited sampling which constitutes the record makes development seem more of a series of abrupt changes than is really the case. Our account must preserve the essential continuity of the developmental process whilst at the same time coming to terms with the 'fact' of change. Further, the account must be more than a mere chronological succession since this, of itself, tells us little.

In the preceding section we examined an account of the development of social interactions which sought to establish continuity by tracking functionally similar situations through the first year. One of the major difficulties with this procedure stems from the strong interpretative element involved. This may be illustrated by reference to the development of particular gestures which are seen during the latter part of the first year. Initially the child's reach for objects during exchange consists of a simple arm extension and manual grasp, bringing the object towards the body. At a somewhat later age he may point towards the object before reaching, or may point without reaching at all. These behaviours occur within the same situation, that is to say within a sequence of object-exchanges, but can they be said to be within the same functional system of action? This is, as Langer (1969, p. 3) remarks, '... a logical interpretive issue'. It is a matter of opinion whether the behaviours are part of the same system whose forms change over time or behaviours from two different systems (such as, 'manipulation' and 'reference'). The notions of 'change' and 'system' are theoretical ones. In dealing with change we are faced with two issues. One is to assess the validity of our own interpretation as outside observers and the other is to posit the nature of continuity.

The interaction which is observed cannot be understood purely by reference to immediately apparent contextual features, either behavioural or aspects of the physical environment. What occurs is more or less influenced by what has happened between infant and parent in a variety of preceding situations to which the observer has no access. The problem is particularly acute in the case of infant social behaviour since, by and large, the infant lacks conventional forms of expression, thus idiosyncratic behaviours are interpreted by the parent in the light of previous interaction. The observer lacks this information and for this reason is (or should be) forced to concern himself with the parent's interpretation of the infant's behaviour. This might be indirect, by inference from the parent's responses to the baby, or it might be via direct questioning, perhaps also asking the parent to view a videotape. But what status is to be assigned to these interpretations in the account of what the infant is doing? Are they to be the main description or purely supplementary? What if there is a conflict of opinion between the observer's analysis and the parent's interpretation? And, if we settle upon a policy of minimum obtrusion, avoiding direct questions to the parent, are there problems caused by the different levels of description of the behaviour of the participants? That is to say that we assume we can make sense of the parent's behaviour directly but the infant's behaviour only indirectly.

The resolution of these problems is not immediately obvious and much depends on the theoretical analysis of the parental role. To impose a categorical distinction between parents and ourselves as observer/interpreters of the infant's behaviour can lead to accepting the position that the parent has some special insight into what the infant is 'really' doing. Rather what must be recognized is that the parent is better described as being in a position of having to make some response to the infant's behaviour. The parent may act *as if* what the infant is doing is, say, offering an object without necessarily believing this to be the case. There is a clear example of this during the course of object-exchange at around nine months when the infant will hold out objects towards the parent. Quite often an attempt by the parent to take the object is resisted by the infant who may withdraw his arm only to hold the object out again a few seconds later. We, as observers, might wish to say that the infant was not 'offering' the object, basing this interpretation on the infant's resistance to actual exchange. However this sort of analysis by results does not lead very far in understanding what was occurring. There is, for instance, little in such a description which would tell us why the participants acted in that particular fashion. It should also be remembered that appeal to agreement of a majority of observers where interpretation is in doubt may only reveal that people can agree to make the same mistakes given a sufficiently similar body of tacit knowledge and overt directions.

There are further difficulties in assessing change that stem from the ambiguity of measurement procedures. Especially in those cases where we are investigating process change, we must rely on inferences from measurement procedures which can rarely be exact. Werner (1957) points to a possible confusion which can occur between the quantitative and qualitative aspects of development. To talk of continuity or discontinuity in quantitative terms is to be concerned with '... measurement—in terms of gradual or abrupt increase with time—of magnitude, of efficiency, of frequency of occurrence of a newly acquired operation ...'. The qualitative aspect of change, however, concerns '... the question of the reducibility of later to earlier forms—emergence—and the transition between later and earlier forms—intermediacy' (p. 133). Werner argues that there is a danger of conflating changes which are 'really' discontinuous with ones that are not (in the sense above) simply because the former might emerge slowly and perhaps imperfectly. In other words we should not expect qualitative change (discontinuity proper in Werner's view) to be necessarily manifested in a sudden and fully fledged manner.

These comments are apposite in discouraging the use of facile empirical evidence as indicative of process change. However a central problem remains. We can in fact usually attribute *some* sort of continuity but the level and type of specification is what counts. Werner himself recognized this when he stated that '... it is the universe of discourse, the interpretational frame within which the material is grasped, that often determines the ordering in terms of continuity or discontinuity' (p. 135). As an example we may return to the relationship between joint action and early language discussed previously. Without wishing to get involved in prolonged discussion on the relationship between language and thought it seems reasonable to accept that the child's early language reflects his knowledge of the world he lives in, just as his actions also do. At this extremely general level, there is a continuity of development. But what specifically might we be able to say about the way in which prelinguistic knowledge is helpful to language acquisition? One thing we *cannot* say is that there is something significant in the ordering of early utterances which is isomorphic to the perceived temporal structure of action. The claim that there is a universal agent–action ordering in two-word combinations may be valid but there is no such ordering in the perception of the world. Agency is contemporaneous with action; one does not precede the other. The agent–action distinction has nothing to do with temporal organization in any sense relevant to the analysis of cognitive structure and thus cannot provide a model for privileges of occurrence in language production or comprehension. Indeed, even if this were not so, the basic problem of how the child recognizes that the language he hears relates to the concepts he has would still remain—just as it does for nativist formulations of language acquisition.

Can we say anything about continuity at the level of specific behaviours, not forgetting Werner's cautions mentioned above? Beyond admitting that similar sorts of knowledge are involved, what detailed relationships could be postulated between two behaviours which emerge at different ages and which seem to serve similar functions? This sort of question is often put in the form of distinguishing between precursor and prerequisite relationships. The former link is simply an assertion that one behaviour precedes the other in time, fulfilling the same function and, usually, being replaced by the later behaviour. To speak of prerequisites, however, is to assert that the earlier form is essential for acquisition of the later form. In the example of object exchange we might hypothesize that the child has to master (non-verbal) demand gestures before he can develop the appropriate linguistic form to request objects. Bruner (1975b, p. 260) goes so far as to state '... for a precursor utterance to become psychologically and linguistically interesting, it must be shown to be an instrumental prerequisite to a more evolved utterance'. However such strong claims cannot be empirically supported for we have no way of varying the infant's development (apart, perhaps, from attempts to train him to see if this has any facilitatory effect). We can only suggest prerequisite status in our account, although we can actually show a precursor relationship.

These problems arise most acutely in the sort of analysis, like the joint action/case grammar example, which focus on (the development of) infant abilities, rather than the process of interaction itself. It is, perhaps, partly because of these problems that research has now shifted to attempts to characterize the social environment in terms of the encouragement and assistance it offers the infant, rather than speculating about specific links. Concern is with parental strategies in adapting to the infant's needs and developmental level, and how these relate to the infant's acquisition of relatively abstract communication skills (see Hymes, 1971, above). We have examined some of the theoretical arguments for this enterprise in a previous section and noted that, by and large, they attach great importance, at least ostensibly, to the bilateral nature of social exchanges. The description of development is often within the context of particular routines but the analysis is at a fairly abstract level, emphasizing non-specific features like timing, ritualization and variability. This is illustrated in Urwin's (1977) study of the social development of two babies followed from seven to twenty months. (These infants were blind but the approach is still representative.) The following is part of her description of the evolution of play routines.

As the children got older, some of the early established routines declined, and new forms emerged. But for both children, particular routines persisted to become generative ... Functioning to sustain heightened social contact, predictable procedures maximised opportunities for building expectancies and anticipation. This allowed and required the parent to exploit new variations. Since many routines involved touching, speaking and physical contact, an element of one could be substituted for another. The babies' development in other spheres opened new contexts for the routines to be exploited ... But within the familiar interchange frames themselves, as the babies showed increasing anticipation and control, the parents began to push them towards making their intentions explicit.

What we have here is an account that emphasizes the mutual influence of developmental change and the parents' structuring of the situation. The parent provides a consistent framework assisting development (for example, by making the infant's interpretative task easier) which is modified as the baby demonstrates increasing competence. The infant's development, then, both gives direction to the interaction and provides its own momentum for differentiation. It is thus both the lability of the interaction and its element of control that enables the child to learn something of the rulebound nature of social exchange. These sorts of considerations, concentrating on how understanding is actually achieved in the dyad seems, at present, to be the most fruitful way to proceed in understanding infant social development. This is not to say that we should discontinue taking account of individual cognitive development for we cannot. Nor have we yet come to terms with the problem that we completely lack any definition of rule or convention which is easily generalizable to infants. For instance, as Collins (1968) pointed out for his (non-linguistic) bees, we have severe problems in distinguishing rule-governed behaviour from behaviour that is merely regular, that is, a consistent response to predictable events in the world. However we may at last have arrived at a position where there is a recognition that without some element of caution we run the risk of confusing models of behaviour with the behaviour itself. It is an unfortunate comment on the state of the study of social development that this has been the norm rather than the exception.

ACKNOWLEDGMENTS

I am grateful for discussion of various points in this paper with J. Churcher, A. Garton, J. Hornak, N. Ratner and C. Urwin.

References

Ainsworth, M. D. S., Bell, S. M. and Stayton, D. J., 1974, Infant–mother attachment and social development: 'socialisation' as a product of reciprocal responsiveness to signals, in M. P. M. Richards (ed.), *The Integration of a Child into a Social World*, pp. 99–135, London: Cambridge University Press.

Austin, J. L., 1962, *How to Do Things with Words*, Oxford: Oxford University Press.

Bernal, J., 1974, Attachment: some problems and possibilities, in M. P. M. Richards (ed.), *The Integration of a Child into a Social World*, pp. 153–165, London: Cambridge University Press.
Brown, R. and Bellugi, U., 1964, Three processes in the child's acquisition of syntax, *Harvard Ed. Review*, 34, 133–151.
Bruner, J. S., 1975a, The ontogenesis of speech acts, *J. Child Language*, 2, 1–19.
Bruner, J. S., 1975b, From communication to language—a psychological perspective, *Cognition*, 3, 255–287.
Bruner, J. S., 1976, On prelinguistic prerequisites of speech, Conference paper, University of Stirling, June, in R. Campbell (ed.), *Recent Advances in the Psychology of Language, Vol. 1.*
Bruner, J. S., 1977, Early social interaction and language acquisition, in H. R. Schaffer (ed.), *Studies in Mother–Infant Interaction*, pp. 271–289, London: Academic Press.
Clarke, A. M. and Clarke, A. D. B., 1976, (eds.). *Early Experience: Myth and Evidence*, London: Open Books.
Collins, A. W. (1968), How one could tell were a bee to guide his behaviour by a rule, *Mind*, 77, 556–560.
Collis, G. M. and Schaffer, H. R., 1975, Synchronisation of visual attention in mother–infant pairs, *J. Childhood Psychology Psychiatry*, 16, 315–320.
Dore, J., (1975), Holophrases, speech acts and language universals, *J. Childhood Languages*, 2, 21–40.
Fantz, R. L., 1961, The origin of form perception, *Scientific American*, 204, 66–72.
Garvey, C., 1974, Some properties of social play, *Merrill-Parlmer Quarterly*, 20, 164–180.
Grice, H. P., 1957, Meaning, *Philosophical Review*, 68, 377–388.
Grice, H. P., 1968, Utterer's meaning sentence, meaning and word meaning. *Foundation of Language*, 4, 1–18.
Hinde, R. A., 1972, (ed.) *Non-verbal Communication*, London: Cambridge University Press.
Hymes, D., 1971, Competence and performance in linguistic theory, in R. Huxley and E. Ingram (eds.), *Language Acquisition: Models and Methods*, pp. 3–28, London: Academic Press.
Ingleby, D., 1974, The psychology of child psychology, in M. P. M. Richards (ed.), *The Integration of a Child into a Social World*, pp. 295–308, London: Cambridge University Press.
Jakobson, R., 1960, Linguistics and poetics, in T. A. Sebeok, (ed.), *Style in Language*, pp. 350–377, Cambridge, Mass.: MIT Press.
Langer, J., 1969, *Theories of Development*, New York: Holt, Rinehart and Winston.
Lorenz, K., 1966, *Evolution and Modification of Behaviour*, London: Methuen.
MacKay, D. M., 1972, Formal analysis of communicative processes, in R. A. Hinde (ed.), *Non-verbal Communication*, pp. 3–25, London: Cambridge University Press.
McNeill, D., 1970, *The Acquisition of Language*, New York: Harper and Row.
Newport, E., 1976, Motherese: the speech of mother to young children, in N. J. Castellan D. B. Pisoni, and G. R. Potts (eds.), *Cognitive Theory, Vol. 2*, Hillsdale, NJ: Lawrence Erlbaum Associates.
Newson, E. and Newson, J., 1963, *Infant Care in an Urban Community*, London: Allen and Unwin.
Rafky, D. M., 1973, Phenomenology and socialisation: some comments on the assumptions underlying socialisation theory, in H. P. Drietzel (ed.), *Childhood and Socialisation*, pp. 44–65, New York: Macmillan.
Richards, M. P. M., 1974 (ed.), *The Integration of a Child into a Social World*, London: Cambridge University Press.

Rosenthal, R., 1976, *Experimenter Effects in Behavioural Research* (2nd ed.), New York: Halsted Press.

Ryan, J., 1974, Early language development: towards a communicational analysis, in M. P. M. Richards, (ed.), *The Integration of a Child into a Social World*, pp. 185–213, London: Cambridge University Press.

Schaffer, H. R., 1971, *The Growth of Sociability*, Harmondsworth: Penguin.

Schaffer, H. R., 1975, Social development in infancy, in R. Lewin, (ed.), *Child Alive*, pp. 32–39, London: Temple Smith.

Tinbergen, N., 1963, On the aims and methods of ethology, *Z. Tierpsychology*, 20, 410–433.

Trevarthen, C., 1975, Early attempts at speech, in R. Lewin (ed.), *Child Alive*, pp. 62–80, London: Temple Smith.

Urwin, C., 1977, The development of communication between blind infants and their parents, in A. Lock (ed.), *Action, Symbol, Gesture: the Emergence of Language*, London: Academic Press, (in press).

Valentine, C. W., 1942, *The Psychology of Early Childhood*, London: Methuen.

Wells, G., 1974, Seminar, Oxford University.

Werner, H., 1957, The concept of development from a comparative and organismic view, in D. B. Harris (ed.), *The Concept of Development*, pp. 125–148, Minneapolis: University of Minnesota Press.

6

THE EFFECTIVE USE OF ROLE-PLAYING IN SOCIAL PSYCHOLOGICAL RESEARCH

G. P. Ginsburg

The use of role-playing in social psychological research has become a topic of considerable controversy during the last decade. The controversy emerged initially over the use of role-playing as a substitute for deception in dissonance experiments, and focused attention on the sort of knowledge generated by role-playing in contrast to that generated by deceptive procedures. Gradually, however, interest spread beyond deception techniques in dissonance experiments to social psychological experimentation in general; and the analyses of role-playing became increasingly sophisticated. The controversy has been beneficial, and in at least two ways. First, it has brought about a re-examination of our investigative techniques and revealed limitations on the sorts of knowledge generated by them. Second, analytical frameworks have been constructed for role-playing procedures in general, and not only for those designed as substitutes for deception, thereby broadening considerably our understanding of the strengths and limitations of such techniques. The major objectives of this chapter are to clarify the issues involved in the use of role-playing and to provide guidelines for its effective use in the generation of social psychological understandings.

A grasp of the strengths and limitations of role-playing requires an appreciation of the place of models in scientific thinking, since any appropriate use of role-playing constitutes a construction of a model about social life. Therefore, attention will be given to the nature of science and the importance of models, and to the nature of social psychological theories and procedures in particular. These considerations will shed light on the social psychological knowledge we generate by our investigative techniques and will enable useful comparisons between role-playing and other, more conventional procedures. We will then turn to a detailed analysis of role-playing strategies and a specification of guidelines as to their effective use.

THE HISTORY OF ROLE-PLAYING IN SOCIAL PSYCHOLOGICAL RESEARCH

Role-playing has a fairly long history of use in psychology and social psychology, and during most of that history its use has been free of controversy. I have traced that history in detail elsewhere (Ginsburg, 1978), and the following few paragraphs are offered only to provide some framework for subsequent discussion. *

Role-playing has been used as an assessment technique and as a therapeutic procedure for decades. It also has been used extensively in psychological and social psychological experiments, ranging from attitude formation and change studies through investigations of group processes. The controversy about role-playing erupted when it was recommended (and used) as a substitute for deception, especially in cognitive dissonance experiments.

Proponents of role-playing generally took issue with the use of deception. They claimed that it is unethical; that it denies participants the opportunity to exert the capacities to grapple actively with the problem being studied, thereby producing information grounded in a model of man with unrealistically limited powers of thinking, manipulating his environment, or comprehending his circumstances and taking consequent action; and that it produces widespread expectations of deceit throughout the population of potential subjects, thereby augmenting design and subject artifacts. Opponents of role-playing generally supported the need for and use of deception. They criticized role-playing as a method which accepts a person's statement of what he would do as equivalent to his actual performance of the act; as not being spontaneous but rather being contrived, and generated in a context of pretence; as highly susceptible to the influence of social desirability and similar artifacts; and as being incapable of reproducing the more subtle interactions found in some deception studies.

---

* Specific references to the various uses of role-playing include:

Assessment: Borgatta, 1955; Leibowitz, 1968; Mann, 1956; McReynolds and DeVoge, in press; McReynolds *et al.*, 1976; Trower, Bryant, and Argyle, 1977.

Therapy: Goldstein and Simonson, 1971; Mann, 1956; Moreno, 1946; Trower *et al.*, 1977.

Conventional psychological and social psychological experiments: Blascovich, Ginsburg, and Veach, 1975; Colby, Lanzetta, and Kleck, 1977; Davis *et al.*, 1975; Davitz, 1964; Ginsburg, Blascovich, and Howe, 1976; Janis and King, 1954; Janis and Mann, 1965; Lanzetta, Cartwright-Smith, and Kleck, 1976. Illustrative only; other examples in text of chapter.

Controversy—opposed to deception; favourable toward role-playing: Argyris, 1975; Bem, 1967, 1972; Forward, Canter, and Kirsch, 1976; Gadlin and Ingle, 1975; Ginsburg, 1978; Hamilton, 1976; Harré and Secord, 1972; Jourard, 1968; Kelman, 1967; Mixon, 1971, 1972, 1974, 1976, 1977a, 1977b, and this volume; Ring, 1967; Schultz, 1969.

Controversy—opposed to role-playing: Aronson and Carlsmith, 1968; Freedman, 1969; Holmes and Bennett, 1974; Miller, 1972; West, Gunn, and Chernicky, 1975; Willis and Willis, 1970.

A careful review of these arguments reveals that we do in fact limit the expression of important personal and social capacities by using manipulative experimental designs, and especially deception. This same issue has been raised by Gibson (1963, 1966) regarding perception and by Jenkins (1974) with respect to memory. In each case, experimental procedures which severely restricted the exercise of natural capacities by the experimental subjects—preclusion of active search in perception studies, and preclusion of receipt and comprehension of words or sentences in context in memory studies—produced simplistic and inaccurate models of living persons. Unfortunately, the same is likely to be true of the pictures generated by conventional social psychological experiments.

Data generated by deception experiments cannot be used as criterial data, against which the data from other research strategies must be compared. Deception designs contain an inherent ambiguity which precludes the assignment of criterial status to them.

Finally, role-playing may entail great personal involvement, an absolute absence of pretence regarding each action or reaction, and real displays of the behavioural variable of interest. Such reality and spontaneity is not guaranteed by role-playing, but neither is it precluded. In fact, under close examination the difference between actions in role-play contexts and actions in routine circumstances of social life becomes very unclear.

Thus, the initially sectarian arguments about the substitutability of role-playing for deception in dissonance experiments have led to much broader and more serious questions about the nature of the understandings we generate through our investigative procedures. These questions must be considered, at least briefly, before role-playing can be compared with more conventional experimental approaches. They will be considered in the next two sections, which set a paradigmatic context for the rest of the chapter.

THE NATURE OF SCIENCE AND THE ROLE OF MODELS

Control and prediction are often cited as the ultimate objectives of science, but that clearly is incorrect. The ultimate objective of science is the generation of accurate and effective explanations, the creation of understandings (Toulmin, 1961). Prediction and control allow us to assess and advance our understandings; they are means to an end.

Harré (1976) characterizes scientific theories as the extended statements of our understandings, but points out that theories must be preceded by recognition of a non-random pattern which requires explanation. Often, considerable research is necessary to establish the existence of a collection of events as a non-random pattern and to identify its form. Harré and Secord (1972) refer to this as a stage of critical description. More research then is needed to specify the range of conditions under which the pattern holds. The most creative aspect of scientific activity is the construction of a model of a mechanism which presumably generates the identified non-random pattern under the range of known conditions of occurrence of that pattern. This step is crucial and requires some elaboration.

An explanatory statement in science should contain an identification of the phenomenon (the non-random pattern) and the range of conditions under which the phenomenon is known or believed to occur. Usually, the phenomenon is a change in state or form of some entity, system or substance, which also is identified. In recent writings, Harré and his colleagues (Harré and Secord, 1972; Harré and Madden, 1975) have taken the strong position that mechanisms which generate the observed pattern under the observed conditions inhere in the nature of the substance, entity or system whose behaviour constitutes the non-random pattern. The entity, for example, may have certain capacities or powers which generate the phenomenon (an explosion, for example) under the observed conditions; or it may have certain liabilities which make it susceptible to the specified conditions in the fashion manifested by the non-random pattern (trees bowing or cracking in a high wind). This view constitutes a theory of natural powers and is directly opposed to the more conventional Humean concepts of causality and explanation (see Harré and Madden, 1975, for a detailed development, and Harré and Secord, 1972, for an earlier version applied primarily to social psychology). The creative task of the scientist involves the construction of a model of the entity whose behaviour is of interest. The model should specify the nature of that entity, describing its powers and liabilites as they relate to the focal phenomenon and the conditions of occurrence. Usually, the model is an analogue, in that the poorly understood entity or process is modelled after an entity or process which is well understood, as in the older switchboard theories of the brain, although sometimes it is a simplified representation of the subject matter on which the model is based, as in an idealized model of the circulatory system based on knowledge of cardiovascular anatomy. The analogical type of model is the more important for purposes of this chapter.

Further research and technological advances may lead to establishment of the actual existence of the mechanisms—the things or processes— hypothesized by the model. In that case, the theory would no longer involve a model, but a description of the thing itself.

Any model must be compatible with the known instances of the phenomenon—Harré (1976) refers to this as 'adequacy'. Moreover, it must not be incompatible with contemporary knowledge ('plausibility'). The acceptance and applicability of a theory depends in large measure on its plausibility, its compatibility with what is believed to be obviously real. However, beliefs about reality change over time, within scientific circles and within whole cultures, so that even our most firmly established scientific laws are dependent upon the metaphysics of the period (Harré, 1976, p. 39). Barry Schlenker (1974) also argues that laws and theories are man-made interpretations of the world as we know it and that scientific laws are statements about patterns.

It is becoming increasingly clear that scientific activity does not involve the discovery of natural laws, but rather the discovery of non-random patterns and the creation of models which explain those patterns in a manner which is compatible with fact. We will return several times to the themes of discovery of patterns, identification of the range of conditions of occurrence, creation of models, and application of adequacy and plausibility as criteria.

THE NATURE OF SOCIAL PSYCHOLOGICAL THEORY, RESEARCH AND KNOWLEDGE

Social psychology is a science, and research within its domain can be carried on in a scientific manner. However, the subject matter of the field has certain features which impose distinguishing characteristics on its theories and research processes. These distinguishing characteristics are worth noting, but since I have developed them in detail elsewhere (Ginsburg, 1978), I will only summarize them here.

As in all sciences, research activity in social psychology involves the construction of models. But the focal phenomena of social psychology—those non-random patterns which we have noticed and wish to understand—are human actions. We are not interested in reflexes, for example, except as part of the proposed mechanism by which an action may be explained. Human actions are *situated* actions (see Argyle, this volume) which take place within sets of interlocking roles and are guided—not determined—by a variety of cultural rules. Moreover, they are embedded in meaningful contexts, and they are feignable (Mixon, 1976) in that most actions of interest are within the capacity of the person to perform or not, as he chooses.

Our objective in understanding a situated action includes the desire to generalize beyond the setting in which we gathered the data, whether field or laboratory. But it is essential to recognize that such generalization implies the extension of our understanding to other settings in which similar actions are known or believed to occur. We cannot generalize abstractly as though the actions were processes existing independently of situations. In contrast with most single organism research in psychology and physiology, we cannot presume that the organism's performance reveals some internal process universal across the type of organism. Further emphasis to the situational grounding of social psychological understandings is given by Mixon's (1976) argument that the feignability of most actions which we wish to explain precludes any claim to general processes; and this is implicitly acknowledged by our interest in behaviours which do vary across situations, and our focus on controlling conditions, contingencies and person-by-situation interactions.

The settings across which we wish to generalize our understanding of an action must be assessed for similarity in their role/rule structures, since a given behaviour or a given style of behaving may be appropriate within one framework and not in another. The notion of rules is complex (see the volume edited by Collett, 1977, and especially his introductory chapter), but apparently essential to an understanding of situations (Argyle, this volume). In addition, actions are components of delineable episodes (Argyle, this volume; Harré and Secord, 1972). An episode unfolds or develops over a real time-interval and is constructed of component actions, but those actions derive their meaning in large part from the episode which their performance is accomplishing. Therefore, it is important to identify the episode which performance of the action is helping to construct. Finally, an understanding of the meanings which the episodes and their component actions have for the participants is essential (Kendon, this volume; Mixon, 1976; Shotter and Gregory, 1976). Jenkins (1974) has pointed out cogently that it is the meanings of events which are important in memory performances, and there is no reason to believe the same is not true for other types of performances in social life. In fact, a perusal of the discussion sections of social psychology journals will reveal the importance of meanings in our understanding of experimental subjects' actions. The experimenter's interpretations often extend far beyond his operational definitions and depend upon his knowledge of cultural meanings—which he presumes his subjects share. As Mixon (1971 and subsequently, including this volume) has argued concerning Milgram's work on destructive obedience (1963, 1974), and as Blascovich and I have demonstrated for risky shift research (Blascovich and Ginsburg, 1978), the experimenter's implicit assumptions about the meanings of the experimental events for the subjects may be far astray—to the detriment of the understandings he generates. The implication is that we must take the meanings of episodes and their component actions into account—and it is better to do so systematically rather than haphazardly, as is common today.

Thus, the phenomena which social psychology wishes to understand and explain are human actions. These actions appear to have a natural structure which should not be ignored, either in the description of the actions or in the construction of models to explain them. The structural features include meanings of the actions for the participants, sequential occurrence of actions in the production of episodes, feignability, and situational location. To ignore the nature of the phenomena of interest is to distort those phenomena, and consequently to preclude the construction of adequate and plausible explanatory models.

ROLE-PLAYING AND CONVENTIONAL SOCIAL PSYCHOLOGICAL EXPERIMENTATION

Role-playing is part of the conventional research armamentarium of social psychology. This was demonstrated in the brief review offered earlier of the history of role-playing as a research tool. However, as noted above, it received special and highly critical attention when it was proposed as a substitute for deception. Critics contended that role-playing was passive and devoid of spontaneity, and they cited empirical comparisons in which role-play designs were not able to replicate the results of deception designs.

On the particular matter of passivity and lack of spontaneity, the critics were wrong. Several papers have appeared which attest to instances of great involvement and spontaneity in explicitly role-play circumstances (Baron, 1977; Forward et al., 1976; Ginsburg, 1978; Hendrick, 1977; Mixon, 1971, 1977), citing such examples as the Stanford prison study (Haney, Banks and Zimbardo, 1973), the simulated attack and defence of Grindstone Island staged by the Canadian Friends Service Committee (Olson and Christiansen, 1966), and the discomfort and ambivalence displayed by Mixon's own subjects in various role-play replications of Milgram's (1963, 1974) studies of destructive obedience. Role-playing of the non-active sort, in which subjects are given a description of some social setting, such as an experiment, and are asked to predict how the participants will behave certainly does not engender behaviours of the sort the subjects are asked to describe; it simply engenders writing behaviours, as requested by the investigator. However, non-active role-play studies can be valuable if conducted properly and for appropriate reasons. Mixon (this volume) discusses the technique at length, and attention will be given to it later in this chapter as well; but for the moment it suffices to say that even non-active role-playing can produce informative descriptions and accounts of actions in other social settings.

The empirical examples in which role-playing did not replicate data generated by deception experiments raise the question of whether such comparisons should have been made. A generally negative answer to the question is called for, and on several grounds. First, as Mixon (1976), Forward et al. (1976) and I (Ginsburg, 1978) already have pointed out, deception designs involve an inherent and irresolvable dilemma which logically prevents unambiguous inferences, deriving from the different and incompatible definitions of the subject's actions as given to the subject through the cover story and as held privately by the experimenter. Second, deception experiments, whether laboratory (Hamilton, 1976) or field (Ginsburg, 1978), are simulation studies themselves, and thereby not categorically different from role-playing studies. In fact, Mixon (1977) argues that most social psychological experiments are simulations, since almost all involve commitment to temporary false beliefs by at least some of the participants, including experimenters and confederates. Third, deception experiments require secrecy and control for internal validity (Argyris, 1975), and they require naive subjects who will respond only to the intentionally manipulated variables (Aronson and Carlsmith, 1968) and not to the experimenter as such. However, considerable evidence has been amassed in recent years which makes clear that these conditions simply are not met, and that we cannot discriminate when they have been from when they have not (see Ginsburg, 1978, for a review). If we knew the meanings which the experimental events had for the subjects, perhaps we could reduce the ambiguity (Weber and Cook, 1972); but we usually do not seek or obtain meanings within conventional experiments, and especially not within deception frameworks, even though we presume shared cultural meanings in interpreting our subjects' actions. Ambiguity of meanings, then, constitutes a fourth ground for rejecting data from deception experiments as criterial.

A final ground is the fact that subjects and experimenters appear to have a framework of role expectations and related rules concerning experimental settings (Epstein, Suedfeld, and Silverstein, 1973; Farr and Seaver, 1975; Shulman and Berman, 1975). Unfortunately, the contents of such role/rule frameworks are largely unknown. Our research orientation generally constrains us from trying to discover the role/rule expectations (Friedman, 1967; Harré and Secord, 1972), which in turn leaves partly unclear the reasons for our experimental results and makes it difficult to specify the natural settings to which our results might apply.

Thus, on several grounds the empirical comparisons of role-playing with deception studies were ill-conceived, although understandable in terms of the controversy. They were ill-conceived because both groups of protagonists treated role-playing as a possible substitute for deception, and deception data were presumed by deception supporters to be 'real' and role-playing data as highly suspect. Instead, role-playing and deception procedures are mutually complementary strategies, each producing useful but somewhat ambiguous information, and each containing within its domain the potential for useful or useless results, depending on the quality of the particular design.

Alexander (Alexander and Scriven, 1977) has argued that role-playing is an essential partner to conventional social psychological experimentation, primarily because of its capacity to reveal the contents of relevant role/rule frameworks which guide the subjects' self presentations. In fact, role-playing procedures provide us with a wide range of tools for enhancing our understandings of human behaviour. Role-playing is not a methodological panacea, but neither is any other strategy by which we generate the knowledge of our field. If used properly, role-play procedures afford us great control over the episode we wish to study. We will deal directly with these matters in the next two sections.

AN ANALYSIS OF ROLE-PLAYING

Starting with Mixon's seminal paper in 1971, several excellent treatments of role-playing have been published. The analysis presented in this section draws selectively upon a number of these (especially Forward *et al.*, 1976; Hamilton, 1976; Mixon, 1971 and this volume; also Baron, 1977; and Hendrick, 1977), as well as upon my own work (Ginsburg, 1978); but obviously the other authors cannot be held responsible for my interpretations of their arguments.

Conceptual context

Any analysis occurs within a conceptual context. It is better for that context to be made explicit than to be vaguely implied by the analysis itself.

First of all, I presume that as social psychologists we wish to understand non-random patterns of human action. Human actions are situated (Argyle, 1975 and this volume) and should be studied in the type of context in which the actions of interest has been noted to occur naturally, or in a defensible facsimile of it. This requires an anthropological understanding of the structure of the natural context (see Marsh, 1976; and Marsh, Rosser, and Harré, 1978, for illustrations concerning aggression and the rules of disorder). The understanding of the context should include but not be restricted to identification of the framework of roles involved in that context and the rules which guide the role performances and negotiations conducted within it (Argyle, this volume). The social psychological understandings which we obtain through our research, including experimentation, can be reflected back to the natural contexts of observed occurrence of the actions to the extent that our contexts of research are functionally similar in structure, especially role/rule structure, to the natural contexts. The very dependability of our understanding is essentially an issue of generalizability (Cronbach et al., 1972), as will be seen later, but for the moment it is sufficient to stress the importance of understanding both the natural and the more controlled, investigative contexts of the non-random pattern of interest.

An observed non-random pattern of human action usually requires considerable exploratory and descriptive effort before its form and its conditions of occurrence are known. Harré and Secord (1972) call this stage of activity 'critical description', and both they and Forward et al. (1976) emphasize the need for it in social psychology. In practical terms, it is necessary to demonstrate that the suspected non-random pattern does occur under specified conditions. This typically requires modifying one's experimental conditions, or the script of the simulation, until the sought pattern indeed occurs dependably—or until one gives up (see Collins, et al., 1970, for an interesting example of difficulties with the forced compliance effect). Once the pattern's existence has been established, it is necessary to conduct further observations, and to modify the set of experimental conditions or the script, to identify the range of conditions under which the pattern occurs. An understanding of the form of the phenomenon emerges through the pursuit of these steps of critical description. As knowledge of the form of the pattern and its conditions of occurrence develops, the researcher becomes capable of creating a model of a mechanism which generates the phenomenon under its known and presumed conditions of occurrence.

The proposal of a generative mechanism directs the investigator's attention away from the form of the pattern and the range of conditions of its occurrence, and more toward the nature of the entity whose activities constitute that pattern. For our purposes in social psychology, that entity may be a person or other organism, or an interlocking system of organisms. In his subsequent research, the investigator will try to discover the capacities, susceptibilities, processes and structure of that entity. This will allow him to test his model mechanism against relevant empirical findings, and to modify the model until it constitutes a description of the generative mechanism instead of an analogue of it.

Very often, social psychologists presume sufficient knowledge of the form and range of conditions of occurrence of the pattern to justify immediate development of an explanatory model. Their next step is to devise one or more demonstrations of the phenomenon in specified experimental conditions and claim this as evidence of the correctness of the model. However, without careful, critical description of the form of the pattern and its range of conditions of occurrence, it is possible that the experimental results occurred independently of the presumed determining conditions. In human action, most of which is within the capacities of the person to produce or not, this is very likely to happen through rule-guided character management or face presentation by the subjects and even the experimenter. The continuing series of studies of situated identity by Alexander and his colleagues provides indisputable evidence of this point (Alexander and Knight, 1971; Alexander and Sagatun, 1973; Alexander and Lauderdale, 1977; Alexander and Scriven, 1977).

Impatience with critical description reflects a contemporary presumption of the existence and value of universal processes, with a focus on the proposal or discovery of such processes. Current and historically recent examples in cognitive social psychology include dissonance, balance, symmetry, reactance, congruity, consistency and objective self-awareness. However, we always discover conditions under which the presumptive universal process does not work, and qualifications are added, or are built in at the outset. Sometimes, as with the 'mutually related cognitive elements' requirement in dissonance theory, the qualification cannot be tested independently of the effects produced by the proposed mechanism. It seems better to engage in critical description prior to and overlapping with model construction, thereby minimizing such difficulties.

It should be kept in mind that the 'conditions of occurrence' of human actions refers to the structure of the settings in which the actions occur. As noted earlier, most of the actions which we wish to understand are within the capacity of the person to perform or not. Therefore, we must attend closely to the settings of actions, even if we continue to subscribe to the belief that the explanation for a particular action resides within the individual rather than within the setting or the system of interacting persons. The location of the generative mechanisms of human actions and the priority assigned to the search for universal processes are legitimate and unresolved theoretical issues; but they do not obviate the importance of two themes developed above: we must focus on the settings of action, and we should devote greater efforts toward a critical description of the purported non-random patterns of interest.

The structure of role-playing

Role-playing, used as a research tool, is a deliberate simulation technique, as opposed to the incidental simulations of social life involved in conventional experimentation. A script is constructed, in greater or lesser specificity and completeness, and is used to generate a scenario. The actions of the performers of the scenario are guided to various degrees by the script, but never fully determined by it. The performances are interpreted or evaluated, either by the investigator or by other participants. In the latter case, the judgements of those participants—an audience to the scenario—are then interpreted or evaluated by the investigator in accord with his research objectives. The scenario to which an audience responds may be a live performance, a videotape or ciné film, still photographs, or a written or verbal description. The scenario may contain acts which were begun and completed within it, or completed but not begun, or begun but not completed, and the audience may be asked to complete it verbally. The performers and the audience may be the same persons or different. The variety of possible role-play designs is immense, but each instance constitutes a deliberate simulation of situated human action (Hamilton, 1976; Mixon, this volume). The effective use of role-play techniques requires a recognition of various questions which must be answered in order to adopt a technique on a rational basis.

What is the purpose of the simulation?

An investigation can be undertaken to discover something, such as the process by which an observed outcome occurred, or the unknown outcome of a specific combination of circumstances, or the mere presence or absence of a non-random pattern in some little-known setting. On the other hand, an investigation can be undertaken to verify an interpretation or hypothesis. Although Cooper (1976) argued that role-playing should be used only in a context of discovery and not in a context of verification, more knowledgeable analyses obviate his argument (Baron, 1977; Forward *et al.*, 1976; Mixon, 1976). An investigator may attempt to verify his understanding of the mechanisms by which an obtained non-random pattern was generated, or he may wish to verify a description of the form of the pattern or of the conditions of its occurrence.

A role-play study by Smith (1975) is a good example of a 'discovery' approach. Smith used loosely formulated scripts and pairs of performers to create scenarios in which one performer challenged the attitude of the other. The patterns of interaction, especially the attitude change strategies used by the performers, were the data. Smith found that all contemporary theories of attitude change were represented by the strategies used by the performers, in one or another of the scenarios, but he also discovered several strategies which did not fit any of the current theories.

In contrast, Strickland, Barefoot, and Hockenstein (1976) used a role-play strategy to verify their understanding of a prior finding that people who are told to monitor one person more than another will elect to continue to do so and may never come to trust him. They interpreted the elective continuation of disproportionate monitoring as being due to time pressure or role overload on the supervisor, leading him to monitor his subordinates differentially, with more monitoring devoted to the less trusted of the two. Strickland *et al.* verified this interpretation in a non-active role-play study in which they described the work and required surveillance episode, and then asked their subjects to specify how many out of a second series of ten working periods they would spend monitoring one or the other subordinate. If the subjects were told, in the scenario description, that they, too, would have a task to perform during the second work series, then they said that they would spend more sessions observing the subordinate whom they had monitored more frequently in the first series than they would the other subordinate. However, subjects who were not told that they would have a work task during the second series did not differentiate between subordinates in terms of monitoring time. Strickland *et al.* not only verified their interpretation of the original surveillance findings, but resolved an inconsistency which had arisen in the published literature.

Discovery and verification are not the only categories into which the purpose of a study can be partitioned. An independent consideration is whether one wishes to *analyse* a phenomenon or its development, or to *synthesize* it. The distinction is important, since both our investigative procedures and our evaluative criteria may depend on whether we are breaking something apart to identify its component structure, or combining components in an effort to produce something. Analysis and synthesis are differentiated purposes in other sciences, and the distinction deserves better recognition in social psychology. As Harré has noted (1976, p. 40), the crowning achievement in organic chemistry and biochemistry is the synthesis of those compounds which the chemists have come to understand through analysis. Harré cites Mixon's 'all or none' approach (1972, 1976) as a start toward the 'replication of reality', and it serves as an excellent example of deliberate synthesis through a role-play procedure.

Based on a series of exploratory role-play studies with an analytical emphasis, Mixon felt that he understood the situational basis for Milgram's (1963, 1974) destructive obedience findings. He constructed two scenarios, with carefully devised but different scripts, each of which stopped short of the point where the performer would have to choose whether to stop issuing shocks to the 'learner' or go on to the dangerous voltage range. In one scenario, almost all of the performers continued to give the hypothetical shocks; in the other scenario, none did. The success of his all-or-none synthesis, combined with his previous analytical studies, allowed Mixon to modify Milgram's interpretation of his findings, placing much more weight on the role/rule framework of the setting and less on weaknesses in human nature.

Mixon's use of an all-or-none strategy reflects a synthesizing approach within a verification context. Synthesis also can be applied within a discovery context, in which an investigator wishes to discover what a particular combination of interesting factors will produce, either in terms of the generated process or the ultimate product.

The application of role-playing for the purpose of analysis also is important, and probably more frequently appropriate than synthesis. We seldom have an understanding sufficient to allow synthesis, but we often wish to determine the component facets of some social entity or process. Role-playing can and has been used to advantage here. For example, role-playing has been used to identify the rules of self presentation that appear to operate on specific social occasions, such as an experiment (as noted, this is the focus of Alexander's work on situated identity; Alexander and Scriven, 1977). Braver et al. (1977) used non-active role-playing to determine whether targets of persuasive attempts are aware of the different evaluations which persuaders and observers apply to resisters and yielders, and to identify the contents of those presumed evaluations. In other words, non-active role-playing was used to analyse the meanings of resistant and yielding actions in a persuasion setting, with attention given to the various perspectives extant in such a setting.

Thus, a rational construction of a role-play design requires a specification of the purpose of the study. Purposes can be partitioned in terms of at least two mutually independent pairs of categories: discovery versus verification, and analysis versus synthesis. The simulation procedures used will depend on the purposes of the simulation, and so will the evaluation procedures and criteria.

What is being simulated?

The deliberately simulational character of role-playing forces attention to the specific aspects of the original situated action which will be simulated in the role-play setting. Several aspects are worthy of note.

The investigator may wish to simulate a particular action, or the larger act of which it was a part. The action may be the behaviour of a single person, or the behaviour of a system of interacting persons; and he may focus on character management behaviours or on instrumental behaviours. Any of these reflect an interest in simulating the non-random pattern itself. But the investigator also may wish to simulate the conditions which be believes characterized the setting of the original occurrence of the phenomenon, or other conditions under which it may occur. If the researcher attempts to simulate both the action pattern and its conditions of occurrence, then he is undertaking critical description of the situated phenomenon. For example, Davis and his associates use an active role-play strategy for the investigation of the decision-making actions of participants in mock juries of various sizes and operating under various sorts of decision rules. Davis *et al.* (1975) used six- and twelve-person juries, and required either unanimity or two-thirds majority for the issuance of a verdict. Davis *et al.* contend that '... the mock jury is well suited to at least the preliminary examination of changes in existing law' (p. 11), and they see their role-play approach as providing information that is useful for understanding the natural setting by virtue of the descriptive information they generate about the processes of deciding under controlled and replicated conditions.

Similarly, our work on risk-taking in a blackjack gambling setting used active role-playing to identify a set of necessary and sufficient conditions for the occurrence of a shift in the bet level of a player. We found (Blascovich, Ginsburg, and Veach, 1975) that the opportunity to compare one's performance with those of others was necessary and sufficient for shifts in risk levels to occur, and that discussion of bets or play among the players was not necessary. This, too, reflects the use of role-playing for critical description of the situated phenomenon.

On the other hand, an investigator may be sufficiently advanced in his knowledge of the phenomenon and its conditions of occurrence to be able to develop a model of the entity and its generative mechanisms. The symbolic statements of the model, whether verbal, mathematical or pictorial, will reflect the powers and liabilities inherent in the entity's nature: the entity's resources or capacities to perform, and its susceptibilities to react.

The entity modelled may be a single person, or a set of interacting persons. Kendon (Chapter 4, this volume), in his use of context analysis for analysing films of social interaction, strongly recommends that the system of interacting persons be construed as the entity to be analysed. This view is held by many microsociologists and symbolic interactionists, and is the major theme of the recent text by Sampson (1976). However, single individuals continue to be the more common entities of interest, even in interactional processes, and an understanding of social behaviours usually is sought in the nature of the individual person. For example, Harré (1977) argues that the task of social psychologists is to discover the cognitive resources of persons which allow them to act knowledgeably and comprehensibly in social settings. The whole range of consistency theories of attitude formation, attitude change and attitude–behaviour relationships (Abelson *et al.* 1968), including dissonance theory, constitute intraindividual models which propose internal mechanisms for the generation of situated social actions. The same is true for current theories of attribution. Although it will be argued later that these models may not meet the test of plausibility, they have produced an immense array of studies which focus on generative mechanisms. Bem's (1972) use of interpersonal simulations, a form of non-active role-playing, was designed to demonstrate alternatives to dissonance reduction as generative mechanisms; and an interesting dissertation by Touhey (1973) used role-playing techniques to demonstrate that the apparently inconsistent results of attitude change studies based on dissonance versus incentive theories were due to differences in instructions. Specifically, incentive and dissonance instructions respectively entail the enactment of somewhat different roles. Both dissonance and incentive instructions generate self-referent and problem-oriented actions. However, dissonance instructions are enacted with reference to anticipated responses of others; they create conditions under which the participant expects to be held accountable. Incentive instructions create roles in which the reason for the action is clear and accounting for it unnecessary (see Touhey, 1973, pp. 98–99 for further details).

Quite often an investigator is interested both in clarifying the conditions of occurrence or the nature of the phenomenon and in assessing a proposed generative mechanism. The series of studies of facial expression and pain by Lanzetta and Kleck and their associates illustrates such combined simulations. Colby, Lanzetta and Kleck (1977) had participants pose augmented or subdued expressions of pain while receiving occasional electric shocks. They found that skin conductance responses were positively related to the pain level of the expression, but only if shock was being received on that trial. This finding specified a limiting condition for the relationship between facial expression and autonomic activity. In addition, the study revealed that the link between facial expression and autonomic reactions was not due simply to an expressive or communicative process, and that changes in expression were able to modulate but not to create the level of autonomic arousal involved in a painful experience. These findings, in conjunction with prior work (see Lanzetta, Cartwright-Smith, and Kleck, 1976), clarified part of the mechanism involved in the emergence of the painful experience. The posed expressions are an active form of role-playing.

Before leaving the question of what is being simulated, two complicating matters should be mentioned. First, the assessment of a model often requires manipulation of conditions of occurrence, so that assessment of the model often leads to changes in the critical description of the situated phenomenon. Second, the investigator's conception of the entity influences the possible nature of that entity. For example, a conception of the person as a passive entity whose behaviours are due to the pushes and pulls of environmental stimuli precludes deliberation, focused thinking and planning from inclusion in the nature of the entity. Thus, those powers would not be eligible as generative mechanisms in the model. On the other hand, a dramaturgical conception of the person, as adopted by Goffman (1959) and as recommended as a starting point by Harré and Secord (1972), emphasizes the capacities to plan, to monitor one's actions and the impressions one makes, to set and strive for goals, and to discern and follow rules. Such a conception allows situational and cultural rules to be used as generative mechanisms, but omits such liabilities as habitual responding, species wide reflexive reactions, classically conditional reactions and rapid, relatively automatic modes of information processing. The beliefs about the real nature of people which are current in a culture, and those which are current in an investigator's scientific subculture, have an important and unavoidable influence on the sorts of mechanisms that can be included in the explanatory models he creates.

How is it being simulated?

The investigator has a wide variety of simulation procedures at his disposal, regardless of whether his purpose is discovery or verification, or analysis or synthesis, and regardless of whether he intends to simulate the phenomenon, its conditions of occurrence, or its possible generative mechanisms. The variety of procedures imposes upon the investigator the task of choosing among them, and the task might be eased by considering each of several necessary choices separately.

First of all, the *mode* of simulation may be verbal description, whether written or oral, or it may be active display. If active display is chosen as the simulation mode, there is the further choice of live display or cinematic display, either on film or videotape. Most attempts to compare role-playing with deception have used verbal descriptions as the mode of simulation (see the studies by Willis and Willis, 1970, and by West *et al.*, 1975) and have been interpreted as faring poorly. However, those simulations generally were inadequately designed and conducted. Several examples of effective simulations using the verbal mode have been mentioned already: the study by Strickland *et al.* (1976), clarifying certain matters of the effects of surveillance on trust; the series by Alexander and his colleagues concerning situated identity and its influence on the outcomes of experiments (Alexander and Scriven, 1977); and Mixon's (1972; also in this volume) discovery of situational factors that may have generated Milgram's (1963, 1974) destructive obedience results. The series of interpersonal simulations by Bem (1972) constitute another illustration. In fact, the verbal mode of simulation is relatively common.

The active mode of simulation is also common in contemporary research. The jury simulation studies by Davis and his colleagues (Davis *et al.*, 1975) and the risky shift studies of blackjack playing (Blascovich, Ginsburg, and Veach, 1975) were cited earlier. Runyan (1974) also has used active role-playing in the study of risk. However, in these examples the role players are the participants themselves; they perform the simulation which had been designed and scripted by the investigator. It also is possible to use participants as judges, just as in non-active role-playing, and use actors or other participants as the performers of the social act being simulated. The presentation may be live or on film or videotape, as noted above. Examples of the use of an audience in role-play studies will be given later in this section.

It also is worth noting that live and filmed forms of simulation in the active mode can be combined. Participants can role-play actively, and then observe a videotape replay of their performance and provide commentary or make judgments. Storms (1973) did that when he took videotapes of pairs of experimental subjects engaging in an assigned 'get acquainted' conversation. For some of the dyads, he replayed the tape, so that each participant saw either his partner, as he had during the conversation, or himself. The latter case amounted to a shift in visual point of view, which Storms found had a strong influence on the causal attributions he was investigating. Thus, Storms had people role-play an episode; that live simulation served as one data source; those same role-players then viewed their active role-play on a videotape replay, and provided still further data. Both the live and video displays constituted forms of an active simulation mode.

The nature of the *script* poses another set of decisions for the investigator. The script is the written text of the simulation. It may be highly specific, allowing the performers no discretion at all, except for the expression of character; or it may specify no more than a task, or an objective, or a setting, or a theme. The study by Storms (1973), mentioned above, used a loosely specified script for part of the simulation, namely a 'get acquainted' conversation. Mixon (1972; also see this volume), on the other hand, used a set of detailed scripts which varied in minor wordings uttered by the 'experimenter' or 'subject', and only the final action by the participant was left unspecified. The degree of specificity to be desired in a script depends in part on the purpose and topic of the simulation, and upon the investigator's knowledge. For example, verification of a model, especially through synthesis, will usually call for considerable specificity, while a more exploratory objective will allow greater discretion.

The matter of script specificity is critical in role-play studies, because it constitutes a major technique of experimental control. Although the mere act of constructing a script will usually reduce the ambiguity of the ultimate results, mainly by revealing instances in which a participant is following more than one script or playing more than one role simultaneously, deliberate consideration about the desired level of specificity will further draw the investigator's attention to possible sources of ambiguity.

The script also controls the rate at which the episodes being simulated unfold, and the amount of time covered by the simulation. Thus, a script which takes ten minutes to perform may simulate a two-minute episode of violent action, but seen from each of several perspectives. On the other hand, a ten-minute script may simulate a year of a person's life. A brief script may simulate a series of actions which together accomplish an act of much greater time-span, such as a courtship, but do so by displaying only the highly informative transition points (Newtson, Engquist, and Bois, 1977) of the linked actions. Deliberate control of the rate at which the simulated episode unfolds is used well and frequently in theatre and literature, but appears not to be appreciated by social psychologists. The recognition of role-playing as an explicit simulation strategy brings with it the ability to control the extent and flow of time within the simulated episode.

The actual time allotted to the simulation is also specified by the script. Although brief simulations are the rule in social psychology, there are exceptions.

Baron (1977) makes the interesting observation that 'passing'—for white when one is black, for male when female, for rich when poor—constitutes an extended form of role-playing, obviously with a loosely specified script. The period of time allotted to the simulation should be specified in the script, since extended time-periods might introduce important factors (as in the Stanford prison study; cf. Haney *et al.*, 1973).

Finally, the experimenter should be careful to include his role and his actions in the script, if his actions are part of the simulation. There is no question that the experimenter is part of the social act within which the simulation is being produced (Friedman, 1967), and that fact must always be kept in mind. However, the experimenter may or may not be part of the simulation itself; but if he is, then his actions must be included in the script.

Decisions also must be made about the *setting* of the simulation. Where will it take place? And in how complete and detailed a manner will it be staged? A simulation can be conducted in the natural setting of the phenomenon of interest, as in the deceptive simulations by Piliavin and Piliavin (1972) of collapsing passengers on New York subway trains. Basic training in the armed forces usually involves active role-playing in natural settings, as when trainees must crawl through mud and under barbed wire while machineguns are fired over their heads and explosives are detonated nearby. However, the natural setting is difficult to control; and it is not necessarily the optimal location for the investigation of situated actions. Natural settings contain a multitude of features, only some of which are likely to be directly pertinent to the actions of interest. It is the pertinent features—or those which the investigator believes to be pertinent—which should be incorporated into the simulation, and the natural location may interfere with the investigator's ability to accomplish that selective incorporation (Aronson and Carlsmith, 1968, make a similar point in their biased criticism of 'mundane realism').

Similar issues arise when the detail and completeness of the setting are considered. A review of Argyle's analysis of situations (Chapter 2, this volume) is helpful in identifying the various situational features upon which a situated action may depend. Certain actions require props if they are to be performed, although the props may be simulations of the natural props. Mixon (1972; also see this volume) used a simulation of the shock board that had been a critical prop in Milgram's destructive obedience scenario (1963), but Blascovich and I use actual casino props for our gambling research, including a blackjack table, gambling chips, cards, carpet, and black apron for the dealer (Blascovich *et al.*, 1975). Beside props, Argyle also directs attention to elements and sequences of action, roles, rules, knowledge and skills, all of which constitute features of the situation, even though each is made manifest through the meaningful actions of the participants. The investigator's decisions about which features to include in the simulation, and in what form, will depend on his knowledge and understanding of the situated action and upon the purpose of the simulation.

As with other decisions discussed in this section, there are no simple rules for inclusion of props and details in the scripted scenarios, nor for choosing the location of performance. However, the decisions have to be made, and it is better to do so deliberately and reflectively. If they are made haphazardly or by default, the link between the simulation and the naturally situated phenomenon may be tenuous at best. This appears to have occurred in an interesting role-play study by Baxter and Rozelle (1975), who wished to understand some of the dynamics of encounters between police and citizens. They examined non-verbal aspects of the interaction when the 'policeman' and 'citizen' were at various distances from each other, using an outline script to guide the simulation, and found that crowding in upon the 'citizen' generated fragmentary protective and escape movements. Since these could be interpreted by a policeman as indications of guilt, but were actually reactions to invasion of space, Baxter and Rozelle urged that the 'conditions of interaction' (p. 53) be taken into account by police in such encounters. The results are interesting and potentially informative, but their linkage to the natural setting of interest is ambiguous, because insufficient information is given about the pertinent—and perhaps critical—features of confrontations between police and a citizen. For example, what are the rules governing interpersonal distances in such situations, especially when heated? What would a distance of 8 inches (200 mm) mean then—a physical threat, or an expression of status? Would approaching to 8 inches (200 mm) constitute the breakage of a rule, as it might in the experimental setting unless otherwise specified, or would it be a device for redefining the situation and switching to a different set of rules? The role-play study was not 'unreal'; it simply stands in unclear relationship to the situated phenomenon which it was designed to simulate. Reduction of that ambiguity would have required an analysis of the features guiding the performance of acts in confrontation episodes and explicitly choosing which to incorporate in the simulation.

The investigator must also decide upon the *performers*. Most active role-play studies have used experimental subjects as performers, but a few have used trained confederates or actors, or the experimenter himself. Carpenter and Darley (1977), for example, used actors when they videotaped different versions of a chase and fight episode in order to explore the cultural meaning of 'legitimate counter-aggression'. In our own laboratory, Ross Crosby and Karl Kosloski (1977) have constructed eight videotaped versions of a shoplifting scenario as part of their investigations of the behavioural and moral rules by which such actions are comprehended and evaluated. The use of trained confederates in conventional experiments is common, and their potential as actors in role-play simulations of social episodes is at least as great.

In non-active role-playing, the experimental subjects are usually the audience to a simulated act. The act may be presented in the active mode, as in the examples just cited; but by far the more common practice is to present it as a verbal description, usually in written form. The performers in the written description generally are presented as being similar to the subjects, as in Bem's (1972) interpersonal simulations of dissonance experiments, although they also can be presented as specific characters. In any case, they are presented within particular roles, embedded in settings.

To whom is the simulation being presented?

As I mentioned earlier in the chapter, role-playing strategies are deliberate simulations. The simulations are presented to people, and the reactions of those recipients constitute, directly or indirectly, the bases for interpretation and evaluation of the simulation. It is important to recognize the variety of possible recipients, and to choose among them rationally.

The recipient may be the investigator, or his confederates. This is common when an active, live mode of simulation is used and the performers are experimental subjects. However, in the verbal description mode, the recipients usually are a conventional audience, typically composed of experimental subjects. The same is true of most instances of active display using film or video, although the study by Storms (1973), cited earlier, used the role-players themselves as an audience with respect to videotaped replays of their own performances.

The recipients of a simulation are part of the simulation setting, much as an audience is part of a theatre setting, and there is no *a priori* reason to expect that different recipients—the investigator, an audience, or the performers recast into the role of audience—will react similarly to the simulation. The investigator should choose recipients in terms of the knowledge and perspectives he needs his recipients to have, and the roles which he wishes them to enact. Most of the recipients of a theatrical presentation are members of an audience, but some are theatre critics. The roles and perspectives of the two categories are quite different. As Miller (1972) has pointed out, the audience must share the semantic system being used for representation on the stage; its members must unselfconsciously use the 'paradigm which confers distinctive meaning upon the . . . gestures and inflections that are raised to the status of signs . . .' (p. 367). Mixon (1977b) develops a similar theme by arguing that disbelief can be and often is temporarily suspended—a theatre audience participates actively in the creation of the staged illusion, and responds in relatively unselfconscious fashion. The active participation by the audience in the creation of an illusion requires skills, or role competence; for example, a Western audience would see Chinese theatre, with its 'discontinuous succession of discretely coded gestures' (Miller, 1972, p. 367), as a stilted version of the familiar semantic system of Western theatre and would be unable to participate in the creation of the illusion.

The theatre critic, on the other hand, must both share the semantic system being used on the stage and retain a critical stance. That is, he must perform a detached but knowledgeable analysis. Thus, different recipients of simulations occupy different roles within the simulation setting. The investigator should choose carefully the role which he wants the recipients to enact, and he should ensure that the people he uses as recipients have the competencies required by the role.

What is the recipient of the simulation to do?

The functions of the recipient depend in part upon the purpose, focus and display mode of the simulation, and upon the identities of the performers and recipients. The recipients may be asked to record features of the simulation, or to offer predictions. They also may be asked for interpretations, judgments or evaluation of the actions being simulated; or they may be asked to evaluate the simulation itself.

Recipients of written scenarios are often asked to predict how the characters described in the script will complete the act in which they are engaged. As I noted earlier, Mixon (1972) asked whether the character in his script would agree or refuse to give an ostensibly harmful shock to another person; Willis and Willis (1970) asked their subjects whether a described character would conform to the judgment of another; and West *et al.* (1975) asked their simulation recipients to predict whether the described character would agree to participate in a burglary. However, prediction should be used in role-playing with caution; the investigator must make clear, to himself and to the recipients, the type of character about whom the prediction is to be made. Several authors (see Hamilton, 1976; Hendrick, 1977; Mixon, 1971) already have emphasized the importance of distinguishing between oneself, a specific other, and an 'everyman' or generalized other as the scripted character. Their concern is well deserved, although I think they all err in believing that recipients actually can predict the actions of an 'everyman' (Mixon, 1971) or 'generalized other' (Hendrick, 1977) without further specification of the identity, character, role or status of that person. The investigator must provide the role-play recipients with sufficient information about the situated identity of the character in the script to allow them to predict that character's behaviour; otherwise, the recipient will create an identity on his own initiative which will be unknown to the investigator.

It also is common to assign recipients the task of interpreting or judging the role-play simulation, usually along dimensions prescribed by the investigator. Alexander has found this very useful for revealing the structure of evaluative norms which appear to guide actions in experimental settings (Alexander and Scriven, 1977). Attribution studies frequently require interpretive judgments; the recipients of brief written scenarios are asked to assign the reasons for a target action either to the character or the situation (see McArthur, 1972, 1976; Storms, 1973). In general, these procedures involve an interpretation and evaluation of actions contained within the scenario—that is, of the simulated actions.

Recording by the recipients of the role-play simulation is a complicated topic, because recording frequently involves interpretation and judgment. Furthermore, it is interwoven with the units of study, which will be discussed shortly. Recording refers to marking the occurrence or non-occurrence of events within the scenario, regardless of whether judgment or interpretation is needed to recognize such occurrences. The events may cover very brief or relatively long intervals of time, and may be physical movements, meaningful actions, or completed acts or episodes. The recording may be accomplished by a direct coding process, using any of several notational systems currently available (see Duncan and Fiske, 1977, for a recent review), or the scenario may be recorded on film or tape for later analysis (again, see Duncan and Fiske, 1977). Kendon (this volume) strongly recommends that the perspective from which the recording is accomplished be chosen to reveal as much as possible, but once chosen be held constant. Although he is referring to film recording, the recommendation should apply to the directly coding observer as well. The only exception should be when perspective is a variable within the simulation itself, as in the case of attribution studies of actor and observer perspectives (cf. Storms, 1973, already mentioned; also see Arkin and Duval, 1975; Regan and Totten, 1975; Taylor and Fiske, 1975; all varied either physical or psychological perspective).

In contrast to evaluation of the simulated actions, recipients may be asked to evaluate the simulation itself. This usually is seen as the task of the investigator, but an audience also can be given the task. Specifically, an audience may be asked to judge both the *sensibility* and *sensitivity* of a simulation. To the extent that the investigator has created an adequate and plausible simulation in his scenario, and to the extent that the audience is comprised of competent members of the culture represented by the simulation, that scenario should be intelligible (sensible) to them and should reveal subtle properties or generative mechanisms of the situated actions (sensitivity). The investigator would treat these evaluations as data and would condense and analyse them in conventional statistical fashion; but he would have capitalized upon the tacit knowledge of competent members of the culture to assist him in his evaluation of the simulation. I do not know of any studies in which this was undertaken systematically, although post-experimental questionnaires sometimes serve a comparable function haphazardly. It does appear promising and worthy of development.

Interesting uses have been made of audiences in recent role-play studies. Carpenter and Darley (1977), in the study mentioned earlier, used two videotaped versions of a scenario containing a fight sequence to examine the views of their audiences about the legitimacy of aggression. In one version, a man was shown chasing, catching and beating a second man; in another version, an earlier sequence was shown in which the second man participated in an assaultive robbery of the first man. The audiences were asked a number of questions pertaining to aggression and its potential justifiability. Although Carpenter and Darley construe their work as revealing the 'naive' psychology of a professionally unsophisticated audience, their study also can be seen as using an audience of competent members of the culture to reveal situated rules which guide the performance and evaluation of aggressive acts. That is, rather than disclosing psychological processes, Carpenter and Darley's study can be interpreted as revealing an aspect of social structure.

Selby, Calhoun, and Brock (1977) studied the reactions of men and women to a videotaped, explicitly simulated interview between a 'police officer' and a 'rape victim'. The audience provided judgments on rating scales concerning causality and severity of consequences. Male members of the audience assigned relatively more causal responsibility to the victim, who was a woman, than did the female members of the audience. Selby *et al.* interpret the results as reflecting gender similarity to the victim and a greater expectation by women than by men of being raped. However, it should be noted that the act itself is different for the two sexes: by common cultural definition, for a man the act of rape is something that can happen 'to them', inducing an observer's perspective; for a woman, it is something that can happen 'to me', thereby carrying an actor's perspective. The relative differences might have disappeared if 'prison rape' had been used, since that is perpetrated on both men and women. Furthermore, the authors should have modified the script until *no* differences occurred between men and women in the audience; a comparison of that 'null script' with the original would have facilitated identification of the normative or role/rule basis for the differential reactions of the audience to the original script.

Turner and Shosid (1976) used written scripts to test and extend their role-based theory of attribution. They scripted two basic dialogues, each in two versions. In the basic versions, one person offered to help a second, or to serve as a leader, and the second person accepted the offer; in the alternate versions, the same utterances of the first person were used, but the second person refused to accept the first person's helper or leader role. The recipients were asked to identify the role being performed by the first character, that character's attitudes and aims regarding the second person, and the type of person the first character is. The audience's responses were coded and examined with respect to the hypotheses, which are not pertinent here. On the other hand, it is worth emphasizing the procedure that Turner and Shosid used: they compared scripts that varied in a fashion explicitly dictated by their model of a social process of attributional acts.

Finally, the role-playing aspect of the cross-cultural work by Paul Ekman and his colleagues on facial expression of emotion is worth noting (see Ekman, 1971). For example, members of the Fore tribe in New Guinea were asked to produce facial expressions appropriate to the feelings or mood of the person in a story. The role-play expressions were videotaped and presented without editing to a US audience for judgment about the emotions being displayed. The Fore tribe member was role-playing, and the US audience was a source of cultural information. The role-play strategy was used to reveal both the meanings of actions, such as facial expressions and reactions to emotional stories, and the rules of interpretation, as reflected by the judges' capacities to evaluate the expressions of the performers and the performers' capacities to reveal the emotional meanings of the stories. The design of the study allowed a demonstration of cross-cultural comparability in the meanings and the interpretative rules.

These examples illustrate the potential for role-play studies of using an audience as competent members of the culture, having at least tacit knowledge of the rules which guide and evaluate situated actions. However, an audience should be used deliberately and rationally, keeping in mind the role requirements and skills discussed a few paragraphs above. That is, does the proposed audience have the skills needed to meet the requirements of the study? Are those requirements compatible with the perspectives and performances involved in the audience role? In the detached audience, or critic, role? The switches in perspective entailed in a move from performer to audience or detached audience roles may involve both changes in focus of attention (for example, as in Objective Self Awareness; see Wicklund, 1975) and changes in modes of information processing (Cupchik and Leventhal, 1974). These changes should not be incompatible with the informational needs of the investigator.

What are the units of study?

The selection of units of study is by no means a decision unique to role-playing, but some discussion is necessary to demonstrate the range of possibilities available to the investigator in a role-play context. The units of study—or units of analysis—should be distinguished from the object of analysis. The latter refers to the formal topic of the simulation: the phenomenon, the conditions of occurrence, or the generative mechanisms. The units of analysis constitute the components in terms of which the objects of analysis are conceived and examined. The units may be construed formally or substantively; but they pertain to features of the simulation and not to the behaviours of recipients of the simulation. Furthermore, they may be manipulated, or observed.

On a formal plane, the investigator may be interested in elements of action, sequences of elements, or nested structures of elements or sequences which are embedded in larger elements or sequences. These reflect the formal structure of social action. Both Argyle (this volume) and Clarke (also this volume) deal with formal structure, and I will add only a few comments. Sequences of elements may be examined either within or between performers (cf. Argyle's typification of interaction structures, Chapter 2 of this volume; also see Kendon's chapter for a discussion of systems of interactors). Nesting refers to the hierarchical structure of behaviour and action, and it is discussed by Argyle, Clarke, Forgas and Kendon respectively, all in this volume. An excellent treatment of hierarchy as an organizing principle in behaviour has been published recently by Dawkins

(1976); and the work of Newtson and his colleagues (Newtson *et al.*, 1977) on the inherent units of action is a pertinent example of empirical work, as is the recent report by Duncan and Fiske (1977). Sequences and nestings are especially useful units because they emphasize the temporal structure of action.

A wide range of substantive units of analysis is available to the role-play investigator. *Non-verbal behaviours* were studied in a role-play design by Rosenfeld (1966a and b). Each subject was asked to interact with another person and to elicit various degrees of liking from him. The units of study were the non-verbal behaviours of the subject as he performed the role-play task. *Physiological* variables also have been used as units of study, as in the work of Lanzetta, Kleck and their colleagues on the influence of expression of pain on autonomic processes. For example, the study by Colby, Lanzetta, and Kleck (1977) reveals a modulating effect of the level of pain displayed facially on the skin conductance response to electric shock. On the other hand, Kopel and Arkowitz (1974) found that enacting a calm or upset role in the presence of electric shock did not differentially influence pulse rate. Both studies dealt with physiological variables in a role-play context.

The *utterances* of the performers, including expressions of their states of feeling and their opinions, can be used as units of study. Mixon, for example, varied the utterances of the 'experimenter' across the different scripts he used for his replications of Milgram's studies (see Mixon, Chapter 7 of this volume). Notice that the units of study were manipulated, and not simply observed or recorded. Clarke (Chapter 3 of this volume), on the other hand, has dealt observationally as well as manipulatively with utterances in his investigations of the rules of sequence in conversations.

More commonly, *actions* constitute the unit of study in role-play investigations. In Mixon's work (1972), the completion of the shock sequence was the action of interest. In the experiment by West *et al.* (1975), the unit of study was the prediction by role-players of the proportion of deceived subjects who would complete the episode by agreeing to participate in a burglary. Runyan (1974) focused on the amount of risk being recommended for another person, and it was the performers who produced those recommendations. *Whole acts* or *episodes*, rather than component actions, also may constitute the units of study. For example, when Davis *et al.* (1975) investigate the decision processes of mock juries, one unit of study is the whole decision act. Although that act is subjected to analysis in terms of units of more narrow scope, one basis of comparison across groups is the decision itself, classified as Guilty, Not Guilty, or Hung Jury. The use of acts or their embedded actions as units of study may require classification according to a coding or content analysis scheme, applied by the recipients of the simulation. The recipients must be demonstrably competent in the use of the coding scheme, in terms of either what to look for in an active display or how to code a written, verbal display.

The growing interest in accounts (Harré, 1977; Harré and Secord, 1972; Scott and Lyman, 1968), speech acts (see Clarke, Chapter 3 of this volume) and statements of causal attribution (Jones, 1976; Kelley, 1967, 1973) is likely to bring these special categories of actions to the fore in role-play research, and a few comments about them are in order. First, they must be coded in order to be useful, and the coding scheme must meet the usual requirements of mutual exclusivity, exhaustiveness and intercoder reliability (Muehl, 1961), even when used by other investigators. Second, it is important to recognize the various actions about which accounts can be offered (Harré and Secord, 1972): specifically, actions of the past (retrospective accounts), of the present (concurrent commentary), and of the future (anticipatory accounts). Retrospective accounts raise problems of memory and adequate reconstruction of the prior context (see Jenkins, 1974). One illustration of the difficulties inherent in using a retrospective account as an adequate explanation of a prior action is the review by a performer of a videotape replay of his previous actions. At the time he performed those actions, they served as components in an as yet incomplete act; but at the time of review and accounting, those actions are embedded in an already completed act and have meanings deriving from it. The meanings of the actions comprising a completed act simply are different from those of actions which are components of the process of constructing an act, and account givers and seekers must be instructed carefully about this distinction (see De Waele and Harré, this volume).

A related point, also introduced by Harré and Secord (1972), is that of negotiation of accounts. There is no *a priori* reason why the account given by a performer is inherently 'correct', or adequate as an explanation of his action, even though it may be a necessary component of an explanation. In addition to the distinctions in the preceding paragraph between retrospective, concurrent and anticipatory accounts, the earlier discussion of performer and audience perspectives and the role requirements of the latter also is pertinent (the actor–observer distinction in current attribution theory is comparable, but has not been applied to the same issue; see Jones and Nisbett, 1972). No single participant in a simulation setting, whether performer or recipient, will have full information of the conditions, meanings and potential ramifications of the performed actions (Nisbett and Wilson, 1977, review experimental evidence supportive of this point), so that the negotiation of accounts may be useful in the generation of an explanation of the actions. However, accounts may be used for other purposes than the construction of explanations (Harré, 1977). For example, a content analysis of accounts can reveal the cultural rules within which the questioned actions are made intelligible and are warranted, regardless of whether the accounts represent the performer's reasons for the actions.

Thus, accounts and attributional statements constitute social actions of considerable potential for facilitating our understanding of other social actions, and they can be useful units of study in role-play investigations. But they must be elicited and used with care.

None of the units of study discussed so far are intraindividual in nature. That is, I have not dealt with tacit knowledge (Baron, 1977), resources (Harré, 1977), character (McReynolds and DeVoge, in press; McReynolds *et al.*, 1976), or cognitive processes (Baron, 1977), all of which have been suggested as either units or objects susceptible to study through role playing. Each of these intrapersonal qualities must be inferred from more directly observable units of study, which have been the emphasis of this section. Techniques for the exploration of both cognitive structure and the products of cognitive processes are common in social psychology, and some of the chapters in this volume focus on them (see the chapters by Collett and Forgas for psychometric approaches, and that by De Waele and Harré for an assisted autobiographical approach). Such techniques can be incorporated into role-play designs, but I do not think that role-playing provides any special advantages for their use. If anything, the use of role-playing to discover dispositional qualities of the performer may interfere with its potentials by making the display of socially desirable qualities salient to the performer.

It is my view that role-play techniques are especially useful for disclosing the situational features, including the role/rule framework, which constitute the conditions under which actions occur and by which the actions are guided. Role-play techniques also are useful for investigating the sequential and hierarchical organization of action. But we are unlikely to achieve special insight into cognitive *processes* through role playing. On the other hand, the tacit knowledge (Baron, 1977) and resources (Harré, 1977) of the performer certainly may be revealed through a person's performance or his evaluation of a script; and role-playing clearly can reveal *social* processes, including the negotiation of meanings of actions. Any of these can serve as inferentially based units of study; but the disclosure of cognitive processes through role-playing is unlikely, and I do not recommend attempts to use such processes as units of study.

Finally, the various units of study should not be presumed to correlate with each other. As Bem (1974) made clear in his discussion of response classes, we should never presume the equivalence or correlation of different classes of units, even if we believe them to be equivalent manifestations of a common state or process. Statements of attitude, behavioural choices in an attitudinally relevant situation, and physiological responses in that situation are examples of different response classes, or units of study, presumptively tied to a common construct, the attitude; but their actual relationships are problematic and should be established empirically.

This section of the chapter has involved a detailed discussion of the structure of role playing as a class of simulation techniques. The discussion was organized around a set of decisions which the investigator must make in order to construct a role-play study on a rational basis. However, the decisions must also take into account the potential utility and grounds for evaluation of role-play studies. These matters are considered in the following section.

THE EVALUATION OF ROLE-PLAY STUDIES

In any science, the utility of a research design is manifested in its capacity to reveal features and relationships, to rule out rival interpretations or explanations, and to allow generalization beyond the immediate setting, procedures and measures of the investigation. This is as true for role-play designs as for any other. However, role-playing is a deliberate simulation strategy, and this raises additional evaluational considerations.

General evaluational considerations

The elimination of internal confounding is treated adequately in the conventional literature by Aronson and Carlsmith (1968) and Campbell and Stanley (1966) under the rubric 'internal validity'. The primary procedure for ensuring internal validity is the random assignment of conditions to subjects, thereby preventing the occurrence of constant errors (biases) and allowing the use of conventional statistical analyses. The proper use of control conditions and the avoidance of reactive procedures and measures also are important for the protection of internal validity.

The issue of internal validity has been developed and rationalized within the framework of manipulative studies, in which an intervention, or experimental manipulation, is imposed upon certain participants during the course of the experiment. The effect of the imposed manipulation is inferred from differences in the subsequent behaviours of the manipulated participants, relative to other behaviours used as a comparison. Obviously, if one wants to infer that some change in behaviour or state is due to an imposed experimental treatment, alternative explanations of that change must be ruled out. In recent years, experimental social psychologists have shown great concern over experimenter bias, demand characteristics and subjects' roles (see Weber and Cook, 1972) as likely sources of rival explanations. The situated identity research of Alexander and his colleagues, mentioned earlier in this chapter, support those concerns.

On the other hand, a good bit of role-playing research is better characterized as 'structural' (Duncan and Fiske, 1977). Primary interest is in discovering or verifying the patterns and sequences of events and processes within a particular type of episode, or in identifying the role/rule framework relevant to the episode. No manipulative interventions are imposed during the course of the study, and no special effect of a manipulation is sought. Nevertheless, internal confounding still is possible, and steps should be taken to avoid it. More than one form of a scenario should be used, and they should be assigned randomly to the participants, who may be serving as performers or as audience. That is equivalent to the random assignment of treatments to subjects in manipulative experiments.

Similarly, control or comparison scenarios are necessary to rule out historical, maturational and instrumentation factors as the bases for the observed structure. All of these factors are extraneous to the simulated setting and episode, and it is important that the observed structure be inherent in the simulation and not be a product of those extraneous factors.

A second major evaluational consideration is the dependability of measures. Role-play studies frequently involve judgments by an audience along scales prescribed by the investigator. The estimated dependability of judgments within a scenario is taken into account automatically in any statistical comparison between the means of the judgments of the various scenarios, in the form of within cell variation. However, the dependability of coders and coding schemes, of instruments, of observers and the rules by which they record events, sometimes goes unquestioned. This is especially true when the investigator constitutes the recording instrument. The observed outcomes or structural features of a role-play study may be chance occurrences, and information about the dependability of the measures is necessary to evaluate that possibility.

The dependability of measurements also pertains to the third major evaluational consideration—generalizability. This is the issue of external validity. In external variable studies (Duncan and Fiske, 1977), in which outcomes are correlated with variables external to the process leading to the outcome, it is posed in terms of the range of circumstances across which the obtained relationship between the experimental manipulation and the observed effect can be expected to hold. Uncertainties about the range of applicability can be reduced through randomization and the use of control conditions; identification of limitations on generalizability is provided by some forms of interaction effects, which indicate conditions under which the obtained relationships do and do not hold (see Campbell and Stanley, 1966). The issues of external validity and dependability of measures overlap considerably, because the dependability of a score is potentially limited to the time, place, persons and procedures involved in its original generation, except in the face of evidence to the contrary. Therefore, it is important to determine whether the score of a person is dependable under different times or places of measurement, or using different but related items, or different raters or observers. These are a subset of the questions involved in external validity, and they are pursued in detail by Cronbach and his colleagues (1972).

The issue of generalizability is important for structural studies, too, and the same sorts of steps should be taken to reduce uncertainty about the range of applicability of the observed structure and to identify the combinations of conditions under which the observed structure does and does not exist. Randomization and the proper use of control or comparison scenarios will reduce the uncertainty, and a multifactor design will allow the identification of structures which are specific to certain combinations of the factors.

Thus, role-playing studies are subject to evaluation by the same general criteria as other types of studies: internal validity, dependability of measures, and generalizability.

Special evaluational considerations

The deliberate simulational character of role-playing raises additional issues for the evaluation of role-play studies. First, there should be reasonable grounds for assuming similarity between the simulated setting and the natural setting within which the action of interest is believed or known to occur. The similarity may be established either explicitly or implicitly by the script, and may be enhanced by the use of props. Similarity in the structure of roles and related rules probably is most critical. There is no simple procedure for establishing similarity, nor is there a formula for assessing its adequacy. Instead, the investigator who uses role-playing has the responsibility of specifying the structural features common to the natural setting and the simulation, and the rationale for their selection. It is essential to recognize that the ability to specify the relevant features of the natural setting and to claim their adequate representation in the simulated setting requires considerable anthropological understanding of the natural setting—what might be called 'local ethnography': knowledge of the roles, rules and meanings of the setting. The investigation by Peter Marsh of violence among young fans at British football games is an excellent illustration of such an approach (Marsh et al., 1978).

In a similar fashion, the action of interest in the simulation must be domonstrably similar to the natural action of which it is claimed to be an analogue. The considerations mentioned above are applicable here, too; but it must be kept in mind that the action under examination is the one being simulated, and not necessarily the actions of the experimental subjects. For example, in our studies of risk-taking (Blascovich et al., 1975), we use blackjack playing by participants in our laboratory, where they are given gambling chips and do not win or lose money, as an analogue of blackjack playing in a real casino, where players do win and lose money. We have compared the results of playing for chips alone with those obtained when players had to buy the chips with their own money and found them to be very similar. Therefore, we have some confidence, for low stake betting, in the similarity of our simulated action to the natural action of interest. In our case, the simulated action is performed by the experimental participant.

On the other hand, the simulated action may be performed by a character in a written script, and the experimental participants may comprise an audience whose task is to judge or rate the scripted action. The structural similarity must be between the scripted action and the original action of interest. For example, in the study by West and his colleagues mentioned earlier (West et al., 1975), an audience was asked to predict the proportion of people who would agree to participate in a burglary, under each of several scripted scenarios. The original action occurred in a deception study, when each deceived subject was asked by a member of a burglary team with which he was meeting privately whether he would agree to participate in a particular burglary at some later time. The deceived person was probably under pressure to agree to discuss the matter and to agree to later participation. Those more qualified actions should have been built into the script given to the audience, rather than the simplistic description which was included.

The investigator may be sufficiently advanced in his knowledge of the form of the phenomenon and the range of its conditions of occurrence to construct a model of the behaving entity. His objective would be to discover or verify the generative mechanisms of the situated action, as deriving from the powers and susceptibilities inherent in the modelled nature of the entity. For example, the performer can be construed, through the script, to have certain bits of knowledge, certain skills, and certain prejudices. His final action in the simulated episode may be left open by the script and interpreted as a product of the operation of the modelled powers and liabilities within the simulated conditions of occurrence. Under these circumstances, both the action of interest and the processes of production of that action should be evaluated in terms of their adequacy and their plausibility. The adequacy of the model pertains to its compatibility with known or believed occurrences of the action. That constitutes a positive criterion. The plausibility of the model constitutes a negative criterion: the model must not be incompatible with common scientific knowledge and beliefs about the entity. For example, if a model of causal attribution contains reflective, linguistic, logical thinking as the process by which attributions are generated, and we know that some causal impressions are achieved much more swiftly than a verbally based process would allow, the plausibility of the model would be brought into question.

Another evaluational consideration is whether the action, and if appropriate, the generative process, can be simulated using different role-play strategies. If not, then the understanding gained may reflect only the particular methods of simulation, and not the inherent features of the situated actions being simulated. This raises again the matter of dependability, since it pertains to the range of conditions across which the features, patterns or structures remain stable.

Dependability, generalizability and variations in procedures

Critical description of a situated action requires modification of the conditions of occurrence until the action no longer occurs. This helps to establish the limits of the range of conditions of occurrence, and sheds light on the form of the action itself. Thus, a limit on generalizability is not undesirable; rather, it is informative. On the other hand, if a simulated action, or the structure of a simulated setting, is replicable only within one role-play strategy, that constitutes a highly undesirable specificity. Specificity that is method-related is undesirable, whereas that which is tied to conditions of occurrence is informative.

Therefore, the evaluation of data and understandings based on role-playing should be based in part upon the range of strategies in which the phenomenon was dependably produced. For example, if the original simulation used a nonactive display, can the action or structure be produced in an active display? If experimental participants were performers and the investigator the recipient for the original simulation, will the simulation be replicated if the investigator or his confederates serve as performers and the experimental participants constitute an audience? The favourable evaluation of an understanding based on a role-play simulation presumes continued adequacy and plausibility of that understanding when the simulation strategies and the conditions of occurrence are altered—a point made forcefully by Hamilton as well (1976). Clearly, this is an issue of the generalizability of the understandings.

Representativeness revisited

As a final consideration in this section, it might be of value to summarize the comments I have made at various locations in the chapter about statistics, individual differences, and representativeness. Specifically, one may ask whether the recipients and performers of a simulation should be construed as samples of populations, and whether the measurement procedures, the allowable behaviours, the modes of simulation, or the features of the scripts, should be seen as samples of universes. The answer to such questions depends heavily on the investigator's conceptual perspective. If a facet of the design, such as the performers within a given scenario, is construed to contain units of a larger universe over which the investigator intends to generalize, and if the units are presumed to differ from each other on grounds that are not subject to practical control, then a conventional, error-theory statistical approach is appropriate. As a rule, the members of an audience are construed to reflect individual differences not subject to practical control. Similarly, performers whose performances are not guided by tightly woven scripts will reflect presumably random differences. Items or scales in terms of which a performance is rated may be construed as units which differ randomly from each other but are all members of some universe of content-related items. Measurements made by one or more observers within a presumably stable portion of an act might be construed similarly. In all of these cases, representativeness is an appropriate concern, and related statistical analyses are applicable.

On the other hand, the simulated setting in a role-play study should *not* be construed as a representative unit from a universe of settings, and no attempt should be made to sample such a universe. Instead, the simulated setting must be recognized as a deliberate simulation of the structure of a natural setting in which the action of interest is known or believed to occur. The simulated setting is a deliberate reconstruction of the natural setting, not a sample of a universe. Furthermore, generalization from the simulation is not to some abstract universe, but to other natural settings having structural features in common with the original setting. Sample considerations and related statistics are not relevant.

The same is true for most scripts. They are usually constructed in deliberate fashion and do not represent some universe of script contents. On the other hand, performances of actions not specified by a script may be aptly construed as units of a population. For example, Mixon (1972, and this volume) suggests the use of an all-or-none procedure to test one's understanding of the generative process underlying an action. Two scripts should be written, one which should always lead to the action and one which never should. This is analogous to the biochemist's attempt to synthesize a molecule, in that the synthesis of a social act is attempted. However, if the investigator considers his control to be less than perfect, he may tolerate deviation from the predicted outcomes of the two scripts as long as they are not statistically significant in number (significantly different from one hundred per cent and zero per cent, respectively).

Thus, the issue of representativeness in role-play studies must be viewed in terms of the conceptual perspective and potential control of the investigator.

CONCLUSIONS

The objectives of this chapter have been to shed realistic light on the considerable potentials and variety of role-playing as an investigative strategy in social psychology, and to suggest guidelines for its use. I hope that the reader will finish this chapter with several recognitions: that all of our research procedures generate somewhat ambiguous information; that no one technique should be used as an absolute criterial procedure; that the difference between performances in role-play and non-role play settings is not very clearcut; and that the careful use of role-play procedures can add significantly to our understanding of social life and social processes—and perhaps of psychological processes as well.

References

Abelson, R. P., Aronson, E., McGuire, W. J., Newcomb, T. M., Rosenberg, M. J., and Tannenbaum, P. H. (eds.), 1968, *Theories of Cognitive Consistency: A Source-book*, Chicago: Rand McNally.

Alexander, C. N., and Knight, G. W., 1971, Situated identities and social psychological experimentation, *Sociometry*, **34**, 65–82.

Alexander, C. N., and Lauderdale, P., 1977, Situated identities and social influence, *Sociometry*, **40**, 225–233.

Alexander, C. N., and Sagatun, I., 1973, An attributional analysis of experimental norms, *Sociometry*, **36**, 127–142.

Alexander, C. N., and Scriven, G. D., 1977, Role playing: An essential component of experimentation, *Personality and Social Psychology Bulletin*, **3**, 455–466.

Argyle, M., 1975, Do personality traits exist? *New Behaviour*, **31 July**, 176–179.

Argyris, C., 1975, Dangers in applying results from experimental social psychology, *American Psychologist*, **30**, 469–485.

Arkin, R. M., and Duval, S., 1975, Focus of attention and causal attributions of actors and observers, *Journal of Experimental Social Psychology*, **11**, 427–438.

Aronson, E., and Carlsmith, J. M., 1968, Experimentation in social psychology, in G. Lindsey and E. Aronson (eds.), *Handbook of Social Psychology* (revised edition), Vol. II, Reading, Mass: Addison-Wesley.

Baron, R. M., 1977, Role playing and experimental research: The identification of appropriate domains of power, *Personality and Social Psychology Bulletin*, 3, 505–513.

Baxter, J. C., and Rozelle, R. M., 1975, Nonverbal expression as a function of crowding during a simulated police-citizen encounter, *Journal of Personality and Social Psychology*, 32, 40–54.

Bem, D. J., 1967, Self-perception: An alternative interpretation of cognitive dissonance phenomena, *Psychological Review*, 74, 183–200.

Bem, D. J., 1972, Self-perception theory, in L. Berkowitz (ed.), *Advances in Experimental Social Psychology*, Vol. 6, New York: Academic Press, pp. 2–62.

Bem, D. J., 1974, Discussion, in H. London and R. E. Nisbett (eds.), *Thought and Feeling: Cognitive Alteration of Feeling States*, Chicago: Aldine-Atherton.

Blascovich, J., and Ginsburg, G. P., 1978, Conceptual analysis of risk taking in 'risky shift' research. *Journal for the Theory of Social Behaviour*, 8, 217–230.

Blascovich, J., Ginsburg, G. P., and Veach, T. L., 1975, A pluralistic explanation of choice shifts on the risk dimension, *Journal of Personality and Social Psychology*, 31, 422–429.

Borgatta, E. F., 1955, The analysis of social interaction: Actual, role-playing and projective, *Journal of Abnormal and Social Psychology*, 51, 394–405.

Braver, S. L., Linder, D. E., Corwin, T. T., and Cialdini, R. B., 1977, Some conditions that affect admission of attitude change, *Journal of Experimental Social Psychology*, 13, 565–576.

Campbell, D. T., 1957, Factors relevant to the validity of experiments in social settings, *Psychological Bulletin*, 54, 297–312.

Campbell, D. T., and Stanley, J. C., 1966, *Experimental and Quasi-experimental Designs for Research*, Chicago: Rand-McNally.

Carpenter, B., and Darley, J. M., 1978, A naive psychological analysis of counteraggression, *Personality and Social Psychology Bulletin*, 4, 68–71.

Colby, C. Z., Lanzetta, J. T., and Kleck, R. E., 1977, Effects of the expression of pain on autonomic and pain tolerance responses to subject-controlled pain, *Psychophysiology*, 14, 537–540.

Collett, P. (ed.), 1977, *Social Rules and Social Behaviour*, Oxford: Blackwell.

Collins, B. E., Ashmore, R. D., Hornbeck, F. W., and Whitney, R. E., 1970, Studies in forced compliance: In search of a dissonance-producing forced compliance paradigm. *Representative Research in Social Psychology*, 1, 11–23.

Cooper, J., 1976, Deception and role playing: On telling the good guys from the bad guys, *American Psychologist*, 31, 605–610.

Cronbach, L. J., Gleser, G. C., Nanda, H., and Rajaratnam, N., 1972, *The Dependability of Behavioural Measurements: Theory of Generalizability for Scores and Profiles*, New York: Wiley.

Crosby, R., and Kosloski, K., 1977, A role play analysis of shoplifting. Unpublished manuscript, Department of Psychology, University of Nevada, Reno.

Cupchik, G. C., and Leventhal, H., 1974, Consistency between expressive behaviour and the evaluation of humorous stimuli: The role of sex and self-observation. *Journal of Personality and Social Psychology*, 30, 429–442.

Davis, J. H., Kerr, H. L., Atkin, R. H., and Meek, D., 1975, The decision processes of 6- and 12-person mock juries assigned unanimous and two-thirds majority rules, *Journal of Personality and Social Psychology*, 32, 1–14.

Davitz, J. R., 1964, *The Communication of Emotional Meaning*, McGraw-Hill.

Dawkins, R., 1976, Hierarchical organisation: A candidate principle for ethology, in P. P. G. Bateson, and R. A. Hinde (eds.), *Growing Points in Ethology*, Cambridge: Cambridge University Press. pp. 7–54.

Duncan, S., Jr., and Fiske, D. W., 1977, *Face-to-Face Interaction: Research, Methods and Theory*, Hillside, NJ: Lawrence Erlbaum.

Ekman, P., 1971, Universals and cultural differences in facial expressions of emotion, in J. K. Cole (ed.), *Nebraska Symposium on Motivation, 1971*, Lincoln, Neb.: University of Nebraska Press, pp. 207–283.

Epstein, Y. M., Suedfeld, P., and Silverstein, S. J., 1973, The experimental contract: Subjects' expectations of and reactions to some behaviors of experimenters, *American Psychologist*, **28**, 212–221.

Farr, J. L., and Seaver, W. B., 1975, Stress and discomfort in psychological research: Subject perceptions of experimental procedures, *American Psychologist*, **30**, 770–773.

Forward, J., Canter, R., and Kirsch, N., 1976, Role-enactment and deception methodologies: Alternative paradigms? *American Psychologist*, **31**, 595–604.

Freedman, J. L., 1969, Role playing: Psychology by consensus, *Journal of Personality and Social Psychology*, **13**, 107–114.

Friedman, N., 1967, *The Social Nature of Psychological Research: The Psychological Experiment as a Social Interaction*. New York: Basic Books.

Gadlin, H., and Ingle, G., 1975, Through the one-way mirror: The limits of experimental self-reflection, *American Psychologist*, **30**, 1003–1009.

Gibson, J. J., 1963, The useful dimensions of sensitivity, *American Psychologist*, **18**, 1–15.

Gibson, J. J., 1966, *The Senses Considered as Perceptual Systems*, Boston: Houghton-Mifflin.

Ginsburg, G. P., 1978, Role playing and role performance in social psychological research, in M. Brenner, P. Marsh, and M. Brenner (eds.), *The Social Contexts of Method: Readings in the Sociology of Methodology*, London: Croom-Helm, Ltd., pp. 91–121.

Ginsburg, G. P., Blascovich, J. J., and Howe, R. C., 1976, Risk taking in the presence of others, in W. Eadington (ed.) *Gambling and Society*, Springfield, Ill: Charles C. Thomas, pp. 336–346.

Goffman, E., 1959, *The Presentation of the Self in Everyday Life*, Garden City, NY: Anchor Books, Doubleday.

Goldstein, A. P., and Simonson, N. R., 1971, Social psychological approaches to psychotherapy research, in A. E. Gergin and S. L. Garfield (eds.), *Handbook of Psychotherapy and Behavior Change*. New York: Wiley, pp. 154–195.

Hamilton, V. L., 1976, Role play and deception: A re-examination of the controversy, *Journal for the Theory of Social Behaviour*, **6**, 233–250.

Haney, C., Banks, W. C., and Zimbardo, P. G., 1973, Interpersonal dynamics in a simulated prison, *International Journal of Criminology and Penology*, **1**, 69–97.

Harré, R., 1976, The constructive role of models, in L. Collins *The Use of Models in the Social Sciences*, London: Tavistock Publications, pp. 16–43.

Harré, R., 1977, The ethogenic approach: Theory and practice, in L. Berkowitz, (ed.), *Advances in Experimental Social Psychology*, Vol. 10, New York: Academic Press, pp. 284–314.

Harré, R., and Madden, E. H., 1975, *Causal Powers: A Theory of Natural Necessity*, Oxford: Basil Blackwell.

Harré, R., and Secord, P. F., 1972, *The Explanation of Social Behavior*, Totowa, NJ: Rowman and Littlefield.

Hendrick, C., 1977, Role-taking, role-playing, and the laboratory experiment. *Personality and Social Psychology Bulletin*, **3**, 467–478.

Holmes, D. S., and Bennett, D. H., 1974, Experiments to answer questions raised by the use of deception in psychological research: I. Role playing as an alternative to deception; II. Effectiveness of debriefing after deception; III. Effect of informed consent on deception, *Journal of Personality and Social Psychology*, **29**, 358–367.

Janis, I. L., and King, B. T., 1954, The influence of role playing on opinion change. *Journal of Abnormal and Social Psychology*, **48**, 211–218.

Janis, I. L., and Mann, L., 1965, Effectiveness of emotional role-playing in modifying smoking habits and attitudes, *Journal of Experimental Research in Personality*, **1**, 84–90.

Jenkins, J. J., 1974, Remember that old theory of memory? Well, forget it! *American Psychologist*, **29**, 785–795.

Jones, E. E., 1976, How do people perceive the causes of behavior? *American Scientist*, **64**, 300–305.

Jones, E. E., and Nisbett, R. E., 1972, The actor and the observer: Divergent perceptions of the causes of behavior, in E. E. Jones *et al.* (eds.). *Attribution: Perceiving the Causes of Behavior*, General Learning Press, pp. 79–94.

Jourard, S. M., 1968, *Disclosing Man to Himself*, Princeton, NJ: Van Nostrand.

Kelley, H. H., 1967, Attribution theory in social psychology, in D. Levine (ed.), *Nebraska Symposium on Motivation*, University of Nebraska Press, pp. 192–238.

Kelley, H. H., 1973, The processes of causal attribution, *American Psychologist*, **28**, 107–128.

Kelman, H., 1967, Human use of human subjects: The problem of deception in social psychological experiments, *Psychological Bulletin*, **67**, 1–11.

Kopel, S. A., and Arkowitz, H. S., 1974, Role playing as a source of self-observation and behavior change, *Journal of Personality and Social Psychology*, **29**, 677–686.

Lanzetta, J. T., Cartwright-Smith, J., and Kleck, R. E., 1976, Effects of nonverbal dissimulation on emotional experience and autonomic arousal, *Journal of Personality and Social Psychology*, **33**, 354–370.

Leibowitz, G., 1968, Comparison of self-report and behavioural techniques of assessing aggression, *Journal of Consulting and Clinical Psychology*, **32**, 21–25.

Mann, J. H., 1956, Experimental evaluations of role playing, *Psychological Bulletin*, **53**, 227–234.

Marsh, P., 1976, Careers for boys: Nutters, hooligans and hardcases, *New Society*, **13 May**.

Marsh, P., Rosser, E., and Harré, R., 1978, *The Rules of Disorder*, London: Routledge and Kegan Paul.

McArthur, L. A., 1972, The how and what of why: Some determinants and consequences of causal attribution, *Journal of Personality and Social Psychology*, **22**, 171–193.

McArthur, L. Z., 1976, The lesser influence of consensus than distinctiveness information on causal attributions: A test of the person–thing hypothesis, *Journal of Personality and Social Psychology*, **33**, 733–742.

McReynolds, P., and DeVoge, S. in press, The use of improvisational techniques in assessment, in P. McReynolds (ed.), *Advances in Psychological Assessment*, Vol. 4, San Francisco: Jossey-Bass.

McReynolds, P., DeVoge, S., Osborne, S. K., Pither, B., and Nordin, K., 1976, *Manual for the Impro-I (Improvisation Test for Individuals)*, Reno. Nev. Psychological Service Center, University of Nevada, Reno.

Milgram, S., 1963, Behavioural study of obedience, *Journal of Abnormal and Social Psychology*, **67**, 371–378.

Milgram, S., 1974, Obedience to Authority, New York; Harper and Row.

Miller, A. G., 1972, Role playing: An alternative to deception?: A review of the evidence, *American Psychologist,* **27**, 623–636.

Miller, J., 1972, Plays and players, in R. A. Hinde, (ed.) *Non-Verbal Communication,* Cambridge: Cambridge University Press, pp. 359–372.

Mixon, D., 1971, Behaviour analysis treating subjects as actors rather than organisms. *Journal for the Theory of Social Behaviour,* **1**, 19–32.

Mixon, D., 1972, Instead of deception, *Journal for the Theory of Social Behaviour,* **2**, 145–174.

Mixon, D., 1974, If you won't deceive, what can you do? In N. Armistead (ed.), *Reconstructing Social Psychology,* Baltimore, Md: Penguin Books, Inc., pp. 72–85.

Mixon, D., 1976, Studying feignable behaviour, *Representative Research in Social Psychology,* **7**, 89–104.

Mixon, D., 1977 (a), Temporary false belief, *Personality and Social Psychology Bulletin,* **3**, 479–488.

Mixon, D., 1977(b), Why pretend to deceive? *Personality and Social Psychology Bulletin,* **3**, 647–653.

Moreno, J. L., 1946, *Psychodrama.* New York: Beacon.

Muehl, D., 1961, *Manual for Coders.* Ann Arbor, Mich.: Institute for Social Research, University of Michigan.

Newtson, D., Engquist, G., and Bois, J., 1977, The objective basis of behavior units. *Journal of Personality and Social Psychology,* **35**, 847–862.

Nisbett, R. E., and Wilson, T. D., 1977, Telling more than we can know: Verbal reports on mental processes, *Psychological Review,* **84**, 231–259.

Olson, T., and Christiansen, G., 1966, *The Grindstone Experiment: Thirty-one Hours,* Toronto: Canadian Friends Service Committee.

Piliavin, J. A., and Piliavin, I. M., 1972, Effect of blood on reactions to a victim, *Journal of Personality and Social Psychology,* **23**, 353–361.

Regan, D. T., and Totten, J., 1975, Empathy and attribution: Turning observers into actors, *Journal of Personality and Social Psychology,* **32**, 850–856.

Ring, K., 1967, Experimental social psychology: Some sober questions about frivolous values. *Journal of Experimental Social Psychology,* **3**, 113–123.

Rosenfeld, H. M., 1966(a) Approval-seeking and approval-inducing functions of verbal and nonverbal responses in the dyad, *Journal of Personality and Social Psychology,* **4**, 597–605.

Rosenfeld, H. M., 1966(b) Instrumental affiliative functions of facial and gestural expressions, *Journal of Personality and Social Psychology,* **4**, 65–72.

Runyan, D. L., 1974, The group risky-shift effect as a function of emotional bonds, actual consequences, and extent of responsibility, *Journal of Personality and Social Psychology,* **29**, 670–676.

Sampson, E. E., 1976, *Social Psychology and Contemporary Society* (2nd ed.), New York: Wiley.

Schlenker, B. R., 1974, Social psychology and science, *Journal of Personality and Social Psychology,* **29**, 1–15.

Schultz, D. P., 1969, The human subject in psychological research. *Psychological Bulletin,* **72**, 214–228.

Scott, M. B., and Lyman, S. M., 1968, Accounts. *American Sociological Review,* **33**, 46–62.

Selby, J. W., Calhoun, L. G., and Brock, T. A., 1977, Sex differences in the social perception of rape victims, *Personality and Social Psychology Bulletin,* **3**, 412–415.

Shotter, J., and Gregory, S., 1976, On first gaining the idea of oneself as a person, in R. Harré (ed.), *Life Sentences,* London; Wiley, pp. 1–9.

Shulman, A. D., and Berman, H. J., 1975, Role expectations about subjects and experimenters in psychological research, *Journal of Personality and Social Psychology*, **32**, 368–380.

Smith, J. L., 1975, A games analysis for attitude change: Use of role-enactment situations for model development, *Journal for the Theory of Social Behaviour*, **5**, 63–79.

Storms, M. D., 1973, Videotape and the attribution process: Reversing actors' and observers' points of view, *Journal of Personality and Social Psychology*, **27**, 165–175.

Strickland, L. H., Barefoot, J. C., and Hockenstein, P., 1976, Monitoring behaviour in surveillance and trust paradigm, *Representative Research in Social Psychology*, **7**, 51–57.

Taylor, S. E., and Fiske, S. T., 1975, Point of view and perceptions of causality, *Journal of Personality and Social Psychology*, **32**, 439–445.

Touhey, J. C., 1973, An attribution theory analysis of attitude change in a forced compliance paradigm, unpublished Ph.D. dissertation, University of Nevada, Reno, Nev.

Toulmin, S., 1961, *Foresight and Understanding*, Hutchinson.

Trower, P., Bryant, B., and Argyle, M., 1977, *Social Skills and Mental Health*, London: Methuen.

Turner, R. H., and Shosid, N., 1976, Ambiguity and interchangeability in role attribution: The effect of alter's response, *American Sociological Review*, **41**, 993–1006.

Weber, S. J., and Cook, T. D., 1972, Subject effects in laboratory research: An examination of subject roles, demand characteristics, and valid inference. *Psychological Bulletin*, **77**, 273–295.

West, S. G., Gunn, S. P., and Chernicky, P., 1975, Ubiquitous Watergate: An attributional analysis, *Journal of Personality and Social Psychology*, **32**, 55–65.

Wicklund, R. A., 1975, Objective self-awareness, in L. Berkowitz (ed.), *Advances in Experimental Social Psychology*, Vol. 8. Academic Press, pp. 233–277.

Willis, R. H., and Willis, Y. A., 1970, Role playing versus deception: An experimental comparison, *Journal of Personality and Social Psychology*, **16**, 472–477.

7

UNDERSTANDING SHOCKING AND PUZZLING CONDUCT

Don Mixon

What we observe, the products of our research and experimental manipulations, are always understood in terms of and in relationship to something else. Schedules of reinforcement are related to baselines, treatment groups to control groups, and all groups to sophisticated statistical models. Very likely all understanding, not simply scientific understanding, comes from relating one thing to another, from relating something we wish to understand to something we think we already understand. The general terms for this process is 'analogy'.

What is an analogy? An analogy is a relationship between two entities, processes, or what you will, which allows inferences to be made about one of the things, usually that about which we know least, on the basis of what we know about the other (Harré, 1972, p. 1972).

The term 'analogy' can be and is used in divers ways. In this paper I shall concentrate on a particular function suggested in Harré's definition, a function that often receives insufficient attention. *Relationship* commonly is emphasized—and quite properly so. But while acknowledging the necessity of accurately establishing the relationship between two entities, processes, etc., I shall point to how important it is for one of the two to be well understood. Whereas it may be the case that relating two ill-understood things to each other sometimes can throw new light on each, analogy gains its greatest power when the thing we wish to understand is related to something well and thoroughly understood.

Scientists generally make more explicit and careful use of analogy than is common in everyday thought and discourse. Models represent the apogee of scientific use of analogy. The term 'model' as used in this paper refers to what Harré calls *iconic models*—roughly, 'real or imagined things and processes which are similar to other things and processes in various ways, and whose function is to further our understanding' (Harré, 1972, p. 174). Examples of scientific models are many and various, ranging from Watson and Crick's celebrated use of model building to understand DNA to such lesser known examples as Darwin's use of a model of deliberate selection in the construction of his Theory of Natural Selection (Harré, 1972). In recent years philosophers of science Mary Hesse and Rom Harré have elaborated the function of models in scientific practice. Harré in fact makes a good case for the proposition that the proper use of models is the very basis of scientific thinking (1970. 1972).

If models are examples of an analogy's potential to improve understanding, other uses of analogy in scientific practice are less exemplary. For instance, Tinbergen claims that psychiatric research on autism has ignored the commonsense but sound warning of Medawar, namely, that 'it is not informative to study variations of behaviour unless we know beforehand the norms from which the variants depart' (Tinbergen, 1974, p. 21). It appears that researchers are so struck by dramatic differences between ordinary behaviour and autistic behaviour that they fail to see the need to pause and carefully study and articulate the differences. This can be done only by establishing a well-observed and thoroughly understood baseline of normal behaviour to relate to the autistic behaviour. Lacking such a baseline researchers proceed much like the non-scientist; they make use of analogy, but the analogy is intuitive and unexamined.

Behaviour can appear striking and strange only if it differs in some way from commonplace behaviour. Non-scientists and some researchers often are content simply to state the fact of difference. Everyday language provides a rich catalogue of descriptive terms ranging from 'uncommon' and 'puzzling' to 'shocking', 'weird', and 'bizarre'; from 'wrong' to 'immoral' and 'evil'. An important part of scientific practice is to move from the largely intuitive understanding expressed by such words to a careful and explicit use of analogy so that we can discover wherein seeming differences lie. The purpose of this paper is to suggest some extensions of the use of analogy in social psychological research.

CONTROL GROUPS

Social psychologists ordinarily study variations in the behaviour of groups of people produced by experimental manipulations or treatments called independent variables. The effects of such manipulations are revealed by comparing groups who receive experimental treatments to one or more control groups. The common experimental control group, since nothing special is done to it, seems to have the status of a naturalistic behavioural sample. As such it can provide 'the norm from which the variants depart', and thereby serve as the better understood of the two entities of processes in an analogy. At its best the control group furnishes a sample of how a representative group of people behave in a particular, well-understood context, and thus throws into sharp relief the action of the deliberately manipulated independent variables.

Though an example of a rather modest use of analogy, control groups rarely fulfil their full analogic function. One obvious shortcoming lies in the fact that they are seldom a good *sample* in the sense that it is difficult to determine what, if any, larger population the group represents. Exigencies of experimentation usually prevent the control group from being a random or otherwise representative sample of a clearly defined population. The same of course is true of the experimental groups. The lack of a clear relationship to a larger population is one of several factors which make generalization difficult and often dubious. Although the problem is well known to experimentalists it does not always succeed in dampening their zest for making general statements.

If control groups can be poor behavioural samples because the sampling is faulty, at times they also can be faulted because the behaviours and situational contexts which they purport to sample are unclear. The situational context and the behaviour sampled must be well understood for the control group to fulfil its analogic function. The fact that the situational context and behaviour in control groups is sometimes puzzling may be due to a simple failure to see a necessity for clarity. What I mean by 'puzzling' and 'unclear' is that sometimes the nature of the situation and the meaning of the behaviours are not self-evident and need explanation. The explanation cannot come from the theories being tested, for social psychological theories are usually designed to account for the behaviour of the experimental groups, not control groups. In order to fulfil the analogic potential of control groups, what occurs and the situational context in which it occurs must be perfectly clear and entirely non-problematic. How this is to be done is another matter. It depends certainly both on type of experiment and on particular problems connected with specific experimental contexts. The improvement of control groups appears to offer no insoluble difficulties, but it does require that investigators recognize and take seriously the analogic function of such groups.

RANDOM MODELS

Models of random events are by far the most universally employed models in social psychological research. And random models are excellent examples of a well-understood half of an analogy. In fact, I know of no other sort of model on which so much careful attention has been lavished. The literature on random models is voluminous and the mathematical sophistication possible is truly impressive. If other sorts of models were half so well understood there would be no occasion for this paper.

Unfortunately, I suspect that the triumph of random models leads to uncritical use—that the resolve to employ a random model in many cases is not a decision but a reflex. Lancelot Hogben has commented regarding another discipline: 'We get the impression that recourse to statistical methods is prerequisite to the design of experiments of any sort whatever. In that event, the whole creation of experimental scientists from Gilbert and Hooke to J. J. Thomson and Morgan has been groaning and travailing in fruitless pain altogether; and the biologist of today has nothing to learn from well-tried methods which have led to spectacular advances of the last three centuries' (n.d., p. 29). Of course not all psychologists find models of random events relevant to their research interests. Radical behaviourists, for example, have developed a notable research repertory founded for the most part on behavioural baseline, not random, models. Also, a number of interests in social psychology seem unlikely candidates for illumination by random models. For instance, faced with the task of understanding anomalies in conduct governed by roles and rules, an investigator would find a model of random events of little help, but a properly constructed role/rule model would be an essential first step toward comprehension.

PUZZLING AND SHOCKING CONDUCT

Conduct governed by roles and rules can be distinguished from other sorts of behaviour in a number of ways. One simple test is that it has moral content; people are willing to say of an action that it is right or wrong, bad or good. Even in an age many believe excessively permissive, people make moral judgments as a matter of course. Judgments can be personal (I should or should not have done something) or social (he or she should or should not have done something). Such statements can refer to past, present, or future actions and can range from matter of fact comment to cries of outrage and horror. Whenever we make moral judgments we hold either implicitly or explicitly a model of right or proper conduct, for how else can we know an act is good or bad? Social scientists also make moral judgments, but—at least in their professional capacity—not very often. In social psychology such judgments are fairly rare, due partly to a prevailing notion that value judgments are extra-scientific. I am not alone in thinking (cf. Dewey, 1922; Scriven, 1974) that value judgments can be made in a scientific fashion, that indeed a science of morals is not only possible, but of singular importance. However, this paper is not an argument for a science of morals; it is rather an account of how, when social psychologists feel obliged to make moral judgments, such judgments can be given some scientific substance by making the models on which the judgments are based explicit and the relationship between model and behavioural sample clear.

Most of the time we do not make moral judgments about the behaviour of participants in experiments. In fact the form of social psychological research is such that moral judgments are difficult to make even were we so inclined. Studies ordinarily deal with groups of people doing things that have little or no moral content. It would sound quite strange to say 'group X was immoral to change its mean attitude $+0.5$ points after a persuasive communication'. Another factor may inhibit moral statements. Strictly speaking a moral judgment is apropos only regarding 'activity into which alternative possibilities enter' (Dewey, 1922, p. 257). Many popular views of determinism deny possibility. In an effort to be consistent scholars who hold such views may inhibit moral comment, for it would hardly do to call a person's action either 'immoral' or 'good' if the person could not possibly do otherwise.

Though inhibitions are strong, the temptation to offer moral comment sometimes cannot be resisted, and moral judgments do crop up in the experimental literature. The experimenter is not in every case the one to make the judgment, but moral evaluation becomes part of the context in which experiments are discussed. For example, it is often assumed that a participant *should* refuse to conform in a conformity study, *should* disobey in an obedience study, *should* help in a bystander intervention study. It is quite proper and necessary to make such judgments, and social psychologists should study behaviour with moral content; *but* the models on which we base our judgments must be overt and so carefully constructed that the basis for the judgment is clear enough to be challengeable. Unless we do so our judgment has no more (or no less) warrant than common everyday comments. Today warrant is lacking because ordinary experimental procedures cannot tell us why a participant should not conform, should not obey, should help.

In order to claim a person should not conform in a particular situation we must refer to some model of how one should behave; models are similarly necessary to make claims that a person should refuse to obey or should help in certain contexts. Such models ordinarily are not built into experiments, but are held implicitly by experimentalists. The usual control group or baseline tells us only how people behave, not how they should behave. Models of proper conduct are based on social rules. When, where, and how we conform, obey, or help is governed by rules that are specific to the roles we perform. Such rules do not demand that *some* of the people in particular roles and in specified contexts should conform, obey, help; they specify that *all* people in particular roles and contexts should conform, obey, help. When people fail to do so as we consciously or unconsciously expect them to, when they appear to break a rule, reactions can range from puzzlement, to annoyance, to shock, to outrage—or, on occasion, to smiles, laughter, applause, and cheers. When someone breaks or appears to break a rule, people usually want to know why. Any experiment in which people do not behave as we think they should demands careful explanation. Behaviour governed by roles and rules is non-problematic only when people do as they are supposed to do.

It might be argued that the fact that experimental participants fail to behave as they should is *not* puzzling and does not require special explanation. After all, most of us all too frequently fail to do what we should do. Often our failure is so total that we do not even realize what we should do until after the occasion has passed. And while we may flog ourselves for our failure, the fact of failure remains. People who appear to behave badly in experiments may be examples of this common human phenomenon. The line of reasoning is compelling, indeed so persuasive that it can obscure the need to look further. What can be clearer than the fact that there is often a great gap between what we think we should do and what we do, between what we wish to do and what we can do? The gap between wish and execution seems the obvious explanation; but before accepting it an alternative interpretation must be eliminated.

Suppose that the experimenter and those who read the experimental report are wrong, that it is not clear what one should do in the experimental situation, that for reasons that are not apparent there is room for disagreement concerning the proper way to behave. How could this be? Quite simply the behaviour occurring in the experimental situation may not be an example of the sort of behaviour condemned by the rule or model of right conduct held by experimenter and reader. In order to demonstrate what I mean, suppose that the rule informing our judgment of participant conduct in an obedience experiment goes something like: 'A person should not obey a command to seriously harm another'. It is obvious that not all commands are examples of such a rule. No matter how compelling the appearances we should look into whether or not the particular command in the experimental context is an example of the verbal rule. But how could a command that looks like an example of the rule fail to be one? In some cases in social life it is self-evident when an action in a situation is an example of a rule. In others it is not. Many common social situations are filled with ambiguity and an agreed-upon definition may be difficult or even impossible. There are peculiar reasons why the definition of an experimental situation may be uncertain. One reason is connected to the fact that the experimental situation is a very special one in which actions often take on meanings other than the 'same' actions in other contexts. For example, Orne and Evans (1965) found that throwing acid in a person's face has a radically different meaning (because of assumed safeguards) in an experimental context than it has in ordinary circumstances. A second reason attaches to those experimental situations that are a product of complex deceptions. When an action is assumed to be wrong in a deception experiment it is wrong because its wrongness follows from the experimenter's definition of the experimental situation. But the experimenter defines the situation for himself and his readers in a different fashion than he defines it for participants. This in fact is the heart of the deception manoeuvre. It is thought, for example, that one cannot tell participants that pushing a shock lever is an act of destructive obedience; it must be defined as a routine part of a learning experiment. To become morally wrong the routine part of a learning experiment must be clearly transformed by the experimental scenario into an act of destructive obedience. Readers of deception experiments generally assume that such a transformation takes place. The assumption may be wrong.

Consider the fact that in Milgram's basic obedience experiment (1963) he was outvoted. Milgram was certain that the right thing to do in the context was to defy the experimenter, yet sixty-five per cent of his participants by their actions voted for obedience. In terms of what most people did, the conduct of twenty-five of the forty people sample indicated the rule governing the scene was 'obey'. If the conduct of sixty-five per cent of Milgram's subjects declares obedience appropriate why do we take his word rather than their actions? Well, for one thing the written and filmed accounts are very powerful. The agonized involvement of participants is so dramatically compelling as to seem to permit no other explanation. But the very fact that appearances are so unusually dramatic is reason enough to look closely at how the scene was produced.

ROLES, RULES, AND MODELS

It has become apparent in recent years that if we are to comprehend social behaviour we must understand rule-governed conduct. One of the several ways the term 'rule-governed' is used refers to the fact that a large part of social life appears sufficiently regular to be described by brief verbal prescriptions or rules. For example, when someone offers a hand to shake, shake it. The regularity can be due to people consciously following such rules or can be a customary practice so habitual as to be automatic. The term 'role' is sometimes added to 'rule-governed' to emphasize the fact that social rules are role and situation specific. For example, although general rules of great antiquity and the Highest Authority (Thou shalt not kill, for example) can be pointed to, people have devised enough ingenious exceptions to general rules to make even 'Thou shalt not kill' role and situation-specific (for example, Thou shalt not kill unless ordered to in certain circumstances by a superior officer).

An empirical study of rule-governed conduct always involves translation: a concrete situation must translate accurately into a brief prescription or rule; a rule must translate accurately into a concrete situation. The general rule 'Do not harm another' might be made into the role-specific rule 'Do not as subject obey an experimental command to harm another'. Once made role-specific the rule must translate into the concrete detail of a particular experimental situation. Such translations, like any translation, can be well or poorly done. An intermediate operation also needs to be taken into account. We frequently judge situations on the basis of descriptions. In other words, we do not actually see the scene ourselves, but must rely on a descriptive account of what occurred. All description is, of course, selective and what is selected depends upon interpretation. If the person describing a scene has decided that the scene is an example of a particular rule, the description will reflect that fact.

Descriptive translations are a primary source of information concerning rule transgressions. Newspaper and magazine accounts of alleged rule transgressions may shock and puzzle, but with sufficient exposure take on an inevitable regularity of their own. We read of so many individuals allegedly breaking similar rules that we not only come to expect a daily diet of rule transgressions, but see the transgressions themselves in role terms—embezzlers, confidence men, rapists, robbers. Interestingly enough some of the most shocking and puzzling descriptions of social conduct are found not in the daily newspaper but in the experimental literature (Milgram, 1963; Orne and Evans, 1965; Haney, Banks and Zimbardo, 1973). One reason apparent rule transgression in an experimental context has power to shock is that an experimenter can so standardize a situation that we read of person after person apparently breaking the same rule in the same context. This is particularly perplexing because people in experiments behave in full view of the experimenter and are presumably on their best behaviour. Why when so exposed do they break the rule? And if most of them break the rule that we think should govern the situation, what do we make of the rule that in terms of empirical regularity apparently does govern the situation?

MILGRAM'S OBEDIENCE STUDIES

One of the best-known series of experiments in the social psychological literature was also notably shocking. I refer to Stanley Milgram's obedience studies. While most commentators find the studies shocking, they have not been sufficiently puzzled by them. The fact that sixty-five per cent of Milgram's subjects apparently broke an important social rule not to harm others is indeed puzzling. Part of the force of the study comes from the fact that the rule in terms of what participants did (regularity) is in sharp contrast to the rule people thought should govern the situation. I propose to methodically examine Milgram's study. By applying analogical principles, by paying careful attention to the problem of translating scenes into empirical models, I hope to show how puzzles concerning conduct governed by roles and rules can be resolved. The method demonstrated can be used both to reanalyse experiments involving social rules and as a coherent means of studying social conduct. In earlier efforts to work out problems connected with this type of analysis I called the general method the 'all-and-none' procedure (Mixon, 1972, 1974, 1976).

Since Milgram's research has been widely discussed, the studies reprinted in more than one hundred books of readings, and a two-hour fictionalized account shown on national television, I probably need not remind many readers why people were shocked by his results. In the context of attempting to understand why Nazi orders to slaughter millions of innocent people in the Second World War were obeyed, Milgram created what he took to be a laboratory analogy. Experimental subjects were ordered to administer what appeared to be seriously harmful shocks to another person. Milgram and his readers were horrified when substantial proportions of subjects obeyed.

The form of Milgram's series of experiments is important to this discussion. Milgram began by creating an experimental situation that served as a baseline for three further experiments. In other words, rather than the usual practice of establishing a control group or baseline and doing variations in a single experiment, the first study (Milgram, 1963) served as baseline and the three experiments that followed had the status of experimental variations. He then created a new baseline situation and thirteen further experiments were variations on the second baseline (Milgram, 1974). In Milgram's first baseline situation (later called the 'remote' condition), the only feedback from the 'victim' that indicated harm was the sound of pounding on the wall after a 300 volt shock followed by no further responses on the learning task. The second baseline is the scene familiar to those who have viewed Milgram's film. Feedback from the victim was vocal. Protest began with groans at the 75 volt shock and became increasingly agonizing and frantic as the shocks increased in intensity. Percentage of obedient subjects was the same in each 'baseline'—sixty-five per cent or twenty-six or forty subjects. I put 'baseline' in quotation marks because neither situation can serve as a baseline in the sense of being the half of an analogy that is well understood. Far from comprehensible, the behaviour of subjects in both 'baselines' is shocking and puzzling, not understood at all. Such 'baselines' can scarcely be expected to throw much light on experimental variations.

I shall examine Milgram's first (1963) 'baseline', hereafter referred to as his basic scene. The basic scene involved two actors and one naive subject. One male actor played the part of 'experimenter', the other, also male, the 'learner' in a learning experiment. The naive subject (male, except in one experiment) was led to believe he was taking part in an experiment designed to assess the effects of punishment on learning. By a rigged drawing each naive subject became the teacher in the pretend learning experiment. His experimental task was to administer a memory test involving word pairs to the learner who was strapped to an electric shock apparatus in another room. If the learner gave a wrong answer (communication was electronic) the experimental procedure required the teacher to administer an electric shock; further wrong answers were to be punished by increasing the amount of shock by 15 volts each time a mistake was made. The shock generator had a horizontal row of thirty switches with a separate switch for each shock level beginning with 15 volts and increasing in 15 volt steps to 450 volts. Verbal warning labels were inscribed on the generator to give specific meaning to the voltage—from 'Slight Shock' at the 15 volt end to 'XXX' at the 450 volt end. The memory test was to continue until the learner gave the correct answer to all word pairs. The actor playing the learner gave a standardized sequence of wrong answers, but after receiving the 300 volt shock and pounding on the wall ceased giving any answers at all. If the teacher asked questions or protested going on with the learning experiment the actor playing the experimenter had a set of contingent responses, including: 'If there appears to be no answer from the learner, then wait for five or ten seconds. If there is still no answer, then treat the absence of a response as a wrong answer and follow the usual punishment procedure, increasing the shock level each time the learner fails to respond correctly'. A teacher was judged obedient if he continued with the learning experiment to the final 450 volt lever of the shock generator; he was judged defiant if he refused to continue at any point prior to the 450 volt level.

I have gone into particulars because the details of a scene give it its meaning and because of special translation problems connected with deception studies. Because Milgram's study is usually interpreted in terms of his 'real' experiment it is particularly important to have a clear picture of the pretend learning experiment. The teacher of course was not involved in a learning experiment at all. The experimenter and learner were actors, the shock generator only a realistic stage prop. But if the deceits were successful and naive subjects believed they were involved in a learning experiment, then their actions must be judged within the context of the learning experiment. Milgram and his readers assumed that obeying commands to give increasingly severe shocks to a learner in a learning experiment was an example of obeying a command to seriously harm another. I take that assumption to be problematic and will demonstrate a method of determining if the learning experiment is in fact a good translation of a rule enjoining a person to disobey experimenter orders to harm another in an experimental context.

How do we determine if a situation is a good translation of a particular rule? An experimenter might look carefully at the situation and state or claim that it is, but such authoritative statements are rightly met with scepticism. A better means is to translate the concrete situation into a description of the situation and then ask people about the description. Milgram did something of the sort in the course of his study. As a means of determining 'expectations' concerning his experimental scene Milgram translated the scene into a description and presented the description to various groups of people. 'The experiment is described in detail without, however, disclosing the results in any way. The audience is provided with a schematic diagram of the shock generator, showing verbal and voltage designations. Each respondent is asked to reflect on the experiment, then privately to record how he himself would perform in it' (Milgram, 1974, p. 27). If all of the 'respondents' give much the same answer we can assume that the situation described is governed by a rule. The answer they give will tell us what the rule is. Milgram reports that each of one hundred and ten judges (thirty-nine psychiatrists, thirty-one college students, and forty middle-class adults) sees himself disobeying the experimenter at some point. Given such unanimity and regularity it seems correct to infer that the one hundred and ten judges saw the scene described as being an example of a verbal prescription or rule such as 'refuse to obey an experimenter's command to seriously harm another person'. But the fact that the scene *described* is an example of a particular rule does not mean that the scene itself is an example of the same rule. A description can fail to represent a scene. Since Milgram kept no record of the words used to describe the scene* we cannot directly assess the content of his verbal model. The best we can do is to make inferences about the nature of his description after examining some problems connected with verbal models.

---

* Personal communication from S. Milgram, 23 November 1970.

Because the unanimous results connected with Milgram's description imply the existence of a rule, the verbal model could serve as an analogic baseline. Apparently, albeit unconsciously and implicitly, it has served that function. That is, if Milgram's experimental situation is in fact an example of the rule 'refuse to obey an experimenter's command to seriously harm another', the conduct of obedient subjects can be understood as transgressions of that rule. This is precisely how the experiments have been interpreted. Milgram has taken the results of his verbal model as supporting the assumption that his experimental situation does involve commands to do serious harm, and has taken the discrepancy between what people say they would do on the basis of description and what people do in the experiments as evidence of the power of the situation to make people behave badly. The presumed discrepancy gives the study much of its drama and power. His experiments appear to be examples of situations in which people behave badly in spite of themselves.

I think it is clear that Milgram's verbal model—his written description of the experimental scene—functioned as an implicit baseline. However, I shall show that it is not a proper baseline because in all likehood it described not just the learning experiment, but the 'real' experiment as well.

VERBAL MODELS

Models can be constructed in various ways. At times—the Inter-Nation Simulation, for example—people are the model's primary components. Electronic components are the basic stuff of computer models. Still other models involve an interaction between human participants and a computer. But whatever its components, the purpose of a model is to construct something that in particular aspects is like something else, hoping that by understanding our construction we can come to understand that which we modelled. The components of a verbal model are words selected to stand for concrete events.

Models must be tested. If I make a model of a flying machine I cannot simply claim that my small-scale model has incorporated all of the flying characteristics of the object modelled. I must test it in some medium capable exhibiting its flying properties. A verbal model must also be tested in an appropriate medium. So if the claim is that the verbal model is a translation that incorporates the essential properties of a particular rule-governed situation it must be tested in a medium capable of examining the claim—in this case the judgments of people.

Though called something else, verbal models are not unknown to social psychology. Daryl Bem (1967) made extensive use of a particular sort of verbal model in his controversy with cognitive dissonance theorists. Some of the early attempts to find a 'role-playing' alternative to deception studies in fact were verbal descriptions and as such were more or less successful attempts to construct a verbal model of a deception experiment. The status of such verbal descriptions, because of claims of equivalency to deception experiments, has aroused considerable controversy (Freedman, 1969; Miller, 1972). By conceiving of the descriptions as models their status becomes clear: verbal models have the status of any other model. The resemblance of the model to the thing modelled is contingent. A model is never identical to the thing modelled or it would cease being a model and become the thing itself. However, the mark of a good model is that it will simulate accurately whatever it is it was designed to simulate. The problem comes in distinguishing good models from bad. The discussion that follows suggests criteria for identifying good verbal models of moral conduct.

In assessing a verbal model two criteria are important. The first is that the model's relationship to the thing modelled must be clear. The second criterion concerns the necessity for identifying in some fashion what it is about the description that affects and informs the judgments of the people testing it. Critics can judge success in meeting the first criterion only if the model is available for inspection. This is especially important because a scene can be described in one thousand and one ways. One way of meeting the second criterion is to test a series of closely related models in such a way that the judgments of the testers will point to what informs their judgment. The examples that follow are intended to demonstrate how the criteria can be met.

MODELLING MILGRAM'S BASIC SCENE

Only if Milgram's verbal model is an accurate representation of his mock learning experiment can it serve as an analogic baseline for interpreting experimental variations. Since his model is unavailable, one way of making inferences about its accuracy is to make new models and see if they are judged in the same way. The verbal models I shall describe were part of a larger project designed to answer a number of questions about role-playing methods (Mixon, 1971, 1972).

Before attempting verbal models I worked with a model of another sort—an active role-playing or acting model. For the acting model I obtained a script of Milgram's study containing all the words of the actor/experimenter, the memory test, the programme of wrong answers, the contingent responses, etc. By playing both experimenter and learner in forty tests of the acting model I became thoroughly familiar with the script and experimental routine. Faced with the problem of writing a verbal model I was struck with the difficulty of describing the experiment without revealing to judges what Milgram took such pains to hide from his subjects. Recall that Milgram was very careful to keep his subjects from suspecting that he was interested in destructive obedience. Subjects were led to believe they were taking part in a learning experiment; it was assumed that if they suspected it was a study of destructive obedience similar to that which permitted horrors in Nazi Germany they would defy the experimenter. Since Milgram constructed the pretend learning experiment solely to keep subjects from discovering his true interests, an accurate model of the learning experiment must be equally successful in keeping judges ignorant of his interests. I suspected that the reason Milgram's verbal description produced unanimous judgments of defiance is that he failed to hide the purpose of his study and in effect described both the mock learning experiment and the 'real' experiment. One reason for my suspicion was that I found that great care is needed to keep from revealing Milgram's definition of the situation. Even if you carefully describe the learning experiment up to the point of pounding on the wall and then ask 'What would you do?' or 'What would he do?', violence is done to the situation as experienced by naive subjects. This is because there was no point in the learning experiment at which there was any question concerning what to do. The experimenter always behaved as if the situation were normal and would continue in a routine fashion. The best I could do to keep from suggesting that the teacher has a choice was to stop my description at the time of the pounding and as, 'Can you at this point describe the rest of the experiment for me?'

Each of the eight verbal models was tested by reading the description to ten male students, one at a time. Each participant was told that he would hear an account of an experiment that had been performed many times at other universities, that the reading would end before the experiment was complete, and that he would be asked to describe the rest of the experiment. At appropriate times during the reading the participant was handed the materials necessary (shock generator diagram, word lists, instructions) to understand the experimental routine. The account of the learning experiment ended just after the sound of pounding occurred.

I based the first model (DM-1) on the acting model script, but used an abbreviated version which I thought would provide judges with an adequate picture of the experimental episode. Script DM-1 contained full details of the general instructions to subjects, but only a short description of the task instructions to the teacher and even briefer reference to the events in the learning experiment. When the model was tested four out of ten participants judged that the teacher would follow experimental procedure and continue administering shocks to the end of the shock generator (450 volts, XXX). In striking contrast to Milgram's description, script DM-1 produced contradictory judgments. Since it appeared possible to describe the mock learning experiment without revealing the actual experiment, I decided to try more models in order to see how additional detail and varied emphasis would affect the conclusions of judges.

In case the instructions to the teacher in the first script had been too brief to be fully comprehended, I added full and detailed teacher task instructions to DM-1 in order to produce script DM-2. Judges listening to DM-2 heard as much detail concerning general instructions and teacher task instructions as Milgram's deceived subjects had heard. However, the actual events of the learning experiment were only briefly described as in the first script. Five out of ten judges thought the teached obeyed.

A detailed, step-by-step account of the events in the learning experiment constituted the major change that distinguishes the third script, DM-3. Included in the description was the duration of each shock administered by the teacher. Emphasis was placed on the fact that the length of each shock was at the teacher's discretion. Teacher control of duration gives the learning experiments its rationale, because without such control the procedure is so automatic that a teacher is superfluous. Eight out of ten judges said the teacher obeyed.

Script DM-3 had emphasized the control the teacher exercises over shock *duration* at the expense of *level* or amount of voltage over which the teacher has no control. One more bit of detail was added to the script in order to change the emphasis. In script DM-4 each time the teacher administered a shock the voltage level was mentioned, always 15 volts greater than the previous shock. This was done in order to give greater prominence to the inevitable progression of voltage increase built into the experimental design. Five out of ten judges thought the teacher would be obedient. Since there were no further details or change of emphasis that interested me, I decided to use script DM-4, the most detailed of the four scripts, as my verbal model (basic script) of Milgram's basic scene.

The four verbal models demonstrate a number of points. First and most obviously they show that verbal descriptions of the learning experiment can produce contradictory judgments. The contradictory judgments suggest that no clear social rule governs the experimental situation in question. The fact that Milgram's description got unanimous, not contradictory, results is an indication that his description may have revealed his definition of the situation, for once it is known that an experiment is assessing destructive obedience, it is quite clear that everyone should defy it. That *judges* could not agree on how the experiment ended strongly suggests that Milgram's subjects were not simply swept away by the power of the situation and forced to behave badly. The judges were not in the situation; they were merely assessing it.

The next move toward improving our understanding of why some people in Milgram's basic scene obeyed and some defied is to construct two analogic baselines: *two* baselines because the behaviour in the experiment was dichotomous. Needed is one obedience baseline and one defiance baseline. Each baseline situation should be as close to the basic scene as possible but embody a rule that produces obedience in the first case, defiance in the second. By the time I came to construct the baselines I had questioned forty people who took part in the acting model and forty more who served as judges of the first four scripts. With their help I identified a number of sharply conflicting cues in Milgram's experiment. The means I chose to produce the baseline models was to systematically make the cues less conflicting.

OBEDIENCE BASELINE

I did not in fact need to construct a model of unanimous obedience, for Milgram had already provided a baseline. In a pilot study he found that 'virtually all subjects, once commanded, went blithely to the end of the board, seemingly indifferent to the verbal designations ('Extreme Shock' and 'Danger: Severe Shock')' (Milgram, 1965, p. 61). The single difference between the pilot study and the basic scene is that the pilot study had no feedback from the learner suggesting harm. The learner in the pilot study did not pound on the wall after the 300 volt shock nor did he cease responding to the memory test. Although not meant to be a model, the unanimity Milgram found in his pilot study makes it an adequate obedience baseline from which to judge his basic scene.

I have claimed that when everyone follows a rule a scene is non-problematic. What sort of rule might Milgram's subjects have been following in the pilot study that makes their behaviour understandable? At the time Milgram conducted the pilot study the rule probably was not apparent, for research still in progress in the early 1960s (Orne, 1962; Rosenthal, 1963) was just beginning to reveal the roles and rules of the psychological experiment. The work of Martin Orne is especially relevant to the study of obedience, for much of his research represents an unsuccessful quest for an experimental task subjects will refuse to perform. From boring and repetitious tasks to apparently vicious acts—nothing Orne attempted elicited refusal. In an experiment close in subject to Milgram's, Orne and Evans (1965) found that virtually all subjects would obey an experimenter's command to throw a flask of fuming nitric acid in the face of an assistant. When asked why they were willing to engage in such a repugnant act subjects answered that they assumed that the experiment was conducted by responsible experimenters and that safety precautions had been installed to protect the assistant. Briefly, from the range of work done on the social psychology of the psychological experiment we know that for many years now people have been making a number of (correct) assumptions about the experimental context—in particular that things are not always what they appear to be and that safety precautions protect participants from harm. Because of these assumptions almost any conceivable experimental command will appear legitimate, giving a curious twist to the rule that appears to govern the experimental context: 'Obey legitimate commands'. Though the seeming indifference of Milgram's pilot subjects to the verbal warnings on the shock generator might have surprised him in the early 1960s, today the behaviour is perfectly understandable. Pilot subjects were given no indication that the generator would do what the labels suggest or that safety precautions were not in place.

Although I could have used the pilot study as an obedience baseline I was curious about one thing. When Milgram added feedback to his pilot study he produced the contradictory behaviour of his basic scene. The feedback gave new meaning to the events in the study and to such components as the verbal warnings on the shock generator. The feedback suggested that the consequences of the shock might in fact be what the warnings suggest. I was curious to see how far this might work in reverse and decided to use the basic script with feedback but remove the verbal warnings from the diagram of the shock generator handed to judges. In other words, how powerful is the feedback without verbal warning labels to give the pounding and silence a particular meaning? Condition DM-5 used the basic script (DM-4) and a shock generator diagram with all the verbal warnings removed. Nine out of ten judges concluded that the teacher would continue giving shocks to the end of the board.

DEFIANCE BASELINE

Three attempts were needed to establish a defiance baseline. Each script introduced only slight modifications because I wanted to reach unanimous defiance with as little change in the basic script as possible. Before describing the changes in each model it is necessary to give an account of why I made the sort of changes I did.

The obedience baseline (Milgram's pilot) is an example of how experimenter commands are assumed legitimate even when apparently destructive or antisocial. Milgram produced defiant behaviour by introducing a novel sort of feedback from the learner: pounding on the wall followed by no further response or sign of life. This reaction on the part of the learner in effect strongly challenges the notion that safeguards to protect subjects from harm are functioning. It certainly appeared that the learner was hurt and the complete lack of response suggests he might be unconscious or even dead. Given the apparent situation why did only fourteen out of forty subjects defy the now certainly illegitimate commands to continue?

When I questioned the forty people who took part in the acting model of the basic scene and the fifty people who acted as judges of the first five scripts, most of them were puzzled or struck by the behaviour of the experimenter. Why, when it appears that the learner may be seriously hurt or even dead, does the experimenter show no concern? Why does he claim 'Although the shocks may be painful, there is no permanent tissue damage, so please go on'? How can he *know*, without even moving from his chair to check, that the learner is unharmed? Such questions point to sharply conflicting cues in the experimental scenario. While labels on the shock generator ('Danger: Severe Shock'; 'XXX') clearly indicate serious consequences, while the pounding followed by ominous silence suggests terrible consequences, the experimenter, just as clearly, contradicts such an interpretation. Both with words and non-verbally the experimenter calmly indicates that the learner has not suffered and cannot suffer harm. Pain, yes. Pain was part of the experimental contract. But harm? Of course not.

The conflicting cues in the experimental situation can explain why many participants in both my acting model and Milgram's basic scene showed such marked distress. They found themselves in circumstances profoundly mystifying and disturbing. Their extreme emotional reactions were not due to the certain knowledge that they were inflicting serious harm, but to the fact that they could not be certain. The evidence of their senses told them they were, but background expectations and the expert responsible for the wellbeing of participants told them they were not. A more complete account of the conflicting cues can be found in an earlier paper (Mixon, 1972).

Stated simply, given the dramatic indication of serious harm occurring in the midst of an experiment, the experimenter behaved in a curiously implausible fashion. He failed to behave as if the shocks were, or even could be, harmful. In terms of scenario construction, the shocks will appear incontrovertibly harmful only if the experimenter behaves as if they are. Better playwrighting is the clue to producing a defiance baseline: the experimenter must react in a more believable fashion to the indications of harm. He could do this, of course, in a number of ways. I chose to try first to have the experimenter react as subtly as possible to the feedback on the assumption that the less change needed in the basic script to produce a defiance model, the more strongly supported is my interpretation.

Script DM-6 was produced by making two small changes in the basic script. The experimenter was described in the basic script as being 'open, assured and firm'; script DM-6 describes him as 'competent but a bit cold'. The second change involved the description of the experimenter's behaviour after the pounding occurred. Instead of being calm and confident, the experimenter was described as 'surprised and a bit worried and agitated' and 'decidedly worried'. Two out of ten judges thought the teacher would be obedient in these circumstances.

The experimenter in script DM-6, despite being 'worried and agitated', continued to use the standard experimental prod 'Although the shocks may be painful, there is no permanent tissue damage, so please go on!' In order to remove that bit of inconsistency the experimenter in script DM-7 was made to appear nervously indifferent to the learner's well-being. When asked by the teacher if it were possible that the learner had suffered physical injury, the experimenter is made to reply: 'The learner's health is irrelevant. Experimental procedure requires that you treat the absence of a response as a wrong answer and continue as directed. Please go on!' Only one out of ten judges though the teacher would be obedient.

I had thought that cues were consistent enough for script DM-7 to become my defiance baseline. The single judge who said the teacher would obey pointed to a remaining inconsistency. When the experimenter strapped him in the electric chair 'he assured the learner that although the shocks could be painful, they would not cause any permanent damage or injury'. The judge remembered that assurance and gave it more weight than all of the contradictory evidence which followed. Script DM-8 was exactly the same as DM-7 except that the sentence containing the experimenter's assurances was removed. None of the ten people judging script DM-8 thought that the teacher would obey. I had a defiance baseline, a second model of regular, understandable behaviour.

How is the regular behaviour exhibited in the defiance baseline to be understood? Pain is a legitimate part of many experiments. But whereas pain is legitimate, harm is not. No one in an experimental context has the right to harm a subject or to order harm done to a subject. So long as it was possible to believe that the shocks involved pain but not harm some subjects continued to see the experimenter's commands as legitimate. Script DM-8 was designed to make it clear that the experimenter believed the learner might be harmed. Once he appeared to believe harm might occur his commands to continue giving shocks became clearly illegitimate. Judges appear to believe that participants will follow the rule: 'Defy illegitimate commands'. While it is not surprising that people will defy illegitimate commands, it is disconcerting to find how much care must be taken to make a command clearly illegitimate.

The defiance and obedience baselines are scenes very similar, very closely related to the basic script (and, of course, to Milgram's basic scene). A brief description of the three scripts might be descriptions of the same scene. They differ little in detail, but the small variations make all the difference in the way people interpret the scenes. The regularity of behaviour in the obedience and defiance models make them good analogic baselines. The conduct in the two scenes is comprehensible and clear and can serve as twin anchors of understanding from which to examine Milgram's basic scene with its shocking and puzzling conduct. Though I claimed earlier that non-problematic models can give warrant to moral judgments, I find myself reluctant to exercise that warrant. Milgram's basic scene was not a good translation of the rule enjoining us not to harm another. Participants were caught up in a deeply ambiguous situation with few clear guidelines. By what *should* a person do in such a situation? They should turn on the experimenter and refuse to cooperate further until he makes clear precisely what is going on. But I hardly can condemn them for failing, because with all our vaunted individualism it seems that in some circumstances we have no rule directing us to defy authorities when the legitimacy of their command is dubious (Mixon, 1972, 1976).

RELATIONSHIP BETWEEN DESCRIPTIONS AND CONCRETE SCENES

One question about the use of verbal descriptions that has troubled various writers is the relationship of the judges' assessments to what would happen if the description were translated into a concrete situation. Would people behave the way judges say they would? No unqualified statement about the relationship can be made. It depends. It depends upon what sort of behaviour is being judged and on the quality of the translations. The answer is in part empirical, just as the question of the precise content of a defiance baseline is in part empirical. It is not sufficient simply to claim that *if* the experimenter's behaviour can be made consistent with the feedback, *then* people will judge defiance. The empirical part involves doing it. Constructing a defiance baseline is a translation problem—how *descriptively* to make the experimenter's conduct consistent with the feedback.

To go from description to a concrete situation is similarly a translation problem—how *behaviourally* to make the experimenter's conduct consistent with the feedback. In other words, there is no way automatically to go from a description to a concrete scene and guarantee the same results—any more than you can guarantee a certain script will get particular results.

Are there any special reasons to think that if script DM-8 were translated into a behavioural baseline all experimental participants would defy the experimenter? Because script DM-4 was a fairly successful verbal model of Milgram's basic scene and script DM-8 is a carefully and only slightly modified version of DM-4 there is a strong presumption that successful translation from a description into an active scene would not prove difficult. But it is presumption only. Unfortunately, at the time I constructed the defiance baseline I did not see the need to attempt the translation.

However, I discovered three years after building the verbal model that someone earlier had done experiments that followed the prescription used for DM-8 and had indeed found unanimous defiance. That someone was none other than Stanley Milgram. The prescription I used to construct the defiance baseline was a simple one: if the experimenter behaves as if *he* believes the shocks are or can be harmful, his commands will appear illegitimate and people will defy him. Such a prescription could be filled in many ways other than the one I chose; that is, the experimenter could indicate his belief in the harmfulness of the shocks in many different ways. In 1974 Milgram published a book that included experiments done in the early 1960s but previously unreported. Three of those experiments—even though they were variations of his second 'baseline'—filled my prescription.

In the first of them (Experiment 12: Learner Demands to be Shocked)

> the experimenter called a halt to the study, stating that the learner's reactions were unusually severe and that, in view of his heart condition, no further shocks should be administered. The learner then cried out that he *wanted* to go on with the experiment, that a friend of his had recently been in the study and had gone to the end and that it would be an affront to his manliness to be discharged from the experiment (Milgram, 1974, p. 91).

There was more give and take between the experimenter and learner. Important in view of my prescription is that throughout the exchange the experimenter behaved as if he believed the shocks might cause harm. None of the twenty subjects serving as teacher continued to give shocks.

Milgram's Experiment 14 (Authority as Victim: An Ordinary Man Commanding) had a complicated plot with the experimenter ending up in the electric chair in order to give a demonstration to the learner of the harmlessness of the shocks. At the 150 volt level the experimenter demands to be released. Again there is considerable dramatic give and take, but the crucial point is that in demanding to be released the experimenter implicitly indicates that higher shocks might harm him. None of twenty subjects continued to administer shocks.

Milgram added a second experimenter to Experiment 15 (Two Authorities: Contradictory Commands). At the 150 volt level, after the learner makes a strong protest, one experimenter tells the teacher to continue the experiment, the other experimenter tells him to stop. In other words, one of two experimenters behaved as if further shocks might cause harm. None of twenty subjects gave shocks beyond the 165 volt level.

The three experiments were the only experiments reported by Milgram that produced unanimous defiance. In each of them he changed his 'baseline' more drastically than I changed my basic script, but each can serve as a behavioural defiance baseline. Thus, the defiance model which I had constructed earlier can be seen as receiving support for its accuracy from some of Milgram's later experimental variations.

UNDERSTANDING PUZZLING AND SHOCKING CONDUCT

Behaviour shocks and puzzles when it fails to conform to some model of right and proper conduct. This paper has argued the necessity of establishing explicit, empirical models of regular conduct to serve as baselines from which to examine the behaviour which shocks. Eight verbal models were described in some detail as an example of a procedure suited to examine shocking and puzzling scenes. The example was rudimentary, the procedure incompletely filled out. As described it lacked symmetry, for two translations were left undone. A behavioural example (Milgram's pilot study) was used for the obedience baseline and a verbal model (DM-8) for the defiance baseline. To give the procedure symmetry and to tackle all of the translation problems, a verbal model of Milgram's pilot and a translation of DM-8 into a behavioural (active role-playing) baseline is needed. Such a step, when successful, would demonstrate how a prescription or rule translates into a verbal description *and* into a concrete scene for both analogic baselines. The more complete the mastery of the translation problems, the more convincingly demonstrated is the claim that the scenes are well understood.

When first reported in the 1960s, the method employed in the obedience studies seemed to offer social psychologists a means of study puzzling and shocking conduct. The method involved establishing a baseline of dramatic, fully involved behaviour, followed by experimental variations of the baseline designed to discover and specify situational conditions that produce obedience and defiance. The method failed to fulfil its promise for two reasons. The first involves the fact that the deceptions used to produce the often agonized involvement touched off a storm of intense moral concern that rightly has inhibited potential imitators. In previous papers (Mixon, 1972, 1976) I have argued and demonstrated that involvement fully equal to that brought about by deception can be produced by active role-playing methods and that such methods can be responsive to moral concerns.

A second reason that the form of research initiated by Milgram has not been taken up by others is that his grasp of the baseline's analogic function was at best intuitive. By failing to develop a means to understand the conduct of people in his baseline scene, he insured an unsound comprehension of the variations on the baseline. The importance of accurately understanding baseline conduct has been a major theme of this paper. Although the discussion has been devoted to problems of concept and method, one result of the suggested procedures —understanding—speaks also to one of the moral questions raised by the obedience studies. At the end of each experimental session Milgram took care to see that subjects were informed about the nature of the experiment. The 'debriefing' included an account of the 'real' definition of the situation and an interpretation of subject conduct. But because their conduct was not understood, their behaviour was carefully explained to them in a way that made what they had just done appear worse than in fact it was: a gratuitous burden for subject, and experimenter. Active role-playing methods, combined with the sort of analogic models described in this paper, offer a possibility of investigating—and understanding—shocking and puzzling conduct.

ACKNOWLEDGMENT

Warm thanks are due to Dennis Byrnes and Gerald Ginsburg for thorough and helpful comments on an earlier draft of this paper.

References

Bem, D. J., 1967, Self-perception: An alternative interpretation of cognitive dissonance phenomena, *Psychological Review*, **74**, 183–200.
Dewey, J., 1922, *Human Nature and Conduct: An Introduction to Social Psychology*, New York: Holt.
Freedman, J. L., 1969, Role playing: Psychology by consensus. *Journal of Personality and Social Psychology*, **13**, 107–114.
Haney, C., Banks, W. C., and Zimbardo, P. G., 1973, Interpersonal dynamics in a simulated prison, *International Journal of Criminology and Penology*, **1**, 69–97.
Harré, R., 1970, *The Principles of Scientific Thinking*, London: Macmillan.
Harré, R., 1972, *The Philosophies of Science*, London: Oxford University Press.
Hogben, L., no date, *Statistical Theory: The Relationship of Probability, Credibility and Error*, New York: Norton.
Milgram, S., 1963, Behavioral study of obedience. *Journal of Abnormal and Social Psychology*, **67**, 371–378.
Milgram, S., 1965, Some conditions of obedience and disobedience to authority. *Human Relations*, **18**, 57–76.
Milgram, S., 1974, *Obedience to Authority*, New York: Harper and Row.
Miller, A. G., 1972, Role playing: An alternative to deception? A review of the evidence, *American Psychologist*, **27**, 623–636.
Mixon, D., 1971, *Further Conditions of Obedience and Disobedience to Authority* (Doctoral dissertation, University of Nevada, Reno) Ann Arbor, Mich.: University Microfilms, No. 72–6477.

Mixon, D., 1972, Instead of deception, *Journal for the Theory of Social Behaviour*, **2**, 145–177.
Mixon, D., 1974, If you won't deceive, what can you do? In N. Armistead (ed.) *Reconstructing Social Psychology*, London: Penguin Education.
Mixon, D., in press, Studying feignable behavior, *Representative Research in Social Psychology*.
Orne, M. T., 1962, On the social psychology of the psychological experiment. With particular reference to demand characteristics and their implications. *American Psychologist*, **17**, 776–783.
Orne, M. T. and Evans, F. J., 1965, Social control in the psychological experiment: Antisocial behavior and hypnosis, *Journal of Personality and Social Psychology*, **1**, 189–200.
Rosenthal, R., 1963, On the social psychology of the psychological experiment: The experimenter's hypothesis as unintended determinant of experimental results, *American Scientist*, **51**, 268–283.
Scriven, M., 1974, The exact role of value judgments in science, in K. F. Schaffner and R. S. Cohen (eds.), *Boston Studies in the Philosophy of Science* (Vol. XX) PSA 1972. Dordrecht, Holland: D. Reidel.
Tinbergen, N., 1974, Ethology and stress diseases, *Science*, **185**, 20–27.

8

AUTOBIOGRAPHY AS A PSYCHOLOGICAL METHOD

J.-P. De Waele and R. Harré

INTRODUCTION

This chapter introduces the assisted autobiography as a psychological method. In it we describe the ways an individual person is assisted by a well-trained team in the production of a document which is a representation of how he views his own life-course, his own knowledge, beliefs, interpretative schemata, and principles of action and judgment. Our method should be distinguished from any form of biography, that is from all forms of accounts of the lives and psychological resources of individual people produced by other people without a working and continuous consultation with the subject of the study. In general, biographies rely upon first person information in the form of documents produced by the subject of the biography but whose interpretation is undertaken by the biographer. The biographer's interpretations usually draw upon a system of concepts which are imposed upon the material rather than drawn out of the living experience of the subject of study and are worked out with respect to the theories of social action of the biographer rather than the object of the biography. An assisted autobiography does not have a subject as such; instead, it is a work of cooperation, an endeavour to reveal the life-conceptions of the central participant.

An autobiography must also be distinguished from a diary. The former is a recollection and interpretation of life-episodes and the author's relation to them. The latter is a record compiled at the time of the incidents recorded, necessarily employing the conceptual resources of the diarist as they were at the time of writing.

Neither the writing of autobiography nor the idea of basing a psychology upon the lifespan of human beings is new. It is the combination of these ideas into a union which radically modifies each that is the innovation to be described in this chapter. Autobiography is transformed through the introduction of the team of trained assistants who work with the participant to create the document that represents his conception of his life. In this way something by way of a true *psyche-logos* is created. On the other hand, the universalistic assumptions of much that has been attempted in 'lifespan' psychology are avoided, since the ethogenic method by which the assisted autobiographical studies are conducted deliberately takes an idiographic form. If there are universal features to the historical development of human lives, they will need to be demonstrated in detail by the comparison of the documents recording individual lives with respect to the various themes upon which their construction has been based.

THE NEGLECT OF THE AUTOBIOGRAPHY AS A PERSONALITY RESEARCH PROCEDURE

An autobiography is an individual's written report of his own life, told in his own manner. Usually, though not always, autobiographies are retrospective accounts formulated at some moment during the life-course. Autobiographical accounts are also basic constituents of self-conceptions and involve some kind of self-presentation. Self-conception as it is investigated by means of other techniques (for example, the 'Who Am I') mostly reflects aspects of the synchronic, or current, structure of the self. But the self-conception as it is investigated by means of the autobiography refers predominantly to the diachronic, or historically developed, aspect of personality. Therefore one can also speak of an 'autobiographical self', which is the individual's conception of his own history. In autobiography, this autobiographical self leads to a more or less pronounced 'self-presentation' which can be made more explicit by concentrating on the participant's various uses of language and reference. Indeed, the accounts embedded in an autobiography appear in the course of an individual's interpretation of his past experiences.

As was suggested by Annis (1967), the type of information provided by the autobiography not only depends upon the kind of instructions given by the investigator, but also upon the instructions the person gives himself in responding to the task, the kind of relationship existing between the investigator and the writer, the institutional situation in which a personal document is being collected, and the degree of motivation and the ability of the individual to divulge information about himself.

> Obviously, the veridicality, personal involvement, and degree of self-disclosure in the autobiography, will be a function of the combination of operative motives. Knowledge of these motives will place the reader in a better position to view the autobiographical communication from the author's frame of reference. If the analyser of the autobiography is oblivious to the motives operating, he is treading on precarious interpretative ground (Annis, 1967).

But, conversely, it can also be asserted that the selected themes of which the autobiography is composed, as well as the structure and the content of the accounts, and the audience to whom it is explicitly or implicitly addressed, provide a direct access to the author's cognitive matrix, which is the organized system for social knowledge and belief upon which he draws in acting and accounting for action, and his system of prevailing motives. Thus, the autobiography is an important source of information, and distinct from such other sources as diaries and biographies.

Still, in spite of its being an important source of information for the study of personality, considered in both synchronic and diachronic perspectives, the autobiography has generally been ignored by psychologists. There are several reasons for this neglect.

The first reason is to be found in misplaced criteria, originating in psychometric theory. Questions of objectivity, reliability and validity have been raised as to the usefulness of autobiographical material. However, the writing of an autobiography can hardly be compared with a psychological test, and the analogy collapses completely as soon as the production and analysis of autobiographies is placed in its proper context, that is the reconstruction of individual conceptions of life-courses. When the task of autobiographical reconstruction is undertaken, the first source to consult is the participant himself by asking him to write his own story. This naive autobiography is the indispensable first step in personality assessment, but it is only the first step. The naive autobiography should not be considered as a goal on its own, but as a means towards biographical reconstruction. As will be described in detail later in this chapter, the naive autobiographical data should be further investigated through a series of specially designed focused interviews (Focused Account Eliciting interviews). The accounts offered by the participant should then be compared with data stemming from other sources (observation, biographical inventory, social enquiry, problem and conflict situations). Among these sources of data, the autobiography distinguishes itself by being centred on the individual person, considered in his historical aspects. However, it is only on condition that the autobiography be integrated with other conceptually homogeneous data, that it is possible to perform the comparisons and checks necessary to establish the meaning of the information it conveys. In this way, the synchronic and diachronic aspects of personality may be brought together.

The value of published autobiographies is often impaired by the absence of supplementary case material which may help to fill some gaps and serve as a check on the authenticity of the story so as to make possible a more adequate interpretation of the experiences and situations described in the documents. However, the validity and value of a personal document is not dependent upon its 'objectivity'. Besides, it is highly desirable that the autobiography should reflect the personal attitudes and interpretations of the participant, for it is just these personal factors which are diagnostically relevant. Consequently, selective emphasis on certain topics, exaggerations, fabrications, self-descriptions and descriptions of others, rationalizations, prejudices, and excuses and justifications, are quite as valuable as objective descriptions, provided of course that these aspects are identified when analysing the personal documents. The participant's view of his life situation is a very important element for interpretation, because any specific act can only become comprehensible in the light of its relation to the sequence and articulation of past experience.

Another reason for the neglect of autobiography is to be found in a lack of interest in the 'whole person', as has been noted by Carlson (1971). Much contemporary research leads to an atomistic, fragmented collection of unrelated facts about personality and fails to integrate the diachronic and synchronic aspects of personality. Longitudinal studies are still scarce. Autobiographies contribute to a holistic sketch of the individual because the understanding of a human being requires the knowledge of his whole life history. In this way the use of autobiographies has considerable advantages toward correcting the weaknesses of contemporary personality research and assessment.

The behaviourist ideology of contemporary research also has had an effect, in that little attention is directed toward subjective reports from 'subjects' about their own interpretations of their existence. As a general consideration relevant to many kinds of research problems, Carlson (1971, p. 215) notes, '. . . it is safe to assume that most subjects are willing to tell us much more than our current research designs ask about their experiences and the personal meanings of these experiences'. The autobiographical approach certainly is a way to get those personal meanings. Moreover, Carlson distinguished the contractual and collaborative models of subject–investigator relationships in current psychological inquiry. The autobiographical method is an example of the collaborative relationship in which the 'subject' is more like a colleague than is true under a contractual relationship, in which the 'subject' is more like an employee. Only the collaborative model involves personal subject–investigator relationships, and is consequently capable of providing valid information about the ways of organizing experience. As a result, the autobiographical method is one that benefits both the investigator and the participant: while the investigator learns about the dynamics and organization of personality, the participant learns about himself.

The autobiographical investigation of the individual's past transcends itself continuously during the process of negotiation of accounts with the participant, in the course of the Focused Account Eliciting (FAE) interviews. Inferences about past events, made by the participant and the investigator, lead to more remembering and to accounts which may be used to amend and modify the earlier constructions, thereby eliciting new memories. Moreover, the individual's past is not a relic carried along from early to later periods in the life-course. Quite the contrary, it is part of the living present, continuously affected by actual and future concerns. The individual's past is differentially forgotten and repressed;

what is remembered of it is inevitably subject to continuous modification. Reconstructions about the past are self-transcendent in the light of new data and viewpoints. Thus, the past not only makes us, but we also make it by putting pieces together into a more or less coherent whole.

Still another reason for the neglect of personal documents is to be found in the problems involved in the analysis of the material. The development of objective tests which could be administered quickly to large groups certainly contributed to a loss of interest in the systematic use of autobiographical data. However, one of the distinctive advantages of the autobiography is that it pictures the continuity of an individual's development, an aspect which is missing in most so-called objective methods.

If the autobiography is not widely used, the reason is not to be found in the fact that it cannot be objectively and reliably analysed or interpreted, nor is it because personal documents have nothing to offer which cannot be obtained as easily by other methods. Instead, the one defensible reason for the infrequent use of autobiography is its high cost if one attempts to go beyond the level of general impressions and tries to analyse and interpret the information in it.

Personal documents are difficult to adapt to research purposes and lend themselves little, if at all, to statistical treatment in their original states. Moreover, it is probable that any method of detailed content analysis of such material tends to destroy the important 'wholeness' of the material. Indeed, most applications of content analysis seem to be inadequate for several reasons. First, coding of isolated units does not take into account either the hierarchical structure of temporal processes or the contextual determinants of the communicated content. Furthermore, the usual forms of content analysis ignore the various uses of language that can be found in autobiographical documents, particularly the expressive and performative uses, which often appear in the guise of statements of fact. In addition, the choice of the categories is usually made by the investigator who imposes—without further interviewing—his own typifications on those of the person studied. In contrast, it is one of the autobiography's specific functions to provide a starting point for making explicit the kind of first-order constructs a person uses as well as the background expectancies which underlie them.

PSYCHOLOGICAL METHOD: GENERAL CONSIDERATIONS

The idea of autobiography as a psychological method is to be located in a general point of view concerning both the methodology of social and personality psychology, and the role of that science in the recording, understanding and improvement of the moral and political basis of society. The autobiographical method as we shall outline it is based upon a complex and mutually respectful relationship between those who assist in the creation of the autobiography and the person whose autobiography is being generated in the process. The person concerned must initiate the process by contributing a naive autobiography, from which the assisted creation can begin. But then, as a permanent participant rather than as a mere subject of study, he is involved as a member of the team which creates the autobiography. Autobiographical construction, then, conceived in our way, belongs in that *genre* of social and personality psychology in which the intelligibility of an episode, or of a life, or a social practice, is derived from the interpretation of the folk who live these lives, and is not imposed in accordance with a prior scheme invented by the investigators.

The shift from the use of concepts imposed upon the form of life to an analysis employing interpretations derived from that life-form itself, has two main consequences. First, it leads to a relation of mutual respect between the participant and the investigators. This relation supports a particular moral and political attitude to psychological investigation of other people, namely one of respect for their integrity and point of view. It involves a reluctance to impose meanings and a refusal to manipulate people as subjects in experiments, although participants certainly may agree to subject themselves to experiences devised by other members of the investigative team (Calder, 1976). Still, great care must be taken to avoid impositions. Seemingly inescapable routine features of the conduct of an investigation can all too easily lead to contempt for people and even to oppressive policies. This progression from apparent practical necessities to political oppression has been thoroughly documented by Johnson (1972) in a detailed review of the procedures of gerontological psychology and their practical consequences.

Second, the maintenance of interpersonal respect in the conduct of an investigation is an important foundation not only for a morally acceptable psychology but also for a truly scientific one. By taking participants' interpretations seriously we avoid the falsification of reality which occurs when self-reports are confined to the replies to questionnaires, etc., which have been devised in advance by the investigator. The language of these instruments incorporates unexamined theories and imposes uncriticized interpretations upon the action. Participants, if allowed to construct their own interpretations, often present a range of meanings and reveal implicit theories sometimes widely at variance with those imposed by the investigators. Furthermore, since they may change from time to time, the use of such concepts serves as a precaution against hidden universalistic assumptions. The existence and implausibility of these assumptions and the deeply misleading role they play has been carefully explored by Gergen (1977).

Recognition of the need for a participatory methodology can also be derived from the realization that human social interaction involves a wide variety of interactive mechanisms. On the one hand there are the processes of automatic adjustment and readjustment which, in the ordinary course of events, can form no representations in consciousness. To understand these interactions only the manipulative experiment is required, as in psychophysics. At the other extreme are those interactions which are mediated by intentions, rules, aims, and the like, where social acts are consciously achieved through the performance of the conventional and appropriate actions. Talk frequently accompanies the latter—talk in which what has happened and what might happen is brought to account and justified or explained in some way or another. Only if the participant is free to talk both as actor and as commentator can his interpretative and explanatory schemata be brought to life.

Most social episodes are neither the result of the operation of automatic mechanism nor the outcome of consciously controlled planning and execution of intentions. They are 'enigmatic'. Based upon the two extremal forms of action-genesis psychologists have developed two main paradigms of research. The experiment is the typical empirical procedure should we take the automatic processes as our model. The ethogenic exploration of the social knowledge and competence of the local folk takes precedence if we turn to conscious rule and plan following as a model for the basic form of action-genesis. In our view social and personality psychology should always make a prior attempt to understand enigmatic episodes whose causal mechanisms are unknown on the model of consciously controlled behaviour and speech where the cognitive sources of the action are monitored and recorded in conscious awareness, before falling back on automatisms, whether inherited or acquired.

The ethogenic approach

The maximal utilization of talk, both as a natural occurrence and as something prompted into being, is a central feature of social and personality psychology in the ethogenic style, that is as the investigation of the genesis of accountable behaviour (Harré and Secord, 1972). Members' accounts are taken as serious contributions to the understanding of the action and its genesis. The ethogenic approach is based upon the idea that the cognitive sources of action can only be found by an integrated study of human behaviour and accompanying talk. The approach partitions social performances into those action-sequences in the course of which social reality is created and maintained, and those performances in which that first level of performance becomes a topic, the subject matter of commentary or account.

Action-sequences, the fragments of the mosaic of social life, are usually the result of the interlocking performances of several people, each making a contribution at the right place and time. The first step in analysing these sequences is to try to understand their social form, that is what they bring about socially, by way of the social acts they are used to perform. An episode in which someone comes to the assistance of another has an instrumental structure, that is help was given, but confining oneself to that level of analysis we miss the social features of the episode. The action may have had a further significance through which it produces another effect, perhaps the building of the public character of the helper. If the occasion is treated as an opportunity to patronise the one to be helped, this may merely ratify the social order, or it may change it. Performances at this level of action can be analysed, by the use of sociological models, picking up in this way the social force of the action-sequence, in this case patronage. Thus, actions have the double reality of being both instrumental to a certain practical task and the means for achieving a certain social act, what we have called their social force.

At the same time, those actions are also and relatedly the means by which a public presentation of the self as conforming to a certain kind of persona is achieved. Since self-presentation usually occurs in the manner of the performance rather than in the performance itself, we shall speak of this feature as the presentational or expressive qualifications of the instrumental actions. It is by means of these stylistic qualifications that persona is usually presented and character as public presentation is achieved.

The conventions for the presentation of self derive from the local typology of recognized personas. The conventions can be understood by viewing the stylistic aspect of performance as if it were deliberately staged—the use of a dramaturgical model as a specific, analytical device.

Only three sociological models appear to be required for analysing the social structure of the action sequence of a particular episode and its relation to the episodes of previous and subsequent encounters, at least for our society as it is presently constituted. The old exchange model seems particularly apt for understanding the structure of the early, tentative (negotiating) phases of an encounter that may develop further to a stable relationship. Provided the metaphorical character of the concepts of costs and reward is kept in mind, and provided they are not allowed to fade from attributed meanings into the externalist, positive and negative reinforcement idea, we can usefully see the early phases of a relationship in this matter. A useful schematization of the forms of encounters in the early phases of a relationship derived from exchange theory can be found in Jones and Gerard (1967).

Local customs soon invade private relationships in most human societies. Their presence and effectiveness, particularly as ritual ratifications of the stages of a relationship, have to be understood on a generally liturgical model derived from investigations of the structure and mode of genesis of formal or ceremonial episodes. This constitutes the second type of model.

The possibility of reflection on and planning for the action in an encounter makes necessary a third model—the dramaturgical. This model applies to the whole of what is comprehended under the exchange and liturgical models, and it leads to the use of concepts analogous to staging, plot, role, etc., by which the setting and scene, the action and the actor, can be further understood.

On the basis of these analyses attributions of social competence can be made to individual people. To be competent is to have both social knowledge and social skill based upon that knowledge. We shall speak of the cognitive aspects of this as the resources individuals have for coping with both routine and problematic features of social interactions with others. The analytical schema of observed performance and attributed resources is not unlike the basic methodological framework of linguistics, competence being the linguist's concept of resource. For reasons which are not germane to this paper we prefer the concept of resource to that of competence, but the important point is that an individual's resources for social life are manifested in his performances of sequences of action.

But the performance of sequences of actions is not the only way in which individual resources for social life are manifested in public performance. There is also accounting, speech relevant to the action. Accounting is a public performance, at least in principle, and in so far as speech itself achieves social ends and illustrates character, it is another performance at the level of action. However, the *content* of accounts is a second form of representation of social knowledge. The basic ethogenic principle is simply that the same resources are deployed in action as in the giving of accounts. The analysis of the two taken separately enables us to make independent attributions of cognitive structure, content and organization, to individuals competent in a social world. The concept of resource is not to be understood statically. We would follow Alston (1977), Kelly (1955) and Mischel and Mischel (1977) in thinking of resources as put to work in various ways in various situations, even to the extent of generating different disposition sets in situations taken as socially distinct.

On the basis of joint attribution we propose a general and coarse schematization of resources according to the situations recognized as socially distinct, since the kind of personas we manifest, the arbiters we imagine judging the action, and the rules we can imagine as guiding the action, are largely situation-relative. For example, when an adult confuses a child with its sibling, the action is treated as a demeaning insult in a schoolroom, but as an occasion for merriment in a youth club, by the very same child (Harré and Rosser, 1977). Our empirical studies have shown that the most effective analytical method begins with the identification of distinct situations and proceeds by basing the taxonomy of resources upon them (Harré and Rosser, 1977). The genesis of actions and their justifications in speech is the result of dynamic processes based upon the contents of a cell in the matrix of social knowledge, a cell which contains representations of the resources for both formal and improvised actions which are recognisably social within a socially distinct type of situation. The processes may be of the sort suggested by Kelly's (1955) dynamic cognitive psychology, or by the theory of planning offered by Miller, Galanter, and Pribram (1966). However, we do not address the knotty problem of how an individual's resources actually are represented in his 'internal' psychic structure. It should not be supposed that because we utilize the same form of representation for individual social knowledge as is the natural form for the representation of accounts, namely speech and writing, we presume that the individual's representations are in that medium. At present we have nothing to offer by way of a solution to the problem of how and in what medium representation occurs in individuals.

On the other hand, our general methodological stand does carry implications concerning the relationship of action to life and social psychology to action. To reiterate our main psychological hypothesis, social life is a product created by mutual action and based upon some measure of shared social knowledge. Social knowledge is a complex structure including cloudy representations of the overarching forms of society, the effect of which on individual action is not clearly understood. It involves much specific and precise knowledge of what is required for success in day-to-day practices. Bearing in mind the preponderance of the ritual and symbolic over the automatic in human social adjustment one to another, it becomes necessary to insist that, in general, social competence is an intellectual skill, having more in common with puzzle solving than with, say, skill at a motor task.

Time relatedness of social psychologies: synchrony and diachrony

In relation to our interests, we must make some clear distinctions between the time-relatedness of social psychologies. Synchronic social psychology is the technique for the recovery of the content and organization of the shared social knowledge of individuals forming a social order at some time and for the analysis of the processes by which that knowledge manifests itself in action and speech. In contrast, diachronic social psychology is the study of the change and development of the psychological foundations of social interaction in time, and it has been unduly neglected. Diachronic studies can take two forms. An individual's social competence, his resources, are acquired and developed over time and one aspect of the study of that development is the creation of biography and autobiography, that is of verbal representations of a social life and developing social skill and knowledge. Another aspect is developmental social psychology, the study of the acquisition of the very beginnings of social competence in childhood (Harré, 1974). But social practices and their selection conditions are historically situated and undergo historical change. An historical ethnography directed by an interest in the changing forms of rituals and expressive style and the changing content of legitimate accounts against which individuals' resources can be judged adequate or inadequate must complement the study of an individual's social development. Since social psychology is itself a historically situated social practice it too is subject to the historic process by which such practices change (Gergen, 1973).

As a basis for diachronic studies ethogenics takes for granted a quasi-Darwinian theory of the historical change of social practices. The conditions that lead to the mutation of practices are of a different order from the selection conditions which determine which of those practices survive. In general, we locate macrosocial matters amongst selection conditions. Obviously, the changes which occur in selection conditions cannot be explained in terms of the same type of Darwinian theory by which the explanation of changes in social practices can be undertaken. For instance, the slow changes in social and economic *milieu*, which act as selection conditions within which mutations in social practice survive or fail, cannot be explained by the same fundamental selection environment as the survival of mutant practices. There must be a *finite* set of mutation-selection pairs, the last selection environment of which must either be stable or not selected in a Darwinian way. Continental drift and sunspot activity have that status, with other physical conditions, in evolutionary biology. The corresponding feature of social change dynamics is unknown. Our concern is within a relatively stable, situated ethnography, to follow the development of an individual's resources in the course of 'lived experience'.

The intelligibility of events within a life

The problem of how to render something intelligible is at the root of nearly all scientific enquiry. For social and personality psychology it becomes the problem of how to render some socially defined action intelligible, that is how to construct an acceptable account. Broadly speaking, there are two main ways this can be done. In the one, the event is made intelligible by making clear how it is an instance of a kind of event and showing that the conditions that did obtain prior to that event satisfied a law-like generalization to the effect that under conditions of that kind events of that kind would occur. Such a schema pays no attention to which individual the event involves. This schema has been elevated to the status of an exclusive definition in positivistic theories of science.

On the other hand, an event can also be made intelligible by locating it in a unique sequential and unfolding process, unique with respect to the individuals involved and perhaps the combination of elements forming its stages as well. The sequence of clusters of conditions and events has no exact parallel in other individuals, but it represents a progression of like clusters *in the individual under study*. For this case there is no transindividual covering law from which the intelligibility of an event in particular conditions can be derived. There is, however, a progression within the individual's history of like situations, or situations which progress in some intelligible way, such as increasing intensity. For that individual the description of the progression and sequence of situations constitutes a law of his life. Autobiographies provide the material for the internal, nomothetic analysis of an idiograph, namely a representation of a human life. In our forthcoming *The Psychology of Individuals*, we illustrate the point with a case history in which the intelligibility of a unique murder is achieved by reference to the progression of like situations, unique to a specific human life. If, as seems probable, the very psychology of social life is forever changing, not only will there be no exact contemporary parallels to that life, but no previous or future lives will be exactly like it either. To make a particular contemporary murder intelligible requires an account of a particular contemporary life. It is our contention, and it has been our experience, that the assisted autobiography is a powerful procedure for generating such an account.

AUTOBIOGRAPHY: GENERAL FEATURES

In the foregoing we have argued for the autobiography as the apotheosis of the ethogenic method, that is, of the use of accounting theory as a psychology. Before describing the assisted autobiographical method in detail, it is vital to clear the ground concerning two important features of autobiographies, historicity and idiography, features which often lead to important reservations about the nature of the product of autobiographical investigation.

The historicity of autobiographies

Relation to the events described

We must ask whether autobiographies are representation of sequences of actions in situations as they could have been seen at the time when the actions took place, or whether the autobiography is a representation of past sequences of actions in situations as they are now seen. That is, how far does autobiography reflect the same kind of relationship with action as would a diary? There is a distinct difference between autobiographical representation of events and the representation of those events as they would occur in a diary. The cognitive resources which an autobiographer uses to understand and represent his social past may have evolved and changed in the course of the time elapsed between his involvement in the action and his recording of it. A diarist writes an account in which, to all intents and purposes, the accounting and the action are occurring at the same time. Therefore, the basic ethogenic tenet that action and account derive their content, meaning and structure from the same cognitive resources, must be assumed for a diary, but cannot be taken for granted for the autobiography.

Relation of the author to the proposed reader

A further reservation must be made as to the historicity of an autobiography. Not only may the character of its author change but variations in the content and the form of an autobiography may also derive from differences in the author's conception of the person to whom it is addressed. These variations make the question of the historical exhaustiveness of an autobiography, however detailed, inapplicable, at least in simple form. There is, for example, My History for Me, as Against My History for You, and My History for Anyone. Each of these will involve its own selection criteria and its own interpretative principles. All of these may be differentiated with respect to a number of further considerations which do not occur explicitly in the texts, such as the purpose for which the writing was done in the first place, the degree of collaboration between author and potential reader, and so on.

Multiple perspectives in the text

Since an autobiography, as a social performance by its author, may serve as a device for self-presentation, just as a biography can be used by its author for the expression of hero-worship or for the denigration of its subject, the possibility arises of contradictory presentations occurring in the same text. Helling (1976) has identified such a case in the autobiographies of German carpenters and used Schutz's term 'perspectivity' to describe this feature. In one perspective items are cited as part of a 'Poor-me' presentation and in another as part of an 'I'm the greatest' presentation. Each perspective represents *a* way in which a man views his life. The question as to which of these his life really was (and now is) is without application.

Reflexive effects of autobiographical activities

Lastly, the very act of producing the autobiography may lead to a rapid change in those resources in terms of which the described action is seen and understood in the course of the short time-span during which the autobiography is generated. In a complementary way, my resources for understanding my life may be drastically changed by my reading your interpretation of my life that you have made either for me, or for yourself, or for others. Thus my perception of what it was that happened to me may be drastically affected by *our* reflecting upon it. We shall return to this point in discussing the upshot of the production of a biography as a psychological investigation.

The idiography of biographies

The particularist presumption

An autobiography is a life story of just one human being who is the central character of a life drama as represented in the text. How far can we assume that lives, considered in detail and related to their cognitive and expressive foundations, are based upon universal principles, common traits, common understandings? It is characteristic of the ethogenic approach to psychological investigations to eschew *a priori* universal assumptions, to begin an investigation with no particular expectations of the discovery of universal features common to every human life. Such a stance does not preclude the possibility that universal features of various kinds may emerge in the course of further comparative studies. But apart from a minimal assumption of a limited, initial, common intelligibility of speech and action, and this assumption is very limited indeed, we make no *a priori* prognostications about what is likely to be revealed by comparison of individual lives. We preclude neither the possibility of continuing idiography nor the discovery of universals.

The logic of a science of individuals

A science of individuals raises issues of design strategy and of empirical domains. The design issues concern the logic of intensive versus extensive designs. The distinction between the intensive and extensive designs is based on that elementary property of classes expressed in the well-known qualitative relationship: intension varies inversely as extension. The more proper ties that are used in the definition of a typical member of a class, the fewer individuals are likely to be found exhibiting those properties, and so the smaller the class extension. Each design has advantages and disadvantages, but the disadvantages can be reduced by using the two designs conjointly.

In the ideal form of the extensive design the investigator examines all the members of a class. In practice he examines whatever are available, a subset which is thought to be a representative sample. He *derives* the type by some sort of averaging procedure, working from the properties of the members he has examined. The advantages of the extensive design are that at least some result is guaranteed, however trivial, since all the members, or some suitable sample of the members, have been investigated, and there are sure to be some properties which can be averaged or abstracted as a type. But there are serious risks in this method. If the individuals which constitute the extension of the class are highly variable in their characteristics, the results of the investigation are likely to be trivial since there will be few properties in common to all the members of the extension of the class.

The intensive design, on the other hand, involves the examination of a typical member in an endeavour to discover all, or as many as are practicable, of the properties that that typical member has. In this design the extension of the class is derived as the set of individuals who are like the typical member in relevant respects.

Again, there are both gains and risks. The advantage of the intensive design is that a great many properties can be investigated together, their structural relations and interactions ascertained, and a detailed type-description proposed. There are corresponding risks. The results may be misleading, since the member chosen as typical of the class in which we are interested may not be typical. Since we have no other members under empirical scrutiny, we may generate a type which is a distortion of the typical member of the class we have in mind. However, if we endeavour to resolve this difficulty by analytically defining the class as that set of individuals which is typified by the member we have studied, then the danger is that the class may turn out to be very small and our discovery be trivial.

A resolution of the difficulty occasioned by the advantages and disadvantages of each method comes by the joint use of the extensive and intensive designs. The extensive design enables us to identify a hypothetical typical member from a known extension. Then that member, which we hypothesize to be typical, can be subjected to an intensive investigation to generate a detailed knowledge of the type. This can be subjected to empirical criticism with respect to our original extension by choosing *an* other member and subjecting it to intensive investigation, the two intensive studies acting as potential falsifiers of the hypotheses that each is typical. In this way we can achieve depth and breadth together. In practice, however, the results of the application of the extensive and intensive design have favoured the intensive in that detailed investigations of individuals, as Mixon (1971), De Waele (1971) and others have shown, leads one to be very sceptical indeed about the value of the original extensive class from which, for example, a typical murderer or a typical obedient citizen was selected.

The fact that in practice the intensive design seems to predominate over the extensive as a viable empirical method leads us to be doubtful of the idea that there are wide-ranging categories of human beings, at least as social actors. In the light of this the results of empirical studies should be very carefully distinguished with respect to their domain of application. This point is best made by distinguishing between idiographic and nomothetic studies, that is between detailed studies of single individuals, and summative studies of sets of individuals on the basis of which nomothetic statements, the laws of the many, are to be made.

This distinction and its application to the separation of empirical domains has been worked out in detail by Du Mas (1955). He shows that an idiographic domain can be defined which is not accessible from any extensive design. The argument involves three domains.

1. Domain A: This domain represents all the people and all their properties at one point in time. It is a nomothetic domain with respect to the universe of people.
2. Domain B: This domain represents all individuals across time but only one property. It is also a nomothetic domain with respect to the same universe of people but covers the whole of their lives.
3. Domain C: This domain represents all the properties at all times for one individual. This is an idiographic domain, and the exploration of it is identical with biography.

The complete summation of any one domain will yield exactly the same information as the complete summation of either of the other domains. However, it is not possible to recover the individual biographies of the members of the population from either of the nomothetic domains. That is, the full set of properties across the whole life of a particular person cannot be obtained from the information in either domain A or domain B. Thus, some information can be obtained only by idiographic studies of each individual separately. It should be clear that the exploration of the idiographic domain is identical with successive investigations under the intensive design, though the antecedents of the investigation are different. The idiographic domain is not based upon any hypotheses about typicality of members, but the intensive design can be derived from biographical investigation simply by adding the hypothesis that a member whose biography is being explored is typical of some set of members and perhaps of all. And in accordance with the principles of ethogenic psychology (Harré, 1977) the best method for exploring biographies is by the assisted construction of autobiographies, since these have the status of accounts.

In order to state more precisely the relationship between the idiographic and nomothetic or transindividual characteristics of lives, we have tried to structure our analysis so that it serves to *reveal* diachronic structure in the terms of each biography. That is, the analytical concepts appropriate to revealing the order and systematicity of a life come from the individual's own accounts, though these meanings, as we shall show, are subject to certain kinds of external negotiation. We hope that our practice is so structured that, apart from the commonalities involved in speaking the same language, no structural universals, no semantic universals, and no causal hypotheses of a universal character are *imposed* upon the text of the constructed autobiography.

In analysing autobiography one hopes to move, of course, from a purely idiographic study eventually to something nomothetic, in terms of which some sort of expectation can be derived. However, there are identifiable limits to the generality of autobiographies, and these deserve some comment.

The limits of generality in autobiography

In our autobiographical studies (cf. De Waele and Harré, 1977, for details) we see the nomothetic characteristics of lives in two different contexts. One context is from an earlier to a later stage of the *same life*. This sort of transition can be subjected to quite specific forms of statistical analysis, the so-called Q and P designs. Within the terms of our general theory we would expect to find successful nomothetic transitions within individual lives in that, in all sorts of ways, later stages of a life can be seen to be orderly developments of earlier.

The second nomothetic transition is from one *life* to another, and it is much more problematic and much more difficult to achieve by the use of any statistical method. Indeed, there seem to be very good reasons for thinking that the use of a generally summative method aimed at inducing a common form, in which lives are compared with respect to the features in which they are alike, is unlikely to yield much of interest. As we argue elsewhere (De Waele and Harré, 1977), the most illuminating analogy for biographical investigations is to be found in anatomy, where the anatomical structure of one organism serves as the concrete exemplification of the schema of a species until, by comparison with the anatomical structure of another concrete individual, *prima facie* of the same species, some feature of the first is removed from the schema by eliminative induction. The actual anatomical structure of the second organism now replaces the first as the concrete bearer of the species schema. In the case of biography, any nomothetic transition from one life to another must be established at each stage within the terms available for that stage of the life of the individual; that is, in terms of the available meanings, the isomorphism of patterns is required to be *shown*. We may not read from one life *to* another, imposing the meanings of one *onto* the other. Methodologically we are permitted only to compare lives already analysed within their own terms.

To this point, we have discussed some important, general features of psychological method and of autobiographies in particular. However, the assisted autobiography, as developed in Brussels and which constitutes the basis of this chapter, has features which require more detailed description. The rest of the chapter is devoted to that task; but it might be kept in mind that until very recently the procedure has been used with a special group of participants and for a special purpose. Specifically, the central participants have been convicted murderers. The purpose has been to understand their lives so as to make sense of their acts of murder and to assess their potential for parole in the future.

AUTOBIOGRAPHY AS A CONSTRUCTION: THE BRUSSELS METHOD

The construction of an autobiography is conceived as a cooperative achievement between a team and the participant whose autobiography is to be generated. The team ideally consists of about a dozen people, each bringing to the task a different professional background, such as sociologist, psychologist, social worker, medical doctor, and so on. In the Brussels project the participant, though a prisoner, is a volunteer and receives a salary as a team member. The technique involves three major features. First of all, the process involves continuous detailed negotiation so that accounts are continually being brought under the scrutiny of members of the team, including the participant. In this way, no one way of conceptualizing lives is dominant and in all cases a certain sort of priority attaches to the contributions of the participant himself. But lives are individual, as we have emphasized, and part of the task of autobiography genesis is that of learning an idiography, learning an individual's way of conceiving his situations, understanding his predicaments, and solving his problems. In this respect the team of professionals must stand in a relation of humility to the life form and cognitive resources of the participant. Finally, it is important to realize that any technique that stands a chance of success in a finite time, must make use of and incorporate an enormous body of tacit knowledge and implicit understandings of the social world. The adjustment of that knowledge between the participants in the process is a central feature of the negotiations which occur.

The creation of an assisted autobiography, then, is really a continuous process of negotiated autobiographical reconstruction. There are two strategies by which this may be achieved in practice.

The time-oriented method

The participant is invited to contribute an autobiography written in his own terms, in his own time, and to his own satisfaction. This constitutes a text which then is divided into time-slices corresponding to the number of members in the team. Each member provided with a slice attempts to reconstruct from that slice the rest of the life as it has so far been lived. The production of these narratives begins a process of negotiation in which the people involved, professionals and participant, in turn negotiate their narrative, one with another, leading to a new series of documents in which revisions that are the products of internegotiation, are incorporated. The process is made orderly by negotiations occurring first within professional groupings, such as social worker with social worker, and then in cross-professional groupings, such as medical doctor with criminal psychologist. The final product, including the negotiations with the participant himself, then forms a basic text. This method, while a theoretical alternative, has only just begun to be used in practice. In Oxford, studies have just begun using the time-oriented method but combined with topic-orientations.

The topic-oriented method

In this method the naive autobiography is dismembered and reassembled according to a nine-fold thematic scheme. The analytical scheme to be described has been developed in the Penitentiary Orientation Centre in Brussels. The scheme is a modification of the table of contents of the Biographical Inventory, as shown in the Appendix to this chapter. The Biographical Inventory is a systematically organized collection of open questions, questionnaires and ratings, and serves as an integrating technique for various sources of data, including the naive autobiography, Problem and Conflict Situations (to be described below), the Social Enquiry (a detailed investigation of the social and physical environment of the participant) and observational methods in which a wide variety of opinions about the person are sought. The point of using the topic-oriented scheme is to make the reconstruction of the life-course systematic and to bring together the synchronic and diachronic aspects of personality.

The scheme has two advantages. First, it enables systematic identification of the themes mentioned by the author of the autobiography. Second, by highlighting what is lacking in the autobiography it opens the way to focused interviewing and permits exploration of the reasons for the omissions. This aspect of cooperative self-exploration is as important as what is explicitly formulated.

The scheme consists of a list of topics which can be used by the analyst when reading the autobiography systematically from a number of different points of view. These correspond to the nine main parts of the Biographical Inventory:

Microsociological framework

1. Time perspective
2. Social ecology
3. Socioeconomic living conditions

Social psychological life-patterns

4. Family and groups
5. Cultural pattern of values, norms, expectations and roles
6. The institutional (prison) situation

Individual characteristics: self and personality

7. Self descriptions and interpretations
8. Interests, occupational and leisure-time activities
9. Goals, aspirations and conflicts

Each topic of the scheme has to be connected with the Biographical Inventory. Each topic in the scheme is assigned the number under which that topic is mentioned in the Biographical Inventory. In this way the investigator can proceed to a content analytical comparison between the naive autobiography and the Biographical Inventory, the instructions of which induce the person to 'zoom' on the various aspects of his autobiography.

It is important to note that the scheme does not amount to a quantitative but to a qualitative method. Indeed, its application does not lead to profiles or tables of frequencies, but to an integrated picture of the themes, whether the author mentions them in his naive autobiography, or whether they have to be explored in subsequent discussion. By avoiding translation into numerical representations, an attempt is made not to overlook the specific meaning of the 'data', that is, the meaning the 'data' have for the participant and for the other members of the team.

Application of the conceptual scheme

To put the scheme into practice, about ten successive readings of the basic autobiography are necessary. Nine readings are reserved for the analysis of the nine main parts of it. However, a first reading by the person acting as director is necessary to make himself familiar with the whole autobiography, since any part of it may reflect on any other part. A complete reading also is necessary to draw up some kind of inventory of the themes dealt with in the autobiography and to code the document with respect to the appearances and reappearances of these themes. The number of readings can, however, be limited to one or two when the analyst immediately classifies all autobiographical data under the topics of the scheme. For this purpose he needs to know the structure of the scheme very well. When the scheme is put to use, the data from the autobiography do not have to be literally copied; they can be reproduced synthetically under the topics of the scheme, though, as in all translation, there is the danger of inaccurate representation of meaning.

The topics composing the scheme are not always mutually exclusive. Thus some autobiographical data may be classified under more than one heading. This means that the same 'data' are being considered from different points of view and systematically change their meaning as they are viewed in this or that perspective.

The analyst must also pay close attention to whether or not the subject refers in an explicit or implicit way to the topics of the scheme. By explicit references we mean the 'manifest content' of the autobiography, and by implicit references we mean those topics to which the subject does not explicitly refer but which are supposed to be present by the analyst. This constitutes the problem of the 'latent content' of the autobiography and of the inference the analyst draws to conclude to that latent content. Implicit and explicit references are not always easy to distinguish and it is better to think in terms of a continuum. The investigator is here faced with the problem of the interpretative depth he allows himself when analysing the autobiographical data, as well as the danger of projecting material from his analytical scheme on to the participant. There may really have been a cognitive vacuum corresponding to an element in the scheme. There is no *a priori* way of guarding against the danger of projection, though the multiple negotiations inherent in the method are some guarantee against its gross forms.

Once the autobiographical data have been classified under the different headings of the scheme by the project director, the thematic investigators can proceed to an internal analysis of theme data since each is assigned one of the nine themes. This should lead each thematic investigator to provisional conclusions and hypotheses concerning the longitudinal organizing principles of the life under study. As the analysis deals with explicit as well as with implicit references about incomplete 'data', each investigator can formulate hypotheses which will be put to the test by a comparison with the other sources of data, with the hypotheses of the other thematic investigators, and with the further elicited accounts of the main participant.

In a less intensive case-study, with or without autobiography, the analytical scheme finds its place too. A single investigator may use the scheme as an *aide memoire* for directing his interviews. Such interviews would be directed especially towards those topics of the scheme about which nothing was mentioned in the autobiography or in the interviews.

To the conceptual scheme is appended an interview guide which can be used by each investigator to search for the so-called 'performance modalities' of the written autobiography. Knowledge of the attitude or set adopted by the participant with regard to the task, and of the corresponding motives, place the reader in a better position to view autobiographical communication from the author's frame of reference and to identify those themes whose detailed exploration will reveal the pattern of the participant's life as he conceives it.

As noted earlier, the nine thematic readers and the participant now engage in an ordered sequence of anticipations and negotiations, as each of the readers tries to reconstruct the remaining themes of the autobiography on the basis of his common sense knowledge, his professional expertise, and the information available in his 'slice'. Each of three triads of thematic readers then engages the participant in a further round of negotiations to settle the differences that have emerged in the course of the hypothetical reconstructions. This produces a reconstructed autobiography at what one might call the first level of sophistication. The method by which these negotiations are conducted is described in the next section.

METHOD OF NEGOTIATION: THE FOCUSED ACCOUNT ELICITING INTERVIEW

One of the fundamental rules of the idiographic personality assessment method, of which the biographical interview is a fundamental constituent, is the 'Interviewing Rule'. According to this rule, every answer given to a questionnaire, every meaningful whole of written statements produced by the subject, and all available documents about him must be submitted to an interview in order to make explicit the content and form of the constructs which the participant uses to describe and explain his life. These constructs are likely to be used by him to differentiate socially distinct situations, to identify socially proper action, to arbitrate that propriety, and to indicate the personas he has presented and the conventions governing those presentations.

As happens very often, these interviews will induce the subjects to produce supplementary autobiographical documents. However, to accomplish this task systematically, we have developed an interviewing technique called the Focused Account Eliciting interview. It uses a series of successive focusing procedures to elicit accounts from the participant, and its rationale is based on the aims well summarized in the following citation of Harré and Secord (1972, pp. 9–10).

> If we follow the paradigm of non-positivistic science, explaining behavioural phenomena involves identifying the generative 'mechanisms' that give rise to the behaviour. The discovery and identification of these 'mechanisms' we call ethogeny. We believe that the main process involved in them is self-direction according to the meaning ascribed to the situation. At the heart of the explanation of social behaviour is the identification of the meanings that underlie it. Part of the approach to discovering them involves the obtaining of accounts—the actor's own statements about why he performed the acts in question, what social meaning he gave to the actions of himself and others. These must be collected and analysed, often leading to

the discovery of the rules that underlie the behaviour. The explanation is not complete, however, until differing accounts are negotiated and, further, put into the context of an episode structure. Greater precision of meaning through such procedures is analogous to greater accuracy of measurement in the physical sciences. An important tool in obtaining these meanings is ordinary language, which is well adapted for explaining a pattern of social interaction in terms of reasons and rules. Two cardinal principles in using the concepts or ordinary language as developed by philosophers are:

1. The conceptual system embedded in ordinary language should provide the basis for the concepts employed in a realistic psychology and should serve as a model for other logical connections and new concepts introduced by psychologists.
2. Given the existence of carefully checked description of social behaviour, a detailed exploration of particular cases by the analysis of accounts should next be undertaken. The justificatory context of the accounts is dominant here and leads to the discovery of how behaviour is monitored by the actor, because in such a context he must turn his attention most fully upon what he has done.

Thus, accounts play an important role in creating the intelligibility of action, and a systematic procedure for their elicitation is desirable. In order to enable investigators to make full use of the data afforded by our main sources, an appropriate interviewing strategy should involve a series of successive focusing procedures on the written and spoken statements of the studied person and through them on the various social episodes referred to. This focusing is the first step towards the eliciting of accounts which, if sufficiently explicit, will lead to hypothetical reconstructions of the individual's cognitive resources. This Focused Account Eliciting interview is also applied to the situations in which the subject gave his first answers to the biographical inventory and to other specialized techniques. Moreover, it also is used reflexively in order to analyse the interview situation itself. In both these cases, the subject is induced to adopt the 'dramaturgical standpoint' by stepping out of his temporary role and taking distance from it.

A closely related conception of interviewing was developed by Merton, Fiske, and Kendall (1956). The essential features of both their Focused Interview technique and our Focused Account Eliciting interview can be summed up as follows.

The persons being interviewed by a focused procedure must have experienced one or more particular situations about which they have made a report, either by responding to a questionnaire or by answering some open questions. The significant component of the situation or the social episodes as well as the form in which the subjects have formulated their views has to have been previously analysed by the investigator, who may have other sources of information at his disposal as well. With this preliminary analysis as a starting point, the investigator, by sorting out interesting cross-references in his material, and by setting up some interpretative hypotheses, constructs a specific interview-guide for use during the interview.

The interview itself—which generally speaking is of the non-directive kind—is centred around the subject's experiences, his situational definitions, and the meaning he attributes to the components of the social episodes referred to. As the making explicit of meaning requires exemplification, new data will inevitably emerge on which the interviewer will also have to focus. Far from leading to 'summary generalizations' or 'summary judgments', the focused interview will produce detailed accounts of various situations, role/rule patterns, and persona descriptions which are to be used to verify the initial hypotheses as well as those emerging as a result of the interview.

To be effective, a focused interview has to satisfy a certain number of criteria concerning range, specificity, depth and personal context. Since the interviewee should be afforded maximal freedom to define the contextual meaning of his former experiences, no restrictions should be imposed on the memories evoked, analogies drawn, etc. Neither should the statements concerning his personal reaction be limited in any way. Furthermore, the focused interview should result in specific and detailed reports about the social episodes and the situation referred to in the initial responses, and the interviewee should be given the opportunity to express the emotional impact of the experienced situations as well as his personal involvement in them. Finally, personality characteristics, persona-presentations, role/rule models representing either standard or improvised solutions to past problem situations, as well as the participant's future and past time perspective, should also be explored in order to provide a personal context for his statements.

The accounts which the Focused Account Eliciting interview attempts to elicit are not to be interpreted as introspective, causal explanations, though some accounts may have *inter alia* that character. Primarily, accounts serve to make action intelligible, either by fitting it into the interpersonal life-world and warranting its placement, or by locating it in a structure as part of the biography of a person involving the rituals and forms of our society, or by making it part of the performance of social acts within an episode, creating meanings and defining selves. Ordinary accounts achieve intelligibility for action patterns and styles of performance (a) by settling the meaning assigned to items of the environment and to actions, and (b) by referring to the rules of action and role-requirements followed in monitoring social behaviour.

Meanings may be explicitly formulated in an account (I meant so and so by what I did, or how I did it, or what I said and how I said it). However, they will often be given an implicit explication by successive redescription through two acts of implicit imposition of meaning. The first one consists in the redescription of the actions generated in the language of the intended or meant action. (What may have been described as 'My elbow caught him in the ribs' becomes 'Well, actually I dug him in the ribs'.) But a second act of meaning-giving is possible in which the meaning of an action is specified by mentioning what social act it is meant to accomplish, such as—'I wanted to share the joke with him'. These successive redescriptions embed the descriptive terms in different semantic fields and so relate 'what happened' to different networks of social consequences and to different expectations, all of which create the semblance of a fragment of orderly social life. Since it is only as meaningful acts that what people do can be subsumed under rules, people's accounts of their doings usually involve reference to rules and other normative principles. This is because accounts are largely called for in justification of actions. Therefore, such accounts require the implicit or explicit definition as social actions of the mere happenings done in the performance of acts. A person may indeed also produce accounts in which he identifies himself in the status of a mere thing and all the events referred to are described in the language of mere happenings; that is, they are transformed neither into actions nor acts. However, if the problem of justification of an action is raised, then, as Lyman and Scott (1970) have shown, reference will be made explicitly to rules and other 'normalizing' devices in the pursuit of legitimacy.

The deliberate and technical analysis of accounts involves methodological conceptions that are not common in conventional psychological and social psychological assessment. First, one must consider the types of accounts and rhetorics. Excuses and justifications are, according to Austin's analysis (1961), the two major kinds of accounts which are likely to be invoked when a person is accused of having done something that is 'bad, wrong, inept, unwelcome, or in some other of the numerous possible ways, untoward'.

Excuses are accounts resorted to in order to alternate or relieve responsibility in which it is admitted that an act was wrong or inappropriate while denying that one was fully responsible. Appeal to accidents, to irresponsible biological drives, and scapegoating are some of the concrete forms excuses can take. Justifications are accounts in which one accepts responsibility for the act in question but denies the pejorative evaluation associated with it. Techniques like 'denial of injury', 'denial of victim', 'condemnation of condemners' and 'appeal to loyalties' are all special cases of justification.

Accounts may be organized into coherent conceptual schemes ranging from quasi-logical arguments to arguments based on real structures and the imposition of structure through examples, models, analogies and metaphors (Perelman and Olbrechts-Tyteca, 1970). These 'rhetorics', so called because accounting accomplished by them persuades of the intelligibility and propriety of acts, are systems of linked terms by which social objects are identified and classified and with which go certain implicit theories. Closely associated with the diverse kinds of rhetorics are the various styles with which they are communicated in written or spoken form.

The account analyst also must consider the social role/rule systems. The local role/rule system or local ethnography is often revealed in accounts, and it describes the ideal social competence of a member or participant in the subject's society. Comparison of an individual's accounts with the matter extracted from a great many accounts given by other people can lead one to an understanding of the extent to which an individual's resources for accounting match or fail to match the local role/rule system.

It also is essential to recognize that the accounts generated in Focused Account Eliciting interviews are not 'responses' elicited by 'stimulus questions'. Like all accounts they always occur between persons encountering each other in certain roles. Therefore the nature and types of communication taking place between interviewer and interviewee are regulated by various norms defining whether and in what manner accounts may be asked and given, accepted or rejected. Depending on the degree of acceptance or of rejection of accounts as illegitimate or unreasonable, and eventually as a consequence of the interviewee's use of techniques for avoiding accounts, like mystification, referral to other sources or identity-switching (Lyman and Scott, 1970, p. 134), various processes of negotiation and bargaining will be initiated. The successive reformulations to which they lead will disclose the strategies used by the interviewee. However, in the account-giving situation of the interview, casting the other person into a situationally appropriate role and assuming an identity are indispensable for structuring the negotiation process since only in this way can the social stage for its display be set. Therefore every negotiation of accounts will also be a manifestation of the underlying negotiation of identities.

Moreover, the interview-situation must be recognized as a social episode. The account-giving situation, and consequently the accounts themselves, will be decisively influenced by the kind of social episode they are part of. Either the interviewer or the interviewee, or both, may define the interview situation by subsuming it under certain models. Interviews performed by parole boards, psychiatric committees, or courts, clearly belong to the 'liturgical' model (Harré and Secord, 1972, p. 177). According to this model, each action and saying and its place in the act-action, as well as the actions of each participant and the kind of individual who is permitted to perform a certain role, are all governed by rule and convention. In the context of criminological investigations it frequently happens that delinquents either transfer this interaction model from the judiciary or administrative situations they have been exposed to into the assessment situation by a kind of learned generalization or purposively simulate a misunderstanding of the assessment interview. Diametrically opposed to interviews modelled after ritualistic episodes are those informal interviews taking the form of conversations, that is, episodes having only action structures but no defined outcomes, which do not bring about specific social acts. These conversational exchanges, which make up a great part of the interactions between prisoners and warders, derive most of their value from the fact that they are not systematically planned. Their obvious weakness is that, as they can only be reported after having occasionally taken place, they make high demands upon the reporting skills and the conscious insight of prison personnel.

The assessment situations of interviewing will mostly be patterned after the game or agonistic model made up by a series of moves and countermoves emanating from interactants pursuing partially or completely opposed goals. The game typology proposed by Lyman and Scott (1970), which is based on the goals sought by the interactants, will help an interviewer to diagnose the various aspects of the social episode in which he is involved on the condition that, for each concrete interviewing situation, he should regard these games as being only analytically distinct, but in fact functionally interdependent and empirically overlapping.

In a *face game* two objectives are pursued either singly or together. One can be termed defensive, in which a member attempts to protect his own identity against damage; the other is protective, in which a participant seeks to prevent any spoilage to the identity of the person with whom he is interacting. In *relationship games*, 'the interactants have one of two aims: to decrease or increase social distances. When one of the interactants undertakes a line of action to achieve greater intimacy, he initiates a positive relationship game; when one of the interactants wishes to alternate or terminate an overintimate relationship, he initiates a negative relationship game. In either case the game consists of managing a presentation of self so as to suggest the desired outcome. Since the other player may not share the perspective of the first, this presentation is subject to checks and countermoves as well as supports (Lyman and Scott, 1970, p. 43).

In *exploitation games* the interactants seek to maximize the power they can exert on one another. But, although they hope to achieve control over the beliefs or the actions of their opponent, they are not absolutely sure to attain their goals. *Information games*, which overlap with all the others because information is a fundamental requirement of all social life, are for obvious reasons of paramount importance in the interviewing situation. They arise when one actor wishes to gain access to information concerning another who wishes to conceal it. A sequence of control moves, covering moves, uncovering moves and recovering moves is initiated. A detailed analysis of this kind of game also has been offered by Goffman (1970).

The three stages of the focused account eliciting interview procedure

Properly authenticated accounts have the status of explanations about the genesis and meanings of action. It is through their analysis that the investigator will seek to construct and define an individual's cognitive equipment for social problem solving, in other words, his cognitive matrix as it is attuned to the basic problem situations with which he is confronted. In order to reach that objective, the investigator making use of Focused Account Eliciting interviews will apply a determinate, three-stage questioning procedure. He will start either from a directly observed situation, a document like the autobiography, or from the written answers given by the subject to the questions of the Biographical Inventory. The basic rule involved here is that the investigated subject should initiate a whole series of first moves. This gives the investigator the opportunity to record and analyse the subject's spontaneous interpretations of the questions, in other words, his understanding of the questions is uninfluenced by any covert or overt communication concerning their desirability which may emanate from the investigator. Furthermore, these first answers will constitute the starting point for two kinds of interview questions which correspond to two successive stages of the Focused Account Eliciting interview.

Stage 1: reflexive questions

In the first stage of the interview *reflexive* questions will be asked, that is, questions about the process of interpreting and answering the questions in written form. A few examples will make clear what is to be understood by these reflexive questions.

> What was your reaction when you first read the questions?
> What is, according to you, the purpose of these questions?
> Did it occur to you that these questions might have a hidden purpose?
> Did some questions look to be catch questions?
> Did you notice questions which you had already put to yourself?
> Were there any questions which you had never thought of?
> Which questions were difficult and which were easy to answer? Why?
> Which questions seem to be personally relevant to you and which do you consider irrelevant?
> On which items do you think your answers deviate considerably from those given by other people and on which questions do you think you are in agreement with the majority of people?
> With whom would you be ready to discuss some questions or with whom would you be ready to discuss your answers?
> How would you group together some of the questions and the answers you have given?
> Of whom did these questions make you think?
> Whose answers to these questions would you like to know?
> Whose answers to these questions do you think you could fairly well predict?
> How did you feel when answering these questions?
> What other things were you reminded of when answering these questions?
> Do you think you would always have answered these questions as you have done recently? Why
> Do you think you may eventually answer them differently in the future?

The accounts generated by these reflexive questions constitute a general background which prepares the way for the *direct* inter-questions of the second stage. That these reflexive questions should come first and that the utterances conveying the answers as well as the attendant non-verbal communications should be carefully observed and eventually recorded is made necessary by the fact that all rule and meaning explicating accounts are indexical expressions (Garfinkel, 1967). That is, they cannot be understood without reference to the pragmatic context made up of the person uttering them and of the circumstances of their utterance.

Stage 2: direct questions

Several types of questions belonging to the second stage of the Focused Account Eliciting interview may be distinguished:

1. Information questions whose aim it is to collect further factual information about a given topic.
2. Ordering questions: By these questions the subject is asked

    (a) to make comparisons,
    (b) to classify certain data,
    (c) to rank-order them, or
    (d) to evaluate rewards and costs pertaining to alternatives.

3. Questions about choices between alternatives and possibilities. The general aim of these questions is to induce the subject to give his accounts of the way in which, out of possible alternatives open to him or to others, one finally was realized. Here again one can distinguish

    (a) questions about possible alternatives,
    (b) questions about plans 'rehearsed in the inner theatre of the imagination',
    (c) questions about ideal and real goals,
    (d) questions about reversible developments and points of no return,
    (e) questions about anticipated and improvised plans,
    (f) questions about substitute actions and expressions, and
    (g) questions about person-dependent and role-dependent behaviours.

4. Questions enabling the subject to formulate the conditions under which certain events took place and on what evidence his assertions about them are founded. Here we can distinguish

    (a) specification and exemplification questions,
    (b) questions aiming at generalizations and frequencies, and
    (c) questions intended to elicit statements about necessary, sufficient or counteracting conditions.

These kinds of questions are used for additional analyses of act-action structures.

5. Objections: Alternative accounts are proposed to the subject or flaws in his argumentation are pointed out to him and he is asked to give his opinion on them.

Stage 3: reflexive questions

When several interviews organized along these lines have taken place, the third and final stage of the Focused Account Eliciting interview method has been reached. Once again, it is structured by *reflexive* questions. But this time they are aimed at the second stage of the interviews. Their object is triple. First, the game aspects of the preceding interviews are made the central theme of the interview. Second, the negotiation of accounts and of the underlying identities is explored. Finally, the various types of argumentation and the rhetorics used by the subject are discussed.

The results of Focused Account Eliciting and cross-negotiation between the thematic investigators is a new autobiographical text.

PROBLEM AND CONFLICT SITUATIONS

This new autobiographical text is subjected in the next stage of the investigation to an attempt to identify what one might call authentic longitudinal themes, using locally adjusted conceptions of what the cognitive resources of actions and accounting of an individual might have been at that time. One could speak of these metaphorically as world lines linking formally identical or isomorphic situations.

But lives are not smooth. Their development shows features other than the orderly evolution of themes. In particular, the lives so far studied in Brussels, which are exclusively of those who have committed murders, are characterized by what one might visualize as 'knots' or 'whirlpools' in the smooth flow of life: conflict and crisis situations. Like 'eddies' in the atmosphere they are not readily understood in terms of principles governing the smooth, streamlined flow. The problem for a biographer is to grasp, if he can, the structure of such situations as conceived by the participant and the way he views his attempts to resolve them. The solution of this autobiographical problem is achieved in the Brussels technique by requiring the participant to identify situations in his life which have the same formal characteristics, as far as·he can perceive the matter, as certain standardized situations of conflict and crisis which he has experienced in the prison psychological wing and which have been artificially constructed by the team for his benefit. The participant is asked to experience a range of contrived conflict and problem situations such as a series of tasks of increasing difficulty, the last one of which is insoluble in the given conditions and often highly stressful for the participant. After experiencing these, the participant is asked to find within his life story descriptions of situations that seem to pick out moments in his life which are formally isomorphic to those crises and conflict situations in which he has had to participate in the prison. Interactively, and reflectively, an individual lives through part of his life again, but in terms of common features he identifies for himself.

The autobiography, then, is not a record of happenings and responses to them, but a record of interpretation of happenings, the plannings of responses to them, the understandings of successes or failures in these matters. In short, it provides a cognitive map both of how the individual now represents his life to himself and how he represents his resources by which he sees himself to have coped or failed to cope with the problems and crisis of that life as it unfolded.

REFLEXIVENESS OF NEGOTIATED AUTOBIOGRAPHIES

We must now turn to a clear statement of some of the features of this method which can be sources of misunderstanding. The construction of an autobiography by interaction between the team and the participant is clearly itself a social activity and in the Brussels technique is monitored and recorded by a twelfth member of the team. But it is also reflexive in that the participant, in constructing his own autobiography, is developing himself so that certain cautions as to the epistemological standing of the product must be entered and clearly understood.

Changes occasioned by producing the autobiography

Cognitive resources for understanding and managing social life are changed by the very act of cooperative construction of the autobiography, so that the participant who enters the year-long discussion of his life comes out at the end a different person. The degree of that difference is, of course, beyond any possible monitoring, because it is impossible in principle to distinguish the degree to which what was tacit in his knowledge has been made explicit, that is, what knowledge existed all along, and what new matters he has learned from the rest of the team in the course of the interaction. The final autobiography, then, represents the world of the participant and his interpretive schemata as it exists at the end of the process.

It follows from this that, strictly speaking, the product of autobiography contains a representation of a contemporary synchronic picture of a life and the resources necessary to generate it and cope with it; as a *history* it is problematic. That is, while it is not necessarily false, it cannot be taken to be literally true. Again, we should compare the relation of the text of a diary to the events and interpretations it records, which is very different from the relation of an autobiographical text to like events.

The historicity of the autobiography

Any attempt to improve the historicity of the document involves the comparison of the idealized and constructed 'What happened' contained in the completed autobiography with some other representation of 'What happened'; and that latter representation will have to be reconstructed if it is to be intelligible with respect to the present semantic systems of the individual. There are further difficulties, too. External sources of information about the life history of an individual may seem to be invaluable: for example, such documents as school reports, probation officers' reports, medical files, and so on. However, we know from the findings of ethnomethodology that these cannot be taken unreservedly as standing in a clear and unambiguous relation to the facts that they purport to describe as either lies or truths. They must be subjected to the ethnomethodological critique (Garfinkel, 1967), in that the social processes by which the documents are generated must be examined, and they must be seen as processes not unlike that by which the autobiography under scrutiny and comparison was itself produced. In particular, documents do not stand as fully intelligible in themselves apart from an understanding of the institution which produced them and the interaction of that institution with the institution which is querying their intelligibility. However, it is an essential part of the Brussels method to attempt at least some kind of cautious confrontation of the constructed autobiography with documents which have been reworked ethnomethodologically.

A final caution must be entered. It is certainly sometimes the case that the autobiographer, the subject of the autobiography, who has participated in its construction, may also in earlier times have participated in the genesis of the documents against which its historicity is to be compared. He may himself have stimulated actions to create the documents in question, as for example those which might be found in the archives of a Magistrate's Court.

Finally, it is worth emphasizing that the autonomy of the participant, as someone in good standing as a member of the team, is respected and reflected throughout the process of construction.

CONCLUSION

In this method we are extending and deepening one aspect of the central tenets of ethogenic psychology, since autobiographical reconstructions are accounts, but the most detailed and differentiated accounts of all. They allow us to form a representation of a person's current cognitive resources, including that most important of all personal resources next to one's language, what one thinks one's life-course to have been. It should be clear that our products are not life histories in the conventional sense.

Nor are they to be confused with 'lifespan' studies which use only one schematizing device, the calendar, and one independent variable, namely linear, conventional 'clock' time. Because lifespan studies are generalized across lives they yield at best only the biography of the generalized human being. Our belief is that the generalized biography will turn out to consist almost entirely of biological stages and transitions—since almost everything of social importance is likely to be local and ephemeral, even the meaning to be given to various moments in the biological life-cycle. Only by detailed comparisons of locally validated lives are any deep structural universals likely to be revealed.

References

Alston, W. P., 1977, Traits, consistency and conceptual alternatives for personality theory, in Harré, R. (ed.), *Personality*, Oxford: Blackwell, Chapter 4.

Annis, A. P., 1967, The autobiography: its uses and value, *Professional Psychology*, **14**, 9–17.

Austin, J. L., 1961, A plea for excuses, in J. O. Urmson, and J. G. Warnock, *Philosophical Papers*, Oxford: Clarendon Press, Chapter 6.

Calder, N., 1976, *The Human Conspiracy*, London, BBC, pp. 110–111.

Carlson, R., 1971, Where is the person in personality research? *Psychological Bulletin*, **75**, 203–219.

De Waele, J-P., 1971, *La Méthode des Cas Programmés*, Bruxelles: Dessart.

De Waele, J-P., and Harré, R., 1977, The personality of individuals, in Harré, R. (ed.), *Personality*, Oxford: Blackwell.

De Waele, J-P., and Harré, R., in press, *The Psychology of Individuals*, London: Academic Press.

Du Mas, F. M., 1955, Science and the single case, *Psychological Reports*, **1**, 65–75.

Garfinkel, H., 1967, *Studies in Ethnomethodology*, Englewood Cliffs, NJ: Prentice Hall, Chapter 6.

Gergen, K. J., 1973, Social psychology as history, *J. Personality and Social Psychology*, **26**, 307–320.

Gergen, K. J., 1977, The social construction of self-knowledge, in T. Mischel, (ed.), *The Self-Psychological and Philosophical Issues*, Oxford: Blackwell, Chapter 5.

Goffman, E., 1970, *Strategic Interaction*, Oxford: Blackwell.

Harré, R., 1974, The conditions for a social psychology of childhood, in M. P. M. Richards (ed.), *The Integration of a Child into a Social World*, London: Cambridge University Press, Chapter 12.

Harré, R., 1977, The ethogenic approach: Theory and practice. In Berkowitz, L. (ed.) *Advances in Experimental Social Psychology*, Vol. 10, New York: Academic Press, 284–314.

Harré, R., and Rosser, E., 1977, 'The meaning of trouble', E201, *Personality and Learning*, Block 7, Open University.

Harré, R., and Secord, P. F., 1972, *The Explanation of Social Behaviour*, Oxford: Blackwell.

Helling, I., 1976, Autobiography as self-presentation: Carpenters of Konstanz, in Harré, R. (ed.), *Life Sentences*, London and New York: Wiley, Chapter 6.

Johnson, M., 1972, Self-perception of need amongst the elderly: An analysis of illness behaviour, *Sociological Review*, **20**, 521–531.

Jones, E. E. and Gerard, H. B., 1967, *Foundations of Social Psychology*, New York: Wiley, p. 552.

Kelly, G. A., 1955, *The Psychology of Personal Constructs*, New York: Norton.

Lyman, S. M. and Scott, M. B., 1970, *A Sociology of the Absurd*, New York: Meredith, Chapter 2.

Merton, R. K., Fiske, M., and Kendall, P. L., 1956, *The Focused Interview*, Glencoe, Ill.: Free Press.

Miller, G. A., Galanter, E., and Pribram, K. H., 1966, *Plans and the Structure of Behavior*, New York: Holt.

Mischel, W., and Mischel, H. N., 1977, Self-control and the self, in T. Mischel, (ed.), *The Self: Psychological and Philosophical Issues*, Oxford: Blackwell, Chapter 2.

Mixon, D., 1970, Behaviour analysis treating subjects as actors rather than organisms, *Journal for the Theory of Social Behaviour*, **1**, 19–31.

Perelman, Ch., and Olbrechts-Tyteca, L., 1970, *Traité de l'augmentation*, Bruxelles.

Appendix

OUTLINE OF THE BIOGRAPHICAL INVENTORY

The Biographical Inventory consists of nine main parts which can be summarized as follows:

I. Microsociological framework
  A. Time perspective
  B. Social ecology
  C. Socioeconomic living conditions
II. Social psychological life-patterns
  A. Family and groups
  B. Cultural pattern of values, norms, expectations, and roles
  C. The institutional situation (the prison)
III. Individual characteristics: self and personality
  A. Self-descriptions and interpretations
  B. Interests, occupational and leisure-time activities
  C. Goals, aspirations, and conflicts

The complete form of the Biographical Inventory presently in use comprises more than 600 pages. This extensiveness which contrasts with the length of most schemes suggested for use in case studies results from the fact that, being a technique empirically derived from the study of a large number of individual cases it provides a broad set of possible areas of investigation of which only a limited set are relevant for each individual case. As it is obviously impossible to reproduce here all the questions of the Biographical Inventory in the way they are explained and formulated we shall have to restrict our presentation to a short summary of its sections and subsections. The full Biographical Inventory has been published in Dutch: Pers van de Vrije Universiteit, Brussels, 1977. Interested readers should contact the authors for fuller details and for specific bibliographic references concerning the material in this appendix.

I. MICROSOCIOLOGICAL FRAMEWORK

A. Time perspective

1. Division of the life-course, as described in the Autobiography in subjectively meaningful principal and subordinate parts.
   For each of these parts a detailed description of a typical day is being asked.
2. For each of the discriminated periods, enumeration of fulfilled, not fulfilled, half-fulfilled wants and wishes and presently still existing past wishes.

3. For each of the discriminated periods, enumeration of all known positive and negative authority-figures.
4. For each of the discriminated periods, enumeration of positively and negatively valued peers.
5. Exploration of oldest memories.
6. Exploration of remembered past: ease vs. difficulty of evocation; preference vs. aversion toward remembered episodes; vividness vs. vagueness of recollections, etc.
7. Retrospective wishes for changes in the life-course.
8. Motivation Induction Method (J. Nuttin): fifty incomplete sentences used to explore future time perspective.
9. Attitudes toward time: (a) time-anxiety; (b) time submissiveness; (c) time-possessiveness; (d) time-flexibility.
10. Time preferences: (a) day of the week; (b) week of the month; (c) month of the year; (d) season of the year.
11. Future time perspective: enumeration of a minimum of ten anticipated events.
12. Evaluation of anticipated events.
13. Anticipation of life-situation ten years from present moment.
14. Preoccupation with death (questionnaire by Dickstein and Blatt, 1966).
15. Frustrations and losses inflicted by death (questionnaire by Diggory and Rothman, 1961).
16. Ways of dying: paired comparisons between various ways of dying (Diggory, 1966).
17. Miscellaneous questions about own death, death of relatives, death sentence, suicide, anticipated reactions toward knowledge of date of death.

B. Social ecology

1. Map of neighbourhood and of town or village with localization of own living quarters and of those of friends and relatives.
2. Localization and description of aesthetic activities.
3. Localization and description of business activities.
4. Localization and description of occupational activities.
5. Localization and description of educational activities.
6. Localization and description of activities with nutritional purposes.
7. Localization and description of activities related to dispensing information.
8. Localization and description of activities related to keeping up and improving personal appearance.
9. Localization and description of philanthropic activities.
10. Localization and description of activities which promote or maintain physical health.
11. Localization and description of recreational activities.
12. Localization and description of ideological and/or religious activities.
13. Localization and description of governmental and administrative activities.

For each of the above-mentioned activities (2–12) the following aspects are taken into account:
    (a) Subject's own participation in the activity.
    (b) Participation of relatives and friends.
    (c) Role played and degree of penetration in the activity's setting.
    (d) Duration and frequency of participation in each setting.
    (e) Evaluation of activities, opportunities available, wishes and suggestions for changes.
    (f) Opinion about acquisition of knowledge and learning of skills.
    (g) Successes and failures, satisfactions and frustrations resulting from participation in the activity.

14. Neighbourhood scale (questionnaire Bernard, 1964).
15. Opinions, role definitions, and role expectations concerning neighbours.

C. Socioeconomic living conditions

1. Construction of personal hierarchy and definition of classification criteria. Localization of self, relatives, and friends in the personal hierarchy.
2. Classification of occupations and professions by means of Van Heek's technique (1945).
   (a) Subject's opinion: classification of fifty-six occupations and professions in seven categories according to prestige and ordering of the occupations within each category.
   (b) Definition of the criteria used for the delimitation of the seven categories.
   (c) Definition of positions in the hierarchy:
      —Self
      —Parents and relatives
      —Siblings
      —Level of aspiration of self.
   (d) General opinion as imagined by the subject: classification of fixty-six occupations in seven categories according to prestige and ordering of the occupations within in each category.
   (e) Definition of the criteria used for the delimitation of the seven categories.
   (f) Definition of positions in the hierarchy:
      —Self
      —Parents and relatives
      —Siblings
      —Level of aspiration of self.
3. The Warner Index of Status Characteristics (1949).
   (a) Chronological enumeration of domiciles.
   (b) Description of chronological sequence of occupations.
   (c) Sources of income at each of the places of residence.
   (d) House type at each of the places of residence.
   (e) Description of the dwelling area for each of the places of residence.
   (f) Description of occupation, sources of income, house type and dwelling area considered as ideal.
   (g) Description of occupation, sources of income, house type and dwelling area considered to be attainable goals.
   Occupations, sources of income, house type, dwelling area are rated on a seven-point scale.
4. Description, for each place of residence, of the living room by means of Chapin's Social Status (living room scale, 1945)
   (a) Material equipment and cultural expression of the living room, of the home (cf. scale items).
   (b) Condition of articles in the living room (cf. scale items).
   (c) Uses to which the living room is put.
   (d) Description of ideal living room by means of the Chapin scale.
   (e) Description by means of the same technique of a living room considered to be an attainable goal.
5. Sources of income
   (a) Estimate of available sources of income in family of origin and in own family.
   (b) Structure of budget in family of origin and in own family.

(c) Hypothetical budget structure for a monthly income of X.
  (d) Hypothetical changes in budget structure if monthly income were raised by twenty-five per cent, or fifty per cent.
  (e) Description of savings of expenses in the hypothetical case of monthly income drop of twenty-five per cent, or fifty per cent.
  (f) Decision taking concerning expense items in family of origin, in own family.
6. Pocket and spending money
  (a) Own pocket money: amount received and ways of spending.
  (b) Pocket money of brothers and sisters.
  (c) Pocket money of friends.
  (d) Pocket money of future wife.
7. Salary and pay
  (a) Use of first own salary/pay and further evolution.
  (b) Use of first salary by brothers and sisters and further evolution.
  (c) Use of first salary/pay by friends and further evolution.
  (d) Use of first salary/pay by future wife and further evolution.
8. Saving
  (a) Family of origin: attitude of family members toward saving and actual situation.
  (b) Own family/attitude of self, wife and children toward saving and actual situation.
  (c) Future plans concerning saving.
  (d) Conflict situations between spending and saving.
  (e) Questionnaire on thrift (Bues, 1934).
9. Instalment purchases
  (a) Family of origin: attitude toward instalment purchase and actual situation.
  (b) Own family: attitude towards instalment purchase and actual situation.
  (c) Future plans concerning instalment purchase.
  (d) Conflict situations: Saving vs. instalment purchase instalment purchase vs. direct payment.
10. Debts
  (a) Family of origin: attitude toward contracting debts and actual situation.
  (b) Own family: attitude toward contracting debts and actual situation.
  (c) Future plans concerning debts.
11. Loans and mortgages
  (a) Family of origin: attitudes toward loans and mortgages and actual situation.
  (b) Own family: attitude toward loans and mortgages and actual situation.
  (c) Future plans concerning loans and mortgages.
12. Expenditure of monthly income
  (a) Opinion about complete or incomplete expenditure of monthly income.
  (b) Actual situation.
13. Personal expenses
  (a) Lasting commodities: description of commodities, circumstances of purchase and reason for buying commodities.
  (b) Non-lasting commodities: *idem*.
14. Expenses in family of origin
  (a) Lasting commodities: description of commodities purchases for the family as a whole as well as for individual members; mode of payment; circumstances and reasons for buying these commodities.
  (b) Checklist of non-lasting commodities, charges, rates and taxes which must be paid for in most families.
15. Expenses in own family: same questions as in 14 above.
16. Loss of property, reduction of sources of income.

(a) Famiy of origin: evolution in time, circumstances, effects.
(b) Own family: evolution in time, circumstances, effects.
17. Games of chance
(a) Family of origin: attitude of members of family toward games of chance, and actual situation.
(b) Own family: attitude of members of family toward games of chance, and actual situation.
(c) Questionnaire on games of chance (Bues, 1934).
18. Free insurances
(a) Family of origin: attitudes toward free insurances and actual situation.
(b) Own family: attitudes toward free insurances and actual situation.
(c) Future plans.
19. Compulsory insurances: attitude toward existing system of compulsory insurances.

II. SOCIAL PSYCHOLOGICAL LIFE-PATTERNS

A. Family and groups

1. Family.
   (a) Composition of the family: names and addresses of all known members of the family.
   (b) For each of the persons mentioned available information is asked concerning educational level, interventions of juvenile courts, homes or institutes, previous convictions, vagrancy, vocational training, occupational history, trade-union membership, political activities, religious affiliation, marriage, separation, divorce, notable successes and/or failures, partners, offspring.
   (c) Family of origin
       (i) Cliques and subgroups in the family.
       (ii) Role and prestige of each child.
       (iii) Rights and duties, rewards and punishments that were specific of each child.
       (iv) Tasks and obligations of each child.
       (v) Special privileges enjoyed by some children.
       (vi) Group activities in the family.
       (vii) Age at which each child has left the family; circumstances.
       (viii) General atmosphere in the family.
       (ix) Life-adjustment of brothers and sisters.
       (x) Other persons or relatives belonging to the family circles.
   (d) Specific questions for small or large families.
       (i) Attitudes of parents, brothers and sisters toward:
           —belonging to a small family
           —belonging to a large family.
       (ii) Desired number of children:
           —if previously raised in small family
           —if previously raised in large family.
       (iii) Ideally desired birth order in a family.
       (iv) Ideal composition of a family.
       (v) Affective and economic security afforded by
           —a small family
           —a large family.
       (vi) Importance given to financial resources:
           —in a small family
           —in a large family.

(vii) Distribution of roles and functions
—in a small family
—in a large family.
(viii) Socialization of a child
—in a small family
—in a large family.
(ix) Advantages and disadvantages of being raised
—in a small family
—in a large family.
(e) Investigation of family structure by means of P. G. Herbst's 'A Day at Home' technique (1952). Fifty-six activities (social, economic, household and children-care activities) are rated as to the person responsible for the activity and executing it; the decision-taking procedure and tension generated by decision-taking.
(f) Investigation of the psychosocial field inducing children to participate in family activities by means of P. G. Herbst's questionnaire (1952).
(g) Family-scale (questionnaire by Rundquist and Slette, 1936).
(h) Appraisal of parent behaviour: description of parent behaviour by means of the graphic ratingscales constructed by Baldwin, Kalhorn and Breese (1945).
 (i) Discord in the home (conflict–harmony).
 (ii) Restrictiveness of regulations (restrictiveness–freedom).
 (iii) Readiness of enforcement (vigilant–lax).
 (iv) Severity of actual penalties (mild–severe).
 (v) Democracy of regulation and enforcement policy (democratic–dictatorial).
 (vi) General babying (overheld–withholds help).
 (vii) General protectiveness (sheltering–exposing).
 (viii) Readiness of criticism (critical–uncritical).
 (ix) Direction of criticism (approval–disapproval).
 (x) Solicitousness for child's welfare
  (anxious–nonchalant).
 (xi) Acceptance of child (devotion–rejection).
 (xii) Emotionality (emotional–objective).
 (xiii) Affectionateness (affectionate–hostile).
(i) Attitude toward discipline exercised by parents (questionnaire by Itkin, 1952).
(j) Control exercized by parents toward adolescents (questionnaire by Nye, 1951).
(k) Attitude toward parents (questionnaire by Itkin, 1952).
(l) Parent's judgment regarding a particular child (questionnaire by Itkin, 1952).
2. School training. The first nine questions are to be answered by the subject: concerning himself and concerning his siblings.
(a) Chronological inventory of the schools attended.
(b) Reputation of and attitudes towards each of the schools that were attended.
(c) Circumstances under which change from one school to another took place.
(d) Control over school attendance and scholastic activities.
(e) Description of the contacts between parents and school authority.
(f) Description of values and rules especially emphasized in the school.
(g) School composition of school population.
(h) Description of non-scholastic activities organized by the school.
(i) Description of values and rules considered important by the school and/or parents.
(j) Comparison of non-scholastic activities organized at school and those organized at home.
(k) Comparison of school atmosphere and the atmosphere at home.

(l) Comparison of the demands made at school and those made at home.
(m) Description of the adaptation process involved in each school change.
(n) Questions concerning the role definition of 'a teacher', 'a school director','a pupil', 'a school mate'.
(o) Description of the process of adaptation to the change from kindergarten to the first class.
(p) Indication of difficulties experienced in learning to read and to write.
(q) Indication of failures to pass and classes that had to be repeated.

For each of these classes the number of pupils, the liked and disliked courses, global results, detailed results (for each course), relations with the teacher, own position in the class, groups in which one took part and friends, are inquired into. With respect to all these items it is also asked what influence failing to pass examinations and staying down exerted.

3. Homes and institutions
   (a) Chronological inventory of all homes and institutions in which the subject and siblings resided.
   (b) Opinion concerning the reputation, the objective quality of the homes or institutes.
   (c) Description of the circumstances of the first placement and of the circumstances and reasons of change of institution.
   (d) Control over school attendance and scholastic activities.
   (e) Description of the contacts between the institutional authorities and parents.
   (f) Description of values and rules emphasized especially in the homes and institutions in which the subject and his siblings resided.
   (g) Description of the social composition of the population of homes and institutions in which the subject and his siblings resided.
   (h) Description of non-scholastic activities organized by the homes and institutions in which the subject and his siblings resided.
   (i) Description of things considered important by the home or institutions and/or the parents and the family.
   (j) Comparison of non-scholastic activities organized by the home or institutions and those organized at home.
   (k) Comparison of the atmosphere of the home or institution and the atmosphere at home.
   (l) Comparison of the demands made in homes or institutions and those made at home.
   (m) Description of the adaptation process involved in a change of institution or home.
   (n) Role definition of 'educator', 'director', 'friends' in homes and institutions.
   (o) Questions concerning evaluation of the influence exerted by the homes or institutions, of their programmes, of the interpersonal relations typical for each home or institute, and the attitude towards them.
   (p) Description of the circumstances in which the subject left the last home or institute.

4. Miliary service
   (a) Date of the beginning of military service, unit, functions and promotions.
   (b) Attitudes towards the army and towards military service, held by oneself, one's friends, acquaintances, parents and family.
   Description of first impressions of military life, and of the process of adaptation to it.
   (c) Medical information concerning the period of military service: diseases, accidents and the like. Also: simulation and exaggeration of symptoms.
   (d) Opinions concerning army doctors and other personnel of army hospitals.

(e) Opinions concerning soldiers, non-commissioned officers and officers.
(f) Description of personal experiences during the period of military service: (a) good experiences, (b) bad experiences, (c) special knowledge acquired during military service.
(g) Differential comparison of values and rules considered important in the army, at home, and among friends.
(h) Differential comparison of activities in the army, at home, and among friends.
(i) Description of the subject's relations with his army superiors.
(j) Description of subject's human environment during military service.
(k) Description of leisure-time activities during military service.
(l) Description of sanctions incurred.
(m) Attitude towards staying in the army after one's term.
(n) Subject's opinions concerning the army, military service.
(o) Subject's opinion concerning military service for women.

5. Own family
   (a) Composition of the family: names and addresses of all members of the family.
   (b) For each of the members mentioned information is asked concerning: educational level, interventions of juvenile courts, homes or institutes, previous convictions, vagrancy, vocational training, occupational history, trade-union membership, political activities, religious affiliation, marriage, separation, divorce, notable successes and/or failures, partners, offspring.
   (c) History of relationship with sex-partners.
   (d) Role descriptions.
       Descriptions of good/bad, fiancées, spouses, or concubines and self-description as a partner.
   (e) Description of the evolution of mutual relationships between members of the family.
   (f) Investigation of family structures by means of Herbert's 'A Day at Home' technique; fifty-six activities (social, economic, household and child-care) are asked, checked as to execution, performance, decision-taking, and tension.
   (g) Questionnaire by Nadler and Morrow on 'Attitudes towards Women'.
   (h) Questionnaire by Dean and Allen on 'Antifemininity in Men'.
   (i) Burgess questionnaire: Marriage prediction schedule (prediction of probability of a successful marriage).
   (j) Burgess questionnaire: Marriage adaptation schedule (evaluation of the subject's degree of adaptation to marriage).
   (k) Opinions regarding the bringing up of children (questionnaire by Itkin).
   (l) Survey of opinions regarding the description of children (questionnaire by Itkin).

6. Groups
   (a) Chronological enumeration of all groups in which the subject has participated.
   (b) Application of Hemphill's questionnaire on group dimensions (group goals, Rules and regulations, degree of participation of the members and the subject, organization, relative influence of any member on the others, leadership, social composition, rules of admittance and of exclusion, evolution of the group, cohesion, external relations, degree of intimacy, general group atmosphere, etc.) on each of the groups mentioned under IIA6a.
   (c) Hemphill's questionnaire is supplemented by an extensive interview on each of the dimensions.
   (d) Questionnaire regarding several possible attitudes toward groups and accounts given as backing of these attitudes (groups in which one did not participate are also considered).

(e) Description of roles, related to group leadership functions. Information is gathered on the subject's view about good, mediocre and bad leaders, and a self-description as a group leader is added.

B. Cultural pattern of values, norms, expectations, and roles

1. Prohibitions
    (a) Chronological inventory of all prohibitions to which one has ever been subjected.
    (b) Indication of (a) those prohibitions which were also obeyed by the person imposing them, (b) of those which were not obeyed by the imposing person, and (c) of those which this person only applied to himself.
    (c) Ranking of prohibitions according to their subjective importance.
    (d) Indication for each of the prohibitions of the persons who attached great importance to them.
    (e) Description of disagreement on certain prohibitions and of the disagreeing parties.
    (f) Description of prohibitions to which only the subject was submitted.
    (g) Description of the prohibitions that were clearly formulated (indication by whom), and of those for which justifications were given (indication by whom).
    (h) Ranking of the prohibitions according to their attractiveness and repulsive force.
    (i) Ranking of all prohibitions according to the difficulties experienced in observing them.
    (j) Descriptions of subject's reactions in case of a violation of each rule.
    (k) Description of punishment(s) and reward(s) that followed the violation or the observation of the different rules.
    (l) Indication of the persons who decided to punish or not, and of the executors of the punishments.
    (m) Indication of circumstances under which there was disagreement on the nature and severity of punishment, and indication of the disagreeing persons.
    (n) Ranking of all listed punishments by the subject's sensitivity to them and reasons for this order.
    (o) For each of the prohibitions ranking of all relevant punishments and rewards as to their experienced effectiveness.
2. Prescriptions
    (a) Chronological inventory of all prescriptions to which one has ever been subjected.
    (b) Indication of (a) those prescriptions which were also obeyed by the person imposing them, (b) of those which were not obeyed by the imposing person, and (c) of those which this person only applied to himself.
    (c) Ranking of prescriptions according to their subjective importance.
    (d) Indication for each of the prescriptions of the persons who attached great importance to them.
    (e) Description of disagreement on certain prescriptions and of the disagreeing parties.
    (f) Description of prescriptions to which only the subject was submitted.
    (g) Description of the prescriptions that were clearly formulated (indication by whom), and of those for which justifications were given (indication by whom).
    (h) Ranking of the prescriptions according to their attractiveness and repulsive force.
    (i) Ranking of all prescriptions according to the difficulties experienced in observing them.
    (j) Descriptions of subject's reactions in case of a violation of each rule.
    (k) Description of punishment(s) and reward(s) that followed the violation or the observation of the different rules.

(l) Indication of the persons who decided to punish or not, and of the executors of the punishments.
(m) Indication of circumstances under which there was disagreement on the nature and severity of punishment, and indication of the disagreeing persons.
(n) Ranking of all listed punishments concerning the subject's sensitivity to them and reasons for this order.
(o) For each of the prescriptions ranking of all relevant punishments and rewards as to their experienced effectiveness.
(p) Description of parental attitudes towards their children and of attitudes amongst the children themselves: (a) the subject describes situations of agreement, disagreement, approval, disapproval, punishment and reward; (b) concerning punishments and rewards the subject has to elaborate on the family members that were allowed to punish and reward (and reaction of the others); (c) finally the subject has to indicate the family member who was punished most frequently, and the one who was most often rewarded.

3. Expectations
   (a) Inventory of everything one has ever been expected to do by someone else with indication of persons involved and possible exceptions to these expectations.
   (b) Inventory of all expectations parents had regarding their children but not towards the subject.
   (c) Description of the subject's brother(s) and/or sister(s) compliance with the parents' expectations.
   (d) Description of parental expectations towards their children inspired by a desire either (a) to see their example followed, or (b) to see their children doing better, or (c) to see their children achieve more than they themselves ever did, or (d) to protect their children from unpleasant experiences they had to suffer.
   (e) Indication of all persons (a) that were ever mentioned as an example, (b) of all persons that influenced the subject's parents or any other authority, and (c) of those who followed this example.
   (f) Indication of those expectations that were (a) totally, (b) partly, and (c) never realized.
   (g) Description of realizations which came about without anybody expecting them.
   (h) Description of the subject's expectations towards parents and other authorities that were totally, partly or never realized. Description by the subject of other persons who conformed to these expectations.
   (i) Description of the behaviour or aspects of conduct one ever expected from a 'good' brother, sister, grandfather, grandmother, uncle, aunt.
   (j) Description of the subject's attitude towards his own children: what to forbid (and why), what to impose (and why), how to reward and to punish (and why), persons as examples (and why), expectations regarding offspring.
   (k) Description of the subject's attitude towards his children.
   (l) Description of the attitude of the subject's wife or concubine towards their children.
   (m) Description of the attitude of children towards each other.
   (n) Information is asked on disagreements; encouraged behaviour, discouraged behaviour, punished behaviour, persons involved; rewarded behaviour, child most frequently punished or rewarded, rewarding and punishing attitude of children towards each other.

4. Moral qualities. Making use of a list of explicitly defined moral qualities like unselfishness, trust, courage, devotion, tact, humbleness, self-control, modesty, wisdom, etc. . . . the subject is asked (a) to indicate what persons he ever met who either

exemplified these virtues to a marked degree or who manifested quite the opposite behaviour; and (b) in what circumstances he interacted with these persons.
5. The Rokeach value questionnaire. A questionnaire yielding information regarding the subject's views on a number of values and the appropriate means to reach them. The subject is asked which situations in which he participated did these values exert a guiding influence, and in which ones they did not.

C. The institutional situation: the prison situation

1. Available information concerning the first time the subject has been arrested, the first interrogation, and the first appearance in court as a suspect.
2. Experiences with officials in charge of police and judicial investigations.
3. Description of the circumstances of the arrest subsequent to the 'worst' crime committed. The subject is also asked to describe (a) the first interrogation, (b) subsequent interrogations, (c) his opinions concerning witnesses and experts involved in his trial, and (d) to comment on his file.
4. Description of subject's relationship with his lawyer(s), and of his opinion about him (them).
5. Description of subject's subjective experience of all steps between arrest and conviction, and all persons and institutions involved.
6. Subject's knowledge and opinions concerning the effects of the trial on family members, friends, acquaintances, neighbours, relatives of the victim, and on public opinion.
7. Personal remarks on appearance at court, on the trial.
8. The subject is asked to give a series of role definitions which covers all officials involved in arrest, investigation and trial.
9. Description of subject's first impressions after the first contacts with prison and prison life.
10. Inventory of all prisons where the subject stayed, ranking according to personal preference.
11. The rank ordering of ten important prison activities according to their subjective importance.
12. Description of the unpleasant aspects of prison life and of those aspects which the subject tolerated better than most prisoners.
13. Description of subject's adaptation to prison routine. Comparison of sleeping habits in prison and in normal life, and a description of the evolution of the subject's physical condition in prison.
14. Description of the way in which one keeps track of the course of time (timetables). At this point questions are also asked about the subject's time perspective in prison.
15. Description of subject's contacts with the outside: (a) subject's reactions to visits, (b) to correspondence, (c) to events outside the prison, and (d) opinions of outsiders concerning the subject.
16. Subject's opinion about prescribed activities in prison.
17. Description of subject's contacts with (a) fellow-prisoners, (b) guards, and (c) members of the prison administration.
18. Subject's opinions about a prisoner's fundamental rights and about the way he feels he is actually treated.
19. Description of (a) subject's personal occupations, and (b) of group activities in which he participates.
20. Description of imaginary conditions like high wages, private visit of wife or girlfriend, meals, holidays spent outside, etc. . . . under which the subject would consider the lengthening of his sentence to be a good bargain.

21. Description of the imaginery conditions like hard labour, low wages, compulsory, scientific experimentation, lack of recreational activities, suppression of visits etc. . . which, according to the subject, would justify a shortening of his sentence.
22. Subject's opinion concerning changes in duration of sentence that would be required if (a) a friend, or (b) a relative could be substituted to him.
23. Opinion concerning the conversion of the subject's sentence into a measure which would allow him to stay in prison only during weekends, given that the length of punishment (expressed in days) would remain the same.
24. Descriptions of role definitions of (a) a guard (different hierarchical gradations), (b) a prison director, (c) a prison doctor, (d) a prison psychiatrist, (e) a prison psychologist, (f) a social worker, (g) a fellow prisoner.
25. Opinions concerning (a) the existing judicial system, and (b) concerning some recent innovations in the penitentiary system.

III. INDIVIDUAL CHARACTERISTICS: SELF AND PERSONALITY

A. Self-description and interpretations

1. The body.
   (a) The subject is asked to rate thirty-eight aspects of the body (a) as to their subjective importance, and (b) as to the satisfaction experienced concerning them.
   (b) Reasons for complaints about some parts of the body and about one's physical characteristics.
   (c) Indication of that part of the body which is experienced as the centre of one's person.
   (d) Body Focus Questionnaire (Fisher). Parts of the body are presented in pairs; the subject is asked to indicate the part of which he is actually most conscious).
   (e) The Body Distortion Questionnaire (Fisher). (A list of eighty-two perceived distortions has to be checked).
2. Personal appearance. A series of questions is asked concerning (a) situations in which one was laughed at, (b) nicknames, (c) physical defects and diseases, (d) valued characteristics of a beautiful person and of a beautiful woman, (e) evaluation of physical characteristics shown during certain life periods (puberty, adolescence, adulthood, old age).
3. Peculiar habits. Enumeration of peculiar mannerisms and ticks (picking one's nose, sucking, nail-biting for example) performed in public and/or in private.
4. Questions concerning subject's physical development, after birth, during early childhood and first years of life (description of birth conditions, hygiene, speech development, lateralization, peculiar habits with mention of source).
5. Health. A chronological enumeration of illnesses, hospitalizations and surgical interventions. Furthermore the subject has to relate (a) his personal experience with medical staff during these periods, (b) possible effect of the illnesses, hospitalizations and interventions on his personality, and (c) role definitions of members of medical staff.
   (a) Description of one's play activities and their evolution in time.
   (b) Description of one's sleeping habits and dreams, and their evolution in time.
   (c) Description of one's eating habits and of their evolution in time.
   (d) Description of one's drinking habits and their evolution in time.
   (e) Description of one's evacuation habits and their evolution in time.
   (f) Cleanness of body and clothes. Information is gathered on personal hygiene and

on clothing habits, as well as on their evolution in time and their variations in different settings.
   (g) Description of subject's sexual experiences and attitudes towards sexuality (Eysenck–Wilson questionnaire on sexuality).
6. Emotional reactions and sentiments: The subject is asked to give detailed descriptions of situations in which he experienced: fury, rage, joy, sadness, fear, guilt, remorse, inferiority, pride, jealousy, envy, superiority, admiration, disapproval, compassion, indignation, resentment.
7. Self-description by means of (a) the enumeration, (b) classification, and (c) exemplification of one's important personal characteristics (modification of the 'Who Am I' technique).
8. Self-description focused on elementary school period, indicating the sources of informations.
9. Self-description focused on adolescence period, indicating sources of information.
10. A description of oneself within ten years from 'now' (or at another future moment).
11. Imaginary self-description at the age of sixty-four.
12. Description of other persons: most similar to the subject; most dissimilar to the subject.
13. Subject's description as he imagines it would be given by his best friends; by his enemies.
14. A series of questions is asked concerning one's opinions about (a) one's name, (b) favourite objects, environments and animals.
15. Family relations.
    (a) Names and occupations of all members.
    (b) For each member a series of questions is asked in order to gather information on major events in their lives; date of birth, present address, date of death, physical condition, diseases, medical and psychiatric care, hospitalizations, accidents, physical weaknesses, alcoholism, etc.
    (c) Important personality traits of each family member.
    (d) With respect to the subject's parents questions are asked concerning the evolution of their marriage, also concubines, divorces, and their relations within the rest of the family.
    (e) Interpersonal relations. Questions are asked about (a) preferences for certain members of the family, (b) interpersonal importance of each member, (c) similarities and differences within the family.
    (f) Role definitions. The subject is asked—for each role mentioned in the list below—to give a general opinion about a good/bad father, mother, etc. a personal opinion about a good/bad father, mother, etc.; a description of the corresponding members of his own family; and a self-description as a father, etc.
    (g) Role list: a father, a stepfather, a mother, a stepmother, a grandfather, a grandmother, an aunt, an uncle, a brother, a sister.
16. The 'Self and Others' questionnaire (Berger). Sixty-five items concerning self and other acceptance are to be rated on a five-point scale according to their applicability to oneself.
17. Personality descriptions. Thirty short personality descriptions are presented and the subject is asked to indicate which individuals personally known to him fit the descriptions. The subject is also asked to describe for each person the circumstances of their first contacts and to describe the evolution of their relationship.
18. Profile of mood scales (POMS by Lorr and McNair). Sixty descriptions of mood states are rated on a five-point scale as to their applicability to (a) the real self, (b) the ideal self, (c) the father, (d) the mother, and (e) the girlfriend or wife.

19. Two hundred and sixty items concerning personality characteristics are rated on a five-point scale as to their applicability to : (a) self, (b) ideal self, (c) subject's father, (d) subject's mother, and (e) subject's girlfriend or wife.
20. Psychological rating. Three hundred and sixty-three items concerning psychopathological characteristics are rated as to their applicability to the self.
21. Leary's checklist. One hundred and twenty-eight personality characteristics are checked so as to yield a description of subject's real and ideal self.
22. Adjective checklist (ACL) by Gough. Out of three hundred adjectives those that are descriptive of the self are to be checked (one global scale; eight sub-scales, two factor scores).
23. Buss's questionnaire on Aggression (Seventy-five items).
24. Estimate of various abilities and skills (physical, technical, economical, leadership ability, social, erotic, intellectual, aesthetic and artistic). The subject is asked to give an estimation of his real ability in each of these fields, and to indicate his desired ability level. Besides, the subject has to mention the family members who had (in a particular field) manifested an ability above average.
25. Inventory of the subject's reference persons. A list of role titles is given and the subject is asked to fill in the name of the person he knew who best matched the role title in question. Furthermore he is asked to describe the persons mentioned, to indicate their most salient characteristics, and to describe the circumstances under which the person mentioned and the subject became acquainted.

The following titles are given:
(a) Most peculiar or interesting persons ever met, (b) the most peculiar or interesting persons ever heard of or read about, (c) persons whose advice would be asked, (d) the best friend(s) one had, (e) a friend (role definition), (f) admired public figures (sports, music, painting, etc.), (g) disliked public figures, (h) important persons one would like to meet.

B. Interests, occupational and leisure time activities

1. Interests. The subject is asked to enumerate chronologically all interests he ever had, and to indicate for each of them: (a) the life-period in which he had this particular interest, (b) the favouring conditions, (c) the inhibiting factors, (d) the persons involved, (e) the groups involved, and (f) the influence exerted by each interest on the subject's knowledge and capacities.
2. The centre's questionnaire. Ten statements referring to general professional goals are provided. The subject is asked to rank order them.
3. Employment. The subject is asked to enumerate all his former occupations accompanied by detailed information about: (a) activities, (b) colleagues, (c) staff members, (d) trade-union representatives, (e) discharge, (f) training programme. Then the subject is asked to explain eventual differences between his actual occupations and his preferences given under III.B. 2 above.
4. Job enjoyment questionnaire (Rothe and Brayfield). The subject has to express his degree of agreement or disagreement with eighteen statements concerning each of his former occupations.
5. Job description index. Description of former occupations, the best possible occupation, and the worst possible occupation, in terms of (a) working, (b) wages, (c) promotion opportunity, supervision characteristics and characteristics of work-mates.
6. Role definitions. The subject is asked to give: (a) the general opinion concerning a good and a bad worker, (b) his personal opinion as to what a good worker and a bad worker is, (c) a description of a good, an average and a bad worker he personally knows, (d) a

self-description (even hypothetical) as a worker. The four questions are eventually repeated for a foreman, a boss, an employee or clerk, a head of department, a director, etc. . .
7. Questionnaire on leisure-time activities and enjoyment (Pace, 1941). For each period of life, the subject is asked to indicate the frequency with which he practised any of the forty-eight activities listed and the degree to which he enjoyed them.

C. Goals, aspirations, and conflicts

1. Description of some (at least three) goals easily reached in the past, and of anticipated level of aspiration in future similar situations.
2. Description of some (at least three) goals that were hard to attain, and of anticipated level of aspiration in future similar situations.
3. Description of some (at least three) goals never attained, and of anticipated level of aspiration in future similar situations.
4. Description of some situations in which one could hardly take a decision, and anticipated behaviour in future similar situations.
5. Description of some situations in which it proved to be impossible to take a decision, and of anticipated behaviour in future similar situations.
6. Description of some situations in which one had to chose between two equally attractive goals, and anticipated behaviour in future similar situations.
7. Description of some situations in which one had to chose between two equally unattractive goals and of anticipated behaviour in future similar situations.
8. Description of some situations in which one was equally attracted and repulsed by the same goal, and of anticipated behaviour in future similar situations.
9. Rotter's questionnaire on 'Locus of Control' (external vs. internal—twenty-nine items).
10. Guevara's questionnaire about success-seeking and failure avoidance (twenty-two items).

9

THE REPERTORY GRID IN PSYCHOLOGICAL RESEARCH

Peter Collett

INTRODUCTION

In 1955 George Kelly published a two-volume book entitled *The Psychology of Personal Constructs*. In it he argued that a psychological theory must take account of the fact that people actively make sense of their world. He also made the point that in the daily course of their lives people approach problems much like a scientist: they form predictions, make observations and test hypotheses; and it is by virtue of the fact that men behave like scientists that scientists behave the way they do.

Kelly took great care to explicate the assumptions upon which his theory was grounded. These took the form of three axioms. He proposed, first of all, that the universe is real and not some ghostly projection, and secondly that it is temporally constituted and therefore only properly understood as it exists in time. Finally he suggested that events are interrelated or integral. In positing such a world he also made the point that those interpersonal things that we call beliefs, feelings or whatever are as real and substantial as events which are external to the individual. Man, for Kelly, is not some inert object acted upon by forces external to him (including, paradoxically, the all-knowing investigator), but he is rather an agent, an agent who makes sense of the world by actively construing it. Men can only know the world in terms of the constructions they place upon it, and the limits of men's constructions are the limits of their imaginations. Each man, says Kelly, builds for himself a model that will enable him to understand what happens about him. This representational scheme takes the form of a construct system. It is a *construct* system because constructs are the means whereby he construes the world, and it is a construct *system* because constructs are organized in a coherent fashion.

Kelly called his approach *constructive alternativism*, and this he contrasted with *accumulative fragmentalism*, namely the idea that findings can be collected in piecemeal fashion until they reach some critical mass from which a theory mysteriously emerges. His idea concerning the arbitrariness of construct systems has important repercussions, not only for the notion of a theory, but also for the way one approaches others. More importantly though, Kelly sought to persuade his reader that theories are shortlived and frail. Just as men come to see old facts in a new light, so too established theories must in time give way to new ones. Kelly saw an entrenched theory as inviting replacement rather than respect, and of course he saw his own theory as being liable to the same process of eventual rejection as any other. There are several points in his writings where he makes it quite clear that he expects Personal Construct Theory to enjoy the same fate as other theories. But while Kelly showed himself to be unthreatened by the prospect of having his theory dismantled, many of its later adherents have not.

Kelly was convinced that any psychological theory must be reflexive. Its terms of reference must encompass not only people who are being studied but also those who seek to study them. In this way, and by comparing men to scientists, Kelly tried to provide a theory which would also account for the activities of the investigator. He attempted, furthermore, to offer a conception of the individual. His idiographic perspective was of course consistent with the requirements for a theory about personal constructs, but as Bannister and Mair (1968) have pointed out, it also allowed for comparisons between individuals. Kelly's theory was presented in the form of a fundamental postulate and eleven corollaries which extended the scope of the fundamental postulate. The fundamental postulate was that 'A person's processes are psychologically channelized by the ways in which he anticipates events', and the corollaries described various supposed characteristics of a construct system. By including the term 'anticipation' Kelly placed himself firmly among those who refused to be bothered by the consequences of seeing people as purposive agents (see Bannister and Fransella, 1971).

The cornerstone of the theory of personal constructs is the construct, for it is in terms of constructs that the individual construes certain entities as being similar to or different from each other. Kelly went to great lengths to distinguish the construct from other, closely related notions. It is not, for example, like a concept, for while the concept describes the point at which constructs intersect, each construct defines only one feature of an entity. Furthermore, the construct has categorical properties. It functions in an all-or-none fashion to indicate the perceived value of an entity in relation to just that feature. Constructs do not stand alone, but form a system in which each is related inferentially and by implication to others in a hierarchy. These and other properties of the system were described by Kelly in the eleven corollaries which elaborated and extended the fundamental postulate.

The methodological handmaiden to Kelly's theory was the Role Construct Repertory Test, what is now commonly referred to as the *Repertory Grid*. It is a *repertory* grid because it seeks to disclose the repertoire and the systemic properties of a person's constructs, and it is a *grid* because the method involves a matrix technique. Kelly tried several approaches, and subsequent attempts, most notably those of Hinkle (1965), have endeavoured to tap into the construct system by other means. In this essay, however, our sole concern will be with the grid method, the types of data that can be extracted from the matrix and the various uses to which it has been put. The technique which Kelly developed and others have since refined was by no means novel. Matrix methods were available at the time, and some of the statistical procedures that are now employed were being used, admittedly in a rudimentary fashion, when he wrote his book. Stephenson (1953), for example, had produced a detailed analysis of the Q-sort technique some two years before Kelly, and the availability of these and other techniques may have played some part in fashioning his thinking. It is worth noting that Kelly gave to matrix methods a new and more respectable purpose. He gave it a theory, and in this lies the appeal that it has had. Interestingly, in his later years Kelly paid less attention to the actual method and began to turn his hand more to programmatics. He is reported to have said that had he had his time again he would have dislodged the method from the theory (Hinkle, 1970). But Kelly's later opinions need not detain us here. Rather, what is important is what the method offers us by way of a technique for disclosing the constructions that people place on their world. It is to this general issue that we now turn.

DESIGNING A GRID

The grid method relies on a matrix technique. Not only does the matrix provide a systematic scheme within which to examine a person's constructions, but it also promises to disclose the relationships that obtain among his constructs and among the events which they describe, as well as those which hold between particular constructs and events. A grid is usually assembled with constructs arrayed down the rows and events or *elements* along the columns of the matrix. No particular size of matrix is stipulated, although for certain statistical purposes a grid of no less than eight rows and eight columns should be employed.

In administering a grid the researcher encounters three types of problem. He must decide which elements are to be described, which constructs are to serve this purpose, and the means whereby elements are to be allotted to constructs. Let us deal with each of these issues separately.

Selecting elements

Where the selection of elements is concerned the investigator may either provide elements for the person to appraise or allow him to nominate his own elements. The second procedure usually involves the provision of *role titles*, to which the person is required to fit the names of people who fit the descriptions implicit in the titles. Kelly and those who employ the grid in a clinical context have used this technique extensively. Kelly, for example, would provide his client with role titles like, 'A person of your sex you would enjoy having as a companion on a trip', 'A teacher you like', 'The most interesting person you know', and so on. By eliciting elements in this way one allows the subject to address himself to people who are salient to him, but, against this, there is always the possibility that some of the role titles may be peripheral to the person's concerns. It may, for example, be the case that holiday companionship is not central to the discriminations that certain people make. We see therefore that where role titles include constructs, either expressedly or by implication, then the question of construct salience is liable to apply as much to decisions about which constructs should be used as it does to which elements he should be asked to construe. The other advantage of employing the role title technique is that it allows for standardization. Merely providing everyone with equivalent elements meets the same end, but it does not of course make concessions to the peculiar dispositions of the individual.

Selecting constructs

The distinction between eliciting and providing applies as much to decisions about constructs as it does to elements. As we have seen, elements are elicited by providing role titles. In the case of constructs the picture is more complex and the alternative procedures more numerous. Bannister and Mair (1968) and Fransella and Bannister (1977) have discussed the various ways of eliciting constructs which occupy salient positions in a person's system. The one technique to which they devote most of their attention is the Triadic Method. The procedure relies on the prior determination of elements, and it involves confronting someone with a set of three elements at a time. The investigator asks the person to consider which two are most alike, and then to say how they are similar and yet different from the third. Kelly made the point that not all constructs can readily be verbalized, and some researchers have in fact gone so far as to administer grids without the person having to label his constructs. For the most part, however, the subject is required to be explicit.

The term that someone uses to unite two elements is variously referred to as the *emergent* or *explicit* pole of the construct, and that which defines the third element in the triad as the *submerged* or *implicit* pole of the same construct. In the absence of additional information, this distinction should not be regarded as anything more than a useful heuristic, because the expression which serves to identify two elements will probably depend on which elements have been considered. Short of making it the central focus of an investigation, there is really no good reason to suppose that any reliable inferences can be drawn from the term used as the unifying feature of a construct.

Where constructs are elicited through the triadic method the subject is normally required to offer both the term that unites two elements and its opposite. If, for example, he had announced that two of the people being considered were *kind* and the third was *mean*, then the construct would, for these purposes, be taken to be the *kind–mean* construct. The question of what should be taken as the opposite pole depends on the nature of the allotment system being employed, but that notwithstanding it seems best to take the negative of the first terms as the contrary expression. Instead of pressing the subject for his personal antonym for *kind*, one would merely take its negation, namely *not kind*, as the opposite. The reasons for adopting this procedure are two-fold: Firstly, it obviates the need for having to decide whether to admit both a *kind–mean* and a *kind–inconsiderate* construct in the same grid, and secondly it eliminates the possibility of each term spanning only part of the full array of elements. In other words, while the constructs *kind–not kind* would presumably exhaust the range of elements, a *kind–mean* construct might not, for the simple reason that the subject may feel that there are some people who warrant neither description.

The question whether constructs should be elicited or provided has received some attention. Kelly (1955) was quite insistent that the person be allowed to deploy his own constructs, and to some extent his strictures have been observed. There are, however, many studies where, for reasons of standardization and comparison, subjects have been provided with constructs. This means, in effect, that they are required to use terms which they might normally not apply. This issue has been examined in several ways in order to determine whether grids with provided constructs are any different from those where the subject expresses himself in his own terms. Some studies claim that people handle their own terms with greater proficiency, others that there is no difference between using one's own and the experimenter's labels. Much of the evidence assembled in favour of elicited constructs has been of the self-report type. Investigators have found that subjects regard their own constructs as more 'useful' (Bonarius, 1965; Landfield, 1968) or more 'meaningful' (Cromwell and Caldwell, 1962) than those provided by an experimenter. As it happens, such studies offer no indication of the actual facility with which people handle their own as opposed to others' construct terms, and even as an attempt to uncover people's opinions about their own and other people's terms they are liable to the distortions produced by demand characteristics.

Other studies have discovered that subjects use more extreme points on rating scales when employing their own constructs (Landfield, 1968; Bonarius, 1965), while at least one study has totally failed to uncover any difference at all (Warr and Coffman, 1970). However, as Adams-Webber (1970b) has pointed out, the interpretation of extremity of rating is problematic. What is more, the relationship between extremity and the utility of a construct remains undemonstrated. There is some evidence that the overall distinctions produced in the use of personal constructs offer a better reflection of the groupings produced in a free sorting task (Stringer, 1972), and there are also several studies which show that grids completed with elicited constructs are no more complex than those with provided constructs (Tripodi and Bieri, 1963; Bieri *et al.*, 1966; Jaspars, 1966; McFadyen and Foulds, 1972). The debate about whose construct terms should be employed is far from settled, although as Kelly pointed out there is strong *a priori* argument in favour of examining a person's construct system in its own terms. There are many studies where the subjects are required to use the same constructs. Even though this may occur for quite good reasons, it seems that as a rule it is better to allow the subject to offer his own criteria.

The allotment of elements to constructs

Aside from deciding whether elements and constructs should be elicited or provided, the investigator must also face the question of how the subject is going to describe the relations between the elements and the constructs. There are three common methods from which he may select. They are as follows.

The dichotomous method

This is closest to the heart of Personal Construct Theory. As the title suggests it involves a dichotomous application of constructs to elements, such that the subject is only able to make one or two possible statements about an element and a construct. All constructs, whether elicited or provided, will usually be located along the rows of the matrix. The subject's task is to consider each construct in turn and to say which pole of the construct describes each element. If, for example the subject had offered the construct *kind–not kind* for the first row, he would then be asked to consider the first element—that is, the person whose name appears in the first column—and say whether that person was kind or not. Normally a judgment in line with the emergent pole is recorded with a one (or a tick) in the appropriate cell, while a judgment in line with the submerged pole is recorded with a nought (or a cross). By taking each row separately and by working through all the elements one at a time the investigator and the subject should conclude the session with an array of ones and noughts in the cells of the matrix. No cell should remain empty.

The rating scale method

This involves the subtention of a scale across the two poles of the construct. As with all scalar techniques there is no obligatory number of points, although researchers usually employ either a five or seven-point scale. When the rating scale method is used then the antonym of the emergent pole rather than its negation is located on the opposite pole. Where, for example, the subject has offered the terms *kind* and *mean* to distinguish members of an elicitation triad, then these terms are located at the ends of the scale and qualified with such expressions as *extremely* or *very* in order to distinguish the extremes from the intermediate points. Where a midpoint is included it may be marked as *both* or *neither*, and it is this provision which makes nonsense of any attempt to employ the emergent pole and its opposite. Clearly, the subject's task would be complicated by having to decide whether an element was 'neither kind nor not kind' or whether it was 'both kind and not kind'. Thus, where the rating scale method is used the requirement concerning the use of emergent poles and their opposites must necessarily lapse. There has been some informal debate as to whether the intermediate points on a scale should be labelled. The only appropriate decision here would be one which took account of the predicament of the subject. One vindication of a method is that subjects have no special difficulty working with it.

The ranking method

While the rating method focuses on quasi-nominal relationships, the ranking method is designed to uncover the ordinal relationships between elements. When using the ranking method only one construct pole is employed and the subject is asked to consider all elements in relation to that single expression. The method may involve one or two procedures: the subject may be confronted with an array of cards on which the names of the elements have been written and then asked to nominate the most representative from among the set. That card would then be withdrawn and the procedure repeated until all the cards had been removed. Alternatively the subject could order the elements covertly and then record their rank positions himself. The former method has been widely used within an interactive context (Bannister and Fransella, 1967), the latter where it is assumed that the subject is capable of handling the procedure without the investigator's assistance. Ranking eliminates the problems that might arise from different people placing different constructions on the terms that qualify the scale points. It therefore has the advantage of being better suited to cross-cultural studies where problems of translation equivalence are paramount (see Collett, 1972, 1976).

Before administering a grid the investigator must reach a decision on each of the issues we have discussed. He should decide whether to provide or elicit elements and constructs, and which of the allotment procedures to use.

ADMINISTERING A GRID

For the purpose of illustration, let us suppose that the investigator is interested in discovering how someone construes the members of his family, and that he has discovered that ten people constitute the immediate family of his subject. In drawing up a matrix he would need to include ten columns. Let us also suppose that he decides to have ten rows, one for each construct. He would then have a ten by ten matrix, with the names of the elements arrayed along the top. On confronting the subject, he would briefly outline the procedure to be adopted and then direct his attention to the first construct elicitation triad. The respective triads are usually indicated by circles in the appropriate cells, and if he were following this convention he would read out the names of the people in the first triad. In the case of the example depicted in Figure 9.1 below he would refer the subject to Mother, Tom and Harry.

As decisions about which elements to group into triads tend to be somewhat haphazard, let us digress this point. The first thing to notice is that in a 'square' matrix each element will appear in three triads, and secondly that triads made up of dissimilar elements are more likely to elicit superordinate constructs than those composed of similar elements. In order to extract constructs that occupy varying positions in the hierarchy, it is necessary to constitute triads in such a way that some contain similar and others dissimilar elements. One method of doing this is to have the subject sort the elements into groups on the basis of overall similarity before the session begins. These groupings can then be used to arrange triads which are composed of within- and between-group elements.

A construct is usually elicited through the provision of a triad of elements. The investigator presents the elements one at a time and asks the subject to consider one important way in which two of them are alike and yet different from the third. It is preferable, if not essential, to precede the actual elicitation phase with an illustration of what is required. This should be done with elements which are not already listed. The illustration should show that there are three ways of grouping three people, and that a multitude of labels can be attached to any one distinction. This, the investigator should point out, demonstrates that there are

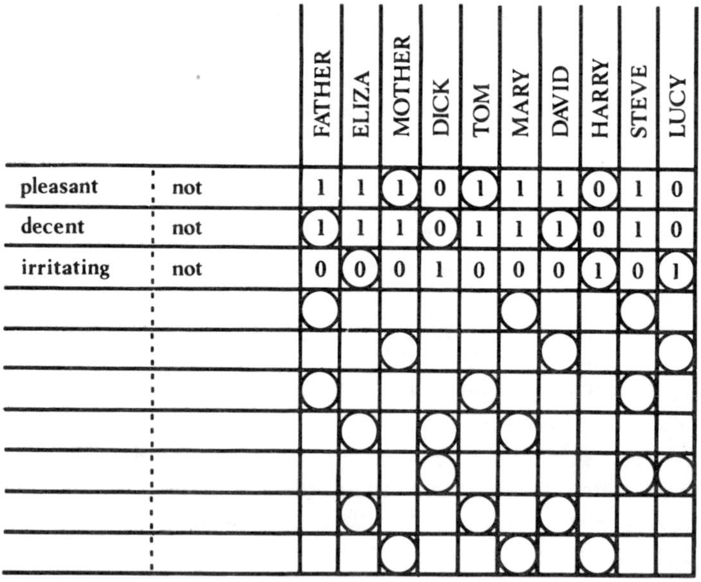

		FATHER	ELIZA	MOTHER	DICK	TOM	MARY	DAVID	HARRY	STEVE	LUCY
pleasant	not	1	1	1	0	1	1	1	0	1	0
decent	not	1	1	1	0	1	1	1	0	1	0
irritating	not	0	0	0	1	0	0	0	1	0	1

Figure 9.1 The format of a grid

different ways of grouping people, just as there are many different reasons for such groupings. There is obviously no single correct way; it all depends on one's point of view. This relative aspect of the procedure should be emphasized in order to ensure that the subject offers his own opinions and that he is not intimidated by the prospects of some veiled test.

Once the subject has indicated that he understands the method, the investigator can proceed to elicit the first construct. In doing so he should check that a distinction has actually been made, and that the subject does not apply the emergent pole to all three elements at some later stage. He should also dismiss all 'double-barrelled' constructs such as *kind and generous* or *clever and shrewd*, as the subject may alternate between the constituent terms of the pair when applying the construct. Bannister and Mair (1968) also suggest that excessively general constructs such as *male–female* and excessively specific constructs such as *wears a monocle–does not* should be excluded from the grid because constructs with limited ranges of convenience cannot be used throughout.

Once a satisfactory construct has been offered, this is recorded in the appropriate space beside the first row of the matrix. Depending on which type of allotment procedure is being used the investigator then either enters the negation of the term or else goes on to elicit the label for the implicit pole. Let us imagine that the investigator has decided to use the dichotomous method and the negation of the emergent pole. He would then take each column separately and ask the subject which term described that element. Responses in line with the emergent pole would be identified with a one, those in line with the negation with a nought. The same procedure would be adopted for all elements and the next triad of elements would then be presented in order to elicit the second construct. Here the investigator would need to ensure that the subject did not offer what appeared to be a synonym for the first construct. If, for example, the constructs *pleasant* and *pleasing* were offered for the first and second triads respectively, then he would ask the subject if *pleasant* people are necessarily *pleasing*, and whether *pleasing* people are necessarily *pleasant*. Were the subject to give an affirmative response to either question then the investigator would have to ask him to offer a different construct. The same applies for all pairs of constructs. The investigator must ensure that identical constructs do not enter the list under the guise of different labels. Once all the required constructs have been elicited and all the elements have been allotted to each construct the investigator should have a matrix full of ones and noughts. At this point the grid is ready for analysis.

ANALYSING A GRID

There is a wide variety of measures to be extracted from a matrix. Although the allotment procedure does influence the kinds of indices that can be extracted from a grid, it is also true that all grids yield much the same information. Kelly made the point that it is possible to analyse a grid without considering the elements and constructs. Figuratively speaking it is possible to take a pair of scissors, remove the elements and construct labels and then scrutinize just the structural properties of the matrix. This suggests that a grid can be treated in one of three ways, either by looking at the constructs irrespective of their relations, by looking at structure independently of content or by examining structural relations in conjunction with the content of the constructs.

Examining content

Where the investigator is interested in the labels that the subject provides he may categorize the elicited constructs according to some pre-established scheme (see Landfield, 1971; Fransella, 1972; Duck, 1973). In Duck's analyses of the relationship between construct similarity and friendship formation, constructs were assigned to various content categories from which it was possible to derive an index of the extent to which two people employed similar constructs.

This procedure raises the question of what it actually means to categorize another's construct terms. In this connection there are two opposing sets of assumptions which underpin quite different arguments. On the one hand there is the suggestion that our manifest success in comprehending each other demonstrates that we use the constituents of language in similar ways. Against this there is a solipsistic argument to the effect that in principle intersubjective identity cannot be demonstrated. Whatever the relative merits of these two positions it is quite clear that any attempt to recover the supposed meaning of a linguistic sign out of context will be fraught with problems. Admittedly there may be some descriptive terms which convey only one meaning, but there will be many more that are liable to several interpretations. In ordinary language use the task of deciding between competing interpretations is performed with reference to the context and the utterance within which the expression is embedded. Even so it is often our unhappy experience that we fail to understand each other. This fact casts serious doubt on the practice of slotting other people's decontextualized terms into different boxes.

Examining structure

Following the administration of a grid the investigator will, depending on the type of allotment procedure used, be in possession of a matrix with ones and noughts or a series of numbers in the cells. There are various measures of the properties of this matrix and they can be extracted as follows:

Measures within a construct or element

Given a completed grid of the sort shown in Figure 9.1, the investigator might wish to derive a numerical index for each construct which could then be related to other measures. One such index, application to the dichotomous and rating scale methods, is the ratio of ones or noughts (whichever is the smaller) to the total number of elements. This type of distributional measure cannot be used when the ranking method has been employed. However, the defining property of a rank, namely its assumed transitivity, does offer another way of looking at the single construct. We will return to this issue later. For the moment it is worth noting that by simply inspecting a row or column it is possible to obtain an index of its 'shape'. Shape can be defined statistically and its relations to other properties of elements or constructs can be explored.

Measures between pairs of constructs or elements

The association between two constructs may be described by a correlation coefficient or a matching score (ratio of agreement to total number of columns). Constructs 1 and 2 in Figure 9.1 would yield a correlation of 1.00 and a matching score of 10/10; constructs 2 and 3 would yield a correlation of -1.00 and a matching score of 0/10. Both pairs of constructs show a strong association, the former positive and the latter negative. Since constructs are bipolar and the poles can be transposed without altering their meanings, the sign of the correlation should be ignored when examining construct associations. However, when element associations are examined the signs must be taken into account (see Fransella and Bannister, 1977).

The question as to what inferences can be drawn from statistical associations is a complex one. First of all it is inappropriate to suppose that a high degree of association between two constructs has anything to do with their substantive semantic content. The most that can be claimed is that they have a particular association, an association which is contingently defined by the range of elements they describe. Construct associations can therefore only be said to hold for a certain range of elements, just as element associations can only be said to hold for a specified sample of constructs.

Secondly, cognitive 'linkages' (Kelly, 1955) and 'relationships' (Bannister and Mair, 1968) cannot be inferred from associations where these are expressed in terms of a single matching score or correlation coefficient. There are at least two ways of determining the relationship between two constructs. The first relies on explicit statements by the subject, the second on inferences by the investigator. In the former case the subject might be asked to describe that probability of one quality implying another (Hinkle, 1965), while in the latter such statements might be inferred from the subject's grid. Suppose, for example, that the subject has allotted a set of elements to two constructs, *healthy–unhealthy* and *wise–unwise*, using a dichotomous allotment procedure. Given this information it would be possible to extract indices of the extent to which *healthy* implied *wise* and *unhealthy* implied *unwise*, as well as the extent to which *healthy* implied *unwise* and *wise* implied *unhealthy*. Notice that we are not interested in relations between poles of the same construct since they are by definition exclusive. Notice also that implications are directional; the presence of *a* may imply the presence of *b*, but not the reverse. Furthermore, implicational relations are context-dependent. Irrespective of what method is used to extract them, it should always be assumed that they depend on the range of elements that has been considered.

Let us now turn to the example offered by Bannister and Mair (1968) in connection with what they call the problem of 'lopsidedness'. They provide an hypothetical case involving two constructs, *clergymen–laymen* and *sex maniacs–normal*, in order to show that a preponderance of ones or noughts can give rise to artefactual and therefore misleading levels of association between constructs. If we look at their example in Figure 9.2 we notice that the two constructs turn out to have a strong statistical association (17/20) despite the fact that none of the clergymen are described as sex maniacs. Bannister and Mair concluded that lopsided constructs could not be handled adequately with the dichotomous allotment procedures. However, the important thing to notice is that a single index of association such as a matching score may fail to capture the details of what the subject is telling us. If, instead of focusing on a unitary index of association, we turn to the set of statements that are implied in the two rows of the example we see that although the emergent poles are not linked, the submerged poles are: that is, there are no implied relations between *clergymen* and *sex maniacs*, but there are implied relations between *normal* and *laymen*.

Several points follow from what we have said so far. First, the overall matching score disguises the actual state of affairs. Given just a matching score it is impossible to tell what kinds of relations hold between the respective poles of two constructs. Second, there is always the possibility that similar matching scores may serve to summarize quite different sets of relations. Another subject might have produced the same matching score while informing us that all clergymen are sex maniacs. It is easy enough to compute an index of association between two constructs. But its conceptual bases will continue to elude us so long as we neglect to examine the actual relations which constitute that index. We can see that an apparently simple union between two constructs is in fact composed of a variety of relations between their poles. Recognition of this fact does complicate the task of the investigator, but it is a complication which is borne of a need to do justice to people's thinking about personal qualities and other people.

Measures of total structure

The total structure of the matrix is most frequently used as the basis for inferring the cognitive complexity or simplicity of the subject. The two most commonly

Figure 9.2 Lopsided constructs (after Bannister and Mair, 1968)

used measures of total structure come from the matching score and the correlation coefficient. Bieri and his colleagues have measured the complexity of a grid by summing the matching scores between all pairs of constructs (Bieri et al., 1966). Their argument is that to the extent that someone's thinking is simple or unidimensional his constructs will be highly related, so a high index of construct matching will indicate simplicity and a low score complexity. Similarly, Kelly's and Bannister's index of *intensity* computes the tightness–looseness of the constructs in a matrix by summing the squared correlations between all pairs of constructs and then multiplying the total by one hundred. The measure of intensity has been widely used within a clinical sphere, where it has repeatedly been found that thought-disordered schizophrenics produce lower intensity scores than normals. These findings have generated some debate about the nature of thought disorder and the relative merits of certain measures of cognitive structure. We will return to this issue again.

Factor Analysis and Principal Component Analysis have also been used to measure total structure. The two measures which we have mentioned so far both involve an aggregation of the degrees of association between all constructs. A matrix in which all the constructs were structurally identical would produce a maximum matching score with Bieri's method and a maximum intensity score with that of Bannister. Were such a matrix to be subject to principal component analysis, we would find that a hundred per cent of the variance was attributable to the first component. Only one factor would emerge and this would account for all of the variance. If, on the other hand, the matrix were altered by lowering the correlations between the constructs then new components would be introduced. The point here is that in a simple structure a high proportion of the variance will be accounted for by the principal component or factor, and this allows it to be used as a measure of structural simplicity–complexity (see Bonarius, 1965; Crockett, 1965; Adams-Webber, 1970a).

These structural measures—the matching score, intensity and the 'explanatory power of the principal component'—all offer a unitary index of the whole matrix, and as we would expect the first two correlate rather well with each other. It is noteworthy that all three measures leave out a great deal of information. For example, two grids of the same size—one in which all the correlations were 0.70, the other in which half were 0.00 and half 1.00—would produce similar matching and intensity scores (but not of course the same proportions of variance on the principal component), and although we might reckon that the two grids were quite different, our computations would not.

There are two ways of looking at the structure of a grid. One consists in merely taking the matrix at its face value and computing some index of its structure—as in the case of the three types of measure enumerated above. The other consists in systematically varying the properties of the grid in order to determine its overall resilience to change. Here the matrix might be altered by removing or collapsing certain constructs and elements on the assumption that different structures are differentially sensitive to such alterations. Let us refer to these two types of measure—that is, those where the matrix is taken at its face value and those where it is altered in some way—as measures of *state* and *stress* respectively.

Stress measures can take a variety of forms. For example, each construct could in turn be removed from the matrix in order to determine the resultant correspondence between the original and the stressed grids. On the other hand certain constructs could be excluded or collapsed by way of examining the impact of such loss of information on the configuration of the elements. This method has been used by Smith and Leach (1972) who began by clustering elements and constructs separately. They then collapsed all constructs above a certain criterion of similarity and cluster analysed the elements again. A half matrix of element similarities, based on a node count, was produced on the basis of each cluster, and a summary index of the differences between the two half-matrices computed as an hierarchical measure of cognitive complexity. Their argument was that the greater the change between the original and the impoverished element clusters the greater the complexity of the original matrix. This measure, incidentally, was found to be unrelated to Bieri's measure of cognitive complexity. It is of course one of several that could be employed, and it seems likely that in time we may see the introduction of other measures of stress. For example, it would be possible to systematically impoverish constructs, or for that matter elements, either by eliminating or collapsing them, on the basis of their relations to other constructs, elements or components. Whatever procedures are employed it is important to ensure that the same number of constructs or elements are altered, and that their relations to other constructs, elements or components are equivalent across all the grids being compared.

Before concluding this section several crucial points need to be made. First of all, measures of structural complexity may be sensitive to the range of constructs being employed or the array of elements being construed. Unfortunately the evidence is somewhat equivocal on this point, and although there have been claims to the effect that different kinds of constructs produce comparable degrees of complexity (Bieri *et al.*, 1966), there is also some evidence that structural complexity varies as a function of the types of elements being judged (Williams, 1971; Smith and Leach, 1972). Secondly, although it is possible to obtain measures of association between both constructs and elements, almost every measure of total structure has proceeded from an analysis of construct associations. Correctly speaking therefore, we should refer to Bieri's *construct* matching score and Bannister's *construct* intensity score. The same applies to the size of the first component. It should be apparent that there is no necessary relation between the proportions of variance accounted for by the first components when the same grid is analysed in construct- and element-space.

Finally, it is worth noting that although certain measures of total structure might be related, their respective originators have not always drawn the same inference from comparable scores. Recall that in the case of Bieri's measure, a high score—produced by high degrees of association between the constructs—is taken to indicate low cognitive complexity. Although Bannister's measure of intensity is also an index of structural complexity, he and his colleagues have not inferred cognitive complexity from structural complexity. Instead a high intensity score is taken to indicate a 'loose' system, one in which the constructs are weakly related to each other. As we mentioned earlier, thought-disordered schizophrenics have been found to be particularly prone to what Bannister regards as looseness. All this presents something of a problem, for Bannister's schizophrenics are, in structural terms, producing fairly complex responses and yet he is unwilling—and rightfully so—to give them the benefit of the doubt. He excuses himself by referring to the fact that schizophrenics also produce low consistency scores. (A consistency score is calculated by correlating the ranks of the correlations between all pairs of constructs in the two grids, where these are aligned by both elements and constructs or just constructs.) In other words, not only are their constructs weakly related but these weak relations are unstable across separate administrations of the same or similar grids. On the basis of this Bannister reasons that the intensity scores of thought-disordered schizophrenics are really no more than the outcome of a confused state of mind. In itself, therefore, the measure of intensity does not provide an unequivocal index of cognitive complexity. Certainly a random process will, as Bannister and others have suggested, produce a seemingly complex structure, and the task of deciding whether a low intensity score is due to some process of confusion or the makings of a complex mind must involve still other measures. We will return to this issue again.

Mapping a space

A completed grid, like any array of data located in a matrix, can be handled by conventional methods of Factor Analysis or Principal Component Analysis. Ever since Kelly analysed his patients' grids by hand these techniques have developed apace, and there is now an extensive range of programs which have been expressedly designed with the grid in mind. Slater has been largely responsible for these advances, and over the years he and Chetwynd have elaborated and refined *Ingrid*, a principal component package, and developed several subsidiary programs for the comparison of grids (see Slater, 1977). *Ingrid* analyses the matrix in construct space, extracting a wide variety of information from the raw data. Not only does it offer a set of orthogonal or independent components, derived in descending order of magnitude, but it also presents the loadings of the constructs and elements on the components, as well as the 'distances' between all pairs of elements and the correlations between all pairs of constructs. Correlations between constructs are expressed in the form of scalar angle scores, and the correlations between each construct and every element are also presented. Among other things the program calculates the percentage variance attributable to each component and on request it will determine the significance of each component. Not surprisingly, *Ingrid* is the most commonly used program for the analysis of single grids (see Fransella and Bannister, 1977, for discussion of other packages).

When mapping the space defined by a set of constructs and elements the axes of the first and second component are usually drawn at right angles on graph paper. However, before this is done the proportion of variance accounted for by each component should be inspected to ensure that the structure resolves without undue loss of information in two dimensions. If, for example, the third component is significant and similar in magnitude to the second then it will be necessary to plot the elements and constructs on three pages—one against two, two against three, and one against three. Alternatively, a solid three-dimensional model can be used or the elements and constructs can be plotted on a hypersphere. Where it can be seen that the first two components will do justice to the data, the elements and constructs may be individually plotted on a single page. Components are usually named or indexed by consulting the loadings of the constructs on the components. Those constructs which load significantly on a particular component, but not others, are taken to define that component. The task of indexing is not without its problems, for even where a construct is found to define one component and not others it is still possible that another semantic criterion, which has not entered the analysis but which correlates with that construct, is the actual aspect under which the elements have been construed. Not only does indexing involve a high degree of interpretation on the part of the investigator, but unless his statements are tempered by caution it also leaves him open to the charge that he has labelled the underlying dimensions without sufficient evidence.

Once the subject's grid has been analysed and each element and construct has been plotted in its rightful place, the investigator will be able to scrutinize the configuration. There is, however, an additional technique which renders the graphic plot even more comprehensible. When the matrix as a whole or the extracted inter-element distances are cluster analysed, the derived clusters can be superimposed on the plot in the form of concentric contours—much like some geographical relief map. This emphasizes the hierarchy of similarities between elements by capturing them in a series of explicitly related groups. Two problems may arise when one tries to overlay clusters on a graph. Firstly, if a structure does not resolve adequately in two dimensions it will be inappropriate to represent it as such. But even if it does there is always the possibility that superimposition of clusters on a graph will produce anomalies in the form of elements being clustered in a manner which differs from the way in which they have been grouped by the principal component analysis. This may occur because information is more readily lost in the construction of a graph than a cluster diagram. Secondly, the investigator has to make assumptions about the type of space and the kind of linkage that holds between elements. Different assumptions may produce different cluster configurations, so whenever a cluster programme is employed it will be necessary to carefully consider which type of space and which kind of linkage is most suitable for the analysis being performed.

APPLICATION OF THE GRID

The grid has been put to a wide variety of uses. Its initiation was, we have seen, within a clinical sphere, and it is here that it has continued to enjoy the most frequent application. Aside from its use as a device for focusing discussion between the therapist and patient (Landfield, 1971; Morris, 1977; Rowe, 1977; Ryle, 1977), it has also been employed as a means of determining the manner in which various clinical groups differ from each other (Bannister, 1960, 1962; Ryle and Breen, 1972; Norris and Maklouf-Norris, 1974). Correspondingly it has been used as a diagnostic tool for identifying members of these groups (Bannister and Fransella, 1966). Elsewhere it has been used to explore friendship choice (Duck, 1973), choice of university (Reid and Holley, 1972), the symbolic value of football 'gear' (Marsh, 1977), the perception of holiday locations (Riley and Palmer, 1977; Pearce, 1977) and the appraisal of environments and architectural constructions (Harrison and Sarre, 1971, 1975; Stringer, 1977; Honikman, 1976). In an ethnographic context it has also been used to investigate the subjective consequences of urbanization (Du Preez and Ward, 1970) and the structure of spirit cosmologies in African communities (Orley, 1977; Collett, 1976). Research in these areas has encountered problems which are both general and at the same time peculiar to particular fields of study. Some of the general problems have already been discussed, but there are others which can best be illustrated by examining its use in specific contexts.

Of all the various uses to which it has been put, the grid has been most widely used in the study of schizophrenic thought disorder; and it is here, rather than any other single sphere of application, that it has generated the most provocative debate. In his early work Bannister (1960, 1962) discovered that when grids were administered to schizophrenics who showed signs of disordered thinking they produced far lower intensity scores than normals, and when successive grids were compared they were also found to have lower consistency scores. On the basis of these findings Bannister concluded that thought-disordered schizophrenics possess 'loose' construct systems, that is, systems in which constructs are weakly related and unstable over time. And this, he proposed, could be explained in terms of the history of the patient and what he called 'serial invalidation'. The idea of serial invalidation may be understood as follows. Someone might begin by regarding his mother as *loving* until she is seen to behave in a manner which is at variance with this description, at which point he may regard her as, say, *hating*. To the extent the subject's expectations about his mother are repeatedly invalidated he will shuttle her back and forth between the poles of the construct. Bannister suggests that repeated invalidations will lower the predictive efficacy of that construct, and so in order to safeguard other constructs which are related to it that construct will be loosened, as it were, from its moorings and set adrift. This will have the effect of producing weaker relations between that and other constructs, and it is this looseness that is later captured in the form of low intensity and consistency scores.

The finding that thought-disordered schizophrenics produce lower intensity and consistency scores than normals has been replicated on several occasions (see Fransella and Bannister, 1977), and a packaged set of instructions and protocols has been marketed to enable the clinician to test his patient and then compare the results against standardized norms (Bannister and Fransella, 1967). In this case the procedure involves the use of specified constructs and the provision of elements in the form of photographs of people. The test is administered by the investigator and elements are ranked in relation to each of the constructs.

In recent years there has been some controversy over the use of this method and the idea of loose construing. Earlier on we suggested that the inference from weak structure to looseness rather than complexity presents something of a problem because without additional information it is impossible to say whether the subject is cognitively complex or just plain confused. To pre-empt this criticism Bannister has examined what he calls consistency, that is, the extent to which the pattern of relationships between pairs of constructs remains stable across separate grids. He has shown that his schizophrenics obtain low consistency scores, and on the basis of these findings has concluded that the weak structure which is manifest in low intensity scores is the product of disordered thinking. This explanation assumes that complex thought involves stable relations between constructs, whereas there are of course good grounds supposing that so-called unstable relations could be due as much to complexity as confusion. In the complex individual, associations between constructs should vary in relation to the range of elements being described; it is he, rather than the simpleton, who should be offering contingent opinions. It seem unlikely that the low consistency scores produced by thought-disordered schizophrenics are due to complexity, but in the absence of some demonstration to that effect Bannister is not entitled to insist that the addition of a second measure, which is liable to different interpretations, disambiguates findings obtained with a measure that is similarly afflicted.

So the problem of distinguishing between complexity and confusion still remains. It remains because there is no way of calling the subject's bluff. When the subject describes the elements his opinions have to be accepted at face value, and consequently there is no way of determining whether or not the resultant matrix is complex. When, for example, the subject is presented with an array of photographs and asked to order them against some criterion he will, if he is obliging, produce a rank. In so doing he will provide a composite statement which may in turn be dissembled into a set of constituent statements. A rank of n elements will contain $n(n-1)/2$ statements, where each of these refers to the relative applicability of the construct label to a pair of elements. Where, instead of being asked to rank the elements in one fell swoop, the subject is required to describe the relations of each pair to the construct he may very well offer a set of statements that accord with those that constitute a rank. On the other hand he may invert one of these statements, thereby producing an *inconsistency*. An inconsistency, or what is called i, requires at least three elements (Slater, 1961). Where, for example, the subject informs the investigator that the father is taller than the mother, the mother is taller than the baby, and the baby is taller than the father, he will produce a *circular triad*, an *intransitivity* or an *inconsistency*. By their very nature ranks disguise inconsistencies and it may be the case that these disturbances, which are not open to inspection when the subject is simply asked to rank elements, are at the root of disordered thinking. To determine whether or not this is the case it is necessary to have the subject compare all pairs of elements in terms of every construct.

This type of study was performed by Haynes and Phillips (1973), although it should be said that the logic of their argument was not the same as that offered above. They suggested that the measures of intensity and inconsistency, as conventionally determined, are artefactually related and that the former contaminates the latter. They also suggested that inconsistency offers a 'pure' test of these two measures. In their study they had subjects rank overlapping subsets of elements, and from the inferred ordinal relations between pairs of elements they were able to compute the number of inconsistencies generated by each subject as well as an intensity score for each grid. The elements were photographs of men and women, and the constructs were provided—effectively the same materials as those used by Bannister. Their analyses produced two important findings. Firstly, it was found that inconsistency served to discriminate more effectively than intensity between thought-disordered schizophrenics and normals, and secondly that when inconsistency was partialled out from intensity the latter no longer distinguished one group from the other. On the basis of these results it was concluded that inconsistent applications of the constructs are responsible for weak associations between the constructs.

In response to this criticism of loose construing Bannister (1972) offered two arguments which, as it happens, are mutually contradictory. He began by dismissing the measure of inconsistency as being unrelated to the main body of personal construct theory, and then went on to claim that the findings of Haynes and Phillips were 'exactly what would have been predicted from a "loose construing" argument' and that their proposed conceptualization was 'the *same* notion at a lower level of abstraction' (413, his italics). For our immediate purposes we can afford to ignore the suggestion that inconsistency is unconnected with the original theory, but it is important that we understand why Bannister is mistaken in supposing that inconsistency can be predicted on the basis of looseness. He is mistaken because intensity is a measure of the relations *between* constructs, while inconsistency is a measure of the structure *within* the construct. And while it is the case that weak relations *between* constructs may be produced by weak relations *within* constructs, it is inconceivable that weak relations within constructs could arise by virtue of weak relations between constructs.

The measure of inconsistency offers a means of looking at the logical structure within a construct. This, we have seen, is done by asking the subject to judge pairs of elements in relation to a construct. It follows that the structure within an element can also be determined by requiring the subject to compare pairs of constructs in relation to an element. Inconsistency within a construct arises when someone produces a set of judgments that result in a circular triad. But what, we may ask, are the psychological sources of an inconsistency? By way of offering an answer to this question Marc Binns and I have proposed a model of various changes that may occur in the production of an inconsistency (Collett and Binns, 1976). The model presupposes that elements are like points, suspended, as it were, in semantic space which, in turn, is crosscut by constructs. Constructs may take the form of lines, surfaces or planes. When someone is asked to compare two elements in relation to a construct he locates their respective projection points on the construct and, having determined which is closer to the marked or positive pole, he then announces which element is best described by the label of the construct. Figure 9.3 offers a rough picture of the model and two processes that may occur when such comparisons are being made. The upper half of the diagram shows that state of affairs which underlies the judgments that A is greater than B, and B greater than C, and how the 'rotation' of the construct's axis through space may produce a judgment that is inconsistent with others. This we call *construct shift*. The lower half of the diagram shows the processes which underlie the judgments concerning A and B, and B and C, and how the 'migration' of one element across the space may produce the same final judgment. This we call *element shift*. In the case of both construct and element

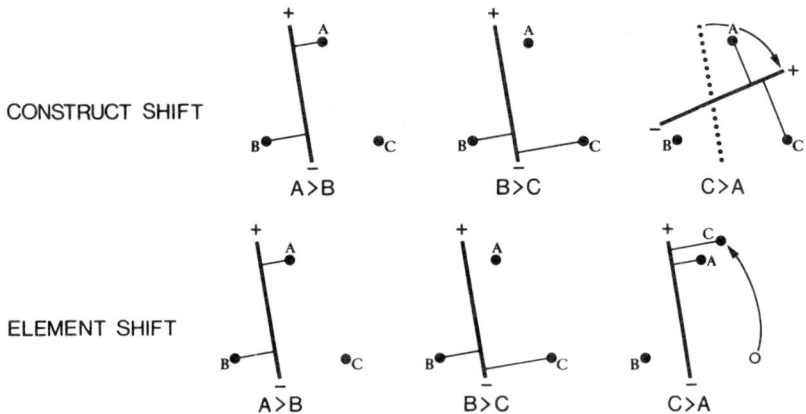

Figure 9.3 Construct and element shift

shift the shift may occur during any one of the three judgments, and in the case of element shift either one or both elements being compared could migrate. We see therefore that there are two phenomenally distinct processes that can underlie the *same* set of judgments. One derives from instability of the construct, the other from instability of an element or elements.

Given just the three statements that comprise a circular triad it is impossible to say which type of shift has occurred and which statement needs to be reversed in order to resolve the inconsistency. Of course where the subject's judgments have some basis in fact—as in the case of height—the investigator will in principle be able to determine which statement or statements need to be inverted. But when the subject has applied a construct which does not involve a reality criterion it will be necessary to have him resolve his own inconsistency. This can be done by having him assign a confidence rating to each of his earlier judgments, and, assuming he has made one rather than two errors, by transposing the statement which is held with least confidence. This procedure enables one to discover which pair of elements was party to the inconsistency and therefore the occasion on which it occurred. This information can then be recorded in a matrix which conforms to the dimensions of the grid and, by comparing the variance of the row and column totals of the entries in the matrix, it is possible to determine whether the inconsistencies were the product of element shift, construct shift, or both. In other words, a preponderance of entries within a particular row is taken to indicate a shift of that construct, whereas a high proportion of entries in a particular column is taken to indicate a shift of that element. This type of pattern analysis allows one to discover whether the subject has trouble entertaining a stable conception of the people he has described, whether he has trouble retaining an enduring sense of the constructs he uses to describe these people, or whether the instability in his system is due to both shaky elements and wavering constructs. It should not in any way be supposed that results obtained through the application of such methods offer any indication of the actual instabilities that are present outside the confines of the study. Rather one can only assume that, by virtue of the demand characteristics of the exercise, the subject will, by being pressed to the limit, reveal the kinds of competencies that inform his thinking elsewhere.

We have argued that inconsistencies may arise as much through the activities of elements as through those of constructs, and the time has come to extend this observation to other aspects of construct theory. The first thing we notice is that elements are defined by their relations to constructs, and that constructs are defined by their relations to elements. It follows that any change in the association between two constructs may produce a corresponding change in the association between the elements, and vice versa. To take a very simple example, if we have a two by two matrix with the same entry, say a one, in each of the cells, and we alter the association between the two rows by changing one of the ones to a nought, then we will inadvertently change the association between the two columns. But what has this self-evident fact to do with construct theory? Well, if we return to the current theory of the genesis of schizophrenic thought disorder we will see that it has serious repercussions for the notion of loose construing.

Kelly wrote at some length on loose construing, which he saw as characterized by changes in the position of an element relative to a construct or constructs. Although he made a passing reference to 'rotation of the personal-construct axes' (1033), and would seem therefore to have considered the possibility of construct shift, nevertheless he adhered throughout to the idea of looseness as being exclusively due to shifting elements. Thus for Kelly, 'a loose construct is one in whose context there is some continual *shifting of elements* from one pole to the contrasting pole' (1058, my italics). The idea of looseness being due to element shift has also been taken up by Bannister and his associates. For Bannister loose construing is brought about by repeated invalidations of an element-construct relationship, one in which the element moves, as it were, back and forth between the poles of the construct. The consequence of this is that the construct is loosened from other constructs and this leads to a weakening of the structure. But if someone discovers that a particular element fails, for whatever reasons, to give consistent readings on a construct, why should he loosen the construct? Could it not be that, instead of his loosening the construct, he directs his attention to the real culprit, namely the element, which he loosens, thereby inadvertently producing weaker relations between his constructs? For example, if his mother repeatedly invalidates his predictions then it seems likely that several constructs will be similarly affected. In which case it would make a nonsense to suppose that a particular construct, rather than that element, was dislodged in the system. And consequently it would be necessary to conclude that the identifying feature of schizophrenic thought disorder is not so much looseness in the application of constructs but looseness in the conception of elements (Frith and Lillie, 1972).

Instability in the system will invariably affect both elements and constructs, and it is the investigator's task to discover whether elements and/or constructs are the victims of this type of process. It is not enough to assume that because Kelly offered a theory of personal constructs it therefore follows that changes or perturbations in the system can adequately be described in terms of their effects on constructs. Because of their mutually defining properties it is important that the systems always be viewed through both the elements and the constructs.

THEORY AND PRACTICE

When Kelly advanced the theory of personal constructs he offered it conjointly with a method. In some ways the theory and the method have enjoyed a fraternal relationship, so that while the grid has been introduced to several spheres of psychology and gained in popularity its more thoughtful brother has gone largely unnoticed. Some psychologists, such as Bannister and Fransella, insist that the method relies on the theory and that both should always be entertained together. However, there are others who argue that the theory offers little by way of advantage to the method. In what remains of this essay I will touch very briefly on what I take to be some of the shortcomings of the theory of personal constructs. In an attempt to be fair I will also suggest that the method, like most favoured brothers, also has certain limitations.

Central to Kelly's conception of man was the idea of anticipation. He made it the cornerstone of the fundamental postulate and traced its implications through several of the corollaries. Given the climate in which he wrote, it is perfectly understandable that he should choose to emphasize the anticipatory component of men's constructions. But man's constructions involve a great deal more than his private projections. Aside from their preoccupations with the future, men are also concerned with the past and the present, and although the method acknowledged this fact, it only achieved a peripheral role in the theory of personal constructs. Hinkle (1970) has put the point rather nicely by drawing attention to the spectator at a cricket match. He makes the point that the spectator is probably less concerned with the business of prediction than he is with what is actually happening on the pitch. This is not to say that the spectator is incapable of surmise or that he cannot identify the purposes of the players, only that in making sense of what is happening he will have to reckon with events as they occur. In fact the notion of anticipation presupposes that of understanding, for it is on the basis of understanding that predictions are made.

Not only did Kelly neglect to articulate the relations between men's conceptions of the past, present and future, but he also failed to identify the regulative features of their thinking and action. The theory of personal constructs offered a model of the way in which someone might construe aspects of his environment. It is a theory which addresses itself to the individual's assumptions about the properties of objects and persons. It is not a theory which seeks to describe what he deems to be required of him in his transactions with others, and therefore while it goes some way towards explaining how he subjectively constitutes the world, it does not account for what he regards as appropriate behaviour in relation to objects and persons that are constituted in the world. The cricket enthusiast must be able to identify the constituents of the game. He must be able to distinguish members of the respective teams, and players from umpires. But over and above this he must be able to understand the activities of players and umpires in relation to the constraints and purposes of the game. These constraints are the rules of cricket, and without some knowledge of the regulations in the rule book and the informal conventions that have grown up over time he will not be able to make sense of what he sees before him (see Du Preez, 1974; Collett, 1977; Young, 1977). Kelly did not reserve a proper place for the notion of rule within his theory. It is interesting that while he saw man as a scientist, making predictions and appraising the evidence of his experience, he failed to observe the highly conventionalized nature of science. Had he extended the analogy he would undoubtedly have noticed that the scientist is far from autonomous. Like the layman, the scientist is bound by a set of established practices that define the ways in which he may and should conduct himself. Kelly once said that men's constructions are limited by their imaginations. He could equally have added that they are contained by the communities in which men live.

The theory of personal constructs has been held up as a highly original formulation. One reason for this, it is claimed, is that Kelly sought to bring a set of hitherto disparate faculties together under one central integrative theory. Kelly lamented the fact that anxiety, hostility, guilt, threat and so on had been separated from each other, and so he set about redefining the various emotions in terms of personal construct theory. For example, he defined guilt as 'the awareness of dislodgement of the self from one's core role structure', and threat as 'the awareness of an imminent comprehensive change in one's core structures'. Without concerning ourselves with the accuracy of these characteristics, it is worth noting that Kelly equated the emotions with different types of awareness. In so doing he identified an emotion as some change in the construct system or as the realization of this change. He did not suggest that such changes are brought about as a consequence of the emotion, and therefore he did not allow that emotions consist of anything more than people's relations to them. In this and other respects Kelly made extravagant claims for the theory. His prime concern had been to produce a theory of the way in which man construes his environment, but not being content with such modest terms of reference he allowed himself to be persuaded that a psychological theory need only be a theory of the person's subjective constructions. In this way he was as guilty of reductionism as those whose conceptions he sought to displace.

Earlier on we outlined the kinds of problems that the investigator encounters in designing, administering and the analysing a grid. We identified the various structural measures that can be extracted from a completed matrix and pointed to some of the difficulties associated with inferring psychological properties from such measures. Aside from these issues there are two other problems that need to be mentioned. The first concerns the type of status that is conferred on the subject's statements. In this connection the investigator may choose either to accept the completed matrix as a summary of the subject's actual opinions or as some convenient expression of what the subject assumes to be required in that situation. The delicate task of deciding between these conceptions is seldom aired by those who work with the grid. In other areas of psychology it is commonly accepted that where the subject is aware of his role as the object of study he may tailor his actions in accordance with what he takes to be the investigator's expectations. There is absolutely no justification for assuming that the grid method is somehow immune to these reactive processes, and it may well be the case that it evokes as much self-presentation on the part of the subject as any orthodox questionnaire. There are, however, instances where the investigator may wish to take advantage of the demand characteristics inherent in the situation. He may, for example, decide that the extent to which someone is inconsistent in his use of a construct during the study bears no relation to the manner in which he normally applies that construct. The investigator may even suppose that someone with a well-articulated system actually tolerates a high degree of inconsistency, but that such a person will be able to produce a set of consistent statements when the situation demands it.

The other enduring problem of the grid is that the method only allows for the specification of one relationship between each element and construct. Where, for instance, the dichotomous allotment procedure is being employed the subject will be able to describe an element in terms of one pole or the other, but not both. Those who have used the grid will have heard the occasional subject complain that both poles of the construct apply equally to an element; one is told that it all depends on the context, the mood of the person being described, or whatever. The inclusion of a midpoint labelled 'both' or a separation of the poles into separate constructs goes some way toward solving this problem, but it does not satisfy the requirement for an examination of this phenomenon in its own right. Quite clearly there are elements which are supposed, by their very nature, to vacillate between contrary descriptions. We know that the ancient Greek pantheon was populated by capricious gods who divided their time between Olympian and earthly pursuits, and who did not therefore admit of any single characterization. We also know that the Greek gods were anthropomorphized and that men and women formed the basis of the analogy. If we believe that people alternate between mutually exclusive states then it seems only reasonable that the methodology should make allowances for this fact. As things stand, while our common knowledge accommodates this belief, the method does not.

In this paper I have tried to describe the kinds of choices that confront someone who wishes to use the grid. I have also discussed the actual mechanics of administering a grid and enumerated the types of measures that can be derived from the completed matrix. In illustrating applications of the method we have explored the ways in which the grid can serve the various interests of the psychologist and we have also attended to some of the problems associated with the theory and the method. My personal feeling is that the theory has been pampered and that this, together with a tendency to use the method in an uncritical cookbook fashion, has constrained advances in this area. My hope, however, is that we will witness a continued interest in those important issues to which Kelly addressed himself.

References

Adams-Webber, J. R., 1970a, An analysis of the discriminant validity of several repertory grid indices, *British Journal of Psychology*, **61**, 83–90.

Adams-Webber, J. R., 1970b, Elicited versus provided constructs in repertory grid technique: a review, *British Journal of Medical Psychology*, **43**, 349–354.

Bannister, D., 1960, Conceptual structure in thought-disordered schizophrenics, *Journal of Mental Science*, **106**, 1230–1249.

Bannister, D., 1962, The nature of measurement of schizophrenic thought disorder, *Journal of Mental Science*, **108**, 825–842.

Bannister, D., 1972, Critiques of the concept of 'Loose Construing': a reply, *British Journal of Social and Clinical Psychology*, **11**, 412–414.

Bannister, D. and Fransella, F., 1966, A grid test of schizophrenic thought disorder, *British Journal of Social and Clinical Psychology*, **5**, 95–102.

Bannister, D. and Fransella, F., 1967, *Manual of the Grid Test of Schizophrenic Thought Disorder*, Slough, Bucks: National Foundation of Educational Research.

Bannister, D. and Fransella, F., 1971, *Inquiring Man; the Theory of Personal Constructs*, Harmondsworth: Penguin.

Bannister, D. and Mair, J. M. M., 1968, *The Evaluation of Personal Constructs*, London: Academic Press.

Bieri, J., Atkins, A. L., Briar, S., Lobeck, R., Miller, H. and Tripodi, T., 1966, *Clinical and Social Judgement*, New York: Wiley.

Bonarius, J. C. J., 1965, Research in the personal construct theory of George A. Kelly, in B. A. Maher (ed.), *Progress in Experimental Personality Research, Vol. 2*, New York: Academic Press.

Collett, P., 1972, Structure and content in cross-cultural studies of self esteem, *International Journal of Psychology*, **7**, 169–179.

Collett, P., 1976, The psychological structure of the Mende spirit cosmology, Oxford: unpublished.

Collett, P. (ed.), 1977, *Social Rules and Social Behaviour*, Oxford: Blackwell.

Collett, P. and Binns, M., 1976, Shifting elements and constructs in schizophrenic thought, Oxford: unpublished.

Crockett, W. H., 1965, Cognitive complexity and impression formation, in B. A. Maher (ed.), *Progress in Experimental Personality Research, Vol. 2*, New York: Academic Press.

Cromwell, R. L. and Caldwell, D. F., 1962, A comparison of ratings based on personal constructs of self and others, *Journal of Clinical Psychology*, **18**, 43–46.

Duck, S. W., 1973, *Personal Relationships and Personal Constructs*, London: Wiley.

Du Preez, P. D., 1974, Action and anticipation in Kelly's theory of personal constructs, Department of Psychology, University of Cape Town, S. Africa.

Du Preez, P. and Ward, D. G., 1970, Personal constructs of modern and traditional Xhosa, *Journal of Social Psychology*, **82**, 149–160.

Fransella, F., 1972, *Personal Change and Reconstruction: Research on a Treatment of Stuttering*, London: Academic Press.

Fransella, F. and Bannister, D., 1977, *A Manual for Repertory Grid Technique*, London: Academic Press.

Frith, C. E. and Lillie, F. J., 1972, Why does the repertory grid indicate thought disorder? *British Journal of Social and Clinical Psychology*, **11**, 73–78.

Harrison, J. A. and Sarre, P. V., 1971, Personal construct theory in the measurement of environmental images: problems and methods, *Environment and Behaviour*, **3**, 351–374.

Harrison, J. and Sarre, P. V., 1975, Personal construct theory in the measurement of environmental images: applications, *Environment and Behaviour*, **7**, 3–58.

Haynes, E. T. and Phillips, J. P. N., 1973, Inconsistency, loose construing and schizophrenic thought disorder, *British Journal of Psychiatry*, **123**, 209–217.

Hinkle, D. N., 1965, The change of personal constructs from the viewpoint of a theory of implications, Ph.D, thesis, Ohio State University.

Hinkle, D. N., 1970, The game of personal constructs, in D. Bannister (ed.), *Perspectives in Personal Construct Theory*, London: Academic Press.
Honikman, B., 1977, Construct theory as an approach to architectural and environmental design, in P. Slater (ed.), *The Measurement of Intrapersonal Space by Grid Technique, Vol. 1: Explorations of Intrapersonal Space*, London: Wiley.
Jaspars, J. M. F., 1966, *On Social Perception*, University of Leiden.
Kelly, G. A., 1955, *The Psychology of Personal Constructs, Vols. 1 and 2*, New York: Norton.
Landfield, A. W., 1968, The extremity rating revisited within the context of personal construct theory, *British Journal of Social and Clinical Psychology*, 7, 135–139.
Landfield, A. W., 1971, *Personal Construct Systems in Psychotherapy*, Chicago: Rand McNally.
Marsh, P., 1977, The symbolic value of 'gear' in the social world of the football fan, mimeo.
McFadyen, M. and Foulds, G. A., 1972, Comparison of provided and elicited grid content in the grid test of schizophrenic thought disorder, *British Journal of Psychiatry*, 121, 53–57.
Morris, J. B., 1977, The prediction and measurement of change in a psychotherapy group using the repertory grid, appendix to Fransella, F. and Bannister D., *A Manual for Repertory Grid Technique*, London: Academic Press.
Norris, H. and Maklouf-Norris, F., 1977, The measurement of self-identity, in P. Slater (ed.), *The Measurement of Intrapersonal Space by Grid Technique, Vol. 1: Explorations of Intrapersonal Space*, London: Wiley.
Orley, J., 1977, The use of grid technique in social anthropology, in P. Slater (ed.), *The Measurement of Intrapersonal Space by Grid Technique, Vol. 1: Explorations of Intrapersonal Space*. London: Wiley.
Pearce, P., 1977, The social and environmental perceptions of overseas tourists, Ph.D. thesis, Oxford University.
Reid, W. A. and Holley, B. J., 1972, An application of repertory grid techniques to the study of choice of university, *British Journal of Educational Psychology*, 42, 52–59.
Riley, S. and Palmer, J., 1977, Of attitudes and latitudes: a repertory grid study of perceptions of seaside resorts, in P. Slater (ed.), *The Measurement of Intrapersonal Space by Grid Technique, Vol. 1: Explorations of Intrapersonal Space*. London: Wiley.
Rowe, D., 1977, Grid technique in the conversation between patient and therapist, in P. Slater (ed.), *The Measurement of Intrapersonal Space by Grid Technique, Vol. 1: Explorations of Intrapersonal Space*, London: Wiley.
Ryle, A., 1977, Some clinical applications of grid technique, in P. Slater (ed.), *The Measurement of Intrapersonal Space by Grid Technique, Vol. 1: Explorations of Intrapersonal Space*, London: Wiley.
Ryle, A. and Breen, D., 1972, Some differences in the personal constructs of neurotic and normal subjects, *British Journal of Psychiatry*, 120, 483–489.
Slater, P., 1961, Inconsistencies in a schedule of paired comparisons, *Biometrica*, 48, 303–312.
Slater, P. (ed.), 1977, *The Measurement of Intrapersonal Space by Grid Technique, Vol. 2: Dimensions of Intrapersonal Space*, London: Wiley.
Smith, S. and Leach, C., 1972, A hierarchical measure of cognitive complexity. *British Journal of Psychology*, 63, 561–568.
Stephenson, W., 1953, *The Study of Behaviour: Q-Technique and its Methodology*, Chicago: University of Chicago Press.
Stringer, P., 1972, Psychological significance in personal and supplied construct systems: a defining experiment, *European Journal of Social Psychology*, 2, 437–447.

Stringer, P., 1977, Repertory grids in the study of environmental perception, in P. Slater (ed.), *The Measurement of Intrapersonal Space by Grid Technique, Vol. 1: Explorations of Intrapersonal Space*, London: Wiley.

Tripodi, T. and Bieri, J., 1963, Cognitive complexity as a function of own and provided constructs, *Psychological Reports*, **13**, 26.

Warr, P. B. and Coffman, T. L., 1970, Personality involvement and extremity of judgement. *British Journal of Social and Clinical Psychology*, **9**, 108–121.

Williams, E., 1971, The effect of varying the elements in the Bannister–Fransella grid test of thought disorder, *British Journal of Psychiatry*, **119**, 207–212.

Young, G., 1977, Social skills and superordinate constructs, paper presented to Second International Congress on Personal Construct Psychology, Oxford.

10

MULTIDIMENSIONAL SCALING: A DISCOVERY METHOD IN SOCIAL PSYCHOLOGY

Joseph P. Forgas

INTRODUCTION

After unprecedented growth in the nineteen-fifties and the nineteen-sixties, social psychology in the nineteen-seventies is characterized by a pervasive crisis of confidence. Many authoritative critics both within and outside the discipline have analysed our current difficulties (Argyle, 1969; Armistead, 1974; Bruner, 1976; Gergen, 1973; Harré and Secord, 1972; Israel and Tajfel, 1972; McGuire, 1973; Levine, 1974). Perhaps the single most important communality between these diverse criticisms is their shared diagnosis that social psychology has been too much concerned with the evaluative, hypothesis-testing stage of research, usually involving controlled experiments, to the neglect of the hypothesis-generating, or exploratory phase, and the integrative, theory-building phase (McGuire, 1973). The predominance of the manipulative laboratory experiment is criticized both on methodological (Israel and Tajfel, 1972) and on epistemological (Harré and Secord, 1972) grounds. The suggested remedies almost always include a call for more naturalistic field studies, and an increased emphasis on the pre-experimental, descriptive stage in the scientific process.

The method to be described, and indeed, advocated here, multidimensional scaling (MDS), is one which is eminently suited to the objectives of the new, emerging social psychology. Its main advantage is that it enables the investigator to quantify and describe extremely complex psychological phenomena which would not be accessible to quantitative analysis otherwise. In essence, this is accomplished by the application of powerful mathematical techniques such as matrix algebra and euclidean geometry to the understanding of psychological relationships. The central assumption underlying the psychological use of MDS techniques is that psychological distance or similarity (between concepts, constructs, persons, traits, social episodes, national stereotypes, etc.) can be represented and analysed in terms of euclidean distance formulations. By bridging the gap between psychological and euclidean distances, 'we have gained enormously in the techniques we have at our disposal for analysing and interpreting psychological data. We can approach with impunity some areas about which we are quite ignorant, armed with methods of great precision and power' (Jackson, 1969, p. 228). By providing a sensitive, multidimensional representation of complex and elusive psychological phenomena, MDS can be an important tool for discovery, and an excellent alternative to the qualitative journalistic, descriptive methodologies currently being advocated by some critics. In the few research areas where MDS has already been applied, such as person perception, political behaviour, the study of social structure, social episodes and the study of self-concept, it has profoundly affected research. It is in this sense that MDS methods can be regarded as more than simply another group of statistical techniques. In a very real sense they constitute a new, emerging research strategy in social psychology.

In this chapter the evolution of MDS methods will be summarized, the various uses of MDS techniques will be discussed, and some of the practical advantages of using this technique will be outlined. In addition, a non-statistical description of the steps involved in using MDS methods will be given, together with a brief summary of already existing studies in social psychology using this method.

In particular, the application of MDS techniques to the study of social episodes will be described in some detail. The study of social episodes is one of the major themes of the 'new' social psychology (Forgas, 1976, 1977; Harré and Secord, 1972; Argyle, this volume). MDS is one of a few techniques capable of providing a quantitative display of people's meaningful construals of social episodes, representing an excellent illustration of the potential of this method.

THE EVOLUTION OF MDS METHODS

Multidimensional scaling is one of a group of multivariate techniques, the principal object of which is the simplified representation (reduction of dimensionality) of complex data sources. However, MDS is easier to use and interpret than the other procedures. Comparison is made with factor analysis later in this chapter; but for detailed comparisons of MDS with factor analysis, cluster analysis, and principal components analysis, see McCallum (1974).

Input data for MDS consist of measures of similarity between all the elements to be scaled, and the aim is to produce an optimal representation of this complex space in a reduced number of dimensions. 'The problem of multidimensional scaling, broadly stated, is to find n points whose interpoint distances match in some sense the experimental dissimilarities of n objects' (Kruskal, 1964, p. 1). The evolution of different MDS techniques can be traced through three distinct stages of development, each characterized by a gradual relaxation of the initially rigid requirements and assumptions demanded of the input data, and an increase in the power and interpretability of output configurations. The number of MDS programs available is rapidly expanding, and only some programs can be mentioned here. A package which may be particularly useful to social psychologists using the SPSS command language, is currently being assembled by Professor A. P. M. Coxon (Department of Sociology, University College, Cardiff, P.O. Box 78, Wales).

The first MDS techniques, often referred to as traditional, fully metric techniques, developed by Torgerson (1952, 1958), Messick and Abelson (1956), and others made rigorous demands on the data. Similarities and distance in space were assumed to be linearly related, and the euclidean nature of the original cognitive space to be scaled was also a prerequisite for the application of these techniques. In essence, fully metric input information was simply represented in a reduced number of dimensions. While statistically unproblematic, the potential usefulness of these techniques for the kind of data social psychologists deal with was also rather limited.

The second stage of development, heralded by Shepard's (1962a; 1962b) papers, was the construction of non-metric multidimensional scaling techniques (Kruskal, 1964a, 1964b; Young and Torgerson, 1967; Lingoes, 1965; McGee, 1968). These techniques 'give us metrically invariant solutions when given only ordinally invariant observations' (Torgerson, 1965, p. 38). In other words, all that is now required of the input data is that rank order relationship between the elements to be scaled should not be grossly violated, while the output configuration remains on an interval scale, in euclidean space; the relationship between input and output data need not be linear, but can be any monotone function. This seemingly unreasonable transformation of rank-order data into interval-scale representations is based on the fact that with a sufficiently large number of points, the ordinal input contains a great deal of metric information as well (Shepard, 1966). The relaxation of the rigid requirements of the earlier, 'classical', methods meant that a much wider range of relevant psychological data could now be analysed using MDS techniques. While non-metric methods are undoubtedly more convenient and applicable to psychological problems than the 'classical' methods, it is important to bear in mind that the statistical techniques used to recover metric information from ordinal data also imply certain limitations; occasionally the configurations obtained will be suboptimal, 'degenerate' or misleading (Torgerson, 1965). Some of these problems will be discussed in a subsequent section.

The third stage of development in MDS procedures was associated with the creation of models which were capable of taking individual differences between the judges into account. One such method, the 'points of view' analysis developed by Tucker and Messick (1963) is based on a two-step procedure: first, typical hypothetical subjects are identified on the basis of a factor analysis of intersubject correlations. The similarity judgments for these 'hypothetical' subjects, each one representing the centroid of a cluster of real subjects, are then subjected to independent MDS analyses, resulting in different stimulus spaces for different 'points of view'. Critics of this model point out that it provides little more information than a number of separate MDS analyses would have done. A different approach was adopted by Carroll and Chang (1970), whc in their INDSCAL model assume that the *same* dimensions underlie the judgments of all subjects, but that these dimensions have different salience for different individuals. The major advantage of the INDSCAL model is that individual perceptual structures can be directly derived from the group stimulus space, and direct comparisons between individuals can also be made. Since this model will be described in more detail in a later section, it will not be discussed further here.

The most recent innovations in MDS techniques appear to be particularly promising for psychological research. The further reduction of the redundancy of information in a complete dissimilarity matrix, containing the whole set of $N(N-1)/2$ judgments, is one of the main objectives. Not only is such a matrix difficult to assemble when more than twenty-five stimuli are involved, but the time and concentration involved in making such a large number of judgments can be tedious and time-consuming for subjects. Several authors (Spence and Domoney, 1974; Young and Cliff, 1972; Baker and Young, 1975; Girard and Cliff, 1976) have contributed to the development of MDS models which would require only a subset of the total number of possible judgments as its input data. The most promising such model was developed by Young and Cliff (1972). Their method, ISIS (Interactive Scaling with Individual Subjects) uses a data collection procedure involving the subject in real-time interaction with the computer in order to determine which of his judgments are crucial to the derivation of a dimensional structure. 'The interactive MDS system allows generalization of current MDS systems in two directions: (a) a very large number of stimuli may be scaled, and (b) the scaling is performed with individual subjects facilitating the investigation of individual as well as group processes' (Young and Cliff, 1972, p. 385). No doubt this procedure will be of increasing importance in the future; the potential representation of intricate cognitive and perceptual structures based on a small number of judgments is of obvious potential importance to social psychology. The shifting emphasis in social psychology towards idiographic rather than nomothetic studies (Pervin, 1976) also promises to create new uses for this technique.

SOME POTENTIAL USES OF MDS TECHNIQUES IN SOCIAL PSYCHOLOGY

The basic argument underlying this chapter is that well tried statistical techniques, of which MDS is a prime example, now exist to serve the changed emphasis on description in current social psychological research. Perhaps it is appropriate at the beginning to be more specific about the kinds of uses to which MDS can be put, and the problem areas to which it can be applied. Four main areas of application will be outlined: the first two are generic to MDS techniques, regardless of the particular problem to which it is applied. The second two are more specifically relevant to MDS application in psychology and social psychology.

The discovery of hidden structures

The first important application of MDS is as an 'analysis for the discovery of previously unknown structure, and hence the achievement of new scientific insight. I still regard . . [this] . . as of possibly the greatest *potential* importance' writes Shepard (1974, p. 374). Perhaps in no other science are 'hidden' structures quite so abundant as in social psychology. As the discipline becomes more cognitively oriented, and with the advent of structuralist thought in its many guises, the discovery and description of cognitive, perceptual, as well as objective structures will be of ever increasing importance. A good case in point is again the study of social episodes. Following the example set by structural linguistics, many social psychologists now argue for a study of the structure of social behaviour. The 'meaning' of a social act, or speech act (Clarke, this volume) derives not only from its invariant features, but also from its position in the structure of events. While sequential analysis may be applicable to the representation of simpler, linear structures, MDS may prove to be the best method for the quantitative representation of the multidimensional structure of whole social episodes. Thus, once all the possible 'units' in an episode are identified their structure could be represented, using frequency of co-occurrence, perceived similarity or other naturalistic observations as input to MDS.

Parametric representation of otherwise inaccessible data

The use of MDS as a tool for data reduction, visual representation and facilitator of effective communication has probably been more important to date than its more substantial uses as a tool of discovery. Nevertheless, this area of application cannot be neglected. The complexity of most psychological phenomena, and none more so than the 'phenomenal' reality studied by the new social psychology, demands effective representation and communication. Much of our knowledge of social behaviour and of the requirements of social situations is implicit, not directly accessible to questioning. Since phenomenologist, and to a lesser extent, symbolic interactionist orientations often rely on precisely this kind of knowledge as their data, the quantitative description of implicit knowledge is of obvious importance. MDS can be a formidable tool in this quest: implicit theories of personality can be reliably represented using this method (Rosenberg and Sedlak, 1972), and representations of implicit perceptions of different social episodes also become possible (Forgas, 1976, 1977, and later in this chapter). The visual–spatial output from MDS, together with the ease of data collection procedures, renders this technique of great value for representations of implicit knowledge (competence) in social psychology.

Taxonomies

As is the case with most relatively new sciences, in psychology there is a vast range of important and relevant phenomena which have never been empirically studied. The endemic custom in social psychology to generate new research areas, concerned with previously uncharted behaviours, is ample enough evidence for this. In many cases, the first step towards an understanding of such a new range of phenomena is concerned with categorization, the analysis of similarities and dissimilarities between the elements—in other words, the development of initial taxonomies. An excellent example is the recent concern of both personality theorists and social psychologists with the role different *situations* play in influencing behaviour. The study of situational characteristics has remained a virtually virgin area in psychology to date, and there is now an overwhelming consensus among researchers in their call for a taxonomy of different kinds of situations (Ekehammar, 1974; Frederiksen, 1972; Argyle and Little, 1972; Mischel, 1973). While other methods, such as factor analysis (Magnusson, 1971), three-way-factor analysis (Frederiksen, 1972) and cluster-analysis are possibly applicable to such a task, the characteristics of MDS make it the ideal method in most cases for such an analysis. With the current reorientation of interests in social psychology, it is likely that the periodic emergence of new phenomena to be studied will be even more frequent. Hopefully, MDS will prove to be a useful aid in the initial classification and categorization of these new variables.

The provision of quantitative descriptive data for further analysis

The first three areas of application of MDS outlined so far were all concerned with facilitating the task of description; it is this fourth area of application, however, which is potentially the most promising for psychological research, since it goes a long way towards enabling investigators to actually test hypotheses about their data. Thus, beyond providing a quantified representation of complex and elusive phenomena, MDS outputs can be subjected to a range of *post hoc* tests. MDS thus makes it possible for the researcher to evaluate hypotheses about a data base which would otherwise be difficult to quantify. An example may better illustrate this point.

Of the many approaches to the study of social structure in small groups, the application of MDS by Jones and Young (1972), Davison and Jones (1976) and Forgas (1976) to this task are perhaps the most effective. At the descriptive level, this method provides a multidimensional, spatial representation of all group members, and their relations to each other on a number of attribute dimensions. In further analyses, however, group members' co-ordinates in multidimensional space can be used to evaluate hypotheses about them. For example, the changes occurring in the group structure over a period of time can be evaluated by calculating a canonical correlation between two structural representations, taken at different point in time (Jones and Young, 1972). The relationship between formal status categories and perceived position within the group can be evaluated, using multiple discriminant analysis (Forgas, 1976b; Jones and Young, 1972). The perceived group structure can be used to predict interpersonal attraction in the group (Davison and Jones, 1976) using a multiple regression technique. Analysis of variance techniques were used by Wish (1976) to evaluate the contribution of different features of communication episodes to their position relative to each other in the MDS structure (Wish, 1976). These analyses only become possible because the often elusive and implicit data base has first been converted into a quantified representation by the MDS technique applied.

SOME PRACTICAL ADVANTAGES OF MDS TECHNIQUES

In advocating the use of MDS techniques for problem areas now emerging in social psychology, such as those mentioned in the previous section, it will be necessary to discuss in some detail those characteristics of the method which represent its main practical advantages. (The steps involved in using MDS will be discussed in more detail in a subsequent section).

Ease of data collection

One of the principal advantages of MDS methods over other descriptive techniques is the absence of rigorous assumptions required from the data. For non-metric MDS, 'all that is required in order to apply it to a given set of N stimuli, is that there be supplied, for each of the $N(N-1)/2$ pairs of stimuli some number specifying how closely those two stimuli are related psychologically. Such given numbers are called proximity measures' (Shepard, 1962b, p. 219). Proximity measures can be operationalized in a number of different ways; most frequently, item co-occurrence, or simple similarity ratings are used. The former measure is readily applicable to an extremely wide range of naturally occurring phenomena. For example, an empirical analysis of Theodore Dreiser's view of women as reflected by the co-occurrence of adjectives to describe his female characters is quite feasible and results in a meaningful representation (Rosenberg and Jones, 1972). The spatial, temporal or conceptual co-occurrence of many groups of psychological variables can be readily established, and the quantitative description of phenomena which would be difficult to operationize otherwise becomes possible.

As for all other analyses, input data to MDS need to be reliable. Although there is some evidence that similarity judgments can be fairly stable over time (Jones and Young, 1972), and MDS structures based on different data collection techniques were found to be quite similar by Wish (1973), it is advisable especially when dealing with complex object domains, to establish the reliability of the input data. The second principal measure of proximity, similarity, gives rise to two further classes of data collection methods. *Objective similarity* of a wide range of phenomena can be empirically measured: body weight, size and shape, the speed and frequency of different gestures, frequency and duration of gaze and mutual gaze, the duration of different social encounters, interpersonal distance, etc., can all serve as objective similarity measures of the variable to be scaled. *Subjective* (perceived) *similarity* ratings of an endless range of phenomena are also relatively easy to obtain: the perceived structure of adjectives, nations, national governments, political leaders, colours, sounds, social episodes, communication situations and many other phenomena have been effectively studied using the raters' similarity judgments as the raw data.

The absence of restrictive assumptions and the ease of data collection for MDS analysis is thus one of the most important reasons for its applicability to the sorts of problems social psychology is concerned with. Since many of the new strategies espouse an essentially phenomenologist orientation, MDS techniques are particularly important as one of the few empirical methods applicable to the representation of internal, perceptual and conceptual structures.

The judgmental procedure

With most data collection methods based on observer or subject ratings, the artefact introduced by the provision of rating scales or other constructs by the experimenter has long been a serious difficulty. As the input to MDS merely requires the subjects to rate the elements in terms of similarity, difficulties associated with preselected rating scales can be completely avoided. In effect, subjects are free to use any cognitive or perceptual dimension which they find relevant in making their judgments—often, the criteria used need not even be explicitly recognized by the subjects. Thus, MDS enables investigators to derive a representation of internal, and often implicit cognitive structures, which are not in any way contaminated by the constructs and/or scales provided by the experimenter. Again, with reference to one of the major objections levelled at 'traditional' social psychology, subjects or respondents are given nearly complete freedom to describe those, and only those, aspects of the real world surrounding them which they implicitly consider important.

Clarity of representation

A further marked advantage of MDS methods is that output configurations are in all cases geometrically representable, providing a concise, clear and visual summary of the structure of the elements scaled. Since often the conceptual space to be explored is inherently complex, and the underlying cognitive dimensions are implicit rather than explicit, visual representation is of particular value. In many cases, the geometric representation is an invaluable asset in the intuitive interpretation and understanding of the underlying cognitive dimensions.

Ready interpretability

The interpretation of output from most data reduction analyses, such as factor analysis, cluster analysis, etc., is usually based on intuitive judgments. Factor loadings are used intuitively to label a factor, and the overlapping 'meaning' of elements within a cluster is sought in order to label the cluster. Of all these techniques, it is in the psychological applications of MDS methods that the most consistent effort has been made to develop empirical techniques for the interpretation of output configurations, and the labelling of stimulus dimensions. While similar techniques, in principle, could also be applied to interpret factors, and Rosenberg and Sedlak (1972) describe an empirical method for labelling clusters, the graphical output provided by MDS has made empirical interpretation the most appropriate, and most widely used, in MDS studies. Depending on the particular MDS programme used, interpretation can be based on the fitting of separately scaled labelling dimensions to the multidimensional space, or in the case of the INDSCAL model for example, MDS dimensions are directly interpretable as psychologically meaningful attribute dimensions.

USING MULTIDIMENSIONAL SCALING PROGRAMS: SOME PRACTICAL POINTS

In this part of the chapter, the use of MDS techniques will be illustrated by describing some of the steps and procedures involved in applying MDS programs in practice. Most of what follows is intended to illustrate the use of two MDS programs, TORSCA 9 and INDSCAL. These programs merit special attention since (a) they are relatively easily obtainable and widely used, (b) they are likely to be of particular relevance to the problems encountered in social psychology, and (c) many of the published articles using MDS methods in social psychology appear to rely on these two programs.

TORSCA 9, a FORTRAN IV program for non-metric multidimensional scaling, was published by Young (1970), based on Young and Torgerson's earlier (1967) TORSCA program. Both of these programs use the method first proposed by Shepard (1962a, b), and later elaborated by Kruskal (1964a; 1964b). TORSCA 9, like all other non-metric methods, 'attempts to provide a scaling solution with ratio properties which is based on data without ratio properties' (Young, 1970, p. 455). This is possible because ordinal information on distances between points in space does in fact contain quite a lot of interval information about the locations of these points.

The TORSCA 9 program is thus a typical representative of non-metric MDS programs in general, and its use is particularly appropriate when the more stringent linear assumptions required by fully metric programs cannot be fulfilled by the data, and when the analysis of individual differences is of little relevance.

The INDSCAL model, unlike most other MDS methods, such as TORSCA 9, allows the analysis of individual differences in the perception of a group of stimulus objects. Input to INDSCAL consists of a series of dissimilarity matrices, each representing judgments by one respondent (or judgments on one of several scales, or in one of several conditions). The program uses the variation between the input dissimilarity matrices to calculate a unique representation of the stimulus objects, as it would be seen by a hypothetical 'average' judge. This stimulus space, unlike the space in other MDS models, is defined by a set of unique axes, which cannot be further rotated, and which can be expected to 'correspond to meaningful psychological dimensions in a very strong sense' (Carroll and Chang, 1970, p. 285).

However, the INDSCAL model also assumes that the dimensions defining the stimulus space are not equally relevant, or salient, to each of the respondents. The model explicitly recognizes that some dimensions will be more relevant to the judgments of some subjects, and some dimensions will be completely irrelevant to others. The output from INDSCAL thus includes, in addition to the multidimensional representation of the stimuli mentioned above, a subject space, in which the respondents themselves are shown in the same co-ordinate framework as the stimuli, placed according to the salience of each of the stimulus dimensions to individual subjects. The co-ordinates of subjects in the subject space, or 'dimension weights', are analogous to partial correlation coefficients, and indicate the relationship between the input dissimilarity matrix for a subject and a dimension of the group stimulus space. By stretching or contracting group stimulus dimensions by a factor proportional to a subject's dimension weight, the stimulus space as perceived by that particular subject can be derived. An illustration of the relationship between the group stimulus space and individual subject stimulus spaces, shown in Figure 10.1, may be helpful in clarifying the model.

Collection of input data

Input data to MDS analysis in all cases consist of a matrix of $N(N-1)/2$ pairwise similarity or association measures between the elements to be scaled. For TORSCA 9, a single such matrix, representing all the judgments of an individual, or the averaged or otherwise summated judgments of a group, is sufficient. For INDSCAL, however, a series of such matrices serve as input, each of them reflecting the judgments of one out of many *individuals*, or the summarized judgments of all individuals on one out of several *scales* or in one out of several *conditions*. INDSCAL can be used to analyse up to seven-way tables, although it is most frequently applied to three-way (individuals x rows x columns) data. 'Instead of dissimilarities, experimental measurements may be similarities, confusion probabilities, interaction rates between groups, correlation coefficients or other measures of proximity or dissociation of the most diverse kind'

(Kruskal, 1964a, p. 1). This broad definition of 'similarity' allows the use of a wide range of data collection methodologies. Three of the most frequently used methods in social psychology, all designed to deal with judgmental data, are outlined below.

Direct similarity ratings

This is the most straightforward method, and simply requires subjects to indicate the perceived similarity of the stimuli, presented pairwise, on a preselected numerical scale. The stimuli can be presented either in the form of a long list of all possible pairwise combinations, in the form of a cross-tabulated matrix, or in discrete pairs. This method is most appropriate when the stimuli are readily

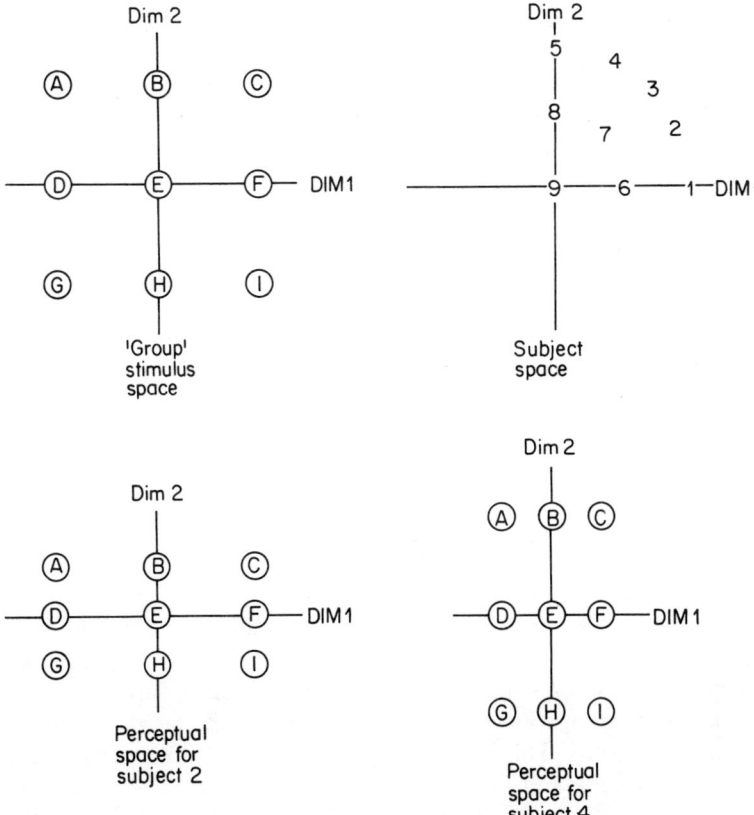

Figure 10.1 A graphical illustration of the INDSCAL model: weights from the subject space as used to stretch or contract the dimensions of the group stimulus space, to produce the individual perceptual spaces of subjects 2 and 4 (after Rosenberg and Sedlak, 1972)

representable, and tangible. For example, MDS studies of group structure, where the individuals to be judged are well known to the judges, tend to use this method.

The multiple groupings technique

In this method, subjects are provided with a set of cards, each bearing the description of one stimulus object. The task is to sort the cards into separate groups, on the basis of perceived similarity, association, etc. For input to TORSCA 9, similarity or strength of association between any two elements may be indicated by a number of subjects from the total sample who have put those elements into the same group—this measure thus involves the aggregation of data over subjects. For input to INDSCAL, individual data may of course be preserved, but individual input matrices from this method will only include binary choices—any two elements can be only related or unrelated, depending on their classification into groups by a particular subject, without any information about the strength of the relationship. This data collection method thus has the advantage of allowing a clear, visual and tangible presentation of the stimuli, with only an easy and meaningful response demanded from the subject. However, the data so derived will contain less information than alternative procedures, if used as individual input. The multiple groupings procedure thus appears most applicable when a number of complex and confusing stimuli need to be presented, and group rather than individual perceptual spaces are of interest as the output. In a study of social episodes, for example (Forgas, 1976), the multiple groupings technique was used since (a) the stimuli were fairly complex and a tangible presentation was preferred, and (b) only the representation of the whole group's judgments was of interest.

Bipolar scales

In some circumstances bipolar scale ratings can provide a suitable, even preferable input to MDS analyses. The usual data collection procedure involves (a) the rating of all stimuli on a number of (usually at least ten) bipolar scales which are hypothesized to be related to the crucial attribute dimensions underlying the stimulus space, and (b) the extraction of similarity matrices for individual subjects or scales from these data, by aggregating ratings over scales or subjects, respectively. This is frequently accomplished by using a profile distance formula (Cronbach and Gleser, 1953; Osgood and Suci, 1952), in which the dissimilarity $\delta_{jk(s)}$ between elements j and k on scale s is expressed as:

$$\delta_{jk(s)} = \sqrt{\frac{1}{N} \sum_{3=1}^{N} \left(X_{ij(s)} - X_{ik(s)} \right)^2}$$

where N is the total number of subjects, and $X_{ij(s)}$ and $X_{ik(s)}$ stand for subject i's ratings of elements j and k on scale s. Using this formula, dissimilarity matrices for every subject, and/or every scale can be obtained.

For TORSCA 9, one single dissimilarity matrix, involving aggregation over both subjects and scales would be derived, whereas for INDSCAL, subject matrices can be used as input. This data collection method, when used in conjunction with INDSCAL, has a further distinct advantage in the interpretation of output configurations, which will be discussed in a subsequent section.

Determining the optimum number of dimensions

In running an MDS analysis it is not normally known in advance how many dimensions will be required in the output configuration to adequately represent the stimulus space. In consequence, some *a priori* estimation of the necessary number of dimensions is made, and then the program is run for a number of dimensions which are more than sufficient to cover the expected dimensionality. In practice, nearly all the stimulus spaces occurring in social psychology are likely to be representable in one to a maximum of five dimensions. Higher dimensionalities would be so complex that little would be gained by their scaling anyway. In effect, then, the program is normally run for one-, two-, three-, four-, five-, and sometimes six-dimensional solutions. The next problem is to decide which of these different dimensional solutions is in fact an optimal representation of the data base.

For non-metric programs, such as TORSCA 9, one guide in determining the optimum number of dimensions is the extent to which the different solutions depart from the monotonicity assumption. Kruskal (1964a) proposed a 'goodness of fit' or stress index, automatically calculated by TORSCA 9, which reflects the extent to which the output configuration is in a monotone relation to the input data. Spence and Ogilvie (1973) published a table of baseline values for stress for different dimensionalities, showing the stress that could be expected by chance. Stress values which are less than expected suggest the presence of some non-random structure in the data.

Beyond maximizing fit (and reducing stress), the *rate* of decrease in stress with increasing dimensionality is also an important indicator: 'For the sake of parsimony, the dimensionality after which there is little improvement in fit is chosen as the optimum dimensionality' (Rosenberg and Sedlak, 1972, p. 243). For INDSCAL solutions, the variance accounted for by the output configuration, and its rate of increase with increasing dimensionality is used in a similar fashion to determine the number of dimensions both necessary (substantial increase in variance accounted for over the previous dimensional solution), and sufficient (little increase in variance accounted for with the addition of a further dimension) to adequately represent the stimulus space.

A second and, in psychology particularly, important criterion for deciding the optimum number of dimensions is the substantive interpretability of the different solutions. The psychological meaningfulness of different configurations is at least as important an indicator of the optimum number of dimensions as the different statistical tests of monotone fit. Indeed, in his recent review of some of the problems associated with MDS techniques, Shepard (1974) argues that 'users, more often than not, are inclined to err in the direction of extracting too many dimensions ... This inclination seems attributable to ... users [tending to] place undue emphasis on the measure of departure from monotonicity (stress) to the virtual exclusion of much more important considerations of the statistical stability and substantial interpretability of the obtained configurations' (p. 385). It is important to note that in decisions about the interpretability of the different solutions, especially in psychology, intuitive notions about the meaningfulness of the different configurations can also be of relevance.

The interpretation of MDS configurations

In many non-psychological applications of MDS techniques, the interpretation of the configurations obtained is often neglected or left to intuition: it is the spatial, metric representation of the data, which is primarily sought. In its psychological uses, however, MDS is unique among descriptive statistical techniques in that we do not know before embarking on a study what the substantive dimensions defining a stimulus space are likely to be, since these are implicit in the subjects' judgments and are not provided by the experimenter in the form of preselected scales. For this reason, it is nearly always important to come to terms with the substantive meaning of the solutions generated. In effect, interpretation normally means the identification and labelling of the dimensions defining the stimulus space. This can be accomplished (a) intuitively, (b) with the help of external bipolar dimensions, or (c) using internal bipolar dimensions, used in the generation of the configurations themselves.

Intuitive labelling

This is the most general method applicable. Knowing the identities of the different stimuli represented, and their co-ordinates on the different dimensions, can serve as the basis for labelling the dimensions themselves, using extremely positioned 'high' or 'low' stimuli as anchor points. This procedure is comparable to the standard interpretative techniques used in factor analytical studies: MDS dimensions are analogous to factors, individual stimuli to tests, and stimulus co-ordinates replace factor loadings. It is important to remember that the stimulus axes derived from most non-metric methods, such as TORSCA 9, are essentially arbitrary, can be further rotated, and are often not directly interpretable. In selecting an intuitively meaningful interpretative axis, it is thus not necessary to collected in the form of bipolar scale ratings. Using this procedure, input matrices representing bipolar scales rather than individual judges are used as input to the INDSCAL analysis: INDSCAL will automatically calculate indices of relatedness between input matrices and stimulus dimensions (dimension weights) which are analogous to partial correlation coefficients, and which thus directly indicate the relevance of a particular bipolar scale to the labelling of an INDSCAL dimension. This procedure is basically similar to the external labelling approach described above, except that the duplication involved in collecting separate bipolar scale ratings can be avoided. The main problem is that this procedure is circular: the same scales which were used to construct the MDS space are used to interpret it. This objection is less damaging when the input also includes matrices other than those representing bipolar scales, such as direct similarity ratings by subjects.

Interpretation based on supplementary analyses

In some cases, the interpretation of configurations obtained from MDS may be facilitated by supplementary statistical analysis of the same input data. Most frequently, cluster analysis is used to discover the categorical structure of the stimuli. Such a categorical representation, superimposed on a dimensional model, may provide new insights into the meaning of the configuration. Cluster analysis may also be useful in detecting the non-dimensional structure of the data to be represented. Other supplementary analyses may also be used from time to time, but only as secondary tools to the primary interpretative techniques outlined above.

Some limitations of MDS techniques

The main emphasis until now has been on outlining the advantages MDS techniques offer to researchers, and pointing out the particular relevance of these techniques to problems now current in social psychology. It is now time to outline some of the very important qualifications and problems which may limit the applicability of these techniques in everyday use.

First, it should be emphasized that even the best fitting and most meaningful euclidean structure constructed by MDS does not prove that the relevant cognitive space is euclidean. 'Such a structure properly represents a tentative theory—a set of hypotheses that should be further confirmed by additional experimentation. The strict interpretation of such a structure is that the data can be represented, to a certain degree of approximation, by a geometric model,' assert Funk *et al.* (1976, p. 128). What MDS does, then, is to provide a more or less well-fitting model of the structural relationship between a set of stimuli which, in the absence of further supportive evidence, should not be mistaken for a direct representation of reality. This 'model' is qualified by another consideration.

In its most common application MDS is used to represent the cognitive structure of a group of subjects, and not individuals. The structure derived can be viewed as the best possible representation of the cognitive structure of a hypothetical, modal subject, representing the group as a whole. The cognitive map of a set of stimuli constructed by MDS suggests that the subjects behaved *as if* they had a cognitive map, but it is not possible to say that they do have one in reality. These points can be important when interpretations of MDS configurations are made. There are some further potential difficulties, more statistical in character.

Because of the limits imposed by computer capacity, most non-metric MDS programs use a method of minimizing departure from monotonicity which may result in a solution representing only a so-called '*local minimum*' rather than the desired global minimum of departure from monotonicity. Because of the complex iterative procedure involved, the possibility of the program being 'stuck' at such a local minimum, and the resulting suboptimal output configuration, is always a possibility. In order to make sure that the optimal global minimum configuration is in fact obtained, it is advisable to run the program more than once, with a number of different random starting configurations. Alternatively, rationally constructed rather than random initial configurations may be used—the description of these is beyond the scope to this chapter, however.

Another possible problem is the so called '*degeneracy*' of some solutions, when although the minimum deviation from monotonicity is achieved, the true structure of the data is not revealed, because the stimuli were too few, or too closely clustered, or the representation has too many dimensions. While the statistical causes underlying this problem can be rather complex, it is generally advisable 'to select objects for non-metric scaling (a) that are not obviously grouped into a few psychologically compact clusters, and (b) that are not fewer than about ten in total number for a two-dimensional solution, or more for a higher dimensional solution' (Shepard, 1974, p. 395).

A further difficulty associated with the use of MDS techniques is that dimensional representations may be intrinsically inappropriate to represent data which are discrete and *categorical*, rather than continuous and dimensional in nature (Torgerson, 1958). This may be a serious problem in social psychological research, since frequently it is not possible to decide in advance whether the relationship between a set of elements is categorical or dimensional. Although strong categorical structures are likely to show up in the form of distinct clusters even in a dimensional representation, the evaluation of the discontinuous aspects of the data from such a configuration may be problematic. It is often useful when in doubt to apply both a dimensional (MDS) and a categorical (for example, cluster analysis) technique to the same set of data. In any case, results from the cluster analysis may help with the interpretation of the MDS results.

The procedure used for the determination of the optimum *dimensionality* can also be a source of difficulty. As was suggested earlier, this decision is usually based on (a) finding the smallest number of dimensions with the best possible fit, such that (b) this configuration is also the most readily interpretable and meaningful. It is normally not too difficult to find such a solution, although this may require the careful inspection of several configurations. Shepard (1974) warns against the tendency to select a higher dimensionality than necessary, and Torgerson (1965) emphasizes the interpretability and stability of the solutions as crucial criteria in deciding optimum dimensionality. Since the number of dimensions chosen is inversely related to the stability of the solution (with higher dimensionality, the structure is less stable), this is an additional reason for being parsimonious in selecting the appropriate number of dimensions. In the absence of more reliable guidelines, the possibility of choosing the wrong configuration is always a danger, which should be borne in mind when using MDS.

A further substantive problem may be associated with the central *assumption* of non-metric MDS models that judgments or observations of similarity and relatedness are monotonically related to distances in the MDS space. 'The monotonic requirements ... means considerably more than just having a set of numbers that one feels must have something to do with similarity' (Torgerson, 1965, p. 382). With judgments involving rather direct perceptual comparisons of simple stimuli, such as pairwise similarity ratings of colours, sounds, etc., 'similarity appears to be a unique relation of stimulus pairs and it does appear to act like a distance' (Torgerson, 1965, p. 382). With stimuli which require subjects to take several perceptual features simultaneously into consideration, however, such as shapes varying in angle, size, and radial line used by Shepard (1964), similarity is no longer an invariant measure as distance is. The multi-attribute cognitive variables most likely to be of interest to social psychologists may not have the invariant characteristics that the distance assumption requires. It seems a reasonable intuitive test of the similarity–distance monotonicity assumption to consider whether similarity judgments of two elements would remain reasonably constant, irrespective of the context, other elements, decision-making strategies, etc.

The monotonicity requirement may not be as restrictive as it appears, however: 'although the similarity structures in the cognitive case do not appear to be inherently spatial or dimensional in nature, yet it does seem that such structures can always be embedded in an appropriate space. This appears to be so, even though the similarity relation itself does not possess all of the properties of a distance' (Torgerson, 1965, p. 390). Thus, most stimulus spaces of interest in social psychology can still be analysed using MDS techniques, if it is kept in mind that although spatial representation is nearly always *possible*, the resulting configuration will not always have the invariant characteristics of points in space. To find out whether the output configuration indeed represents such an invariant structure, it may be advisable to repeat the scaling, using a slightly different task, instructions, a different MDS program, or a manipulation of some other contextual variable. It is encouraging to note, however, that in most multidimensional scaling studies of complex social objects, to be discussed below, stable and invariant stimulus structures were generally obtained, which were not greatly altered by the manipulation of the data collection technique (Wish, 1975).

A BRIEF REVIEW OF SOME EXISTING STUDIES USING MDS IN SOCIAL PSYCHOLOGY

In the previous sections, the major advantages of MDS methods, their most important areas of application, and a description of their uses were covered. The major objective was to demonstrate the relevance and applicability of such 'discovery' methods to problems in social psychology. In the following section, a brief, and by necessity incomplete, review of some studies using MDS techniques to solve social psychological problems will be given. The purpose here is to give some idea by analogy of the range of potential applications of these methods.

Perhaps the most obvious application of MDS methods is in the area of *person perception*: the absence of external constructs provided by the experimenter in MDS, and the ease of data collection make this method ideally suited for the study of social perception phenomena.

In one of the earliest studies, Jackson, Messick, and Solley (1957) asked college students to rate each other for similarity. The resulting dimensions (friendliness, academic interest and status) are surprisingly similar to the dimensions typically obtained in MDS studies of group structure. In another study, Rosenberg and Olshan (1970) asked subjects to describe ten individuals known to them. The cooccurrence of any two traits to describe a person was used as input to a nonmetric MDS analysis, resulting in a three-dimensional space for personality traits, which the authors interpreted as reflecting a strong evaluative component. Mueller (1974) used INDSCAL to analyse the perceptual space underlying judgments of people, and to study the differences between different subject groups in their representations. In this study, it was found that cognitively complex subjects rely less on an affective dimension in their representations while cognitively simple subjects use this dimension overwhelmingly: 'Simple perceptual judgments of people are dominated by the affective dimension' (1974, p. 179). Jones and Rosenberg (1974) used naturalistic descriptions of personality as their raw data in deriving a structural representation. Rosenberg, Nelson and Vivekananthan (1968), in one of the earlier studies of this kind, used Kruskal's (1964) MDS program to analyse the structure of personality impressions; again, they derived their raw data by asking subjects to describe ten other people.

The spreading use of MDS techniques to study person perception phenomena has also affected a related field of study, the study of *implicit theories of personality* (Rosenberg and Sedlak, 1972). Clearly, if an individual's internal representation of different personality traits and their relationship to each other can be quantitatively represented, as MDS enables investigators to do, this structure is likely to reflect the individual's permanent tendencies in associating or dissociating certain traits with each other; in other words, it will reflect his implicit theory of personality. Frequently, trait co-occurrence in naturally occurring descriptions of personality provides sufficient data for such an analysis (Rosenberg and Sedlak, 1972). In an ingenious study, Rosenberg and Jones (1972) used this principle to represent Theodore Dreiser's implicit theory of personality, as reflected in his description of women in *Gallery of Women*. These authors extracted terms and descriptive phrases referring to women from the book, and used trait co-occurrence data as input to an MDS analysis. The property dimensions underlying Dreiser's implicit view of women were interpreted as reflecting male versus female characteristics and conformity (Figure 10.2).

These dimensions, the authors argue, are meaningful in terms of the biographical details known about Dreiser, and his relationship to women.

A third area of application of MDS methods is the study of national and racial *stereotypes*. Perceptions of nations and ethnic groups have always been of interest to social psychologists, and the use of MDS has provided a new dimension to these studies. Stereotype research is an excellent example of a

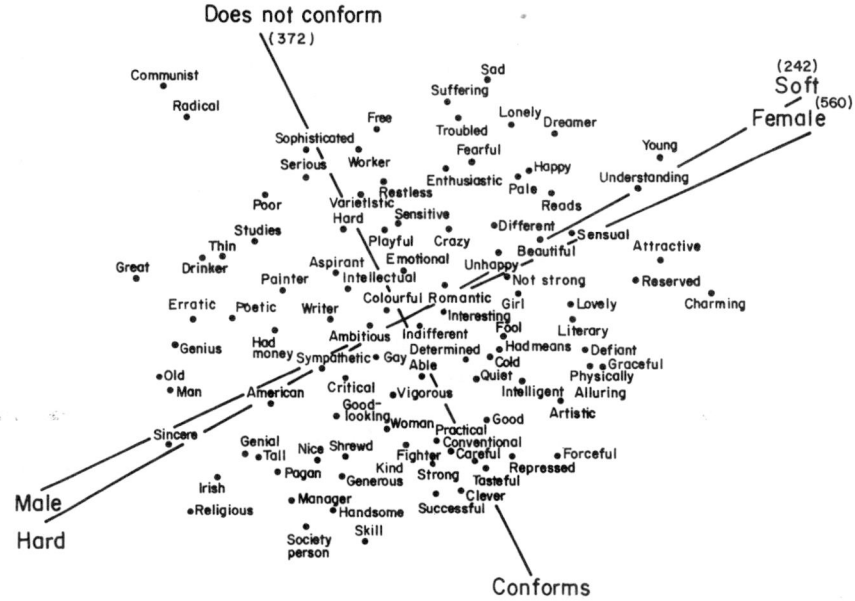

Figure 10.2 Theodore Dreiser's view of women: the two-dimensional configuration of the ninety-nine traits used most frequently in *A Gallery of Women*. Also shown are the best-fitting axes for each of three bipolar labelling dimensions. The numbers in parenthesis show the multiple correlation between coordinates on the MDS axes and the bipolar scales (reprinted from Rosenberg and Jones, 1972, p. 381; copyright 1972 by the American Psychological Association. Reprinted by permission)

research area where the main objects of interest are cognitive structures concerning perceived types of people, yet what is investigated is simple verbal judgments, typically in terms of preselected constructs. 'Stereotype research is in need of a refocusing of interest on the main issue of structure and the utilization of a methodology more suited to this issue', assert Funk et al. (1976, p. 117). In their study, ethnic minorities in the US were found to be clustered in three groups of Asian, European and Spanish and Negro backgrounds. Robinson and Hefner (1967) studied perceptions of different nations, using a sophisticated academic sample, and a random sample of Detroit residents. The cognitive representations by the academic and the random sample were found to be different, reflecting the cultural and intellectual differences between these two groups. Jones and Ashmore (1973) asked college students to sort labels of fifty ethnic groups into categories in terms of similarity. The perceptual space for ethnic groups was found to be three-dimensional, and the three underlying dimensions were labelled as dominant–subordinate, communist–non-communist, and western culture–non-western culture. In another important contribution to this field of research, Wish, Deutsch, and Biener (1970) asked students of different political persuasion and from different countries to rate twenty-one nations for similarity. The conceptual space providing an adequate representation of these nations contained four dimensions, reflecting political alignment and ideology, economic development, geography and population, and race. Important subject differences were also found, with males, political moderates and subjects from developed countries placing more emphasis on the economic development dimensions, while females, political radicals and students from underdeveloped countries perceiving nations primarily in terms of political alignment. In a similar study, Wish (1970) used INDSCAL to analyse the perceptual representation of nations by individuals. In general, these studies yield not only meaningful multidimensional configurations of the conceptual space for nations and ethnic groups, but the cognitive differences between individuals and subject subgroups differing in political allegiance can also be analysed.

A fourth, and related area of application for MDS techniques is in the study of *political behaviour and perception*. In perhaps the first study of this kind, Messick (1961) asked several hundred undergraduates to rate twenty US and foreign politicians for similarity. The MDS analysis of these data yielded a complex, seven-dimensional stimulus space. Tucker and Messick (1963) reanalysed these data, using their more sophisticated points of view analysis. The same program was used by Ahrens (1967) in a study of perceptions of West German politicians, revealing the presence of two 'points of view' in his group. In a more recent study, Sherman and Ross (1972) found a seven-dimensional cognitive space for US politicians, which was related to the liberalism–conservatism of the respondents. Shikiar (1974) derived a representation of eight US politicians and twelve attitude statements in a joint stimulus space. Warr, Schroeder, and Blackman

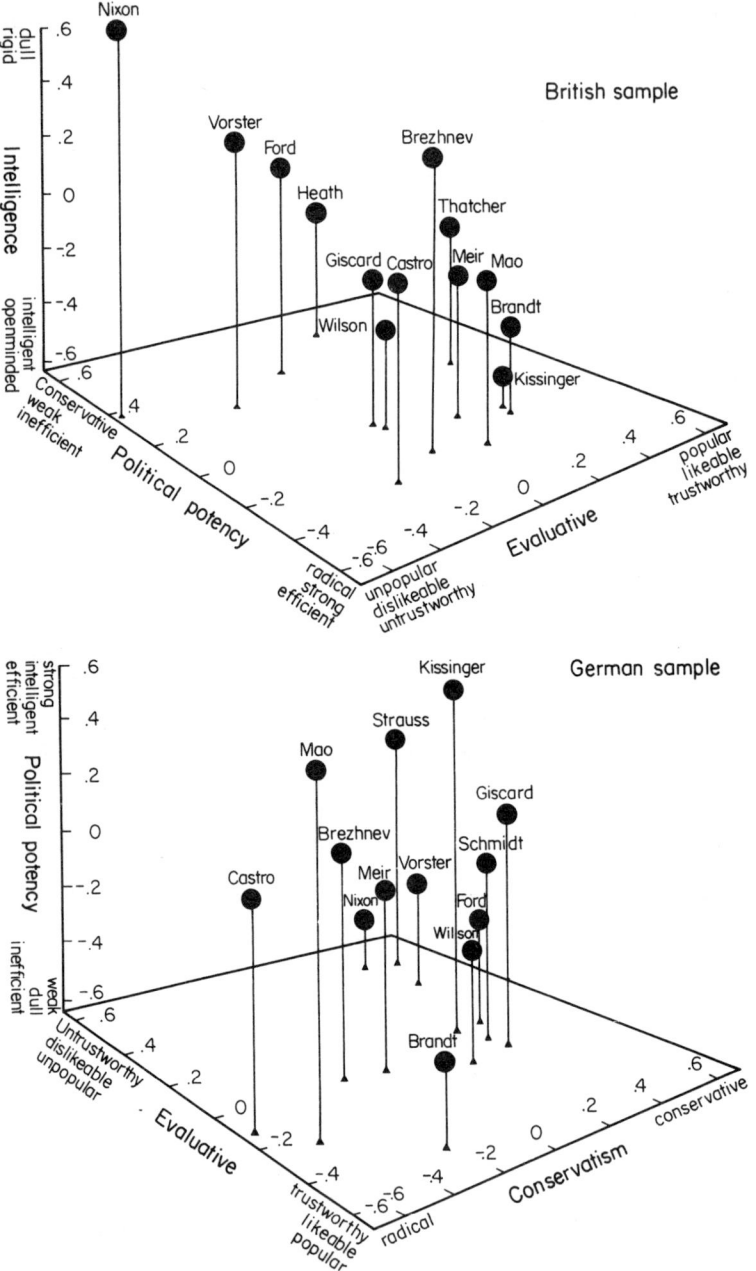

Figure 10.3 The perception of thirteen political leaders by a British and a German student sample in three dimensions, showing the bipolar scales used in labelling the INDSCAL axes (from Forgas, Kagan, and Frey, 1977)

(1969) used left-wing, centre and right-wing subjects and several alternative data-collection techniques in their study of perceptions of national governments. The results of this study showed that even though the 'judgmental structure . . . did not vary as a function of political orientation' (Warr *et al.*, 1969, p. 41), in so far as the same number of dimensions were used by all subjects, the identity of the perceptual dimensions was a significant function of the political orientation of the subjects. The perceptions of political leaders, perhaps the most interesting category of political stimuli, was studied by Forgas, Kagan, and Frey (1977). Student samples in two countries, Britain and Germany, were asked to rate a sample of salient political personalities for similarity. Separate INDSCAL analyses were performed on these data, and the results indicated that the conceptual space for this group of stimuli was three-dimensional, although the identity of the dimensions was again found to be strongly culture-specific. The perceptual space for political leaders is shown in Figure 10.3.

While to date only small-scale studies, frequently using student samples, have used MDS in analysing political perception, the potential of this method in larger-scale, perhaps national, samples is obvious; for the first time, a complex and realistic representation of the conceptual space of large population groups can be derived.

Another research domain where MDS has been extensively employed is the study of the *structure of emotions*. The relationship between different emotions, and the possibility of discovering basic underlying dimensions in emotions has been long pursued as a research area. Abelson and Sermat (1962) in an early study studied the perceptual structure of facial expressions of emotions. More recently, Bush (1973) applied multidimensional scaling to the study of adjectives denoting feelings. A large student sample was asked to provide similarity ratings of emotion-expressive adjectives. The perceptual structure for emotions was found to be three-dimensional in this case, interpreted as reflecting the pleasantness, the level of activation and the level of aggression associated with different emotions. *Post hoc* tests of subject differences also indicated that the race of the respondents has an important effect on their representations of emotions.

A further group of studies using INDSCAL procedures turned towards the analysis and description of *social structure*. While the adequate representation of structure in small groups is a longstanding problem in social psychology, and methods such as Moreno's (1951) sociometric techniques are widely used, the simplicity of the representations, the absence of real spatial relationships, and the frequent imposition of criteria by the experimenter were serious limiting factors. Jones and Young (1972) have managed to overcome all of these difficulties, by using an INDSCAL procedure to represent the structure of an intact academic group. These authors found that the structure of this group, as seen by its members, was readily interpretable in three-dimensional space. Status, academic interests and political persuasion were found to be three basic dimensions defining use the MDS dimensions generated; it is advantageous, however, to keep the dimensions finally selected approximately orthogonal to each other. Since this procedure, based on intuition alone, can be fairly complex, it is generally advisable to use one of the empirical methods described below to interpret TORSCA 9 outputs. For INDSCAL solutions, on the other hand, stimulus dimensions are *not* arbitrary, need not be further rotated, and should reflect underlying psychological characteristics of the stimulus field; their interpretation by intuitive methods is thus much more straightforward.

External labelling

This is much more frequently used than the intuitive method, and is often used to substantiate it. It is essentially based on the analysis of the empirical relationship, by correlation or regression analysis, between MDS stimulus spaces and separately scaled property dimensions, or bipolar hypothesis scales. In interpreting a TORSCA 9 configuration, the separate ratings of the same set of stimuli by the same or comparable group of subjects on a number of bipolar scales are collected first. In the next step, a unique axis in multidimensional space is located which optimally corresponds to a separately rated bipolar scale. This is accomplished by using the stimulus co-ordinates of the MDS solution to predict the mean or median of judgments on the relevant bipolar scale. This multiple regression procedure provides a set of regression weights for each of the MDS dimensions. These weights are used as direction numbers to determine the slope of a unique axis in the MDS space corresponding to a bipolar scale. Once such an axis for each of the bipolar scales is found, the best fitting and approximately orthogonal axes are selected as an interpretative framework for the stimulus space. Other, non-linear methods for fitting property axes to MDS configurations were also proposed (Carroll and Chang, 1966), but are only infrequently used in psychology.

The interpretation of INDSCAL configurations using external property dimensions is considerably more straightforward, thanks to the direct interpretability of the stimulus dimensions. Rather than locating external axes in multidimensional space, it is sufficient to establish an empirical relationship between INDSCAL dimensions and the different property dimensions used to label them. Usually, correlation coefficients, partial correlation coefficients or regression analysis are used to establish such a relationship. The bipolar dimension(s) most closely related to a particular INDSCAL dimension are then used to label that dimension.

Internal labelling

This is an even more simple and accurate technique applicable to the interpretation of INDSCAL outputs, but only when input data were originally an individual's position within the group. Faculty, research students and staff were also found to be significantly differentiated in this three-dimensional space. In addition, these authors have studied the longitudinal stability of this structure, and found that a one-year interval and minor changes in membership failed to significantly affect the group structure. Davison and Jones (1976) used a similar method to represent the perceived structure of a small group, and to successfully predict interpersonal attraction from this structure. A similar procedure was used by Forgas (1978) to study the structure of an intact research group. In this study, group structure was defined by evaluative, conventionality and dominance dimensions. In addition, it was found that an individual's position within the group in terms of these dimensions was significantly related to his representation of social episodes within the group. The perceived structure of this academic group is shown in Figure 10.4.

In recent years, several further ingenious applications of MDS techniques have

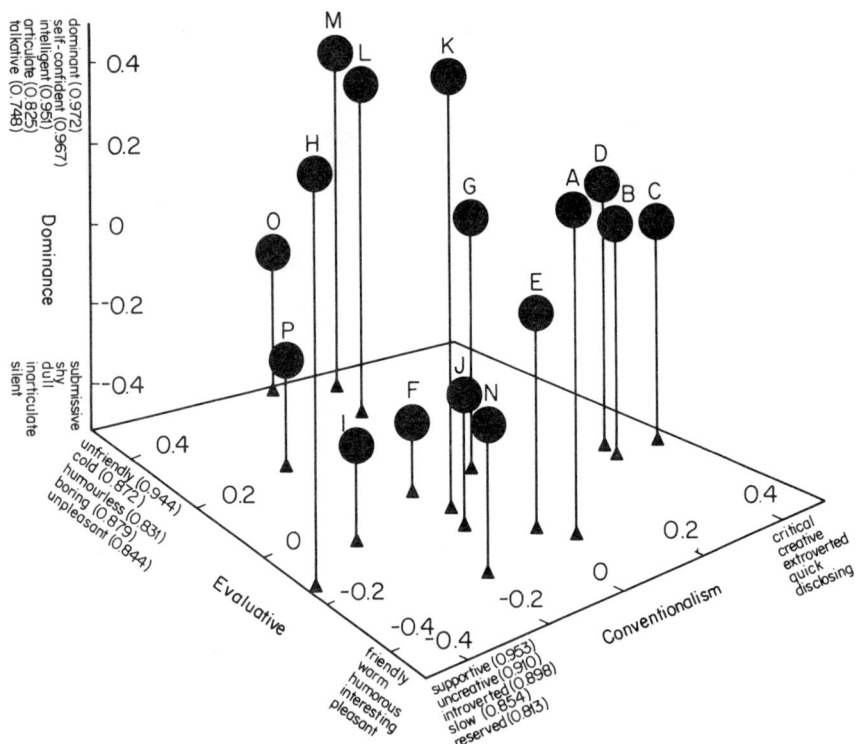

Figure 10.4 The three-dimensional representation of an academic group's sociometric structure, showing the bipolar scales used to label the INDSCAL dimensions. (A–E: faculty members, F–M: research students, N–P: other staff); (Forgas, 1978)

been proposed. In the sociological sphere, Sherman and Dowdle (1974) used MDS to represent perceptions of different crimes and punishments, and Coxon and Jones (1974) used MDS to study subjective perceptions of different occupational groups. Friendly and Glucksberg (1970) studied the acquisition of a specific subcultural lexicon of slang words in Princeton students, by representing the cognitive space for slang words for freshmen and seniors respectively. Jones, Sensenig and Haley (1974) applied MDS to the study of self-descriptions of a large sample of college students. An interesting application of MDS methods is in the area of experimental aesthetics, where perceptions of a sample of landscape paintings were found to reflect attributes such as degree of realism, degree of clarity of detail, and balance or symmetry (O'Hare, 1976a). Further, judges trained in art were found to differ significantly from untrained judges in their weighting of perceptual dimensions (O'Hare, 1976b).

MDS STUDIES OF SOCIAL EPISODES

This leads us to the final, and perhaps most promising area of application of MDS techniques, the study of *social episodes*. The study of social situations and social episodes is a recent development in social psychology, which can be directly linked to the major shift of orientation currently taking place (Argyle, this volume). Initially, concern with the study of social episodes (Harré and Secord, 1972) yielded little more than a spate of speculative, *ad hoc* taxonomies proposed by researchers who often did not even consider the applicability of quantitative techniques to this difficult area. It is only very recently that the first attempts at quantitative taxonomies, significantly, using MDS techniques, have begun to appear (Forgas, 1976; Wish, 1976). Early studies of social episodes used factor analytical methods to represent the perception of different social situations (Magnusson, 1971). More recently, Wish (1975) studied the internal representations subjects had of different communication episodes, using an INDSCAL technique. He varied communication episodes in terms of (a) the *relationship* between the interactors (for example, between husband and wife, supervisor and employee, you and your supervisor), and (b) in terms of the *situational context* (at a large social gathering, working together for a common goal, etc.). Subjects rated each of these episodes on fourteen bipolar scales, and similarity measures were derived from their ratings using the procedure outlined earlier in this chapter. The cognitive representation of communication episodes appeared to be five-dimensional in this study, reflecting co-operativeness, intensity, equality, formality and task orientation. The contribution of the *relationship* and the *situational context* to the position of an episode on each of these dimensions was also evaluated, using an analysis of variance technique. It was found that the perceived co-operativeness, intensity and task-orientation of the episodes depended more on the situational context, while equality and formality were largely dependent on the role relationship between the in-

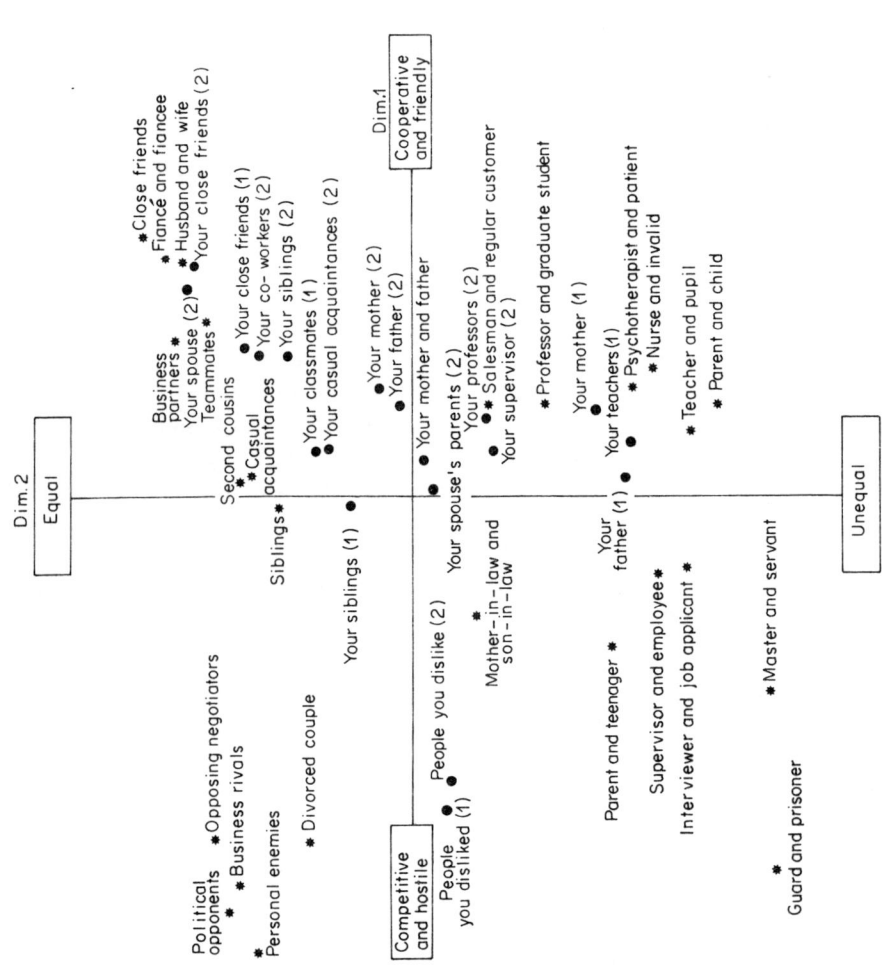

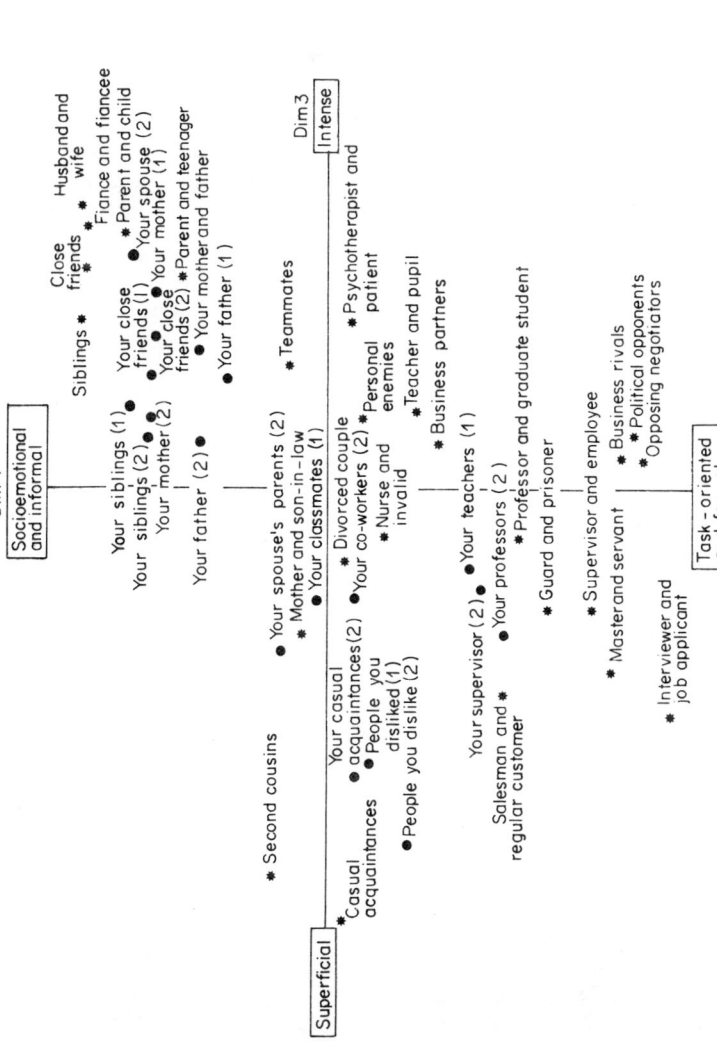

Figure 10.5 Dimensions 1, 2, 3, and 4 of the four-dimensional INDSCAL solution, showing the perception of twenty-five 'typical' and nineteen 'own' interpersonal relations (from Wish, Deutsch, and Kaplan, 1976; copyright 1976 by the American Psychological Association. Reprinted by permission)

teractants. Since individuals' perceptions of different kinds of communication episodes have obvious relevance to their actual behaviour in those situations, this study is promising in pointing the way towards the eventual quantification of these 'subjective' elements in social behaviour. In a similar study, Wish, Deutsch, and Kaplan (1976) addressed the problem of which dimensions underlie the perceptions of dyadic relationships, an important component of the definition of an episode. Students rated dyadic relationships such as 'between casual acquaintances', 'between business rivals', 'between you and your classmates', etc., on a set of bipolar scales. Similarity judgments were extracted from these data and subjected to an INDSCAL analysis, resulting in a four-dimensional solution defined by the equality, competitiveness, intensity and formality dimensions (Figure 10.5).

A rather different task was addressed by Forgas (1976), who undertook to analyse subcultural representations of social episodes in two different social milieus, amongst students and housewives. A representative range of episodes, selected on the basis of an open-ended pilot study, were used as stimuli (see Table 10.1), and a multiple groupings task provided the input data to a TORSCA 9 MDS analysis. The two-dimensional episode space for housewives was interpreted by fitting separately scaled bipolar scales to the MDS space, which are shown in Figure 10.6. The first dimension was found to reflect the

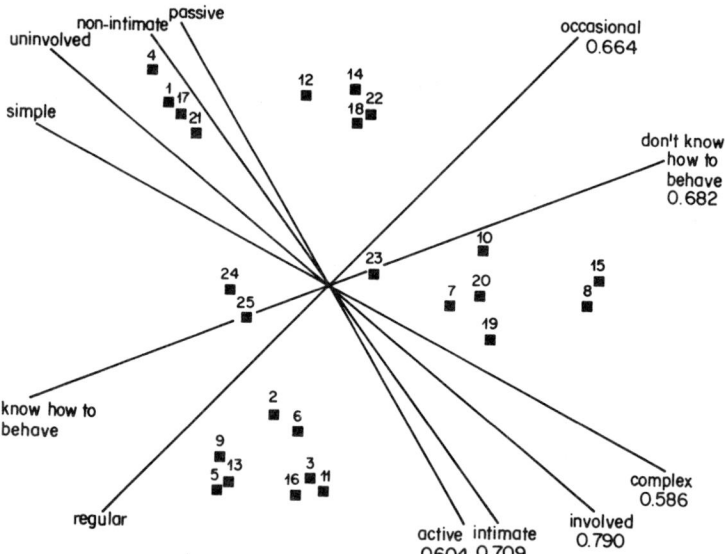

Figure 10.6 The two-dimensional configuration of twenty-five soical episodes as perceived by housewives, with six hypothesis scales fitted (for episode labels see Table 10.1) (from Forgas, 1976, p. 204; copyright 1976 by the American Psychological Association. Reprinted by permission)

Table 10.1

Housewives ($n = 25$)	Students ($n = 23$)
1. Having a short chat with the house delivery man	1. Having morning coffee with people in the department
2. Playing with your children	2. Having a drink with some friends in a pub
3. Your husband rings up from work to discuss something	3. Discussing an essay during a tutorial
4. Having a short chat with the shop assistant while shopping	4. Meeting an acquaintance while checking your pigeonhole for mail in college
5. Having dinner with your family	5. Going out for a walk with a friend
6. Shopping on Saturday morning with your husband at the supermarket	6. Shopping on Saturday morning with a friend at the supermarket
7. Attending a wedding ceremony	7. Acting as a subject in a psychology experiment
8. Having a drink with some friends in the pub	8. Going to the pictures with some friends
9. Washing up dishes after dinner with family help	9. Having a short chat with the shop assistant while shopping
10. Chatting over morning coffee with some friends	10. Getting acquainted with a new person during dinner in hall
11. Reading and talking in bed before going to sleep	11. Going to JCR meetings
12. Chatting with an acquaintance who unexpectedly gave you a lift	12. Chatting with an acquaintance before lecture begins
13. Watching TV with your family after dinner	13. Discussing psychology topics with friends
14. Having a short chat with an acquaintance whom you unexpectedly met on the street	14. Meeting new people at a sherry party in college
15. Going to the pictures with some friends	15. Visiting your doctor
16. Discussing the events of the day with your husband in the evening	16. Chatting with an acquaintance who unexpectedly gave you a lift
17. Talking to other customers while queueing in a shop	17. Visiting a friend in his college room
18. Talking to a neighbour who called to borrow some household equipment	18. Going to see a play at the theatre with friends
19. Having guests for dinner	19. Going to the bank
20. Visiting a friend in hospital	20. Having an intimate conversation with your boyfriend or girlfriend
21. Chatting with others while waiting for your washing in the coin laundry	21. Having a short chat with an acquaintance whom you unexpectedly met on the street
22. Talking to a neighbour through the backyard fence	22. Chatting with others while waiting for your washing in the coin laundry
23. Playing chess	23. Attending a wedding ceremony
24. Going to the bank	24. Watching TV with some friends
25. Visiting your doctor	25. Playing chess

From Forgas (1976). Copyright 1976 by the American Psychological Association. Reprinted by permission.

perceived intimacy and friendliness of episodes, and the second dimension showed the subjective self-confidence or competence of actors, related to the regularity of the episodes. For students, a more complex, three-dimensional representation was found to be defined by three bipolar scales, involvements, pleasantness and knowing how to behave (Figure 10.7). The differences in the complexity of the episode spaces, and the quality of the underlying dimensions were found to reflect the different social and cultural environments of the subjects.

For example, students seemed to regard episodes involving entertainments and socializing with friends with great self-confidence (episodes 2, 8, 18, and 24), in strong contrast to housewives, who viewed similar episodes with a lack of self-confidence. While 'socializing with friends' for students appears to be a natural, self-selected entertainment, for housewives it may be a more demanding, formal and organized affair, involving an element of self-presentation. Since these

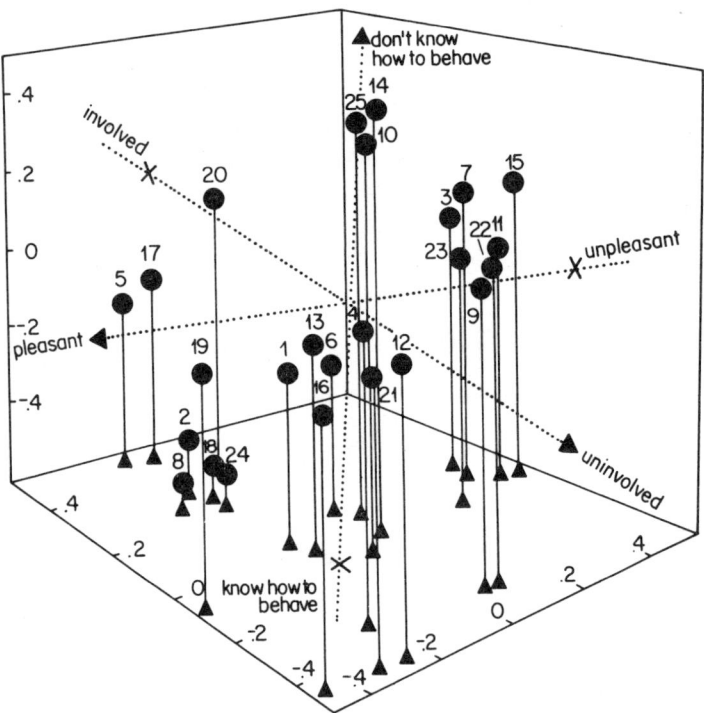

Figure 10.7 The three-dimensional representation of twenty-five social episodes as perceived by students, with three hypothesis scales fitted (for episode labels, see Table 1) (from Forgas, 1976, p. 205; copyright 1976 by the American Psychological Association. Reprinted by permission)

techniques appear to be extremely sensitive to subcultural differences in episode perception, they may also be usefully employed to study individual differences. For example, socially skilled and socially unskilled individuals could be expected to show marked differences in episode perception, a possibility which holds important implications for social skills theory and therapy.

In another study, an MDS technique was used to represent and contrast the perception of social episodes in two small groups—two college rugby teams in Oxford (Forgas, 1977). It was found that even though the two teams as social units were quite unrelated, their perception of social episodes was very similar, reflecting their similar social milieus. The more cohesive team which met regularly for training and on other occasions had an episode space in which task-related (sport) and other episodes were not significantly differentiated. In contrast, these two kinds of episodes were significantly differentiated in the episodes space of the less cohesive team, where training and other group interactions were less frequent and regular.

In a subsequent study (Forgas, 1978), it was shown that an individual's cognitive representation of typical episodes in his social environment is affected not only by the particular social milieu, but also by his status and structural position in his immediate reference group. In this study INDSCAL was used to construct a sociometric representation of the structure of the academic group studied (see Figure 10.4). Similarly, the group's perception of its social episodes was also represented yielding a four-dimensional episode space. In secondary analyses, an empirical relationship between an individual's sociometric position and his perception of social episodes was established. Formal status differences between members of this group were also found to be related to differences in episode perception, as Figure 10.8 shows.

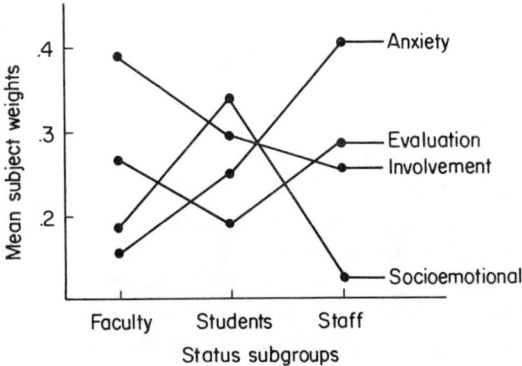

Figure 10.8 Differences in episode perception as a function of status: the mean salience of four-episode perception dimensions to faculty, student, and staff members in an academic group (from Forgas, 1978)

Thus, anxiety was a highly salient dimension to staff, but not for faculty, reflecting perhaps the different social skills of these subgroups. Faculty, presumably often engaged in less than fully involving encounters, found involvement the most salient dimension, while students were most sensitive to the work or purely social character of episodes. This study is an interesting illustration of how elusive aspects of social behaviour and perception can be studied, using quantitative descriptive techniques such as MDS.

The potential for further studies of social episodes and the factors affecting their perception using MDS techniques is obvious: these methods are ideally suited to the study of different aspects of social perception, and to the establishment of relationships between aspects of a social environment which were previously regarded as too difficult to quantify for empirical study.

SUMMARY AND CONCLUSIONS

It was argued in this chapter that the common feature of 'new' strategies in social psychology is their espousal of descriptive analysis of everyday social behaviour, as an alternative to the up-to-now typical manipulative laboratory experiment. The catalysts in this reorientation were, not surprisingly, researchers such as Goffman who provided new insights into social behaviour relying on descriptive, interpretative methodologies. It was emphasized here that description can be quantified rather than anecdotal or journalistic, and that statistical techniques such as MDS are capable of opening up new avenues of research merely by enabling investigators to represent quantitatively otherwise inaccessible phenomena. It is for this reason that studies in social psychology using MDS techniques can be said to constitute a unique, and substantially different research strategy.

As this necessarily brief review of the field suggests, in the diverse areas in which MDS has been applied to social psychological phenomena, substantial new insights have been gained, and productive new research areas have been opened up. The study of perceived social structure, of implicit theories of personality, and of perceptions of social episodes are examples of research areas commonly relying on this new strategy. In each of these three areas, the initial task was simply the description and quantitative representation of otherwise elusive, cognitive structures. Once such a representation proved possible, secondary analyses, using a wide range of statistical techniques followed. With the growing interest in how a person comes to represent his social environment cognitively, studies of this kind will inevitably become more numerous, providing an alternative to the predominantly journalistic and anecdotal modes of description advocated by many today.

However, the potential range of application of MDS techniques is much more extensive. Nearly all the studies mentioned here rely on judgmental data to represent implicit cognitive structures. Other measures of relatedness, such as objective measures of similarity or objective measures of co-occurrence, were not used consistently to date. Just as judgmental data have provided new insights into the structure of cognitive representation of social phenomena, different objective measures can provide new insights into the structure of naturalistic social behaviour. Many aspects of such behaviour can be recorded and measured, and the similarities or dissimilarities between these elements of behaviour can be used as input to MDS to represent the structural relationship between them. As far as the study of social episodes is concerned, existing studies were primarily concerned with the representation of perceived differences *between* different episodes. An equally fruitful, and as yet unexplored, area where MDS techniques can be potentially applied is the study of the internal behavioural structure *within* a particular episode.

Multidimensional scaling as a method is still evolving today. Increasingly convenient and useful variants of the technique are being constantly developed. Interactive programs, such as Young and Cliff's (1972) ISIS, will undoubtedly be of increasing importance in social psychological research. If this chapter has been successful in arousing some interest in the creative uses to which MDS can be put, and the new insights which can be achieved with the help of this technique, then its inclusion here may not have been in vain.

References

Abelson, R. P. and Sermat, V., 1962, Multidimensional scaling of facial expressions, *Journal of Personality and Social Psychology*, **63**, 546–554.

Ahrens, H. J., 1967, Zur Systematik der Urteilsbildung bei der Beurteilung westdeutscher Politiker, *Archive fur die gesamte Psychologie*, **119**, 57–89.

Argyle, M., 1969, *Social Interaction*, London: Methuen.

Argyle, M. and Little, B. R., 1972, Do personality traits apply to social behaviour? *Journal for the Theory of Social Behaviour*, **2**, 1–35.

Armistead, N. (ed.), 1974, *Reconstructing Social Psychology*, Harmondsworth: Penguin.

Baker, R. F. and Young, F., 1975, A note on the empirical evaluation of the ISIS procedure, *Psychometrika*, **40**, 413–414.

Bruner, J., 1976, *Psychological Theories and the Image of Man*. Herbert Spencer Lectures, University of Oxford.

Bush, L. E., 1973, Individual differences multidimensional scaling of adjectives denoting feelings, *Journal of Personality and Social Psychology*, **25**, 50–57.

Carroll, J. D. and Chang, J. J., 1970, Analysis of individual differences in multidimensional scaling via an N-way generalization of 'Eckart–Young' decomposition, *Psychometrika*, **35**, 283–319.

Coxon, A. P. M., 1974, *Multidimensional Scaling*, ECPR Summer School of the University of Essex, monographs on social science data analysis.

Coxon, A. P. M. and Jones, C. L., 1974, Occupational similarities: subjective aspects of social stratification, *Quality and Quantity*, **8**, 139–157.

Cronbach, L. J., 1957, The two disciplines of scientific psychology. *American Psychologist*, **12**, 671–684.

Cronbach, L. J. and Gleser, G. C., 1953, Assessing similarity between profiles. *Psychological Bulletin*, **50**, 456–473.

Davison, M. L. and Jones, L. E., 1976, A similarity-attraction model for predicting sociometric choice from perceived group structure, *Journal of Personality and Social Psychology*, **33**, 601–612.

Ekehammar, B., 1974, Interactionism in personality from a historical perspective, *Psychological Bulletin*, **81**, 1026–1048.

Forgas, J. P., 1976, The perception of social episodes: categorical and dimensional representations in two different social milieus, *Journal of Personality and Social Psychology*, **33**, 199–209.

Forgas, J. P., 1977, The perception of social episodes in two sports teams: a multidimensional approach, *Journal of Social Psychology*.

Forgas, J. P., 1978, Social structure and social episodes in an academic setting: the social environment of an intact group, *Human Relations*.

Forgas, J. P., Argyle, M., and Ginsburg, G. P., 1976, The effects of the situational context on person perception judgements: the fluctuating structure of an academic group, unpublished manuscript, Oxford University.

Forgas, J. P., Kagan, C. M. and Frey, D., 1977, The cognitive representation of political personalities: a cross-cultural comparison, *International Journal of Psychology*, **12**, 19–30.

Frederiksen, N., 1972, Towards a taxonomy of situations, *American Psychologist*, **27**, 176–179.

Friendly, M. L. and Glucksberg, S., 1970, On the description of subcultural lexicons: a multidimensional approach, *Journal of Personality and Social Psychology*, **14**, 55–65.

Funk, S., Horowitz, A. D., Lipshitz, R., and Young, F. W., 1976, The perceived structure of American ethnic groups: the use of multidimensional scaling in ethnic research, *Sociometry*, **39**, 116–130.

Gergen, K. J., 1973, Social psychology as history, *Journal of Personality and Social Psychology*, **26**, 309–326.

Girard, R. A. and Cliff, N., 1976, A Monte Carlo evaluation of interactive multidimensional scaling, *Psychometrika*, **41**, 43–64.

Harré, R. and Secord, P., 1972, *The Explanation of Social Behaviour*, Oxford: Blackwell.

Israel, J. and Tajfel, H. (eds.), 1972, *The Context of Social Psychology: A Critical Assessment*. London: Academic Press.

Jackson, D. N., 1969, The multidimensional nature of human social perception, *Canadian Journal of Behavioural Science*, **1(4)**, 227–261.

Jackson, D. N., Messick, S., and Solley, C. M., 1957, A multidimensional scaling approach to the perception of personality, *Journal of Psychology*, **44**, 311–318.

Jones, R. A. and Ashmore, R. D., 1973, The structure of intergroup perception: categories and dimensions in views of ethnic groups and adjectives used in stereotype research, *Journal of Personality and Social Psychology*, **25**, 428–438.

Jones, R. A. and Rosenberg, S., 1974, Structural representations of naturalistic descriptions of personality, *Multivariate Behavioural Research*, **9**, 217–230.

Jones, R. A., Sensenig, J. and Haley, J. V., 1974, Self-descriptions: configurations of content and order effects, *Journal of Personality and Social Psychology*, **30**, 36–45.

Jones, L. E. and Young, F. W., 1972, Structure of a social environment: longitudinal individual differences scaling of an intact group, *Journal of Personality and Social Psychology*, **24**, 108–121.

Kruskal, J. B., 1964a, Multidimensional scaling by optimizing goodness of fit to a nonmetric hypothesis, *Psychometrika*, **29**, 1–27.

Kruskal, J. B., 1964b, Nonmetric multidimensional scaling: a numerical method, *Psychometrika*, **29**, 115–129.

Levine, M., 1974, Scientific method and the adversary model, *American Psychologist*, **29**, 661–677.

Lingoes, J. C., 1965, An IBM 7090 program for Guttman–Lingoes smallest space analysis—I, *Behavioural Science*, **10**, 183–184.
McCallum, R. C., 1974, Relations between factor analysis and MDS. *Psychological Bulletin*, **81**, 505–516.
McCallum, R. C., 1976, Effects on INDSCAL of non-orthogonal perceptions of object space dimensions, *Psychometrika*, **41**, 177–187.
McGee, V. E., 1968, Multidimensional scaling of N sets of similarity measures: a nonmetric individual differences approach, *Multivariate Behavioural Research*, **3**, 233–248.
McGuire, W. S., 1973, The yin and the yang of progress in social psychology: seven koan, *Journal of Personality and Social Psychology*, **26**, 446–456.
Magnusson, D., 1971, An analysis of situational dimensions, *Perceptual and Motor Skills*, **32**, 851–867.
Marriott, F. H. C., 1974, *The Interpretation of Multiple Observations*, London: Academic Press.
Messick, S., 1961, The perceived structure of political relationships. *Sociometry*, **24**, 270–278.
Messick, S. J. and Abelson, R. P., 1956, The additive constant problem in multidimensional scaling, *Psychometrika*, **21**, 367–375.
Mischel, W., 1973, Towards a cognitive social learning reconceptualization of personality, *Psychological Review*, **80**, 252–283.
Moreno, J. L., 1951, *Sociometry: Experimental Method and the Science of Society*, New York: Beacon House.
Mueller, W. S., 1974, Cognitive complexity and salience of dimensions in person perception, *Australian Journal of Psychology*, **26**, 173–182.
O'Hare, D., 1976a, Dimensions of perceived similarity of paintings, mimeo, Department of Psychology, University of Exeter.
O'Hare, D., 1976b, Individual differences in perceived similarity and preference for visual art: a multidimensional scaling analysis, *Perception and Psychophysics*, **20**, 445–452.
Osgood, C. E. and Suci, G. J., 1952, A measure of relation determined by both mean differences and profile information, *Psychological Bulletin*, **49**, 251–262.
Pervin, L., 1976, A free-response description approach, to the study of person–situation interaction, *Journal of Personality and Social Psychology*, **34**, 465–474.
Robinson, J. P. and Hefner, R., 1967, Multidimensional differences in public and academic perceptions of nations, *Journal of Personality and Social Psychology*, **9**, 251–259.
Rosenberg, S. and Jones, R. A., 1972, A method for investigating and representing a person's implicit theory of personality: Theodore Dreiser's view of people, *Journal of Personality and Social Psychology*, **22**, 372–386.
Rosenberg, S., Nelson, C. and Vivekananthan, P. S., 1968, A multidimensional approach to the structure of personality impressions, *Journal of Personality and Social Psychology*, **9**, 283–294.
Rosenberg, S. and Olshan, K., 1970, Evaluative and descriptive aspects in personality perception, *Journal of Personality and Social Psychology*, **16**, 619–626.
Rosenberg, S. and Sedlak, A., 1972, Structural representations of implicit personality theory, in L. Berkowitz (ed.), *Advances in Experimental Social Psychology, Vol. 6*, New York: The Academic Press.
Shepard, R. N., 1962a, The analysis of proximities: multidimensional scaling with an unknown distance function—I, *Psychometrika*, **27**, 125–140.
Shepard, R. N., 1962b, The analysis of proximities: multidimensional scaling with an unknown distance function—II, *Psychometrika*, **27**, 219–246.

Shepard, R. N., 1964, Attention and the metric structure of the stimulus space, *Journal of Mathematical Psychology*, **1**, 54–87.

Shepard, R. N., 1966, Metric structures in ordinal data, *Journal of Mathematical Psychology*, **3**, 287–315.

Shepard, R. N., 1974, Representation of structure in similarity data: problems and prospects, *Psychometrika*, **39**, 373–421.

Shepard, R. N., Romney, A. K., and Nerlove, S. B. (eds.), 1972, *Multidimensional Scalings Theory and Application in the Behavioural Sciences, Vol. I*, New York: Seminar Press.

Sherman, R. C. and Dowdle, M. D., 1974, The perception of crime and punishment: a multidimensional scaling analysis, *Social Science Research*, **3**, 109–129.

Sherman, R. E. and Ross, L. B., 1972, Liberalism—conservatism and dimensional salience in the perception of political figures, *Journal of Personality and Social Psychology*, **23**, 120–127.

Shikiar, R., 1974, The perception of politicians and political issues: a multidimensional scaling approach, *Multivariate Behavioural Research*, **9**, 461–477.

Spence, I. and Domoney, D. W., 1974, Incomplete designs for nonmetric multidimensional scaling, *Psychometrika*, **39**, 469–490.

Spence, I. and Ogilvie, J., 1973, A table of expected stress values for random rankings in nonmetric multidimensional scaling, *Multivariate Behavioural Research*, **8**, 511–517.

Torgerson, W. S., 1952, Multidimensional scaling—I, Theory and method, *Psychometrika*, **17**, 401–419.

Torgerson, W. S., 1958, *Theory and Methods of Scaling*, New York: Wiley.

Torgerson, W. S., 1965, Multidimensional scaling of similarity, *Psychometrika*, **30**, 379–393.

Tucker, E. R. and Messick, J., 1963, An individual difference model for multidimensional scaling, *Psychometrika*, **28**, 333–367.

Warr, P. B., Schroeder, H. M. and Blackman, S., 1969, The structure of political judgement, *British Journal of Social Clinical Psychology*, **8**, 32–43.

Wish, M., 1970, Comparisons among multidimensional structure of nations based on difference measures of subjective similarity, *General Systems*, **15**, 55–65.

Wish, M., 1973, Individual differences in perceptions of dyadic relationships. Paper presented at the APA Symposium *Using MDS and Related Procedures in Personality, Social and Consumer Psychology*.

Wish, M., 1975a, The structure of interpersonal communication, *Industrial Research*.

Wish, M., 1975b, Subjects' expectations about their own interpersonal communication: a multidimensional approach, *Personality and Social Psychology Bulletin*, **1**.

Wish, M., 1975c, Role and personal expectations about interpersonal communication, Paper presented at the APA Convention.

Wish, M., 1976, Modality differences in perceptions of communication, *Conference Record, National Telecommunications Conference*.

Wish, M., Deutsch, M., and Biener, L., 1970, Differences in conceptual structures of nations: an exploratory study, *J. Personality and Social Psychology*, **16**, 361–373.

Wish, M., Deutsch, M., and Kaplan, S. J., 1976, Perceived dimensions of interpersonal relations, *Journal of Personality and Social Psychology*, **33**, 409–420.

Young, F. W., 1970, Nonmetric multidimensional scaling: recovery of metric information, *Psychometrika*, **35**, 455–473.

Young, F. W. and Cliff, N., 1972, Interactive scaling with individual subjects, *Psychometrika*, **37**, 385–415.

Young, F. W. and Torgerson, W. S., 1967, TORSCA, a FORTRAN IV program for Shepard–Kruskal multidimensional scaling analysis, *Behavioural Science*, **12**, 498.

11

EPILOGUE: A NEW PARADIGM?

Carl W. Backman

Many readers may wonder if the emerging methods and strategies described in the previous chapters, along with the underlying models of man and science, are not signs of a paradigmatic revolution in social psychology.

It is true that some of these methods and conceptualizations are not new but have been with us for some time. Yet it is well to remember that revolutionary ideologies often contain elements whose appeal is not so much in their novelty but in the fact that at last their time is ripe. A further consideration to keep in mind about revolutions, whether they be political or scientific, is that what is often seen as the main phase of the revolution is the tail end of it, the fireworks accompanying the last resistance to the changes that have in fact occurred. What evidence is there to suggest that perhaps social psychologists are well on their way through a revolution without being fully aware of their progress in this respect?

Certainly we have passed through more than a decade of soul-searching and self-doubt which produced a 'crisis' of confidence (Elms, 1975), particularly among those in the social psychological establishment. In part, this reflected increasing disillusionment with the experimental method as knowledge accumulated concerning the social psychology of the experiment, and in part it reflected a concern that the knowledge produced seemed largely irrelevant to the pressing problems of the day. The currents of doubt, whose origins lay largely in the US, were augmented by developments among some social psychologists in Europe who, having briefly succumbed to the American style of social psychology, reverted back to the more philosophically based critical stance characteristic of the European tradition in the social sciences.

Such periods are typical of the revolutionary process, and while there are some signs of a counter-revolution and an attempt to go back to social psychology as usual, there is also evidence that some basic shifts have occurred. To guage these shifts it will be instructive to return to the initial chapter in this volume and examine the degree to which the basic themes identified by Ginsburg as underlying the contents of these collected papers are reflected elsewhere. These elements along with the increasing use of methods other than the social psychological experiment may constitute the new paradigm. Three themes were identified. One was the view of man as an active agent, 'capable of making plans and pursuing objectives, of acting as well as reacting, of doing things for reasons as well as having been forced to do them by causes'. Second was that the meanings of actions, events, and setting to the participants are important in understanding and explaining their behaviour. The third theme was that there exists an underlying structure to interactional sequences.

The idea that man is an active agent rather than exclusively a product of natural forces impingeing upon him has become increasingly accepted in social psychological circles. For some, their model of man was never otherwise. Others have had to undergo a conversion to a view of science different from that of positivism to enable them to accept this view. Still others, less bothered by the philosophers' concern for consistency, may continue to view themselves as behaviourists in a positivist mould, but at the same time have developed theories and conducted research that makes sense only if man is construed as having some degree of freedom. For example, one could hardly argue that persons actively create an interpersonal environment to support their self-conceptions without losing confidence in a view of man as a billiard ball whose behaviour is simply a function of externally applied forces. The same is true for an investigator who does research on how persons attempt to maximize their outcomes in games or take or avoid risks, or for a researcher who learns that subjects may choose to confirm or disconfirm an experimental hypothesis.

Accompanying the spread of the point of view of man as agent has been the cognitive revolution in social psychology which has made the construction of meaning a central focus. Foreshadowed in the early work on social perception, later in the work of dissonance researchers, and now reflected in the dominance of attribution theory, this development surely has underscored the importance to an understanding of social life of the meanings which people attribute to their own behaviour as well as to that of others. Again, it can be argued that social psychology has moved further along this dimension than many of its practitioners realize, particularly those who still avoid looking into the black box when carrying out their experiments.

Much the same can be said concerning the third theme, situationism. While we have a good way to go in explicitly dealing with the meanings of situations and particularly their rule-governed character, the move away from intraindividual variables to situational ones is unmistakable. While the movement has been well documented in the field of personality studies, one need not look any further than more traditional areas of social psychology for striking examples of this shift. While this trend was acknowledged two decades ago in the study of leadership, a history of the research on attraction would show the same trend. Whether one examines the early days of the sociometric movement or the early studies of mate selection and marital success, the trend of research on attraction was first to emphasize characteristics of the individual, later those of pairs, and now the current emphasis is on situational and process variables (Huston and Levinger, 1978). Another striking example of the move in social psychology from the individual to the situation has been the dramatic change in the treatment of social motives. Aggression, altruism, and to an increasing degree achievement are being explained in situational terms rather than as the intraindividual residues of early experience. In addition, whole new areas of research have emerged within social psychology and closely related fields which start out with a situational focus. Examples are proxemics and environmental psychology. Finally, one can point to a number of metatheoretical movements within both the sociological and the psychological traditions in social psychology, including a heightened interest in symbolic interactionism, the emergence of ethnomethodology in the US and a somewhat independent but clearly related movement, ethogenics, in England. All of these are heavily situational in orientation. They place particular emphasis on the meanings of situations and on their rule-governed character. This focus, along with the influence of linguistics and structuralism in other social sciences, has greatly expanded the conception of the normative structure of social life. In this expanded view, not only is behaviour guided by institutionalized expectations attached to the various social categories recognized in a group, but by other shared rules and meanings as well. Institutionalized expectations regulate behaviour in a moral sense; but rules also serve as cognitive guides in the production of behaviour, such as those underlying various social skills, as well as serving to define activities, as in the case of the rules that define a game.

Whether rules are viewed from the standpoint of these newer schools of thought or from the more traditional viewpoint of those studying aggression, altruism, obedience, or other morally relevant behaviour, it is becoming increasingly clear that the normative structure includes more than just the rules of conduct. It also includes shared understandings about situational and personal conditions that determine their applicability (Backman, 1977). Awareness of the existence of background understandings (Garfinkel, 1972), including rules for the applications of rules, has added a depth to the conception of normative structure which hitherto had gone unrecognized. These developments have emerged in part from the studies of linguistics and in part from sociologists and psychologists studying such diverse topics as moral behaviour, non-verbal communication, strategies of self-presentation, etiquette, ritual, and what Goffman has labelled behaviour in public places. Such studies have underscored a final feature of the normative structure, namely that much of it is only tacitly known. A number of the methods in this volume represent ways of getting at this tacit aspect of the structure of social behaviour. Some of them, such as the Role Repertory Grid and multidimensional scaling, involve rather standardized methods of inferring the structure underlying judgments persons make. Others, such as the video and cinematic techniques, provide ways of obtaining and preserving detailed records of observations that can be systematically searched for patterns. Still others attempt to tap persons' knowledge, whether tacit or consciously known, of the rules governing behaviour. These involve either having persons create episodes of behaviour, as in some forms of role-playing, or having them account for their own behaviour or the behaviour of others, either directly through the solicitation of autobiographical accounts or more indirectly by having them account for the behaviour of others in constructed scenarios.

Symbolic interactionism and such newer traditions in social psychology as the ethogenic and ethnomethodology schools of thought have self-consciously made the meaning of situations central to their explanations of social behaviour. However, many investigators whose works derive from the Lewinian or learning traditions seem to have been much less conscious of how their own research demonstrates the significance of the meanings that persons ascribe to situations. The work of bystander intervention by Latané and Darley (1970) provides a striking example. Subjects in their experiments failed to respond in ambiguous emergency situations because they defined them as non-emergencies. A partial replication of one of their emergency situations by Warner (1976), who varied the degree of ambiguity, showed that to the degree the leeway for defining a situation as not an emergency was reduced, persons responded to the norm requiring intervention. Mixon's chapter in this volume suggests a similar interpretation of Milgram's findings on destructive obedience. To the degree that modifications in the role-playing scenarios of the original Milgram obedience situation reduced ambiguity concerning the likelihood of harm to the victim, persons responded to the norm proscribing the harming of others. In general, insufficient attention to how persons are likely to define situations, particularly when they are subject to cross-pressures, and an oversimplified conception of the normative structure that excludes shared understandings concerning the appropriateness of a given rule has led to an underestimation of the importance of norms.

Others coming out of either the learning or Lewinian traditions have made the person's definition of the situation more central to their work. As examples, Berkowitz (1965) and Walster (1971), following Schachter's (1964) emphasis on the role of attributed meaning in defining emotional states, have developed theories of aggression and romantic love that include this element. One can point to other areas of research in social psychology where definitions of the situation are central. The most general finding of the plethora of studies of two-person games during the nineteen-sixties (Nemeth, 1972) was that the results were a function of such situational factors as experimenter instructions, payoff matrices, and opportunities for communication, all of which affected the participants' definitions of the situation. Similarly, the work on equity in the exchange theory literature has served to underscore that it is not the physical amount of a reward or cost that determines matters but its meaning in a normative context. Despite the developments in the nineteen-sixties and the current dominance of attribution theory in a number of areas of social psychology, most social psychologists seem unaware of the full extent of this increased attention to meanings of situations.

There are probably many reasons why most social psychologists have not fully come to terms with the implications of this trend. One reason perhaps is that as a low status but upwardly mobile segment of the profession of psychology they have tended to overidentify with norms of the more prestigious segments of the profession that proscribed any form of subjectivism. Perhaps a second and related reason is that such conformity was encouraged by a commitment to experimental methods whose validity would be jeopardized if the possibility were entertained that the definitions of experimental subjects were anything other than those which the experimenter intended to create by his manipulations and control of external forces operating on his subjects. Only relatively recently and somewhat grudgingly in the form of post-manipulation checks has the probing of subjects' definitions of the situation become a part of experiments in social psychology. The chapters by Mixon and Ginsburg in this volume suggest both the necessity for and the manner in which this phase of research can be more adequately done, particularly in the early stages of the design of experiments. The latter chapter makes explicit what appears implicit in many of the other papers in this volume—those by Mixon, Clarke, and Argyle—that social psychology might well model itself after the structural sciences rather than what Harré (1977) has recently called the parametric sciences.

1. *Parametric Sciences*
In a parametric study it is assumed that the properties referred to by the variables that describe the system are not internally related, that is, that they can be varied separately while retaining their identity. The gas law $PV = RT$, relating pressure, volume, and temperature, is a relation between parameters such that one can hold constant any one parameter and vary the others, and the property represented by that parameter will remain unaffected by the abstraction. As far as pressure, volume, and temperature are concerned, a gas is not a structure of internally related properties. On the other hand an element of an internally related structure ceases to be that element if detached from the structure. In a parametric process the elements interact causally but retain their identity and do not change in type if detached from the structure. Pressure remains pressure however temperature and volume may vary. In a structured entity the component parts derive their meaning from the other details to which they are internally related. A handshake is not the same action when embedded in a betting routine as when part of a greeting. The frequency of meeting someone is not a social item at all if detached from a particular social milieu from which it can gain significance as a meaningful feature of interaction.

2. *Structural Sciences*
We can readily think of a number of structural sciences. One notable example is molecular genetics, where we explain the anatomical structure of an organism by reference to the structure of the deoxyribonucleic acid (DNA). Anatomical structure is the structured product and DNA is the

structured template—and the one is a replication of the other, since at the end of the process the template still remains in existence. Yet another example is to be found in reactions in organic chemistry where one structure can be transformed into another, for example phenol into C_6H_5OCl. The phenol is not destroyed in the transformation; it is not broken up and reconstituted, and yet it does not exist as a separate entity after the reaction. In both of these cases the structure of the product is somehow represented in the template as a preformed structure of the DNA. One of the social sciences has already taken a structural turn, and that, of course, is linguistics. The discipline instructs us to think in terms of preformed structures which are transformed into the product structure by the following of rewrite rules. But the process by which the preformed structure is produced is something quite different from the process by which the preformed structure is transformed into something manifest and visible, namely, a spoken or written sentence (Harré, 1977, pp. 286–287).

The familiar notion of independent and dependent variables that has guided most experimental social psychological research is consistent with the parametric model of science, and most experimental social psychologists still see their science in these terms. On the other hand, the model of science discussed by Ginsburg in his chapter is clearly of the structural variety. Should this structural view eventuate out of the trends we have previously sketched, then a paradigmatic revolution would surely have occurred. Since this development is a distinct possibility, the remainder of this chapter will be devoted to a discussion of the implications of such a paradigmatic revolution for the future character of social psychological research.

To some extent, one can get a foretaste of the kinds of research that social psychologists might be doing if this emerging approach prevails by examining the research literature that has begun to accumulate in a number of traditions that already share the basic elements of this paradigm. These include the older symbolic interactionist movement in sociological social psychology and two relatively recent developments, the ethogenic movement in England (Harré and Secord, 1972; Harré, 1977) and ethnomethodology (Garfinkel, 1967) in the US. The latter two, while sharing similar philosophic roots, are interesting instances of what appear to have been, initially at least, largely independent developments. Although there are some differences, all three schools of thought include a view of man as an active agent; also, the meaning of situations has been a major focus for analysis; and typically their work has been couched in terms of process. The end result has frequently been a model of the sequences of behaviour that make up an episode. Of the three, the empirical and methodological literature of the older symbolic interactionist tradition is the most extensive, and for our purpose at this point, it might be well to start with this. However, we will touch on some of the studies currently being stimulated by the other two movements, some of which are referred to at a number of points in this volume. The latter contain the combination of the type of model building of structures and processes described previously, and at least in the ethogenic case, quantitative and systematic data gathering techniques have been used.

Over the years, a number of methodological treatises have appeared within the symbolic interactionist tradition. One of the most systematic statements was that of Glaser and Strauss (1967) in their *Discovery of Grounded Theory*. More recently, Lofland, in his *Doing Social Life: The Quantitative Study of Social Life* (1976), has provided a less detailed methodological discussion of a similar approach and has organized and codified more than a hundred studies done in this vein. The emphasis in the Glaser and Strauss work is on a much neglected aspect of the scientific process, that of inductively generating theory through a process of progressive elaboration and refinement of conceptual categories and their relationships in response to the accumulation of data. While these authors are typically concerned with smaller analytical units than the episode, they do deal with units of meaning and properties of episodes. Thus, in a study focusing on the manner in which patients, nurses, relatives, and other individuals cope with impending death of a patient, they progressively develop the concept of social loss which appears to condition the relation of the nurse to the dying patient. Similarly, they focus progressively on awareness contexts. Episodes can be classified according to the degree to which persons share the same information concerning a given state of affairs and the perception that each has of it. Thus, in the context of an episode of interaction with a dying patient, both the patient and a nurse may be aware that the patient is dying, and each knows the other's awareness of this fact. On the other hand, the nurse may know that the illness is terminal, but the patient may not know it; or each may know the facts of the matter but one or both may be unaware of the other's knowledge.

Lofland deals with larger units of interaction, for the most part larger than the kinds of episodes referred to in the various chapters of this volume. He focuses on generic situations and the strategies and tactics which emerge to cope with them. Elsewhere, the basic elements in his approach have been described as 'developing intimate familiarity with people as they carry out their everyday activities, focusing on and delineating prime or generic situations that people continually confront in these activities, delineating the strategies, tactics, or play that people use in dealing with these generic situations and, finally, developing disciplined abstractions of situations and strategies from an analysis of a series of concrete instances' (Backman, 1977). Essentially, this approach is the same as that advocated by Ginsburg (this volume) and others (Harré, 1977; Harré and Secord, 1972), who suggest that the task of social psychology as a structural science is to construct models of structures underlying social behaviour. Most experimental social psychologists would feel uncomfortable with some of the methods that are typically employed by Lofland and others who advocate a qualitative approach to data. Gaining intimate familiarity through the use of such qualitative methods as participant observation, unstructured interviews, personal observation, analysis of documents such as letters, diaries, or published accounts seem more like the field techniques of the anthropologist or historian than the kinds of quantitative and structured methods of observation employed by most social psychologists. Yet this approach does not require exclusive reliance on a qualitative methodology, but can include all of the procedures in this volume. Both qualitative and quantitative procedures have their place in the exploration and delineation of structure. Qualitative procedures are particularly valuable, as Glaser and Strauss have argued, in the generation of theory in the early phase of investigation, whereas the more quantitative structured methods are more appropriate in the verification and refinement of the theory. Not only are many of these qualitative procedures less influenced by the preconceived ideas of the investigator but they are less obtrusive and reactive than most structured procedures. Further, some of them capitalize on the important human capacity to take the attitude of the other and share his definition of the situation, information essential for understanding and explaining behaviour within this view of science.

An excellent example of the use of qualitative procedures for the initial construction of models, later to be refined and verified by more systematic quantitative techniques, is the study of how pedestrians coordinate their behaviour on public thoroughfares. This problem was studied by Goffman (1972) employing the more qualitative methods of direct observation. He produced a model of coordination which later was tested by Collett and Marsh (1974), employing more painstaking, systematic and quantitative methods of analysis of the videotaped behaviour of pedestrians on a London street. The latter analysis extended and corrected the earlier model at a number of points. For instance, the more systematic analysis suggests that coordination in the avoidance of collision is not as dependent on the monitoring of facial cues as had been suggested by Goffman, and that there are distinctive passing patterns for each sex.

More recently, David Clarke's (this volume) method of studying the structure of conversation by having subjects reconstruct previously decomposed conversation has provided a systematic and quantitative way of studying certain regularities in the structure of conversation earlier dealt with by ethnomethodologists in more qualitative terms. In particular, Kent, Davis, and Shapiro (1978) have shown how questions seem both to regulate turn-taking in a conversation and to circumscribe the range of appropriate responses, both of which facilitate the task of the accurate reconstruction of conversations. Interestingly, the study by Kent *et al.* also suggests the truth of the notion that the rules persons use to encode and decode conversations are to some extent culturally bound. Canadian participants were less able to use these guides to the structuring of British conversations than British participants.

Reminiscent of the use of a variety of methods and sources involved in De

Waele and Harré's method of autobiographical reconstruction (this volume), Luckinbill (1977) carefully reconstructed the sequence of events leading up to acts of homicide.

> All official documents pertaining to these cases were secured. The character of the larger occasion as well as the organization and the development of the fateful transaction were reconstructed from the content analysis of police, probation, psychiatric and witness reports, offender interviews, victim statements, and grand jury and court testimony. These materials included information on the major and minor participants; who said and did what to whom, the chronology of dialogue and action; and the physical comportment of the participants. (page 177)

The sequences of behaviours involved in these situated transactions were compared with a model described as a 'face game' by Lyman and Scott (1970) and based in turn on the notion of a character contest drawn from Goffman's work (1967). The series of moves, empirically delineated, for the most part fit the phases described by the model but also served to provide additional details and refinements. Some grasp of the model can be gained from the author's concluding statement:

> On the basis of this research, criminal homicide does not appear as a one-sided event with an unwitting victim assuming a passive, non-contributory role. Rather, murder is the outcome of a dynamic interchange between an offender, victim, and in many cases bystanders. The offender and victim devlop lines of action shaped in part by the actions of the other and focused toward saving or maintaining face and reputation and demonstrating character. Participants develop a working agreement, sometimes implicit, often explicit, that violence is a useful tool for resolving questions of face and character. In some settings, where very small children are murdered, the extent of their participation cannot be great. But generally these patterns characterized all cases irrespective of such variables as age, sex, race, time and place, use of alcohol and proffered motive. (Luckinbill, 1978, pp. 185–186)

The face game as a model of interaction, like most models, contains not only cognitive guides and meanings which persons bring into the situation, but also elements of meaning and behaviour that are constructed as the episode unfolds. While the former elements are easily captured with available quantitative procedures which tap the individual's cognitive resources, such as frames of judgment, rules of conduct and the like, the latter elements emerging out of a series of interactional and situational contingencies are more difficult to capture, examine, and describe, using systematic quantitative techniques. Yet a number of the research procedures described in this volume lend themselves readily to the task of capturing this negotiated character of social interaction. Most obvious in applicability are video and cinematic techniques that can provide data for fine-grained analysis of interaction. Examples of this abound in the chapters by Scaife and Kendon, and our brief discussion of the Collett and Marsh research provides another. While not their purpose, the widely viewed video presentation of the Milgram experiment on destructive obedience provides a good example of how to catch the process of the construction of meaning in situations and the pitfalls to be encountered if we fail to take these processes into account in our explanations of an episode. Blinded by the conviction that the experimental manipulations were such to produce definitions in accordance with the experimenter's intentions, little attention was paid to the negotiation of the meaning of the situation between the experimenter and those playing the role of teacher. As the video record attests, participants in the teacher role frequently attempted to convince the experimenter that their giving of shocks to the learner might be endangering the latter's wellbeing. As Mixon's analysis (this volume) suggests, the apparent lack of concern of the experimenter, along with his inflexibility, may well have resulted in a definition of the situation as one with adequate safeguards to protect the learner. While the behaviours of the subjects in the original studies of emergencies by Latané and Darley were not filmed, the evidence suggests and these investigators conclude that variations in the outcomes were likely due to the manner in which the experimental manipulations affected the negotiation of meaning of an ambiguous situation. The situation was such that it might or might not be defined as an emergency requiring some action on the part of the participants, either to report the possible emergency or to intervene and come to the aid of the victim. In particular, where subjects were paired with a confederate of the experimenter who had been instructed to behave as if nothing were amiss, this inflexible negotiating stance resulted in a large majority not responding, seemingly defining the situation as not requiring action. Where subjects were with one or more naive participants whose behaviour was not shackled by the experimenter's instructions, negotiation proceeded in a more normal fashion, producing more definitions of the situation as an emergency requiring action.

Various forms of role-playing can and have been used to study the way in which persons negotiate the meaning of situations and the kinds of behaviour that the participants will enact. Thus, Blumstein (1973) studied the negotiation process where one party attempts to get the other to play a role contrary to his self-image. As the extensive discussion of actual and potential uses of role-playing in this volume indicates, this technique can be employed both to analyse and synthesize models of episodes and other units of interaction, to discover the role/rule frameworks that persons bring into situations and the modifications of these made in the process of enacting an episode. One important advantage of role-playing techniques which, as Ginsburg notes, has hardly been exploited, is the possibility of studying generative mechanisms and processes that take place over a lengthy period of time in a relationship. The ability to compress in time a lengthy history of interaction, as occurs in the theatre or literature, should release social psychologists from the study of models limited to describing relatively brief encounters. This promises a true breakthrough in studies of interpersonal attraction which have largely had to be confined to studies of first impressions (Byrne, 1971), or at best to periods of a few months of the life of an experimental group (Newcomb, 1961).

The ability to deal with realistic time periods and to examine models of interaction that reflect the complexities of social life should allow social psychologists to overcome a major objection to much social psychological research, in other words, its irrelevance to major problems of human concern.

At the same time this paradigmatic shift will not mean that many of the traditional research areas of social psychology will be abandoned. Rather, viewing these areas from this new perspective may well generate significant advances within them. It has already been suggested that the new paradigm should provide the basis for shift in studies of attraction from the encounter to the relationship. Also, we noted past and current trends in the treatment of leadership and in the study of such social motives as aggression, altruism, and achievement which are in the direction of this new paradigm.

The focus on interaction in these new approaches, and particularly on the social construction of reality through negotiation and other social influence processes, should not only revive interest in the study of these processes but also provide a needed correction to the current tendency among many social psychologists to concentrate on individual cognitive processes and to forget the group. Recent theorizing and research on attribution theory by sociologists working in the symbolic interactionist tradition provides some examples of this. Thus Prus (1975) has extended attribution theory. Using an interactional framework he has argued that attributions are not simply the result of cognitive processes within the attributor, but the outcome of negotiations between him and the target person. The latter, in a variety of ways, attempts to control the attributions concerning him, either by initially controlling the information he provides the other or by denying or calling into question the attribution levelled at him. In particular, where attributions are unfavourable, as in the case of being labelled a deviant, the target of attribution in a variety of ways and with different degrees of success will resist such an attribution. Others (Sagatun and Knudsen, 1977) have shown that the attributions persons make are influenced by self-presentation strategies in the context of norms concerning the manner in which persons are expected to evaluate themselves and others. Sagatun and Knudsen used a passive role-playing procedure and discovered that actors tended to make external attributions of both success and failure events, while observers made internal attributions of success and external attributions of failure. Sagatun and Knudsen explained their findings in terms of a role/rule framework based on the idea central to situated identity theory (Alexander and Knight, 1971) that persons attempt to present the best possible image or 'situated identity' in social situations.

We believe that these findings mean that attributors are subject to complex social pressures that vary by both attributor role and social context. Different attribution norms exist for different people in different contexts. For observers, the cultural demand is one of person orientation and concern for others. Attributing another person's success to internal factors, and his own failure to external factors, fit this model. By attributing the person's success to outstanding abilities and inner motivation, the observer shows himself as a generous person and is likely to be well received because of his explanations. By excusing the other's failure as being caused by circumstances, the observer again shows his concern for others. Similarly, the social expectations for self-explanations of success and failure lead the actor to make external attributions in both situations. In success, the objective fact of success is already there, and the actor will make a good impression by appearing modest and attributing his success to external influences. At the same time, an actor is supposed to believe in his own abilities and not be thwarted by failure. Hence, external attribution of one's own failure will help maintain a favorable impression of the actor. The fact that actors tend to give external attributions in both success and failure conditions, then, does not mean that actors are immune to social pressures. Further, attribution norms for actors point in the same direction for both success and failure. It appears that ego-enhancement motives are indeed powerful influences on attributions, but that social norms dictate that different techniques must be used for actors and observers in order to make the right social impression (Sagatun and Knudsen, 1977, pp. 11–12).

This emphasis on negotiation, along with the expanded view of the normative structure previously noted, should provide for a much more dynamic view of the role of cognitive guides and other shared meanings as influences on behaviour. While constitutive rules are much less subject to negotiation, the operation of regulatory rules is constantly modified during interaction. Persons in interaction arrive at a working agreement concerning the applicability of various rules based on explicit or implicit notions concerning the rules for applying the rules, for example which rule has precedent, and concerning the facts of the situation which make one rule more appropriate than another. Models of role negotiations have been developed (McCall and Simmons, 1966; Secord and Backman, 1974), and hopefully with the expanded array of techniques for studying them further elaboration and verification of them should be forthcoming. In addition, the much expanded conceptualization of the normative structure has already begun to provide some theoretical structure to the study of communication, both verbal and non-verbal, and to various areas of environmental social psychology. With respect to verbal communication, we have already noted one instance where the work of Clarke (this volume) has provided a basis for new work in this area.

The focus on interaction and on bargaining should add further impetus to the renewed interest in power (Tedeschi, 1974). Again, a number of models have emerged that await the kind of testing that the wider range of research techniques favoured by this new paradigm will make possible. Similarly, this new focus should provide renewed impetus to the study of group decision processes. Davis et al. (1975), employing the techniques of active role-playing, has been able to test models based on different decision rules, and Ginsburg (this volume) and his colleagues, using similar procedures, have been investigating models of risk-taking in group situations.

While these developments should spur a revival of the once very active and central area of social psychology, the study of small groups, they should also provide the basis for increased work by experimental social psychologists in an area that has been of a more marginal concern, namely socialization. As Scaife's work in this volume suggests, video procedures can be extremely useful in tracing the development and transformation of structures of interaction among children. Moreover, greater use of autobiographical materials following the lead of De Waele and Harré should allow for the generation and testing of models of development covering longer time-spans.

SUMMARY AND CONCLUSION

This chapter has examined the possibility that experimental social psychology may well have unknowingly passed through the major part of a paradigmatic revolution. The major themes underlying the thinking of the contributors to this volume constitute an emerging paradigm that is already evident in a good bit of social psychological practice, even though most social psychologists may still think in terms of an earlier one. The elements in this new paradigm include the view of man as an active agent, an emphasis on the meanings of events and settings in the determination of social behaviour, and a conception of science in which the goal of scientific social psychology is to generate and verify models of the structure of interaction.

Should this assessment be correct and this new paradigm prevail, it was suggested that social psychological research of the future would involve a blend of inductive model-building, characteristic of the older school of symbolic interactionism and the current ethogenic and ethnomethodology approaches, with the systematic quantitative emphasis of experimental social psychology. But the future research would be buttressed by a much broader array of techniques for model-building, refinement and verification than the experimental method so central to the contemporary, conventional paradigm. Finally, it was suggested that research within the new paradigm may well stimulate investigations in new areas and reinvigorate activities in some of the older areas of social psychology.

Whether or not the trends have been accurately portrayed and the predictions as to the future turn out, only time will tell.

References

Alexander, N. C. and Knight, G., 1971, Situated identities and social psychological experimentation, *Sociometry*, **15**, 65–82.

Backman, C. W., 1977, Do it yourself sociology, Review of J. Lofland, *Doing Social Life: The Qualitative Study of Social Life, Contemporary Psychology*, **22**, 562–564.

Backman, C. W., 1976, Explorations in psycho-ethics: The warranting of judgments, in R. Harré, *Life Sentences: Aspects of the Social Role of Language*, London: John Wiley and Sons, pp. 98–108.

Berkowitz, L., 1965, The concept of aggressive drive: Some additional considerations, in L. Berkowitz (ed.), *Advances in Experimental Social Psychology, Vol. 2*, New York: Academic Press, pp. 301–329.

Blumstein, P. W., 1973, Audience, Machiavellianism and tactics of identity bargaining, *Sociometry*, **36**, 346–365.

Byrne, D., 1971, *The Attraction Paradigm*, New York: Academic Press.

Collett, P. and Marsh, P., 1974, Patterns of public behaviour: Collision avoidance on a pedestrian crossing, *Semiotica*, **12**, 281–299.

Davis, J. H., Kerr, H. L., Atkin, R. H., and Meek, D., 1975, The decision processes of 6- and 12-person mock juries assigned unanimous and two-thirds majority rules, *Journal of Personality and Social Psychology*, **32**, 1–14.

Elms, A. C., 1975, The crisis of confidence in social psychology, *American Psychologist*, **30**, 967–976.

Garfinkel, H., 1972, Studies of the routine grounds of everyday activities, in D. Sudnow (ed.), *Studies in Social Interaction*, New York: Free Press, pp. 1–30.

Glaser, B. and Strauss, A., 1967, *Discovery of Grounded Theory*, Chicago: Aldine.

Goffman, E., 1971, *Relations in Public*, New York: Basic Books.

Goffman, E., 1967, *Interaction Ritual: Essays on Face to Face Behavior*, Garden City, NY: Doubleday.

Harré, R., 1977, The ethogenic approach: Theory and practice, in L. Berkowitz (ed.), *Advances in Experimental Social Psychology, Vol. 10*, New York: Academic Press, pp. 284–314.

Harré, R., and Secord, P. F., 1972, *The Explanation of Social Behavior*, Totowa, NJ: Rowman and Littlefield.

Huston, T. L., and Levinger, L., in press, Interpersonal attraction and relationships, in M. R. Rosenzweig and L. W. Porter (eds.), *Annual Review of Psychology*.

Kent, G. G., Davis, J. D., and Shapiro, D. A., 1978, Resources required in the reconstruction of conversation, *Journal of Personality and Social Psychology*, **36**, 13–22.

Latané, B. and Darley, J. M., 1970, *The Unresponsive Bystander: Why Doesn't He Help?* New York: Appleton-Century-Crofts.

Lofland, J., 1976, *Doing Social Life: The Qualitative Study of Social Life*, New York: John Wiley and Sons.

Luckenbill, D. F., 1977, Criminal homicide as a situated transaction. *Social Problems*, **25**, 176–186.

Lyman, S. M. and Scott, M. B., 1970, *A Sociology of the Absurd*, New York: Merideth.

McCall, G. J. and Simmons, J. L., 1966, *Identities and Interactions*, New York: Free Press.

Nemeth, C., 1972, A critical analysis of research utilizing the prisoners dilemma paradigm for the study of bargaining, in L. Berkowitz (ed.), *Advances in Experimental Social Psychology*, New York: Academic Press, pp. 203–234.

Newcomb, T. M., 1961, *The Acquaintance Process*, New York: Holt, Rinehart and Winston, Inc.

Prus, R. C., 1975, Resisting designations: An extension of attribution theory into a negotiated context, *Sociological Inquiry*, **45**, 3–14.

Sagatun, I. J. and Knudsen, J. H., 1977, The interactive effect of attributor role and event on attributions; paper presented at the annual meetings of the Pacific Sociological Association, Sacramento, California.

Schachter, S., 1964, The interaction of cognitive and physiological determinants of emotional states, in L. Berkowitz (ed.), *Advances in Experimental Social Psychology, Vol. 1*, New York: Academic Press, pp. 49–81.

Secord, P. F. and Backman, C. W., 1974, *Social Psychology, 2nd Edition*, New York: McGraw-Hill.

Tedeschi, J. T. (ed.), 1974, *Perspectives on Social Power*, Chicago: Aldine.

Walster, E., 1971, Passionate love, in B. J. Murstein (ed.), *Theories of Attraction and Love*, New York: Springer Publishing Co, pp. 85–99.

Warner, D. B., 1976, Determinants of bystander intervention: The effects of verbal cues of victims and others present; unpublished doctoral dissertation, Reno, Nev., University of Nevada.

Wolfe, M., 1973, Notes on the behavior of pedestrians, in A. Birenbaum and E. Sager (eds.), *People in Places: The Sociology of the Familiar*, New York: Praeger.

AUTHOR INDEX

Abelson, R. P., 130, 149, 255, 275, 285, 287
Adams-Webber, J. R., 229, 237, 249
Ahrens, H. J., 273, 285
Ainsworth, M. D. S., 94–97, 103, 114
Aldiss, O., 84, 85
Alexander, C. N., 124, 126, 129, 132, 137, 144, 150
Alexander, N. C., 299, 302
Alston, W. P., 185, 208
Altmann, S. A., 32, 34, 56, 64
Ames, L. B., 68, 85, 87
Annis, A. P., 178, 208
Argyle, M., 1, 3, 4, 10, 11, 14, 17, 19, 22, 27–29, 31, 34, 37, 60, 64, 69, 85, 118, 121, 122, 125, 134, 140, 146, 150, 154, 253, 254, 258, 277, 285, 286, 293
Argyris, C., 118, 123, 150
Arkin, R. M., 138, 150
Arkowitz, H. S., 141, 152
Armistead, N., 253, 285
Arnes, L. B., 85
Arnold, P., 49, 65
Aronson, E., 118, 123, 134, 144, 149, 150
Ashmore, R. D., 150, 273, 286
Atkin, R. H., 151, 302
Atkins, A. L., 250
Austin, J. L., 41, 64, 101, 114, 200, 208
Austin, J. M., 74, 85

Bach, K., 23, 35
Backman, C., 10
Backman, C. W., 289, 291, 295, 300, 302, 303
Baker, C., 82, 85
Baker, R. F., 256, 285
Bales, R. F., 15, 35

Banks, W. C., 123, 151, 162, 175
Bannister, D., 226, 228, 231, 233, 235–243, 246, 250
Bar, E., 70, 85
Barefoot, J. C., 128, 154
Barker, R. G., 16, 35
Baron, R. M., 123, 124, 127, 134, 143, 150
Bateson, G., 69, 70, 89, 90
Bateson, P. P., 19, 35
Bateson, M. C., 70, 91
Bauman, R., 74, 85
Baxter, J. C., 135, 150
Bell, S. M., 114
Bellack, A. A., 22, 35
Bellugi, U., 105, 106, 115
Bem, D. J., 118, 130, 132, 136, 143, 150, 165, 175
Benesh, R., 78, 85
Bennett, D. H., 118, 152
Berkowitz, L., 292, 302
Berman, H. J., 124, 154
Bernal, J., 95, 115
Bernstein, B., 74, 85
Biener, L., 273, 288
Bieri, J., 229, 237, 238, 250, 252
Binns, M., 244, 250
Birdwhistell, R., 70, 83, 89
Birdwhistell, R. L., 70, 85
Bjerg, K., 18, 35
Blackman, S., 273, 288
Blascovich, J., 118, 122, 130, 132, 134, 146, 150
Blascovich, J. J., 118, 151
Blumstein, P. W., 298, 302
Bois, J., 133, 153
Bonarius, J. C. J., 229, 237, 250

Boomer, D. S., 69, 86
Borgatta, E. F., 118, 150
Bouffard, D. L., 23, 36
Bouissac, P., 78, 85
Braver, S. L., 129, 150
Brazil, D., 74, 86
Breen, D., 241, 251
Briar, S., 250
Brock, T. A., 139, 154
Brosin, H., 70, 89
Brown, R., 105, 106, 115
Bruner, J., 22, 35, 253, 285
Bruner, J. S., 84, 86, 100–103, 108–110, 113, 115
Bryant, B., 14, 31, 37, 118, 154
Bullowa, M., 84, 86
Bush, L. E., 275, 285
Byrne, D., 299, 302

Calder, N., 182, 208
Caldwell, D. F., 229, 250
Calhoun, L. G., 139, 154
Campbell, D. T., 27, 144, 145, 150
Canter, R., 118, 151
Carlsmith, J. M., 118, 123, 134, 144, 150
Carlson, R., 180, 208
Carpenter, B., 135, 138, 139, 150
Carroll, J. D., 256, 262, 267, 285
Cartwright-Smith, J., 118, 131, 152
Chang, J. J., 256, 262, 267, 285
Chernicky, P., 118, 154
Chomsky, N., 45, 57, 64
Christiansen, G., 123, 153
Chupchik, G. C., 140, 151
Churcher, J., 99
Cialdini, R. B., 150
Clarke, A. D. B., 95, 115
Clarke, A. M., 95, 115
Clarke, D., 69, 85, 257, 293, 296, 301
Clarke, D. D., 4, 5, 19, 21, 23, 32, 35, 39, 47, 49, 50, 64, 140–142
Clarke, F. M., 88
Cliff, N., 256, 285, 286, 288
Coffman, T. L., 229, 252
Colby, C. Z., 118, 131, 141, 150
Coleman, J. C., 86
Collett, P., 1, 9, 13, 18, 23, 25, 35, 69, 84, 85, 86, 122, 143, 150, 225, 231, 241, 244, 247, 250, 296, 298, 302
Collins, A. W., 114, 115
Collins, B. E., 125, 150

Collis, G. M., 98, 99, 115
Condon, W. D., 86
Condon, W. S., 68, 77, 83, 84, 86
Cook, M., 19, 34
Cook, T. D., 124, 144, 154
Cooper, J., 127, 150
Corwin, T. T., 150
Coulthard, R. M., 74, 91
Coxon, A. P. M., 255, 277, 285
Crockett, W. H., 237, 250
Cromwell, R. L., 229, 250
Cronback, L. J., 125, 145, 151, 264, 285
Crosby, R., 135, 151
Crystal, D., 78, 86

Danehy, J. J., 70, 90
Darley, J. M., 135, 138, 139, 150, 292, 298, 302
Darwin, C., 156
Davis, J. D., 296, 302
Davis, J. H., 118, 129, 130, 132, 141, 151, 301, 302
Davison, M. L., 258, 259, 276, 285
Davitz, J., 69, 86
Davitz, J. R., 118, 151
Davy, D. L., 78, 86
Dawkins, R., 19, 21, 35, 56, 59, 64, 141, 151
Dell, C., 86
De Long, A., 82, 86
Deutsch, M., 273, 277, 280, 288
Devoe, S., 82, 91
DeVoge, S., 118, 143, 153
De Waele, J.-P., 8, 142, 143, 177, 191, 192, 208, 296–297, 301
Dewey, J., 158, 175
Dickman, H. R., 18, 35, 51, 64
Dittmann, A. T., 68, 69, 86
Domoney, D. W., 256, 288
Dore, J., 101, 115
Dowdle, M. D., 288
Dowdle, M. M., 277
Dreiser, T., 259, 272
Duck, S. W., 234, 241, 250
Du Mas, F. M., 191, 208
Duncan, S., Jr., 138, 140, 141, 144, 151
Duncan, S. D., Jr., 82, 86, 87
Du Preez, P., 241, 250
Du Preez, P. D., 247, 250
Duval, S., 138, 150

Efron, D., 69, 87

Eibl-Eibesfeldt, I., 68, 87
Ekehammar, B., 258, 286
Ekman, P., 68, 87, 139, 151
Elms, A. C., 289, 302
Endler, N. S., 11, 13, 35
Engquist, G., 36, 69, 90, 133, 153
Epstein, Y. M., 124, 151
Erickson, F., 22, 35, 81, 82, 87
Eshkol, N., 78, 87
Estes, S. G., 69, 87
Evans, F. J., 160, 162, 169, 176
Eysenck, H. J., 222

Fantz, R. L., 97, 115
Farr, J. L., 124, 151
Feld, S., 76, 91
Ferber, A., 21, 36, 73, 81, 84, 88
Firth, J. R., 74, 87
Fiske, D. W., 87, 138, 140, 141, 144, 151
Fiske, M., 198, 208
Fiske, S. T., 138, 154
Flanders, N. A., 19, 20, 29, 35
Flapan, D., 69, 87
Forgas, J., 9, 10, 12, 17, 27
Forgas, J. P., 140, 143, 146, 253, 254, 257–259, 264, 274–277, 280–283, 286
Forward, J., 118, 123–125, 127, 151
Foulds, G. A., 229, 251
Fox, R., 24, 25, 35
Fransella, F., 226, 228, 231, 234, 235, 240–242, 246, 250
Frederickson, N., 13, 35, 286
Freedman, J. L., 118, 151, 166, 175
Freedman, N., 68, 87
Frey, D., 274, 275, 286
Friedman, N., 124, 134, 151
Friendly, M. L., 277, 286
Friesen, W., 87
Friesen, W. V., 68, 87
Frijda, N. H., 68, 69, 87
Frith, C. E., 246, 250
From, F., 69, 87
Fromm-Reichmann, F., 70
Funk, S., 268, 273, 286

Gadlin, H., 118, 151
Gagnon, J. H., 24, 35
Galanter, E., 19, 36, 185, 209
Garfinkel, H., 26, 35, 74, 87, 204, 207, 208, 291, 294, 302
Garvey, C., 22, 35, 102, 115

Geller, J., 91
Gerard, H. B., 29, 30, 35, 184, 208
Gergen, K. J., 182, 186, 208, 253, 286
Gesell, A., 68, 87
Gibson, J. J., 119, 151
Gilbert, 157
Ginsburg, G. P., 1, 17, 27, 117, 118, 121–124, 130, 132, 150, 151, 286, 289, 293–295, 298, 301
Girard, R. A., 256, 286
Glaser, B., 295, 296, 302
Gleser, G. C., 151, 264, 285
Glucksberg, S., 277, 286
Goffman, E., 21, 31, 35, 70, 87, 88, 131, 151, 202, 208, 284, 291, 296, 297, 302
Goldstein, A. P., 118, 151
Goodwin, C., 82, 88
Gregory, S., 122, 154
Grice, H. P., 101, 115
Gumperz, J. J., 74, 88
Gunn, S. P., 118, 154

Haas, H., 18, 35
Haggard, E. A., 68, 88
Haley, J. V., 277, 286
Hall, E. T., 70, 88
Halliday, M. A. K., 74, 88
Halverson, H. M., 68, 87
Hamilton, V. L., 118, 123, 124, 127, 137, 148, 151
Haney, C., 123, 134, 151, 162, 175
Harré, R., 8, 10, 18, 22, 24, 25, 31, 35, 39, 41, 50, 62, 63, 65, 118–120, 122, 124, 125, 128, 130, 131, 142, 143, 152, 155, 156, 175, 177, 183, 185, 186, 192, 197, 201, 208, 253, 254, 277, 286, 293–295, 297, 301, 302
Harris, Z., 69, 88
Harrison, J., 250
Harrison, J. A., 241, 250
Hayes, A. S., 70, 91
Haynes, E. T., 243, 250
Hefner, R., 273, 287
Helling, I., 189, 208
Hendrick, C., 123, 124, 137, 152
Herbst, P. G., 215
Hesse, M., 156
Hinde, R. A., 101, 115
Hinkle, D. N., 227, 235, 247, 250, 251
Hockenstein, P., 128, 154
Hockett, C., 70, 89

Hockett, C. F., 70, 90
Hockings, P., 68, 88
Hoffman, S. P., 68, 87
Hogben, L., 157
Holley, B. J., 241, 251
Holmes, D. S., 118, 152
Honikman, B., 241, 251
Hooke, 157
Hornbeck, F. W., 150
Horowitz, A. D., 286
Howe, R. C., 118, 151
Huesmann, L. R., 33, 35
Hunt, E. B., 88
Hunt, J. McV., 13, 35
Hunt, W. A., 68, 88, 89
Huston, T. L., 291, 302
Hutchinson, A., 78, 88
Hutt, C., 56, 65
Hutt, S. J., 56, 65
Hymes, D., 74, 88, 100, 113, 115

Ilg, F. L., 68, 87
Ingle, G., 118, 151
Ingleby, D., 104, 115
Isaacs, K. S., 68, 88
Israel, J., 253, 286

Jackson, D. N., 254, 271, 286
Jakobson, R., 102, 115
Janis, I. L., 118, 152
Jardine, N., 54, 65
Jaspars, J. M. F., 229, 251
Jefferson, G., 49, 65, 74, 82, 90
Jenkins, J. J., 119, 122, 142, 152
Johnson, M., 182, 208
Jones, C. L., 277, 285
Jones, D., 78, 88
Jones, E. E., 29, 30, 35, 142, 152, 184, 208
Jones, L. E., 258, 259, 275, 276, 285, 286
Jones, R. A., 259, 271–273, 277, 286
Jourard, S. M., 118, 152

Kagan, C. M., 274, 275, 286
Kaplan, S. J., 279, 280, 288
Keenan, F. O., 31, 36
Kelley, H. H., 142, 152
Kelly, D. A., 248, 249
Kelly, G. A., 185, 208, 225–230, 233, 235, 237, 239, 246, 247, 251
Kelman, H., 118, 152
Kendall, P. L., 198, 208

Kendon, A., 5–7, 21, 22, 28, 34, 36, 67, 68, 70, 73, 77–79, 81–84, 88, 122, 130, 138, 140, 298
Kent, G. G., 296, 302
Kerr, H. L., 151, 302
King, B. T., 118, 152
Kingdon, R., 78, 88
Kirsch, N., 118, 151
Kleck, R. E., 118, 131, 141, 150, 152
Knapp, M. L., 82, 91
Knight, G., 299, 302
Knight, G. W., 126, 150
Knudsen, J. H., 299, 300, 303
Kopel, S. A., 141, 152
Kosloski, K., 135, 151
Krause, M. S., 15, 16, 36
Kruskal, J. B., 254, 255, 261, 263, 265, 271, 286

Laban, R., 78, 89
Landfield, A. W., 229, 234, 241, 251
Landis, C., 68, 89
Langer, J., 111, 115
Lanzetta, J. T., 118, 131, 141, 150, 152
Latané, B., 292, 298, 302
Launderdale, P., 126, 150
Laver, J., 74, 89
Leach, C., 238, 251
Leibowitz, G., 118, 152
Leventhal, H., 140, 151
Levine, M., 253, 286
Levinger, G., 33, 35, 291, 302
Leviton, E., 74, 89
Lewin, K., 36
Lillie, F. J., 246, 250
Lindenfeld, J., 68, 89
Linder, D. E., 150
Lindsay, R., 24, 36
Lingoes, J. C., 255, 287
Lipshitz, R., 286
Lipton, L., 74, 89
Little, B. R., 258, 285
Lobeck, R., 250
Lofland, J., 295, 302
Lomax, A., 69, 89
Lorenz, K., 95, 115
Luckenbill, D. F., 297, 302
Lyman, S. M., 142, 154, 200–202, 208, 297, 302

McArthur, L. A., 137, 152

AUTHOR INDEX

McArthur, L. Z., 152
McCall, G. J., 300, 302
McCallum, R. C., 254, 287
McDermott, R. D., 70, 81, 82, 89
McFadyen, M., 229, 251
McGee, V. E., 255, 287
McGuire, W. J., 149
McGuire, W. S., 253, 287
MacKay, D. M., 101, 115
McMillan, R. A., 68, 89
McNeill, D., 100, 115
MacPhail, 18
McQuown, N., 70, 72, 89
McQuown, N. A., 70, 89
McReynolds, P., 118, 143, 153
Madden, E. H., 120, 152
Magnusson, D., 11, 35, 258, 277, 287
Mair, J. M. M., 226, 228, 233, 235, 236, 250
Maklouf-Norris, F., 241, 251
Malinowski, B., 74, 89
Mann, J. H., 118, 152
Mann, L., 24, 26, 36, 118, 152
Marey, E. J., 68, 89
Marriott, F. H. C., 287
Marsh, P., 84, 86, 125, 146, 152, 241, 251, 296, 298, 302
Martin, J. G., 83, 89
Mead, G. H., 69, 74, 89
Meek, D., 151, 302
Mehan, H., 74, 89
Mercer, J., 74, 89
Merritt, M., 21, 36
Merton, R. K., 198, 208
Messick, J., 255, 273, 288
Messick, S., 271, 273, 286, 287
Messick, S. J., 255, 287
Michaelis, A. R., 68, 89
Milgram, S., 122, 123, 128, 132, 134, 141, 153, 163–170, 172–175, 292, 298
Mill, J. S., 65
Miller, A. G., 136, 153, 166, 175
Miller, G. A., 19, 36, 49, 54, 65, 185, 209
Miller, H., 250
Miller, J., 118, 153
Minksy, M., 33, 36
Mischel, H. N., 185, 209
Mischel, W., 185, 209, 258, 287
Mixon, D., 7, 8, 118, 121–124, 127–129, 132–134, 136, 137, 141, 149, 153, 155, 162, 166, 171, 172, 174–176, 191, 209, 292, 293, 298

Moreno, J. L., 118, 153, 275, 287
Morris, J. B., 241, 251
Morse, M. J., 65
Muehl, D., 142, 153
Mueller, W. S., 271, 287
Murray, H. A., 15, 36
Muybridge, E., 68, 89

Nanda, H., 151
Neisser, U., 50, 65
Nelson, C., 271
Nemeth, C., 292, 302
Nerlove, S. B., 288
Newcomb, T. M., 149, 299, 303
Newport, E., 106, 115
Newson, E., 105, 115
Newson, J., 105, 115
Newtson, D., 18, 19, 36, 51, 65, 69, 90, 133, 141, 153
Niederehe, G., 82, 87
Nielsen, G., 69, 82, 90
Nisbett, R. E., 13, 36, 142, 152, 153
Nordin, K., 153
Norris, H., 241, 251
Nuttin, J., 211

Ogilvie, J., 265, 288
Ogston, W. D., 68, 83, 86
O'Hare, D., 277, 287
Olbrechts-Tyteca, L., 200, 209
Olshan, K., 271
Olson, T., 123, 153
Orley, J., 241, 251
Orne, M. T., 160, 162, 169, 176
Osborne, S. K., 153
Osgood, C. E., 262, 287

Palmer, J., 241, 251
Parloff, M. B., 69, 86
Pearce, P., 241, 251
Pease, K., 49, 65
Perelamn, Ch., 200, 209
Pervin, L., 256, 287
Phares, E. J., 30, 36
Phillips, J. P. N., 243, 250
Pike, K. L., 45, 51, 65, 69, 78, 90
Piliavin, I. M., 134, 153
Piliavin, J. A., 134, 153
Pincus, E., 74, 90
Pither, B., 153
Pittinger, R. E., 70, 90

Potter, R. J., 17, 37
Pribram, K. H., 19, 36, 185, 209
Price, R. H., 24, 36
Proshansky, H. M., 12, 36
Prost, J. H., 68, 90
Prus, R. C., 299, 303

Rafky, D. M., 101, 115
Rajaratnam, N., 151
Regan, D. T., 138, 153
Reid, W. A., 241, 251
Reusch, J., 69, 70, 90
Richards, M. P. M., 22, 36, 93, 100, 101, 115
Riley, S., 241, 251
Ring, K., 118, 153
Robinson, J. P., 273, 287
Robinson, P., 25, 36
Rommetveit, R., 33, 36
Romney, A. K., 288
Rosenberg, M. J., 149
Rosenberg, S., 257, 259, 261, 263, 265, 271, 272, 286, 287
Rosenfeld, H. M., 141, 153
Rosenshine, B., 29, 36
Rosenthal, R., 104, 116, 169, 176
Ross, L. B., 273, 288
Rosser, E., 125, 152, 185, 208
Rowe, D., 241, 251
Rozelle, R. M., 135, 150
Rubinow, S., 91
Runyan. D. L., 132, 141, 153
Ryan, J., 101, 116
Ryave, A. L., 84, 90
Ryle, A., 241, 251

Sachs, H., 21
Sacks, H., 74, 82, 90
Sagatun, I., 126, 150
Sagatun, I. J., 299, 300, 303
Sampson, E. E., 130, 153
Sander, L., 84, 86
Sarre, P. V., 241, 250
Saussure, F. de, 42, 43, 65
Scaife, M., 6, 7, 93, 298, 301
Schachter, S., 292, 303
Schaeffer, J. H., 68, 90
Schaffer, H. R., 90, 94, 97–99, 115, 116
Schank, R. C., 19, 36
Scheflen, A. E., 22, 36, 70–72, 79–82, 90
Schegloff, E. A., 74, 82, 90
Schenkein, J. N., 74, 84, 90

Scherer, K. R., 68, 87
Schlenker, B. R., 120, 153
Schroeder, H. M., 273, 288
Schultz, D. P., 118, 154
Scott, M. B., 142, 154, 200–202, 208, 297, 302
Scriven, G. D., 124, 126, 129, 132, 137, 150
Scriven, M., 158, 176
Searle, J., 41, 46, 65
Searle, J. R., 74, 90
Seaver, W. B., 124, 151
Sebeok, T., 70, 91
Secord, P., 253, 254, 277, 286
Secord, P. F., 18, 22, 24, 25, 31, 35, 39, 41, 62, 65, 118–120, 122, 124, 125, 131, 142, 152, 183, 197, 201, 208, 294, 295, 300, 302, 303
Sedlak, A., 257, 259, 263, 265, 271, 272
Selby, J. W., 139, 154
Selfridge, J. A., 49, 65
Sensenig, J., 277, 286
Sermat, V., 275, 285
Shapiro, D. A., 296, 302
Shepard, R. N., 255, 257, 259, 261, 266, 269, 270, 287, 288
Sherman, R. C., 277, 288
Sherman, R. E., 273, 288
Sherzer, J., 74, 85
Shikiar, R., 273, 288
Shosid, N., 139, 154
Shotter, J., 122, 154
Shulman, A. D., 124, 154
Sibson, R., 54, 65
Silverstein, S. J., 124, 151
Simmons, J. L., 300, 302
Simonson, N. R., 118, 151
Sinclair, J. McH., 74, 91
Slater, P., 239, 243, 251
Slater, P. J. B., 36, 56, 60, 65
Smith, B. O., 19, 36
Smith, H. L., 69, 91
Smith, J. L., 127, 154
Smith, S., 238, 251
Solley, C. M., 271, 286
Spence. I., 256, 265, 288
Stanley, J. C., 144, 145, 150
Stayton, D. J., 114
Stephenson, W., 227, 251
Storms, M. D., 132, 133, 136–138, 154
Strauss, A., 295, 296, 302
Strickland, L. H., 128, 132, 154

Stringer, P., 229, 241, 251, 252
Suci, G. J., 262, 287
Sudnow, D., 74, 91
Suedfeld, P., 124, 151

Taba, H., 19, 36
Tajfel, H., 253, 286
Tannenbaum, P. H., 149
Taylor, S. E., 138, 154
Tedeschi, J. T., 301, 303
Thompson, J., 68, 91
Thompson, J. J., 157
Tinbergen, N., 103, 116, 156, 176
Tolman, E. C., 60, 65
Torgerson, W. S., 255, 261, 269, 270, 288
Totten, J., 138, 153
Touhey, J. C., 130, 131, 154
Toulmin, S., 119, 154
Trager, G. L., 69, 70, 91
Trevarthen, C., 84, 91, 94, 96, 97, 103, 107, 117
Tripodi, T., 229, 250, 252
Trower, P., 14, 31, 37, 118, 154
Tucker, E. R., 255, 273, 288
Turing, A. M., 50, 65
Turner, R. H., 139, 154

Urwin, C., 113, 116

Valentine, C. W., 94, 116
Van der Kloot, W., 56, 65
Van Hooff, J. A. R. A. M., 56, 65
Van Vlack, J., 77, 91
Veach, T. L., 118, 130 132, 150
Vivekananthan, P. S., 271

Wachmann, A., 78, 87
Walster, E., 292, 303
Ward, D. G., 241, 250
Warner, D. B., 292, 303
Warr, P. B., 229, 252, 273, 275, 288
Watson, J., 17, 37
Weber, S. J., 124, 144, 154
Wells, G., 106, 116
Werner, H., 112, 113, 116
Wertz, M., 70, 89
West, S. G., 118, 132, 137, 141, 147, 154
Whitney, R. E., 150
Wicklund, R. A., 140, 154
Wiemann, J. M., 82, 91
Wiener, M., 82, 91
Williams, C., 76, 91
Williams, E., 238, 252
Willis, R. H., 118, 132, 137, 154
Willis, Y. A., 118, 132, 137, 154
Wilson, T. D., 13, 36, 142, 153, 222
Wish, M., 12, 37, 259, 271, 273, 279, 280, 288
Wittgenstein, L., 74, 91
Wolfe, M., 303
Wolff, M., 84, 91
Wood, H., 74, 89
Wright, H. F., 16, 35

Yngve, V. H., 82, 91
Young, F., 256, 285
Young, F. W., 255, 256, 258, 259, 261, 275, 285, 286, 288
Young, G., 247, 252

Zimbardo, P. G., 123, 151, 162, 175

SUBJECT INDEX

Accounts, accounting, 62, 141, 142, 185, 199–201, 207
Accumulative fragmentalism, 225
Achievement, 299
Act/action structure, 41, 205
Acting model script, 167
Actor and observer perspectives, 138, 139, 142
Adequacy, 45, 120, 147, 148
Adjacency pair, 21
Affective reactions, 12
Agency, 225
Aggression, 291, 299
Agonistic model, 202
Agons, 18
Algorithm, 61
All-or-none approach, 128, 129, 149, 162
Allotment methods, 229
Alternation of utterances, 33
Altruism, 291, 299
Ambiguity of meaning, 124
Analogic baseline, 166, 168, 172, 175
Analogic function, 157
Analogue, 120
Analogy, definition, 155
Analysis of variance techniques, 259
Anthropology, 68
Anticipation, 226
Anticipatory accounts, 142
Approximation, 49
Assisted autobiography, 177
Association
 inferences from, 235
 measures of, 235
Asymmetrical contingency, 29
Attachment theory and imprinting, 95

Attitude change strategies, 127
Attraction, 290
Attribution theories, 130, 137, 138, 140, 290, 292, 299, 300
Attributional statements, 142
Autism, autistic behaviour, 156
Autobiographical reconstruction, 297
Autobiographical self, 178
Autonomic activity, processes, 131, 141

Balance, 126
Behaviour fitting, 24
Behaviour guiding, 24
Behaviour settings, 16
Behavioural baseline, 174
Behavioural baseline models, 158
Behavioural relationship, 67
Behaviourist ideology, 180
Biographical Inventory, 193–195, 198
Biographical reconstruction, 179
Biomechanics, 68
Bipolar scales, 264, 267, 268
Break-points, 19
Brussels Method, 193, 207
Bystander intervention, 159, 292

Canonical correlation, 259
Case grammar and joint action, 109
Causal attribution, 142, 147
Causal mechanisms, 24
Character management, 126, 129
Charting, 72–73
Chunking, 18
Classifying situations, 13
Clumping, 57
Cluster analysis, 54, 238, 240, 258, 268

Coding scheme, 142
Coding video tapes, 108–109
Cognitive complexity, 237, 239, 242
Cognitive concepts, 17
Cognitive dimensions, 260
Cognitive dissonance theorists, 165
Cognitive map, 206
Cognitive matrix, 179, 202
Cognitive planning, 29
Cognitive processes, 13, 143, 299
Cognitive psychology, 24
Cognitive revolution, 290
Cognitive space, 255
Cognitive structure, 142, 256, 260, 284
Communication episodes, 259, 280
Communication theory, 70
Communications systems, 67
Commutation, 44
Competence, 45
Conceptual analysis, 125
Conceptual space, 273
Concurrent commentary, 142
Conditions of interaction, 135
Conditions of occurrence, 126, 140
Configurations, 266
Conforming study, 159
Confusion probabilities, 262
Congruity, 126
Consistency, 126
Constative aspect of sentences, 41
Constitutive rules, 46, 300
Constructive alternativism, 225
Constructs
    elicitation/provision, 228
    looseness, 239, 241
    lopsidedness, 236
    poles of, 228
    selection of, 228
    shifting, 244
Contending, 80
Context, 44
Context analysis, 69, 71, 72, 74–75, 79
Context theory of meaning, 74
Contextual determinants, 181
Contractual and collaborative models, 180
Contrastive analysis, 70
Control groups, 156
Conversation analysis, 74
Co-ordinates in multidimensional space, 258
Corollaries, 226
Correlation, 56

Correlation coefficients, 262, 267
Creativity, 17
Cricket, 247
Criterial data, 119
Critical description, 125
Cross-cultural comparability, 140
Cross-tabulated matrix, 263
Cumulative presenting, 18
Cybernetics, 69, 70
Cycles of events, 20

Deception, 118, 119, 123
Deception experiment, 165
Deception manoeuvre, 160
Deep structure, 64
Defending, 80
Defiance baseline, 170–172, 174
Degeneracy of solutions, 269
Demand characteristics, 144
Dendrogram, 27, 54
Dependability of measure, 145–148
Descriptive translations, 161
Destructive obedience, 123, 134, 160, 166, 168, 298
Diachronic, 41, 178
Diachrony, definition, 186
Dimensions, determining optimum number of, 265
Discovery, 127, 129
    of hidden structures, 257
Dissimilarity matrix, 256
Dissonance, 118, 119, 126
    reduction, 130
Dominance, 17
Dramaturgical concept of person, 131
Dramaturgical model, 184
Dyadic relationships, 280

Editing tables, 77
Elements
    of behaviour, 14
    selection, 227
    shifting, 244–245
Emic descriptions, 45
Empirical domains, 191
Empirical laws, 24, 25
Empirical regularities, 26
Enigmatic social episodes, 183
Environmental 'press', 15
Environmental psychology, 11, 291, 300
Episodes, 11, 15, 17–34, 122

SUBJECT INDEX

Equity, 292
Equivalence class, 43
Ethnography, 68
Ethnomethodology, 207, 291, 292, 294, 301
Ethogenics, 178, 183, 207, 291, 292, 294, 301
Etic descriptions, 45
Euclidean space, 255
Evaluation, 17
Evaluative norms, 137
Everyman, 137
Evolutionary theory, 95
Exchange model, 184
Exchange theory, 292
Experimenter bias, 144
Experimenter construct artifacts, 259
Explaining, 80
Explanatory model, 126
Exploitation games, 202
Expressive behaviour, 69, 70
External control, 30
External labelling, 267
External validity, 145
External variable studies, 144
Extraversion, 17
Extremity of rating, 229

F-formation, 81
Face game, 202
Face presentation, 126
Factor analysis, 237, 239
  of intersubject correlations, 255
Factor loadings, 261
Film analysis projectors, 77
Film technology, 67, 76–77
Filming for context analysis, 74–76
Focused Account Eliciting, 179, 197, 198, 202–205
Focused Interview technique, 192–198
Following gaze, 98, 99
Formation, 81
Formats, 108
FORTRAN IV, 261
Fourth-order artificial dialogues, 32
Frame numbering, 76, 77
Framing, 22
Functional descriptions, problems of, 110–112
Fundamental postulate, 226

Game typology, 202

Games, 18
Gaze, 19
Generalizability, 145, 146, 148
Generalized other, 137
Generative mechanism, 125, 130, 134, 140, 147
Generative rules, 23
Geometric representation, 260
Gerontological psychology, 182
Goal directedness in communication, 101
Goals of participants, 15
Grindstone Island study, 123
Group decision processes, 301
Group stimulus space, 256

Hierarchical classification, 27
Hierarchical organization, 71
Hierarchical structure, 19, 32, 140, 181
Historical ethnography, 186
Historicity of autobiographies, 187, 206
Homeomorph, 39
Hosting, 18

Icon, 39
Iconic models, definition, 155
Idiographic studies, 256
Idiography of biographies 189
Illocution, 41
Implicit knowledge, 257
Implicit theories of personality, 271–272
Incentive instructions, 130
Indexical expressions, 204
Individual perceptual structures, 256
INDSCAL model, 256, 261, 262, 265–268, 271
Inductive model building, 301
Infant intentions, 101
Infant social behaviour, 22
Information exchange, 71
Information games, 202
Information theory, 69
Instrumental behaviours, 129
Intelligibility of events, 187
Interaction rates, 262
Interaction structures, 140
Interactional synchrony, 84
Interactionist approach, 11
Interactionist equation, 14
Intercoder reliability, 142
Internal confounding, 144
Internal validity, 123, 144, 146

Interpersonal attraction, 259, 276, 299
Interpersonal distance, 135
Interpersonal simulations, 130
Interpretability of output, 261
Interpretation of MDS configurations, 266
Interpretative schemata, 177
Interval-scale representation, 255
Interviewing Rule, 197
Interviews
  biographical inventory, 179
  problem and conflict situations, 179
  social enquiry, 179
Intuitive labelling, 266
Invariant stimulus structures, 271
ISIS (Interactive Scaling with Individual Subjects), 256, 285
Item co-occurrence, 259

Joint action and language acquisition, 112–113

Kinesiology, 68

Laboratory analogy, 162
Language acquisition, 100
Latent content, 196
Learning experiment, 163
Learning tradition, 292
Legitimate counter-aggression, 135, 138
Lewinian tradition, 292
Linguistic philosophy, 74
Listening, 80
Liturgical model, 184, 201
Local ethnography, 146
Local minimum, 269
Log survivor function, 57

Manifest content, 196
Mapping, 73, 77
Markov chain, 19, 32
Measures between elements/constructs, 235
Measures of consistency, 239, 242
Measures of content and structure, 233, 234
Measures of inconsistency, 243
Measures of intensity, 242
Measures of state and stress, 238
Measures of total structure, 236
Measures within elements/constructs, 234
Melody analysis, 59
Metatheoretical movements, 291
Metric techniques, 255

Microanalysis of interaction, 97–98
Milgram's obedience studies, 162–165
Mobile individuals, 27
Mode of simulation, 132
Modelling Milgram's basic scene, 166
Monotone function, 255
Monotonicity assumption, 265
Moral judgments, 158
Morpheme, 39, 41
Mother–infant interaction, 84
Multi-attribute cognitive variables, 270
Multidimensional scaling, 12, 253, 254, 291
  evolution of, 254
  models, 256
  potential applications, 284
  programs, 253, 255, 273
  stimulus spaces, 267
  techniques
    limitations of, 268
    potential, uses of, 256
    practical advantages of, 259
Multiple discriminant analysis, 259
Multiple groupings task, 280
Multiple groupings technique, 264
Multiple reality, 62
Multiple regression, 259, 267
Multivariate techniques, 254
Mundane realism, 134
Mutation-selection pairs, 187
Mutual contingency, 29, 32
Mutually related cognitive elements, 126

Naive autobiography, 179
Narrating, 80
Natural behaviour, two senses of, 102–103
Negotiation, 300
Negotiation of accounts 142
Negotiation process, 298
Nested structures of elements, 140
Nomothetic studies, 187, 256
Nomothetic transitions, 192
Non-metric multidimensional scaling, 255, 261
Non-verbal behaviours, 141
Non-verbal communication, 33
Non-verbal cues, 22
Normative structure, 291, 300
Norms, 25
Null script, 139

Obedience baseline, 168, 169, 174

Obedience study, 159, 160, 162
Objective self-awareness, 126, 140
Objective similarity, 259
Optimum dimensionality, 265, 269
Ordering questions, 204
Orthogonal axes, 267
Overspacing, 57

Paradigmatic relations, 43
Paradigmatic revolution, 289, 294, 301
Paralinguistic phenomena, 78
Parametric representation, 257
Parametric sciences, 293
Paramorph, 40
Parochialism of research perspectives, 104
Partial correlation coefficients, 268
Passive protesting, 80
Perceived structure, 276, 284
Perceptual processes, 69
Perceptual space, 271
Perceptual structure, 256
Performance, 45
Performance modalities, 196
Performative use of utterances, 41
Perlocution, 41
Person perception, 271, 272
Person–situation interactions, 15
Person variance, 28
Persona, 184, 199
Personal construct theory, 225, 246
Perspectivity, 189
Phenomenal reality, 257
Phenomenological approach, 13
Phonemic, 45
Phonetic, 45
Phrasal structure, 68
Phrase boundary analysis, 77
Physiological variables, 140
Plausibility, 120, 147, 148
Point, 80
Points of view analysis, 255, 256
Political behaviour and perception, 273, 275
Position, 80
Positionings, 81
Post-experimental questionnaires, 138
Post hoc tests, 258
Pragmatic tradition, 69
Precursors and prerequisites, 113
Prescribed behaviour, 26
Presentation, 80
Principal Component Analysis, 237, 239

Proactive sequences, 21
Problem and conflict situations, 194, 205
Process variables, 291
Profile distance formula, 264
Property dimensions, 267
Proscribed behaviour, 26
Prosodic phenomena, 78
Proxemics, 291
Proximity measures, 259
Pseudo-contingency, 31
Psyche-logos, 178
Psychological method, 181
Psychometric theory, 179
Puzzling behaviour, 155, 157, 158, 162, 163, 174

Quantitative descriptive data, 258
Quantitative taxonomies, 277

Radical behaviourists, 158
Random models, 157
Rank-order transformation, 255
Reactance, 126
Reactive and other sequences, 29
Reactive contingency, 31
Real-time interaction, 256
Reciprocal control, 71
Reconstruction, 46
Recording (role play), 137, 138
Reflexive effects of autobiography, 189
Reflexive questions, 203, 204, 205
Reflexiveness of negotiated auto-biographies, 206
Reflexivity, 226
Regulatory communication, 82
Regulatory rules, 26, 300
Relationship games, 202
Remedial sequence, 21
Repertory grid, 13, 226
    administration of, 231
    analysis of, 233
    applications of, 234
    design of, 227
Replication of reality, 128
Representativeness, 148, 149
Response classes, 143
Response-matching, 33
Retrospective accounts, 142
Rhythmic nature of social interaction, 96–97
Risk taking, 130, 146, 301
Role competence, 136

SUBJECT INDEX

Role expectations, 124
Role negotiations, 300
Role playing, 127, 165, 166, 174, 298
Role Repertory Grid, 291
Role/rule model, 158, 161
Role/rule patterns, 199
Role/rule frameworks, 298, 299
Role/rule structures, 121, 124, 125, 128, 136, 144
Role/rule systems, 201
Role titles, 227
Roles, 16
Rule-breaking, 13, 23, 25–28
Rule governed, definition, 161
Rule transgression, 162
Rule translation, 164
Rules, 11, 15, 21, 22–34, 50, 247

SPSS command language, 255
Sample, 157
Sanctions, 26, 27
Script specificity, 133
Scripts, 19
Segmental phonemes, 78
Segmentation, 51
Self-conception, 178
Self-confrontation study, 69
Semantic, 41
Semantic differential, 13
Semantic system, 136
Semiology, 42
Sensibility, 138
Sensitivity, 138
Sequence analysis, 19, 21, 43
Sequences in social behaviour, 11, 15
Sequences of behaviour, 31
Sequences of elements, 140
Sequential analysis, 257
Serial invalidation, 241
Shocking behaviour, 155, 174
Signalling of episodes, 22
Significant gesture, 74
Similarity ratings, 259, 263
Simulation, 44, 123
Situated actions, 121, 134
Situated ethnography, 187
Situated identity, 126, 129, 144, 299
Situated transactions, 297
Situational context, 277
Situational variance, 28
Situationism, 290

Situations, dimensions, 11, 13
Skilled play within rules, 11
Skills, 17
  individual performance within rules, 28
Social act, 41
  non-verbal, 14
Social competence, 184–186
Social effectiveness, 30
Social Enquiry, 194
Social episodes, 257, 264, 276–284
Social force, 183
Social interaction, 67, 130
Social skills model, 28
Social structure, 258, 275
Socialization, 14, 301
  definition, 93–94
Socio-cultural view of communication, 100
Sociometric movement, 290
Sociometric techniques, 275
Special effects generator, 77
Specific other, 137
Specimens of behaviour, 67, 69, 73
Speech act, 41, 74, 141
Speech act model and infant social behaviour, 101
Speech situations, 74
Standardized questionnaire procedures, 27
Stanford prison study, 123, 134
Stationarity, 56
Stereotypes, 272
Stochastic models of language, 57
Stress index, 265
Structural features, 122
Structural linguistics, 69, 71, 257
Structural role-play research, 144
Structural sciences, 293
Structuralism, 291
Structuralist, 41
Structure of emotions, 275
Structure of social behaviour, 257
Structuring, 22
Subcultural representations, 280
Subject–investigator relationships, 180
Subjective dimensions, 12
Subjective perceptions of situations, 13
Subjective similarity, 259
Subjectivism, 293
Supplementary analyses, 268
Supportiveness, 17
Supra-segmental phenomena, 78
Surface structure, 64

SUBJECT INDEX

Symbolic interactionist orientations, 257
Symbolic interactions, 291, 292, 294, 295, 299, 301
Symmetry, 126
Synchronic structure, 178
Synchrony, 83
   definition, 186
Syntactic, 42
Syntagmatic, 43
Syntax of language, 13
Synthesis (vs. analysis), 128, 129
Systems of interactors, 140

Tacit knowledge, 143
Tasks, 16
Taxonomy, 52, 258
Taxonomy of resources, 185
Teaching module, 19
Theory, 225, 246
Theory of natural powers, 120
Thought-disordered schizophrenics, 239, 241
Three-way factor-analysis, 13, 258
Time and Motion Study Projector, 77
Time-interval analysis, 56
Time-oriented method, 194
Time scale and speed of viewing, 107
Topic-oriented method, 194
TORSCA 9, 261, 262, 264–267
Tracing behaviour through time, 107
Transcription systems, 78
Transition probabilities, 19
Transitional frequency, 56
Transitional probability, 50
Turing test, 50

Unit-boundaries, 18
Universal categories, 15
Use of elements, 29
Use of episodes, 29
Use of means–end sequences, 29
Utterance sequences, 33

Value judgments, 158
Variance, 237
Venture, 19
Verbal models, 165–166, 174
Verification, 127, 129
Video recording, 67

Waves, 73